Economists at War

Economists at War

*How a Handful of Economists
Helped Win and Lose the
World Wars*

ALAN BOLLARD

OXFORD
UNIVERSITY PRESS

OXFORD
UNIVERSITY PRESS

Great Clarendon Street, Oxford, OX2 6DP,
United Kingdom

Oxford University Press is a department of the University of Oxford.
It furthers the University's objective of excellence in research, scholarship,
and education by publishing worldwide. Oxford is a registered trade mark of
Oxford University Press in the UK and in certain other countries

First Edition published in 2020

Impression: 1

Published in the United States of America by Oxford University Press
198 Madison Avenue, New York, NY 10016, United States of America

British Library Cataloguing in Publication Data

Data available

Library of Congress Control Number: 2019946108

ISBN 978-0-19-884600-0

Printed and bound by
CPI Group (UK) Ltd, Croydon, CR0 4YY

Preface and Acknowledgements

Generals do not win wars on their own. This book recounts the role that seven economists played in six countries during the world's wartime years of 1935 to 1955. It covers the period of the Chinese War of Occupation, the Second World War, and the Cold War. The economists came from different backgrounds, held different positions, and faced different challenges. It is a story of good and bad economic thinking, good and bad policy, good and bad moral positions. Despite the differences, the seven had their similarities and their connections.

1935–55 was a time of conflict, confrontation, and destruction. Up to 80 million people may have died in this period; by that measure it was the worst era in the history of the world. It was also the time when the skills of economists were called upon to finance the military, to identify economic vulnerabilities, to help reconstruction. Economics began to be used as a policy tool, and economists started to gain importance as advisors. Macroeconomics, managerial economics, and computing were all born during this time.

Wartime produces many innovations and advances, and economics is no different. Political economist Robert Dorfman expressed his view of the half-dozen most important economic advances of the twentieth century: Keynesian macro-theory, input-output analysis, national income accounting, linear programming, game theory, and general equilibrium theory (Dorfman, 1995, 305). All of these advances involved the economists in this book and all were developed or used during their wartime struggles.

Some good can come from war. Economists learnt much from their experiences of economic management during World War II. This was the time when the discipline developed from classical laissez-faire principles and ad hoc fiscal management in closed economies to new ways of managing the economy: what we would recognize today as more sophisticated fiscal and monetary stabilization policies, an understanding of the dynamic growth process, international economic interactions within a set of international institutions, using the technical advances of economic theory, computing, and data to model outcomes in a more sophisticated way, with larger government, ultimately after the war, to help achieve better standards of living.

The story focuses on seven economists, all men. (Women also played important analytical, computational, programming, and organizational roles in the economic process, and the text highlights several of them, but more often they worked undocumented and in the background.) These men were Japanese, Chinese, German, British, Russian, and émigré American. Their economic backgrounds differed from self-taught to very academic. Their motives differed from patriotic to self-seeking. Their positions differed from high officials to university-based academics. The roles differed from being at the heart of decision-making to ivory tower thinking.

But they had much in common too. Almost all of them came from middle-class professional families with intellectual parents who had fallen on hard times. Almost all of them had themselves experienced chaos and disruption in their youth, and most endured personal hardship during revolution and war, fleeing at times for their own and family's safety. They were intellectually clever, they had parents who admired and extended them (in particular most of them had a supporting and influential mother), they managed to get excellent educations some-times under extreme conditions, they had mentors who challenged them, most had influencing wives. They had wide interests, and most only came to economics late and by chance. They were intellectually arrogant, they travelled widely at a time when this was difficult and unusual, they had international outlooks, they took risks and were brave and adventurous, they struggled with political realities, and they did not seek to use their economics for war. They were all resilient: insight and influence did not fall easily into most of their laps.

These men all believed in the power of economics to make a difference, they all made their economic contributions, and these contributions all made a difference to political outcomes and military ends. They operated under different paradigms with different ideologies, but each had a strong economic framework of thinking. They were of varying ethnicities but they were all (or became) Christians within a determinist tradition. And in their different ways they were all exceptional people.

None of these economists were 'war-mongers' (with perhaps one exception). Most preferred a quiet study over a battlefield, and a fountain pen over a rifle. They engaged their wartime tasks with determination. But most of them would have been equally content working on economic development, exploring new ideas, making money. They did not go looking for war—war came looking for them.

Most of these economists knew or knew of one another. Did they ever think of themselves as direct rivals, dreaming up new economic weapons to defeat the protagonists' economists on the other side (in the way that General Montgomery placed a photo of General Rommel in his quarters during the North African campaign in World War II)? Probably not, but they all had a keen sense of how their economic contributions could change their country's wartime prospects, and how enemy countries were also using economists.

Their stories are told in approximately chronological order from the 1930s to the 1950s. Each chapter documents the story of one economist, linking him through his experience of wartime, and then tying back to his earlier life and experiences. This book does not offer a complete biography of each of these seven: instead, the narrative focuses on several big economic problems each one of them faced and how they dealt with these, arranging the account in a time sequence and highlighting interactions amongst them.

The story commences with the origins of World War II, and tracks through the Cold War. The first of our economists is Japanese Takahashi Korekiyo; he was older than the others—indeed the book opens with his death, then tracks back to explain how such an important statesman, many times Japanese Finance Minister, a man who had brilliantly pioneered debt markets and later saved Japan from serious depression, could end up in this position in 1936, murdered for his fiscal beliefs. The tale then moves on to the invasion of China and the chaotic life of Finance Minister and Bank Governor H. H. Kung, living amongst soldiers, warlords, and gang leaders, raising wartime revenue in such a disrupted environment, while at the same time lining his own pockets to an extent only dreamt of by oligarchs today. When China needed aid he approached Germany in the form of Hjalmar Schacht, the architect of German economic reconstruction and rearmament, uneasily in bed with the Nazis. Schacht was an autocratic, disciplined, and doctrinaire economist, quite the opposite of Kung, and he watched as the arms he had financed were eventually used to invade Western Europe.

Unprepared for total conflict, the UK had to finance their own war effort, and they relied heavily on the insight of that omniscient, opinionated, economic genius, John Maynard Keynes, who pioneered a new idea of economic management and showed how it could help pay for the war. Europe was now in complete upheaval, and brutal fighting was taking place in the USSR, where a brilliant young economic academic called Leonid Kantorovich found himself perilously in the front lines. He had been pioneering new ways to operate Soviet factories more efficiently, but was prevented by a paranoid Stalin from applying his techniques to the whole economy.

Eventually Germany and Japan were defeated, with the help of American émigré economists Wassily Leontief and John von Neumann, who in their various ways applied their technical economics and mathematics to making bombing more effective and more lethal. At last the Armistice brought peace, but there was an increasingly fragile stand-off between East and West—the confrontation of the Cold War. As the tension grew, American von Neumann and Russian Kantorovich were using their economic ideas to help their countries, while Leontief tried to promote the economics of peace.

These economists were not all moral heroes: without some degree of economic management, major wars could never persist. Might one point to the more sophisticated economic management of World War II as one explanation why so many people came to be slaughtered, so much damage could be done? The Annex outlines the many different ways these economic policies worked (or failed), and also the way the variety of background conditions influenced how effective they could be.

Ultimately this is not an economic history of war, not an academic study of economic policies, not a biographical study, and most decidedly not a guide on how to be economically effective in wartime. Rather it is a description of the complex and sometimes terrible positions these economists found themselves in, and how they used their economics and their personalities to address this. This is a book about economics, but it is also a human story.

The military has always known the importance of manpower, materiel, and supply routes but they do not usually think about how to finance them, nor about how to manage an economy faced with a large military disruption. It is not only tactical generals and clever politicians who win wars. They need top economists too.

I wish to acknowledge the help of all those people with whom I have discussed this project and who have made helpful comments, especially Robert Buckle, Jenny Morel, Albert Bollard, Mark Harrison, Katie Bishop, John Smallman, Oxford University Press, Sharman Buckle, and Michael Janes. In addition, I acknowledge assistance from ex-colleagues in interpretation, translation, and transliteration, particularly relating to the foreign material on Japan, China, and the Soviet Union. Every effort has been made to ensure copyright compliance.

Contents

List of Plates

Recent Books by Alan Bollard

Crisis: One Central Bank Governor and the Global Financial Crisis
The Rough Mechanical: The Man Who Could *(novel)*
A Few Hares Running: The Life and Economics of Bill Phillips
The Code-Cracker and the Tai-Chi Dancer *(novel)*

The Economists' Connections

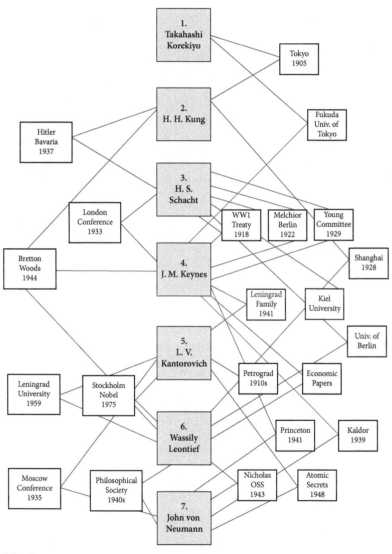

Meetings

Other Connections

Notes to the Diagram

The seven economists lived different lives in different places, but there were physical and theoretical connections among them. The diagram lists the economists in chapter order. The boxes on the left-hand side mark some of the important face-to-face meetings where certain of the economists met together. The boxes on the right-hand side mark other connections: family links, institutional affiliations, cities they both lived in, and work that they had in common.

Notes to the Diagram

'An army nearby causes prices to go up and provisions to be depleted; and this steals from the people.'

Sun Tzu, The Art of War, 5th Century BC

'Every gun that is made, every warship launched, every rocket fired signifies, in the final sense, a theft from those who hunger and are not fed, those who are cold and are not clothed.'

President (ex-General) Dwight D. Eisenhower, 1953

1

Fall Down Seven Times
Get Up Eight?

Takahashi Korekiyo in Japan, 1934–5

How Takahashi Learned His Craft

It was dark before dawn on a freezing Tokyo winter's night. In silence the soldiers prepared their rifles and bayonets. The officers strapped on their greatcoats and swords. They filed in silence out of their barracks and marched down the snow-covered streets. The contingent halted as they reached a beautiful traditional wooden mansion. There was a guard on the gate, and he tried to stop them, but the soldiers knocked him rudely aside and burst past. The guard telephoned desperately for help, but it was too late. The officer barked an order and the soldiers smashed down the front door. They stormed through the house. In a bedroom two officers found an old man asleep in bed. They drew their swords and pistols.

The old man was the venerable statesman Takahashi Korekiyo. He had been Prime Minister of Japan and Minister of Finance seven times. This was the man who prevented his country collapsing into the Great Depression by the combined use of modern fiscal, monetary, and exchange rate policies, perhaps the first in the world to design such a policy package. By 1934, before such policies had been articulated in economic theory, Takahashi had put them into practice. In doing so he had helped Japan build a strong economy. But sadly this economic strength had been used by Japan to build and abuse its military might for war, resulting in the ultimate misery of millions. Takahashi was the only Japanese politician brave enough to stand up to the military and fight against the inexorable slide to militarism in the 1930s, designing a modern disciplined fiscal policy which would put a brake on excessive military spending by 1935. For this he would pay the ultimate price.

Takahashi had learned his craft from his experience in the two major conflicts that had disrupted the region at the turn of the century, and had set the scene for the twentieth century ahead. In the first Sino-Japanese War of 1894–5, Japan dealt a humiliating blow to the declining Chinese Qing Empire and dominated Korea as a client state. The second conflict happened a decade later, when in 1904–5 Japan convincingly defeated the Russian fleets, extended its influence in Manchuria, and bolstered its military.

Takahashi was a quite unique Japanese gentleman of the time, and his life had been an eventful one. He had been born in Edo (the old name for Tokyo) in 1854 and had an unusual upbringing in a country that was undergoing wrenching changes. His father, Morifusa, was a landscape painter in the shogun court at Edo Castle. He was a big-eating, big-drinking, party-going man, famous for his intake of large amounts of sake. Despite having two wives, several offspring and being advanced in age, he impregnated a pretty 16-year-old family maid named Kim, who gave birth to a boy named Wakiji. Wakiji was adopted out to a nearby family named Takahashi, a member of the lowest rank of the samurai clan (effectively the foot soldiers of the Tokugawa regime). There the boy was renamed Takahashi, and brought up by Kiyoko, the widowed grandmother of the house, who was to exert an important influence over him.

In the year of Takahashi's birth, US Commander Perry's ships had breached the self-imposed Japanese foreign blockade, opening up the country, and sparking off major changes. The ruling shogunate gave way to the reinstatement of the Meiji Emperor, recognizing the need to deal with the outside world and to learn lessons from the West. Grandmother Kiyoko was herself a rational, independent, and modernizing person, and she raised Takahashi in this disrupted world. The young boy grew up cute, precocious, and a prodigious learner. He attracted attention from a modernizing senior samurai who sent him, aged only ten, to study with a missionary's wife. Takahashi learned English very fast and very well, engaging enthusiastically with the foreigners he came into contact with. Still aged only 11 he was appointed as a houseboy in the British-owned Chartered Mercantile Bank in Yokohama, the start of his long and colourful financial career.

Most Japanese youths were brought up to be quiet and respectful, but not Takahashi. He was very sociable from a young age. This helped him to learn languages, but like his natural father, he also liked to party, and that soon got him into trouble—drinking, gambling, and joining gangs in Tokyo that preyed on prostitutes. He took up with one of these latter, a young geisha. His family tried to discipline him, but young Takahashi proved irrepressible.

He yearned to travel to see something of the modern world outside Japan, a most unusual possibility for a young Japanese boy. In 1867, still aged only 13, he convinced one of the samurai clan to arrange for him to travel to the US. His grandmother Kiyoko did her best to prepare him for the journey ahead. She even presented him with his grandfather's samurai dagger and taught him how to commit ritual suicide by disembowelling himself, in case he might find this necessary.

It was a rough and difficult voyage crossing the Pacific. Takahashi and another young Japanese travelling companion kept up their spirits by playing pranks on other passengers, which frequently got them into trouble aboard the ship. At last they docked in San Francisco. Takahashi had expected that he would get the opportunity to go to school, but that never happened. Instead he ended up working as a houseboy in San Francisco. Then without realizing what he was doing, he signed a contract committing himself as an indentured servant on a farm in Oakland for some years. He soon had a raging argument with a Chinese cook from the farm who tried to kill him with an axe. The young Takahashi was disciplined by his employer. He tried to run away from the farm, only to be told that he was not allowed to leave. Later he was sold on to another family, a life he described as little better than that of a slave.

Never one willing to be ordered around by others, Takahashi waited for his opportunity to escape, and at last ran away to the Pacific coast. In 1868 he managed to board a ship and head back home to Japan. There he found a country that was in turmoil because the shogun lords were rising up against the new coalition civilian government. The rebellious young Takahashi and his friends joined a local samurai group, and were caught up in opposition to government. For a time they had to flee Tokyo and hide.

Eventually Takahashi Korekiyo settled down to life back in Tokyo. He was offered teaching jobs in missionary schools, where he began first by instructing in English, then extending his teaching into other subjects. He was completely untutored himself, but his outgoing manner and linguistic skills made him an excellent teacher, and no new subject was too difficult for him to learn. However his life continued to drift between missionary discipline and bouts of drunkenness with geisha and gangs.

Before leaving for San Francisco he had wanted to marry Okimi, his geisha friend in the gang. Surprisingly his grandmother gave him permission, perhaps thinking it would settle Takahashi down and ensure he returned. But Okimi had signed another contract as a geisha and her employer would not release her. Now back in Tokyo he was in his twenties, and his grandmother feared his misbehaving again: she arranged a marriage with another young woman, Saigo Oryu. A year later a first son Korekata was born, and several years later a second one, Koreyoshi.

Over the next two decades, Takahashi Korekiyo had worked in several different schools. His natural talents—his language skills, raw intellect, engaging manner, and ability to learn—soon brought him to the attention of some Tokyo government officials. He was invited to take on successive assignments in the Finance, Interior, Agriculture, and Commerce Ministries. He was then appointed to a major agricultural and forestry college, where he established a reputation as an astute administrator. He had a term selling securities for a brokerage firm. This represented a most unusual, varied, and unpredictable career track for a young Japanese official at the time. These diverse roles gave him a very wide exposure to the Japanese government system during an important period of modernization. Takahashi had not settled into a career but he seemed to be prospering.

The chubby youth had matured into a well-dressed young man, still short and portly, losing his hair, but with a smart handlebar moustache and a ready smile. He was now a practising Christian with a happy family life. But in 1884 this happiness was thrown into disarray by the early death of his wife. Yet Takahashi always proved robust in the face of disaster, and three years later he married again, a young woman named Shina.

In 1889, aged 36, Takahashi was assigned by the government to advise on Japan's first Western-style industry policies, taking on the position of Patents Commissioner. He later recalled that his first step was to read the entry on industry policy in the *Encyclopaedia Britannica*. This position gave him the opportunity to visit the US again, this time travelling in more comfort and docking in San Francisco without incident. On the trip his keen mind and engaging manner helped him to learn about intellectual property, industry assistance, and competition policies in other countries.

In the same year he was to have an unusual experience, a very costly one that demonstrated Takahashi's risk-taking nature and resilience. He learnt much from it, though this time his learnings were harsh ones. Japan had few mineral resources but its industry needed raw materials, and for the first time the Japanese were looking abroad for resources. Latin America was a favoured destination for Japanese investment. Takahashi was persuaded to invest in a silver mine in Peru, one sited at high altitude in the remote Andes, and then having invested, he was asked to manage it. He set off on his travels, encountering many dangerous adventures travelling to the Andes—an arduous ocean voyage, followed by a very perilous trek into the high mountains, and tough living conditions at high altitude there. At last he arrived at the site, and very quickly found there was bad news—the mine was exhausted and the commercial claims were largely a hoax.

After a long and dangerous return journey, Takahashi at last arrived back in Tokyo with the bad news about the poor mineral prospects. He worked hard to limit the shareholder losses, learning much about precious metals and trading in the process, but despite his efforts the company went bankrupt. He had personally taken on a loan to invest in the mine, and now he found himself highly exposed, ending up severely in debt to the banks. Reluctantly the family had to tighten their belts. They sold their huge modern Japanese mansion and moved into a small rental property nearby. Takahashi was now unemployed, and with his two sons and their step-mother, he had to eke out a living on a small pension. (He would not be the only economist in this book to experience personal financial problems.)

Takahashi Korekiyo was a resilient man but it took him a long time to recover his health, energy, and reputation. Eventually in 1892, three years after he had set out for Peru, one of his original supporters helped him to find a new job. The Bank of Japan was one of the nation's important modernizing institutions promoting markets and economic growth, and with this in mind, they had embarked on constructing an ambitious Tokyo headquarters in a new style. It was one of the country's first large-scale Western construction projects, and it had run into major architectural, engineering, and financial difficulties. Takahashi was hired on contract to sort out the problems. He had never done any such work in the past, but as usual he learned fast, proving adaptable and equal to the task.

The Bank was impressed with his efforts, and they appointed him as regional manager in the south-west Yamaguchi Province. During his time in the south-west, Takahashi experienced his first war. In 1894 fighting had broken out with China, and Hiroshima in Yamaguchi was the key military centre. The Emperor and the Japanese Government relocated there to better supervise the action, and the Diet also held its sessions there. With the country on a war footing, Hiroshima became a bustling port city, busy with ships and troops, linked to Tokyo by the new Sanyo Railway, and the nearest port connecting to Korea and Manchuria. Across the strait lay a subservient Korea and a declining China.

As Western Regional Manager of the Bank of Japan, Takahashi's job was to help finance the industrial and military expansion that was under way. The war cost money, and the government wanted to finance it domestically. It was Takahashi's job to sell war bonds in the region: this required him to persuade or pressure local government and prominent business figures to buy the bonds, then use their interest to sell more bonds to others. He proved very successful at this, reporting that a mixture of war fever and coercion meant there was a much bigger uptake than expected.

But there was also considerable local hardship in the region, with the military requisitioning stores, warehouses, and rice stocks. Takahashi recognized the damage being done by the army and tried to alleviate it. The Sino-Japanese War gave him a foretaste of what would lie ahead: rising Japanese militarism, demands for army expenditure, major debt, and hardship for citizens.

Takahashi was interested in the possibilities of economic policy to improve farmers' productivity, and to establish a stronger industrial base for Japan. He found that the banking system was not very accessible for small local businesses, so he requested permission to commit Bank of Japan funds to assist them. This was turned down by head office, but undaunted, Takahashi worked to help farmers borrow at the lower Tokyo interest rates rather than suffering the traditional regional premium. He also had his first experience of banking problems: when serious floods and financially-leveraged reclamation projects pushed a local bank into difficulties, he committed Bank of Japan funds to keep the local bank operating, but only after careful studies convinced him that, though illiquid, it was still solvent. (This test of economic viability rather than financial liquidity was proposed by Walter Bagehot in the nineteenth century, and it is still the test in use by bank regulators today.)

Takahashi began to see himself as a nationalist, but one interested in economic advancement, not military conquest. The 1895 peace negotiations conducted in Hiroshima imposed harsh penalties on the Chinese: the surrender of Chinese arms, Japanese occupation of several northeast Chinese cities, control over local railways, ceding of the island of Taiwan and also the Liaodong Peninsula (the southern entrance to Manchuria), and privileged access for Japanese investors. In addition an immense indemnity was levied. Takahashi warned the Japanese Government that such a harsh settlement would cause major anti-Japanese sentiment in China, and possibly in the West as well: his internationalist mindset and desire for moderation were to be lifelong traits.

By 1895 Takahashi's unusual talents were being recognized, and he was promoted within the Bank of Japan, appointed Manager of the Yokohama Specie Bank. The Yokohama Bank held much of Japan's official precious metals but it also operated as an export–import promotion bank and it received Chinese war indemnity payments. Takahashi found he had been appointed to an archaic institution and he set about reorganizing it with a will, putting in place new lending practices focused on more modern business and international concepts.

At this time Japan adopted the gold standard. The gold standard was primarily a way to fix exchange rates, but it was also seen as endowing membership of a club of developed nations, demonstrating that Japan should be taken seriously as a world power. There was considerable argument about which standard and which exchange rates to adopt.

In 1898 the Bank sent Takahashi on a major world trip by steamer. He travelled to Shanghai, Hong Kong, Singapore, and then on to London to inspect bank branches and to learn more about modern banking. During the Asian leg of the trip, he saw bustling trading ports and vigorous Chinese merchants. This experience convinced Takahashi that Japan's future should rely more on expanding trade relations with dynamic Chinese entrepreneurs than on military intervention on the Chinese mainland.

In the City of London Takahashi met with a number of bankers and formed very close friendships with some of them. From them he learned about the workings of the London and European sovereign bond markets, including important practices like how to present a bond issue to the market, what would be a fundable amount for a government to seek, what returns and preconditions bondholders would look for, and how to build up an official credit record, all things that were unknown and untested for East Asia, but would later prove to be crucial.

Takahashi travelled on to the Continent and visited the financial markets of Belgium, France, and Germany, then later visited the US again. With his engaging personality, he soon built up a valuable banking network. He was keen for Japan to graduate to a high borrowing status in international markets, in line with its evolving self-perception as a world power. He was also interested in how Japan might use international financial markets to fuel economic development through the purchase of heavy plant and equipment. However to his eventual disappointment, his capital markets experience would be used to finance expenditure for war not for peace.

Shortly after his return in 1899, recognizing his successful international experience, Takahashi was promoted to Vice-Governor of the Bank of Japan, a very senior position. His new role was to handle bank failures on behalf of the central bank. Takahashi was poetic about his first few years as Vice-Governor: 'When I worked at the Yokohama Specie Bank I felt like a chrysanthemum blooming in the fields. I wasn't a gaudy person widely known to the public, but I worked in a comfortable atmosphere. The Bank of Japan, on the other hand, seemed like a beautiful fragrant rose. The work was flashy, and I had a big public reputation. But one could not escape the thorns in the shadows of the flowers' (Smethurst, 2007, 137).

Takahashi had become an established member of the Tokyo community. Having reached a comfortable, if stout, middle age he now had a family of five children. With wealth and standing he built a new house, an innovative fusion of Japanese and Western design, in Aoyama, an upscale district of Tokyo, across from the residence of the Crown Prince. The family also bought a seaside home in Hayama, fashionably close to the Imperial Villa.

As Vice-Governor at the Bank of Japan, Takahashi developed a new policy stance: artificially low interest rates to stimulate the economy and promote trade. This challenged the traditional approach of the government which had taken the Confucian view that overconsumption was morally bad and deflation morally good. Takahashi was not alone in his new views, but it represented a significant break from tradition. During his decade in the role, the Bank of Japan doubled its rate of lending, although maintaining cautious credit standards. His approach was disciplined, but it focused on growth not frugality, aiming to expand the economy and give Japan a stronger place in the world, while still seeking a balanced government budget.

As Japan grew in power and expanded its interests in North East Asia, there had been growing tension with Russia's Far Eastern interests. With the mounting risk of war, Japan began to build its armaments, ordering warships and other weapons from Britain and the West. The Sino-Japanese War had been costly. It had always been understood in Tokyo that to confront Russia credibly would involve major defence expenditure, and that this could not be funded entirely from domestic tax revenue and domestic borrowing, especially within the normal peace-time budget. Takahashi was the man with experience in European capital markets, and despite his own reservations, was sent in some haste back to London to exploit the contacts he had made before in order to raise money for war. It was 1904, and this time he took with him his oldest son Korekata, now in his twenties.

Tokyo estimated that a Russian war would cost about ¥450 million (about $220 million at the time), similar to the war with China. They calculated that at least a hundred million yen would need to be foreign-funded. In some respects this would be a war about funding: Russia (whose national budget was far larger) expected to be able to finance a four-year-long war and anticipated that Japan would not be able to match this. In Tokyo many were pessimistic about the prospects for raising significant loans, especially as their own domestic reserves had halved over the previous year.

Takahashi was told that the fate of Japan rested on his efforts. He analysed the options. There had been hopes of a loan from the British Government, but the connections between the British and Russian royal families now made this unlikely. Thinking tactically, he arranged to meet some key British, American, and German Jewish bankers who were strong opponents of Russia's treatment of Jews, and they were prepared to assist. He proved very adept at building relations with key personnel in the City of London, and later in the New York markets. For months he lobbied bankers, financiers, journalists, and officials, including such luminaries as Jacob Schiff on Wall Street, the Rothschilds of London, and ultimately even King Edward VII of England, in order to put together the case for lending to Japan. With his London contacts he constructed a bond issue for £10 million (around $US 1 billion today). This was the first issue of this type for any such country, and Takahashi had to do much to sell the image of Japan as a reliable debtor in the face of opposition from Russia. At last the bonds were issued, and they proved surprisingly popular in international secondary markets, helped by a media perception of a plucky Japan, and victories in some key early military skirmishes.

In 1904 the Japanese Navy seized the initiative and attacked the Russian Eastern fleet at Port Arthur across the Yellow Sea in Manchuria. Two days later Japan declared war on Russia. Having crippled Russia's Pacific Fleet, they waited eight months for the arrival of Russia's Baltic Fleet sailing to punish Japan. Once again the Japanese Navy attacked, and catching the Russian fleet by surprise, sunk it in only two days. This represented a major victory for Japan. The war resulted in the ceding of Russia's leaseholds in Manchuria and the southern half of Sakhalin Island.

The victory brought admiration from other Asian countries who saw the first defeat of a Western power, and also recognition by Western Europe and the US of growing Japanese strength; in addition it hastened the 1905 Russian Revolution. There was an outpouring of national pride within Japan, feeding the ultra-nationalist views of Japanese superiority and their assumed place in the world. However the war and its aftermath cost far more than anticipated, with years of ongoing military spending. Ultimately it unleashed the darker forces of Japanese militarism that would cause such suffering in the twentieth century.

By the year's end Takahashi thought Japan had borrowed enough, and he wanted to return home. But he was to be disappointed. With the war proving much more expensive than expected, he was ordered by the government to stay and arrange a further loan. Takahashi managed a quick visit to his home and his family during this time, but spent most of three years working on the international loans overseas. Eventually he succeeded in putting together four war loans totalling ¥800 million, somewhat against his better judgement. These were on increasingly tough terms, which ultimately involved committing Japanese customs duties, tobacco, and liquor monopoly revenues as security.

The tough terms of the fourth final loan had spelt lender resistance, and they were resented in Japan. The country also now found itself under pressure from the West not to demand Russian indemnities, an approach that Takahashi supported (and a position which he shared with British economist Maynard Keynes who argued similarly after World War I). The 1895 war with China had cost ¥250 million. In the end the 1905 war with Russia cost nearly ¥2,000 billion, of which three-quarters had to be financed through public bonds, half of it borrowed overseas by Takahashi.

On his eventual return to Tokyo in 1907, Takahashi's major contribution to the war was recognized by a grateful nation: he was appointed to the Upper House of the Diet, and endowed with the title of Baron. More importantly, he also returned with a rare insight into the way the West was thinking and the value of its financial system—he knew that Japan could not have won this war without European and US finance which had been used to pay for British warships, Shell Oil's petroleum, and Western arms. He also feared that Japan would now face difficulty in servicing its huge new foreign debts and controlling its military spending in the future.

The Japanese economy was becoming more developed. Per capita income had doubled since the Meiji Restoration, primary schooling had become the norm, healthcare and transportation had improved, and the process of government was starting to democratize. But this evolving government still lacked a disciplined budgetary process.

In 1911 Takahashi received a significant promotion: he was appointed Governor of the Bank of Japan with control over interest rates and banking. At home economic concerns had moved on to domestic issues, such as the planned nationalization of the railway system. Takahashi had seen the importance of rail in bringing prosperity to Hiroshima, but felt this should be the business of private industry and that the government should avoid increasing its debt. However he thought the role of government should be to promote low interest rates and low business taxes in order to encourage business investment, and he advocated government funding for transport and agriculture infrastructure projects. Gradually the larger municipalities followed Takahashi's example and also raised loans abroad to finance their local infrastructure.

As someone who had struggled so long to raise public funds, Takahashi had a realistic view about the need to control government spending and repay foreign debt. This reinforced his opposition to excessive military spending, and he opposed the policy of military expansion, arguing instead that Japan should focus on the trade opportunities of the region. But this was not yet a popular view in cabinet. Under the Meiji Constitution the Japanese Armed Forces had the right to operate independently of the Prime Minister. In the 1912 Taisho Political Crisis, the army effectively held the cabinet to ransom until they agreed to extra military spending in the colony of Korea.

This was a politically unstable period in Japanese politics: governments were short-term and weak—averaging less than two years' duration in the first two decades and only half of that in the 1930s. Takahashi was not a particularly political animal, but in 1913 he joined the Rikken Seiyukai Party, one of the two main parties that would dominate Japanese governments for half a century. Incoming Prime Minister Gonnohyoe appointed Takahashi as his Minister of Finance. The Government was short-lived and Takahashi held the post for only a year. However it was to be the first of many reappointments to this post: Takahashi would hold the Japanese finance portfolio a staggering seven times in his career.

Takahashi was out of power when World War I broke out in 1914. Within a month Japan had opportunistically joined the Allies against the Axis powers, primarily in order to seize German holdings in eastern China and in the Micronesian islands. Sensing that the war had disrupted traditional power balances, Japan issued the 'Twenty-One Demands', brazenly insisting that a weakened China should grant it an extension of land, rail, mining, and other holdings in southern Manchuria, actions which would have reduced northern China to a puppet state. The dangers of this were well recognized by Takahashi who labelled the Japanese Foreign Minister's demands as 'absurd'. His concerns were realized when there was a Chinese boycott of Japanese imports and protests by Britain and the United States. But it was one more step in the growing Japanese dominance of China. Sensing more opportunities with the 1917 Bolshevik Revolution, Japan embarked on a further military intervention in Siberia, but this time at great cost in men and yen.

The Japanese economy had started World War I heavily indebted. But as European countries shifted their own industrial production to armaments, so Japan moved into British export markets in Southeast Asia. It benefited from its exploitation of newly accessed resources in Manchuria, and in addition Japan was now building the capacity to produce ships and other heavy industry. Japanese manufactured exports increased by two-thirds during the war, and Japan turned a trade deficit into a large surplus. Japan ended World War I in buoyant economic shape. It had not suffered any structural damage itself, while German and Russian Far Eastern interests had been weakened. But the war left the Japanese military emboldened, with a civilian government struggling to contain them.

Japan's democratic government was still proving very unstable with complex shifting political alliances and coalitions. In this disrupted environment Takahashi's economic expertise and international outlook was much sought after. During the post-war years Takahashi served as Agriculture Minister, Commerce Minister, and repeatedly as Finance Minister: his longest period in that office was from 1918 to 1922. In office he proved a progressive politician, advocating a framework of international economic cooperation for trade, with cuts in military spending, cabinet control over the armed forces, active industry policy, a graduated income tax, and devolution of some taxes and spending to local government. However he was not a natural politician, especially in the difficult Japanese political milieu with its shifting back-room coalitions, military allegiances, and political deals—he was always something of a political outsider and he never established the coalition of interests that would have been necessary to achieve all his economic aims.

Government spending continued to rise. As Finance Minister, Takahashi had initially persisted with big budgets and fiscal deficits, believing that such policies could increase production without triggering inflation, despite the economy showing signs of capacity constraints. But he calculated without the continuing spending demands of the military, which eventually led to inflation and an asset bubble. In March 1920 the bubble broke. Prices fell dramatically and national income contracted. Some industries suffered greatly, and many banks that had been servicing them failed.

Alarmed by the military demands, in 1921 Takahashi sent Prime Minister Hara a memo entitled *An Opinion Concerning the Establishment of East Asian Economic Power*. He argued that Japan should withdraw all its troops and military installations from China, reduce coercion over Chinese economic interests, and cancel forced indemnities. In his view Japan could benefit more from a strong industrializing China than from a weak subjugated one. He promoted the idea of a joint Asian economic bloc, welcoming other foreign capital, an idea before its time, but he could not raise political support for it.

In 1921 Prime Minister Hara was stabbed to death by a right-wing ideologue. It was a harbinger of the dreadful times ahead. Takahashi had been looking forward to his own retirement, but once again he was asked to serve his country. Seeking continuity the cabinet appointed the 67-year-old Finance Minister as a Viscount and as Prime Minister of Japan. Takahashi later wrote: 'when I was received as Prime Minister, I tried to refuse but it was just at the time of the opening of the Washington (Naval Disarmament) Conference and we needed a government as soon as possible…So I had no choice but to become Prime Minister' (Smethurst, 2007, 224).

Takahashi knew he was not a skilled politician and he would struggle to hold a disparate government together; he looked on his seven months as prime minister as an interim appointment. He still wanted to advance his policy ideas, formulating a major restructuring of policies, but he continued to lack the political consensus to implement it. However he did sign the Washington Treaty which limited naval spending, and established international respect for 'the territorial integrity of China'. This improved Japan's international reputation and made the country more attractive to US capital markets and technology. Looking to the post-war success of the US, Takahashi called on Japanese industry to imitate the increased productivity of American industry through larger and more efficient factories. However there was a downside: the limitations on Japanese naval spending imposed in the Washington Treaty were to drive enduring military anger in Japan, and Takahashi was held to blame for this.

After his party had again been out of office a few years, Takahashi was recalled to cabinet in 1924, where for a year he was shunted around among the commerce, industry, agriculture, forestry, and justice ministerial portfolios, giving him wide insights into economic and social policy. In a statement entitled *Speaking of First Principles of Economics: Concerning our Country's Production*, he set out his views on increasing productivity by sharing benefits with workers, rather than concluding that high wages automatically lead to higher prices, and pointing to the important role of capital investment. He foresaw heavy industry and larger factories supported by decentralization of government to meet local needs, to be financed by decentralized land taxes. The government did not last long—the next year it was voted out of office again, and once again Takahashi retired thankfully to his home and garden in central Tokyo.

In 1927 a surge of financial panic sparked off fears of bank failures, partly due to the impending redemption of the Kanto Earthquake Bills, which had been issued following the great Kanto earthquake several years previously. The government resigned and financial panic spread, a period known as the Showa Financial Crisis. A new government was formed and Takahashi (now aged 74 and showing his years) was pulled from retirement and asked to serve again as Finance Minister in the new cabinet. He dutifully but unenthusiastically returned to office. There he proposed a bank moratorium until financial market stability could be re-established, and immediately designed several related bills authorizing the Bank of Japan to make special advances under government guarantee to prop up institutions. Then followed a number of structural reforms to the banking industry, including new capital and governance requirements. This resulted in many small banks having to close down or merge, but the restructuring resulted in a stronger Japanese banking industry a few years later when the Great Depression hit.

These measures had a stabilizing effect and after only six weeks, Takahashi was able to gratefully retire once again, returning to his beautiful home and garden where again he could indulge his favourite hobby—cultivating his collection of intricate miniature bonsai trees at his restful Tokyo mansion. The Buddhist bonsai culture offered him the aesthetic contemplation and calm that he sought in his old age.

But yet again stability proved short-lived. The then Bank Governor particularly admired German Currency Commissioner Hjalmar Schacht with his austere policies to dampen hyperinflation. The Japanese decision to re-join the gold standard was based on a misinterpretation of these policies. In 1929 Takahashi watched the government ignore the advice of Keynes and re-join the gold standard at a high exchange rate, expecting this would 'rationalize' the financial and industrial world, i.e. clean out poorly performing companies, and help Japan take its place as a world power. However joining at pre-war prices implied a revaluation of the yen by over 10 per cent, with monetary and budgetary austerity at home, household frugality, a higher interest rate and reduced government spending. The overall effect on the economy was dire: both trade and prices fell by 20 per cent. Companies laid off workers, wages fell, and investment halted.

Later that year the situation worsened. The shock of the 1929 New York stock market crash swept across the Pacific and through the Japanese economy. Japanese exports had been dominated by raw silk and textile production, much of it for American markets. Within two years Japanese textile exports had more than halved, and the price of raw silk halved, worsened by the growth of synthetic rayon products in the US. The US passed the notorious Hawley-Smoot Tariff Act in 1930, and the UK reinstated its Imperial Preference System. Other nations retaliated to protect their own industries: international trading conditions became very restrictive and international trade declined.

Britain left the gold standard in October 1931. Major financial institutions assumed that Japan would be forced to follow, and they sold their yen to buy US dollars. The Japanese Government tried to put capital controls in place, but could not stem the outflow. To discourage this, they raised the discount interest rate in late 1931, but that only made the economic slowdown worse. Domestic investment dried up, unemployment rose further, while wages and real income dropped considerably. In December 1931 the cabinet resigned: there was a major economic crisis. Gold was flowing out of the country, and exports halved. Gross national expenditure fell by 18 per cent and unemployment rocketed.

Labourers' wages dropped significantly, and indebted farm households lost up to half their income. There was even famine in one province.

The extremist wing of the Japanese military regarded this economic performance as a national insult. In 1930 Prime Minister Hamaguchi had been the victim of a right-wing assassination plot, continuing the ongoing instability of civilian Japanese governments, and pointing to the danger of the rebellious military: the right-wing ultra-nationalists were gaining support and urging more intervention in Manchuria.

A new emergency government was formed at the end of 1931. The new Prime Minister was septuagenarian Inukai Tsuyoshi. He pressured his trusted old colleague Takahashi, now 79, to come out of retirement a further time and re-join the cabinet, becoming Minister of Finance once more. This is hardly what Takahashi had ever envisaged or wanted, but he felt that he owed it to the country. Photographs of the time show him looking hunched and weary.

In September Japanese troops stationed in Manchuria bombed their own railway then blamed this on Chinese rebels, the so-called 'Mukden Incident'. It was becoming clear that the Japanese civilian government could no longer control its own army, which used the incident as an excuse to begin an invasion of North-East China. The Japanese Cabinet ordered a halt to the invasion, but the Kwantung Army ignored the orders and established a puppet state in Manchuria which they named Manchukuo. This continued the serious erosion of Chinese sovereignty that would last until the end of World War II. A month later the 'October Incident' marked another coup attempt in Tokyo. Takahashi and other more Westernized politicians were shocked by these events, foreseeing strained relations with the West and bringing chaos and economic disruption to China.

1934: Saving Japan from Depression

By 1934 the risks of war were spreading across the world. In Europe forces on the far right were demonstrating their military intentions in Germany, Italy, Austria, and Spain. In Germany the 'Night of the Long Knives' was followed by Hitler becoming Head of State and Government.

In Spain the Civil War was brewing. In North Africa Italian forces were gathering to invade Abyssinia. In the Soviet Union fear of National Socialism was only outweighed by the horror of Stalin's domestic purges. Asia was also moving to a war footing. In March the new Japanese puppet state of Manchukuo in China was declared, Japanese aggressive intents were becoming more evident along the Chinese coastline, and in the south the Chinese People's Liberation Army set out on their Long March. Japan itself had been struck by a number of natural disasters: the great Hakodate fire in southern Hokkaido and several typhoons in the Kansai region, each of which killed thousands. By the end of the year Japan had renounced the Washington and London Naval Treaties, and was commencing rearmament.

The Great Depression was now raging through the major economies. The developed world was wracked by protectionism, declining international trade, exchange rate disruptions, financial chaos, business bankruptcies, and very high unemployment. Yet the Japanese economy was growing. It was the foresight and innovation of the elderly Japanese politician, Takahashi, which brought recovery to Japan, as he implemented the world's first concerted reflation programme.

What was it about this 81-year-old man who only wanted to lead a quiet retired life, raising bonsai trees in his garden? As he aged, Takahashi had become increasingly rotund, bald, and white-bearded, with round pebble glasses; in his later years he looked like a wise and benevolent gnome. He dressed carefully in a formal Western Edwardian suit, though he was also pictured in ceremonial official uniform with epaulets, medals, and a cocked hat. Photographs of him at home show him looking comfortable and relaxed wearing a traditional Japanese robe and cloak, smilingly surrounded by a troop of his grandchildren, in the lush garden of his beautiful home in Tokyo.

After returning reluctantly to office in early 1932, Takahashi immediately called an emergency meeting to confront the problem of the Depression. It was a dangerous and volatile time. The right wing ideological arm of the Army was out of control and the political assassinations continued: in 1932 the 'Blood Society Incident' caused the death of a former Finance Minister, and in the 'May 15 Incident' the last Seiyukai Prime Minister, Inukai Tsuyoshi, was assassinated. Having watched the death of his friend and knowing the dangers he faced, Takahashi allowed himself to be drafted in as interim Prime Minister for several weeks before a new coalition government could be formed. Takahashi's cabinet faced a mounting threat: the army declared limitations on who they would support in government, using their effective veto at cabinet level. Eventually a new government was formed, breaking from the ruling Seiyukai party, containing a coalition of military, civil, and party men, headed by Admiral Saito Makoto. This military-dominated cabinet marked the end of Japanese parliamentary democracy until after World War II.

Following the Manchurian invasion, some Japanese bureaucrats had been calling for a command economy with Soviet-style five-year plans to direct the occupied Manchurian and Japanese economies. Takahashi resisted this saying: 'Manchuria is part of China; it is not Japan.' He was neither a free market advocate nor a dirigiste but pursued a middle way, which became known as the 'Takahashi line', committed to what he labelled 'the politics of productivity', i.e. actively supporting the economy while controlling military expenditure.

Takahashi's approach to life had been energetic and bold, and although he was ageing and ailing, he did not abandon his instincts. He was always prepared to trial adventurous policies. Takahashi had been proposing a radical new approach to economic policy, a policy quite different from the austerity under way in most countries.

He adopted a three-pillar approach to get the Japanese economy growing again (Shizume, 2009). He worked closely over the next few years with like-minded colleague Fukai Eigo, Vice-Governor of the Central Bank, to put in place an evolving reflationary programme: Takahashi first devalued the yen by cutting the link with the gold standard. In principle this allowed the currency to float but, fearing the consequences of having no currency anchor at all, he restricted its movements: currency could only be converted with the Finance Ministry's approval, and this was onerous to obtain. The yen was allowed to depreciate very significantly (44 per cent against sterling, 60 per cent against the US dollar) over the year, then as it stabilized at a lower level it was pegged against sterling, with some capital controls in place.

As the yen dropped Japanese exports became far more competitive. The balance of payments soon responded: exports almost tripled by 1935, delivering the first positive balance of trade since World War I. There had been considerable opposition to the devaluation and worries about resulting inflation, despite the prevailing conditions of severe deflation. Takahashi's predecessor as Finance Minister, Inoue Junnosuke, had stoutly defended the gold standard, but there was little concerted opposition after the latter was assassinated. Now when the proposals were debated in the Diet, there was wide support for Takahashi's radical move.

Having reengineered exchange rate policy, Takahashi's second tool was monetary policy. In mid-1932 he moved to substantially increase the money supply to provide liquidity and stimulate domestic demand. He did this by increasing the Bank of Japan's limits on the value of unbacked commercial paper it could issue. As insurance he passed a Capital Flight Prevention Act. The base interest rate fell from 5.8 per cent to 3.6 per cent in two years; this allowed Takahashi to issue government bonds more cheaply, and the lower rate encouraged businesses to borrow and expand.

The third pillar of Takahashi's policies was fiscal policy. Takahashi proposed a financing programme totalling ¥600 million over three years from central government, to be matched by an equivalent amount from local government. In order to get military support for this programme, Takahashi had to agree to commit extra funds to pay for military activity in Manchuria. To fund the extra expenditure the government would sell Treasury bonds to the public to be boosted by the Ministry of Finance selling bonds to the Bank of Japan which could hold them before on-selling. This was potentially risky in that it might have flooded local bond markets, but with his links to the Bank of Japan, Takahashi was confident it could be done. In today's terminology this represents quantitative easing.

Takahashi also linked these moves to more active industry policy, making finance available for importers, reducing interest rates for industrialists, small business and farmers, providing regional banks with cheaper funds, and underwriting problem loans. He wanted to dramatically increase government infrastructure spending, especially on public works and emergency relief (coastline protection, harbour facilities, land reclamation, irrigation, drainage, dikes, new roads, and rail) particularly in rural areas, with the objective of improving competitiveness as well as increasing employment and stimulating demand.

Early in the following session of the Diet, Takahashi gave several major speeches outlining significant proposals to deal with the economic depression. 'We will finance the whole fiscal gap with debt. This is because primary factors of increase in expenditure are temporary, too large to finance with an increase in taxes and other revenues, and because an increase in taxes and other revenues would break the budding economic recovery. This is not yet the right time for a tax increase' (Shizume, 2009, 27). Takahashi noted that if public debt were to become unsustainable, early warnings would appear in the financial markets (meaning there would be a low uptake of bonds and signs of early inflation and exchange rate pressure).

These new measures had a significant economic effect over the next few years. Government expenditure increased by 50 per cent, funded by a big increase in Treasury bonds. Over the period of Takahashi's stewardship the Ministry of Finance issued almost ¥2.8 billion of government bonds, all sold to the Bank of Japan; the Bank successfully on-sold 90 per cent of these, absorbing the excess liquidity. The Bank's Vice-Governor, Fukai Eigo, said that by this method Takahashi 'provided money to stimulate economic recovery, pay for the Manchurian incident, and bring interest rates down—he hit three birds with one stone' (Smethurst, 2007, 263).

Where did these ideas originate? Unlike the other economists in this book Takahashi had no formal higher education, developing his knowledge of economics (and finance, politics, and society) through travelling, talking, and reading. But he was not anti-intellectual: in his twenties he had helped translate Alfred Marshall's *The Pure Theory of Foreign Trade* into Japanese. He had knowledgeable colleagues from the Bank of Japan and the Ministry of Finance who advised him on economic matters, and he corresponded with many foreigners. He was particularly influenced by Maeda Masana, a classically educated Japanese, who studied in France in the late nineteenth century and urged the importance of economic materialism—that the general populace should share in growth, and that industry policy should focus on agriculture and traditional forms of industry.

Takahashi was aware of Keynes's fertile writings at this time: *Tract on Monetary Reform* (1923), *The Economic Consequences of Mr Churchill* (1925), and his later *Treatise on Money* (1930), which had been available in Japanese in time to influence Takahashi's reflationary programme on leaving the gold standard. Discussing the gold standard with his son-in-law, who was an economics graduate, Takahashi said: 'it is best for people to stand in the real world to adopt the best solution to each problem. Theory is for scholars, but not for the rest of us' (Smethurst, 2017, 266). Takahashi's only known direct reference to Keynes was in a 1933 speech where he used the latter's arguments to back up his view that adherence to the gold standard had been one of the causes of world depression. But Takahashi undoubtedly knew more about Keynes. In addition to reading newspapers in Japanese and German, he read *The Times* daily in English, which at this time contained much discussion of Keynes's theories and carried occasional articles by Keynes himself.

In 1929 in temporary retirement, Takahashi had written a long magazine article explaining his misgivings about the pricing and timing of Japan's return to the gold standard. This may have been influenced by Keynes's and Hubert Henderson's pamphlet *Can Lloyd George Do It?*, which had been published the same year, and it contained a cogent explanation of the multiplier effect to be formalized later in Keynesian economics, together with a warning about the pitfalls of falling into a liquidity trap. Takahashi's thinking also reflected the influence of Tameyuki Amano, a Japanese economist and author of several widely used textbooks that contained concepts similar to multiplier analysis and the paradox of saving.

Takahashi explained in his article that if someone saves rather than spends, there is less demand for goods throughout the economy: 'To put it in plain language, if a person goes to a geisha house and calls a geisha, eats luxurious food, and spends ¥2,000, we disapprove morally. But if we analyse how that money is used, we find that the part that paid for food helps support the chef's salary, and the part used to buy fish, meat, vegetables, and seasoning, and the part for transporting it is paid to the supplying merchants. That part then whets the pockets of farmers and fishermen. The farmers, fishermen, and merchants who receive the money then buy clothes, food, and shelter. And the geisha uses the money to purchase food, clothes, cosmetics, and to pay taxes' (Smethurst, 2007, 245).

This article demonstrated an intuitive understanding of the circular flow of income and the stimulating role of multipliers before the formal articulation of these ideas in the 1931 pioneering paper on the multiplier written by Keynes's disciple Richard Kahn in the *Economic Journal*.

When it came to observing New Deal-type policies in major economies, Takahashi was aware of the reflation and expenditure under way in Germany in the 1930s and the new corporate state policies of Mussolini's Italy—both were cited by Western observers looking for new fixes for depression conditions. But he trialled his new macroeconomic policies before the US New Deal was in place.

In a 1933 speech Takahashi cited articles by Irving Fisher of Yale and University of Chicago economists about balancing the budget, not every year, but over a number of years. Much of the economic insight behind this thinking had come from Eigo Fukai, then Vice-Governor of the Bank of Japan. He was also influenced by Tokuzo Fukuda, a Tokyo University professor. (Fukuda's career illustrates some of the international links amongst economists at this time: he had studied at the University of Munich about the same time as Hjalmar Schacht, and his advisor had been Luis Brentano, also Schacht's advisor. He was a follower of the German Historical School, particularly associated with Professor Sombert, Wassily Leontief's supervisor. And he would hear Maynard Keynes discuss his ideas in a conference in Moscow in 1935.)

In the short to medium term Takahashi's policies worked very well from a macroeconomic standpoint. The rapid easing of economic conditions led to a speedy recovery in confidence and activity, with strong growth during the period of the Great Depression. From the early 1930s per capita national income had picked up, growing at an average 6 per cent per annum for five years. With this increase in activity, unemployment reduced markedly so that by 1936 Japan was near full employment. Average wages began to rise and personal income also started to grow again.

Recent studies have estimated which components of policy were most important in this. The fiscal reflation was broadly successful, although there was no formal mechanism to keep the ever-growing military budget in check. One study argued that the fiscal expansion was important in reversing the decline, and that growth was sustained by industry policy, world recovery, and the influence of the nationalistic regime in forcing wage cutting on workers (Cha, 2000). An econometric simulation concluded that the exchange rate adjustment had the strongest effect (Shibamoto and Shizume, 2011).

Overall, this policy programme was even more impressive when viewed from an international perspective. Japan recovered from the Great Depression five years faster than the United States and faster than any other world powers except Germany. Japan expert Hugh Patrick considered it: 'one of the most successful combinations of fiscal policy, monetary policy and exchange rate policy in an adverse international environment that the world has ever seen' (Hadley, 1989).

1935: Disciplining Military Spending

By 1935 Germany was heading towards rearmament in outright contravention of the Versailles Treaty prohibitions, introducing general conscription and passing the Nuremberg Laws stripping Jews of their citizenship. In East Asia the struggle for control over China was intensifying. The Soviet Union had reached an uneasy agreement with Japan, recognizing the latter's control over the South Manchurian Railway and the Soviet Union's control over the China Eastern Railway. In China, the nationalist government had conceded military control of North-East China to Japan, but the Communists were calling for a united front to oppose the Japanese. In Japan increasingly radical and uncontrollable factions of the army mounted coups, continued overseas aggression, and attempted assassination of Japanese politicians who opposed them.

Takahashi was reluctant to return to the finance portfolio: he knew the military would hold an effective cabinet veto over the budget. He had a long record opposing the radical military, and he knew the risks of doing this. In 1931 he had threatened to resign if the Japanese Army carried out its proposed attack on the city of Jinzhou in Manchuria. The following year he had successfully opposed the army's plan to impose the Japanese yen as the currency of Manchukuo, arguing it was really an independent foreign country. He had also argued against Japanese military spending in Manchuria on the basis it would crowd out more important trade with other countries. Once the Japanese attack on Manchuria was under way, Takahashi had called on the Army Minister to bring his troops home, which had brought an outraged military response. To military extremists Takahashi was now marked as an enemy of the Japanese Empire.

Takahashi had always anticipated his fiscal expansion as temporary. In 1934 he terminated a depression relief fund. But it proved very difficult to limit military spending. He consistently offered the army and navy less funds than they demanded, resulting in angry, sometimes public, confrontations with the generals in cabinet. In late 1933 Britain and the US raised tariffs on Japanese goods. Takahashi attributed this partly to the threats made by the Japanese military clique against the Soviet Union and the USA.

From the outset the 1933 budget process had been particularly difficult for all sides. Takahashi was now aged 78 and in ill health. He was unhappy with the whole budgetary process and considered resigning once again, but Prime Minister Saito valued his strength, knowledge, and popularity, and persuaded him to stay. Once more Takahashi agreed, and he tried once more to restructure the budgetary system to limit ministers arguing for their own interests and inflating their own claims. Takahashi wanted a top-down budgetary process, with national priorities to be established first, then with junior ministers becoming involved; however he never received the support that he needed. Indeed the situation had worsened because the military was now appointing hard-line officers as Army and Navy Ministers.

In mid-1934 the Saito Cabinet fell on allegations of corruption, the so-called 'Teijin Incident', where it was claimed that investors had made windfall gains following the government's bailout of a failing industrialist, allegations that later proved to be trumped up by right-wing militants. Several of Takahashi's colleagues were arrested and charged, and it seems that the real target was probably Takahashi himself. But he was not cowed by this attack. His growth policies were still supported by a coalition of large and small businesses, centrist officials, party politicians, and moderate labour unions. But the military and some right-wingers argued for a stronger authoritarian government, larger armed forces, and adventures abroad. The Navy Minister Admiral Okada was selected as the new Prime Minister. Okada asked Takahashi to stay on, but the latter felt bruised by the Teijin Incident and recommended his deputy minister instead. After four very stressful months on the job this successor died. In November 1934, Takahashi, now 80 and continuously in poor health, was pulled back to the ministry for the seventh and last time.

Takahashi's 1934–5 budget ended up conceding more money to the military, an outcome that now seemed almost inevitable. Military spending had grown considerably over previous years and was now absorbing almost half of all government spending. The budgetary process was barely under control, with the nominally civilian government increasingly being held to ransom by military ministers. At least the economy was now growing faster, which allowed for a reduction in bond issuance and a company tax increase, though this latter proved unpopular. Military politicians and radicals continued to threaten their opponents, with propaganda and assassination attempts. They were angry with American trade policies and its treatment of Japanese immigrants, angry about the Great Powers' criticism of Japan's activities in Manchuria, angry about the London and Washington Naval Treaties, angry with the Chinese rebel resistance, and angry with the economic suffering of the Depression years.

Work on the 1935–6 budget began. Takahashi was committed to return to a balanced budget, now that economic growth was improving, inflation was rising, and debt was mounting. He had regularly stated that fiscal stimulus must be thought of as temporary.

The key to Japan's military control over Manchuria lay in the rail network, and the army wanted to expand this. In 1935 Takahashi was the only senior minister to oppose plans to expand the South Manchuria Railway Company's operations, which he saw as advancing Japanese militarism. He seemed to have a clearer view of the military's dependence on Western technology and key materials such as aviation fuel than the military did themselves.

Takahashi had confronted the armed forces publicly in all his last four budgets, in an increasingly difficult atmosphere, given that the budget required unanimous consent of all ministers including the Navy and Army Ministers from the forces. This time the military again opposed Takahashi's proposed budget, demanding unrealistic increases in arms expenditure in a very confrontational way. Takahashi broke off budget negotiations and publicly criticized the insincerity of the ministers. He compared the Japanese economy to a Western one, pointing out the US was nearly ten times higher in per capita income, and much richer in natural resources: therefore Japan could not afford to spend like a big Western power. The army criticized him in the strongest language, declaring: '...our leaders must be completely changed and removed' (Smethurst, 2007, 291).

One of the last photographs of Takahashi shows him reading through-out a noisy budget debate in the National Diet in late 1935 with a bemused smile on his face. This book was *Soviet Communism: A New Civilisation?* by Fabians Sidney and Beatrice Webb. Takahashi apparently arranged for a leading newspaper to publish this photograph quite deliberately and provocatively, because the book had been banned in Japan by government censors for its dangerously Communist tone. Takahashi recognized the risks that he was running, telling others that he knew he could be an assassin's target but felt he had no alternative than to persist.

Finally the Army Minister agreed the year's budget, but it was too late. The military was splitting: one powerful faction was vehemently opposed to any restraints at all on military spending, and they would not compromise. For the next few days long and onerous budget meet-ings were held to try to resolve the impasse. After a 20-hour-long meeting, Takahashi signalled final agreement, earning praise from the newspapers calling him an 82-year-old 'miracle-working daruma'.

In early 1936 Japan woke up to Italy's blatant invasion of Abyssinia. Takahashi was forthright in criticizing it, pointing to the dangers of such aggressive colonialism. The army interpreted this, probably accurately, as renewed criticism of their own Manchurian occupation. On 20 February there was a general election, and Takahashi's stance received public support. But Takahashi was now receiving direct threats on his life from right-wingers.

The Japanese Imperial Army had a history of factionalized protest. A 'Young Officers' movement formed, believing the nation had strayed from its proper destiny. They complained the Emperor was being misled by 'evil advisors around the throne'. (Prominent in their minds was Takahashi.) The Young Officers wanted to purge Western ideas and restore the nation to their notions of traditional purity. The movement was small but had influential sympathizers among the General Staff and the Imperial Family, and had already demonstrated its powers with the Military Academy Incident in 1934 and the assassination of a prominent conservative army general a year later.

The assassinations and uprisings took place under the flag of 'Kokutai', an ultra-nationalist purist Japanese culture. In late 1935 the Young

Officers Movement launched a new plot: in a secret document entitled *Manifesto of the Uprising* they blamed bureaucrats, politicians, and others for endangering the national polity and planned to rid the country of these anti-nationalist enemies. A group of officers would take a contingent of troops to assassinate the most prominent enemies of the Kokutai, control the capital, and submit demands to the Emperor who they believed would be sympathetic to their cause. They prepared a list of half a dozen targets, most of them key senior advisors or politicians, including the Prime Minister. Prominent on that list was the name of Finance Minister Takahashi, accused of 'involvement in party politics, attempting to weaken the military, and continuing the existing economic structure'.

As fears for his life had grown, special precautions had been taken by the civilian government to keep Takahashi safe: he was instructed on how to survive an assassination attempt in his car; there was special security in place in his office; and his home was equipped with special door locks, concealed exits, guards, and a secret escape room. Takahashi was quite aware of the dangers he faced, saying: 'I entered the Government again thinking that this is my last chance to serve. I am prepared to die now' (Smethurst, 2017, 295).

On the evening of 25 February 1936, fatigued from his budgetary marathons, Takahashi returned home early from his offices to see his married daughter who had arranged to visit her parents. The whole family dined together. After dinner, very tired, Takahashi retired early to bed.

On that night, about 1,500 men led by 25 officers prepared for the coup. They adopted the name 'New Righteous Army' and their password was 'Revere the Emperor, destroy the traitors'. They assembled in three barracks in central Tokyo. It was a very cold night and snow was falling. At 5 a.m. in the frigid morning Lieutenant Nakahashi and Lieutenant Nakajima of the Third Imperial Guard marched with 120 men to Takahashi's personal residence, an old-style walled villa only 500 metres from the barracks. Half the contingent of soldiers halted and formed a defensive ring outside. The other half pushed past the guards on the gate. The gatekeeper guard managed to ring a Vice-Minister to warn him what was happening. But he could do nothing to stop the soldiers who smashed through the front gate, kicked their way into Takahashi's house, trampled through the building, and stormed into Takahashi's bedroom where he lay asleep in bed. Hearing the noise Takahashi awoke in confusion, pulled himself upright, and demanded to know what was happening.

Nakajima screamed at him: 'Heavenly punishment!' He unsheathed his sword and hacked at Takahashi's body, almost severing his arm. Nakahashi yelled: 'Traitor!' and fired several bullets into Takahashi's chest and abdomen. Takahashi fell back on his bed, dead. Vice-Minister Tsushima arrived and bravely tried to intervene, but it was too late. The corpse lay motionless on the bed, the pyjamas stained with blood. Takahashi was dead.

Their fanatical mission accomplished, the assassins pushed their way out of the villa, and joined the other armed groups heading to the Imperial Palace. The fanatics continued with their orgy of violence that night: they also succeeded in assassinating a former Prime Minister and another conservative minister.

After the assassinations, the rebel soldiers holed up in buildings in central Tokyo, calling for a military government. But after several days of vacillating, the Emperor refused to condone the assassinations and demanded that the uprising be put down. Now the rebels realized they were defeated. The army was initially unwilling to step in and punish its errant officers, but eventually martial law was decreed and the rebelling soldiers were belatedly arrested and put on trial.

The 26 February Incident ended in failure for the New Righteous Army. After a closed trial, 19 officers were sentenced to death and executed, with many others imprisoned. But the incident also spelt an end to many of the ideals Takahashi had been promoting, including building a modern economy, international economic cooperation, democratic cabinet control, and limits on military spending. The attempted military coup had been suppressed, but nevertheless this event marked the end of the civilian government's control over the forces of the military. The Japanese Cabinet resigned and the incoming Prime Minister was forced to surrender to many of the military demands, including a new requirement that only active officers should serve as Minister of War and the Navy. This meant that if the cabinet did not agree to their funding demands, their commanding officers could order them to resign, thus holding up budgets and causing governments to fall.

Takahashi's disciplined budgetary process was no more. The military increased their spending on rearmament. The following year this spilled over into a full-scale invasion of coastal China, and the formal declaration of war by Japan, the beginning of that terrible period when the world would tumble into war.

Over the next few years unrestrained military spending dominated the Japanese budget, far outstripping the ability of the economy to pay for it, even when additional resources were being seized from the territories occupied by the Japanese Army. Debt rose rapidly and inflation initially jumped to 10 per cent, then rose to astronomical levels.

Tokyo was placed under martial law, and for a month the army prevented Takahashi's family from holding his funeral. When it was finally arranged, no announcements were allowed to be made for fear of stirring further unrest. But somehow news leaked out and it spread rapidly around the community: when they heard of the funeral hundreds of ordinary people lined the streets to see the cortege and to pay their respects to this brave man. In defiance of the army the Empress sent a bouquet of flowers. In the streets the people showed their sadness and respect for the end of a hero, but also for the end of an era.

Takahashi had been a very popular politician, a man who understood the people. Short and stout, his nickname had been 'Daruma', the Japanese traditional doll based on the Bodhidharma monk, usually depicted as a tubby, bearded man, seen as a symbol of perseverance and good luck. Egg-shaped, the dolls are weighted at their base so they will bounce back when pushed over. They are often associated with a famous Japanese proverb: 'nana korobi yaoki', roughly translated as 'fall down seven times, get up eight'. Takahashi was to serve as Finance Minister seven times, but even he could not bounce up again after that.

2

Richest Man in the World?

H. H. Kung in China, 1936–7

H. H. Kung and the First Family of China

News of the death of Takahashi and the 26 February Incident travelled fast. The Nationalist Kuomintang Government of China in Nanjing heard of the assassinations, the Chinese bankers and industrialists in Shanghai heard, the Communists in Yunnan heard. The assassination of the most trusted economic policymaker in Japan, the other deaths, and the attempted Japanese army coup dominated the news. The realistic Chinese knew that the trials and executions would not spell the end of Japan's military ambitions, and they could see that democratic civilian control was crumbling in Tokyo. They understood that this meant China would face more military pressure ahead. The Kuomintang leaders were particularly well informed about these developments in Japan because many of them had lived there in earlier years, either as young radicals fleeing repression, or as young soldiers training in the Japanese military academies. As a military government themselves the Kuomintang could see that the Japanese Army was hardly under control.

One of the most interested and most concerned was Kung Hsiang-hsi, (alternately known today as Kong Xiangxi) commonly called 'HH'. At this time Kung was 55 years old, and serving as both Minister of Finance and Central Bank Governor of China in the Nationalist Kuomintang Government. He knew well the plight of finance ministers in governments with military goals, for he himself was having a very difficult time as he sought to support the currency, stabilize runaway inflation, raise public funds, bolster weak institutions, and restore economic credibility to a government which was fighting wars on several fronts simultaneously. This Chinese Nationalist Government was politically unstable, caught beneath the insatiable and often unreasonable demands of President Chiang Kai-shek, in an era of corruption, profit-seeking, cruelty, and extortion.

Kung had some advantages in this demanding role: unlike Takahashi, he was a trained economist. And unlike Takahashi he was adept at deal-making to support his economic policies. His economic problems were huge, yet Kung was a man who could operate in such a complex environment, attending to his public duties while at the same time using his official position to accumulate huge personal wealth. He saw little conflict in intermingling family and government interests, relying on Chinese resources and labour, helping to fund the fighting against the Communists, but at the same time covertly partnering with Japanese business interests himself. Kung, without Takahashi's sense of moral code or national pride, was an economist who could thrive in such a conflicted and inconsistent world, building relationships, doing government deals, and making something for himself on the side.

In office, Kung spent much of his time raising finance. In 1936, as war looked increasingly likely and there was growing rearmament expenditure by the Nationalist Government, he worked to establish a domestic tax base, a government-owned banking system, and a new currency. From 1937 as conflict spread, he found ways to get arms assistance from Germany and began to channel huge amounts of US aid money.

At the turn of the century the Tokyo of Takahashi had provided an attractive refuge for a new cadre of young Asian nationalists. Japan was riding high on the back of the victory over a major European power. There was a pilgrimage by a new generation of young Asian radicals looking to break the bounds of old imperial traditions and colonial constraints in their own countries. One such was Sun Yat-sen. Sun Yat-sen was a Chinese revolutionary who had mounted several unsuccessful coups to unseat the fading Chinese Imperial Government and the warlords who ruled China immediately afterwards. Hunted by the police, he sought refuge in Japan. In 1905 he travelled to the US, delivering lectures on his vision for a new Republican China and collecting donations for the revolutionary effort from Chinese diaspora there.

That year a young Chinese student studying in the United States journeyed to the bustling industrial city of Cleveland, because he had heard there was to be an important speaker from China at the meeting hall of the local Chinese community. The speaker's name was Dr Sun Yat-sen.

With his revolutionary rhetoric and cosmopolitan background, Sun made a big impact on the young Chinese student that night, and they would later form a close tie.

The impressionable young student was H. H. Kung. He had been born in 1881 in Taigu in Shanxi Province in the north of China to a rich local family. The family wealth came from a string of pawnshops all over China, which made loans to peasants and small business, a crude form of banking. Gradually the Kungs converted their pawnshops into stores and banks. During a bad farming year they would lend generously: those unable to repay lost their land to the Kungs. As a result the family grew very rich over the years, and the money-lending chain grew. Doing business at this time meant reaching accommodations with the local warlords, something the Kungs proved astute at doing, balancing conflicting interests, becoming trusted advisors, and benefiting from the protection and contacts that gangsters offered them. The family was based in Shanxi where they were very powerful, but they were growing their interests all over China, establishing branches as far away as Mongolia, Vietnam, and Japan.

His mother had died when he was very young. The family was very traditional (Kung claimed to be a 75th generation lineal descendant of Confucius), and opposed to Kung having a Western education, but he persuaded his father that education was the new way to get ahead in business life. While the father devoted all his time to the family business, the children were sent to a local missionary school staffed by Americans. There the boy was quick to advance: he learned English and, sensing advantage, he secretly converted to Christianity. In 1896 he moved from his backwater home town to the North China Union College run by missionaries in Tungchow near Peking. There he showed an eager mind as he absorbed courses in mathematics, chemistry, and physics, subjects that had never been part of traditional Chinese education.

Kung was on vacation back at his home in Taigu in 1900 when the Boxer Rebellion erupted in Northern China, then spread across the Shanxi province. The Boxers were radical Chinese patriots reacting against European control of key northern Chinese cities. They went on a bloody rampage through the region, murdering missionaries and local Christians. A missionary tract of 1903 told of the role played by Kung, then a young student of 19. A pro-Boxer mob flocked into Taigu city, emboldened by the talk of massacres nearby. The local and European missionaries knew they would be targeted. Kung armed himself and helped the missionaries to fortify their compound. He did his best to act as a go-between, proving very brave under considerable danger, in the face of taunting by the local Boxers, and ignoring his family's frantic entreaties for him to flee to safety. The Boxers besieged the missionary compound and worked themselves into an hysterical mob howling for blood.

The missionaries saw there was to be no escape from the beleaguered compound, and knowing they were about to die they bravely wrote last letters to their loved ones. At the last moment Kung donned a disguise, took the missionaries' final testimonies, and regardless of the risks managed to steal out of the compound. His family hid him as the mob of Boxers stormed uncontrolled through the city, cruelly killing and beheading all the missionaries and many other Christians. Despite the terrible risks and his family's urgings, Kung refused to recant his Christianity. Eventually, hidden in an ox cart, he managed to flee the region.

When the rebelling Boxers reached Peking and besieged the European settlements there, the weak Manchu Government made the fatal decision to support them. Outraged at the government's complicity and the murder of missionaries, the six occupying European nations sent troops and brutally crushed the Peking revolt, massacring many Chinese and burning property indiscriminately.

After punishing Peking, the avenging Western Force turned their attention to Shanxi Province where many missionaries had been slaughtered. In Taigu Kung helped collect the remains of the dead, distribute famine relief funds, and restore mission property. As a young Christian, he was able to intercede with the commanders of the combined Western forces, persuading them not to carry out executions or sack the towns, offering instead that the province would pay cash reparations and grant concessions to foreign firms. As part of this deal Kung managed to confiscate an extensive property from a pro-Boxer family, and in future years he was to use this land as a site for several schools. His approach was partly that of a good Christian. But it was also about doing favours and using them for personal gain. The Boxer massacres were a disaster, but a disaster that could be leveraged. The Boxer reparations were humiliating, but humiliation could be stomached. Kung was to prove very proficient at such deal-making in his adult years: engaging with difficult, unethical, and unreliable partners, and reaching economic agreements with them, usually with something on the side for himself.

Kung was successful in avoiding further violence and reparations from the region. His clever negotiations came to the attention of the Emperor. As a reward he was decorated and given a passport to study in the US. A missionary educator in Tungchow arranged for him and a fellow student to attend Oberlin College in Ohio, a progressive place of learning affiliated to his old Taigu school. Setting off in 1901 they sailed from Shanghai via Japan to San Francisco. At San Francisco there was a scene reminiscent of young Takahashi's troubles several decades earlier: Kung encountered immigration barriers. He was denied entry to the US, and confined to the ship for a week by the US Immigration Service. There had been an outbreak of anti-Asian sentiment in the US, and Chinese students were not welcome. Released from the ship at last, he found he had to remain in San Francisco for a year, waiting for his immigration papers to be cleared.

He was lodged at a Christian Chinese mission in San Francisco—an opportunity for Kung to work on his English. At last he received permission to attend Oberlin College. Unfortunately the rail line eastward passed through Canada, and on the point of re-entry to the US he was detained yet again by the racist US immigration authorities. He was not released until Oberlin College managed to get their local Congressman to apply political pressure. At last in January 1903 he arrived at Oberlin College, a quiet centre of learning set in a small country town in Ohio, thousands of miles from the chaos and crowds of northern China. At Oberlin Kung decided to study economics as part of the liberal arts degree. He was nothing if not robust and adaptable, and despite his harsh treatment by the US authorities seemed to bear no grudges. Rather, it was a chance to learn how the American system worked, knowledge that he would later use to extract vast sums of money from that country.

Several years later Kung graduated from Oberlin, and thanks to his family's wealth, was able to gain admission to Yale University in New Haven on the East Coast. There he studied for a master's degree in economics. The senior professor of political economy at Yale was Irving

Fisher, a prolific writer, inventor, mathematician, modeller, statistician, and researcher. At the time he was writing books on *The Nature of Capital and Income* (1906) and *The Rate of Interest* (1907), key works which helped develop the quantity theory of money. Fisher's pioneering work would be an important contribution to the economic theories used by several of the other economists in this book. Kung had learned reasonable English and was sufficiently able to pass his university courses. But he was not one to be absorbed by Fisher's economic theories. He displayed more talent for practical economic things: business relationships, banking, deal-doing and money-making.

Armed with his American degrees, Kung returned to China to the family business in Taigu. There he was reintroduced to commercial practices in China, but he also learned about who held power, and how to make himself indispensable to them. It was a very unsettled period with many revolts and uprisings challenging the authority of the fading Qing Dynasty. Soon Kung was appointed as an official advisor, broker, and commercial go-between for a local warlord, Yen Hsi-shan. Yen was a returnee from Tokyo where he had been an admirer of Japanese military efficiency. During the 1911 Xinhai Revolution Kung helped him organize his forces to overthrow the authority of the Qing Imperial Government in Shanxi Province. He also helped him negotiate a position as military governor of the Province with Yuan Shi-kai, the emerging political leader. Yen was known for his charm, guile, and greed, traits that Kung recognized, admired, and was interested to use. In addition to learning the art of negotiation and compromise, Kung also learned from Yen something about the practice of economic development in Shanxi, which was gaining a reputation as a model province despite its poverty and remoteness.

Using the Boxer indemnity lands in Taigu, Kung now helped to establish two new Christian schools for boys and for girls. A few years later he courted a young orphan girl, Han Yu-mei, who he had met at a nearby mission school. They married and began a happy domestic life together on the campus of the new schools which Kung now directed. In a graduation address he spoke on 'The Guiding Compass for a Young Man's Success—careful observation, scientific thinking, prayerful decision, and forceful action', impressive rhetoric although not quite the rules that would guide his own career.

The turbulence continued. Following another uprising, revolutionary leader Sun Yat-sen was elected as the first Provisional President of Republican China in 1911. Two years later Yuan Shi-kai made a bid for total power, turning on his co-conspirators and dispatching assassins to eliminate his rivals. Sun was targeted and he fled back to Tokyo.

Kung had emerged as a natural leader in the community, building a reputation as a young progressive. He served as captain of the local militia—a photograph shows him looking trim and smart in his military uniform. However this stability, prosperity, and family life was brought to an abrupt end: his wife was frail and sickly, and in 1913 she died of tuberculosis, still very young and childless. Takahashi had also suffered the premature death of his young wife, and now Kung was also rudderless. Alone and seeking direction, he resigned as school principal. Eventually he decided to do what other young liberal educated Chinese were doing—travel to the progressive country of Japan to observe that system, while at the same time see whether he might advance the interests of the family business there. In Tokyo his Chinese Christian contacts soon secured him a job as administrator of the Chinese YMCA, a central meeting place for the Chinese diaspora. There Kung found himself in the midst of the Christian Chinese community and among the sympathizers of Sun Yat-sen's Kuomintang party.

At this time Takahashi was also in Tokyo as Governor of the Central Bank of Japan. There is no evidence that they ever met, but a young man with such a questioning commercial outlook as Kung would certainly have heard of Takahashi and probably admired him. He might have ruminated on the fact that China had no such strong civil government, no operating central bank, and no formal economic advisors.

One of the close confidants of Sun Yat-sen was the very wealthy Chinese merchant Charlie Soong, whose daughter Ai-ling worked as Sun's secretary. When Sun Yat-sen fled China, fearing his family might also be targeted by assassins, Charlie and his family took flight too. In China Charlie had used his wealth to help establish the YMCA, so it was no surprise that he too gravitated to the YMCA office in Tokyo. There he met the young Kung. As they conversed, it emerged that Kung had already met Charlie's daughter Ai-ling years earlier, at a student party in New York of all places. Charlie Soong invited the young widower home to dine with his family. Kung, with all his charm, proved a big hit with this powerful commercial Chinese family. As he sat down at the dinner table he charmed Charlie and he charmed his wife, but he especially charmed number one daughter Ai-ling. Seagrave caught the atmosphere:

> HH Kung found himself the captive of Ai-ling Soong. Kung was the answer to her prayers. Chunky, puppy -like, and humble in his manner, he was unprepossessing in the extreme. But, if he was far from glamorous, so was she. He was a link to reality in the midst of a travelling sideshow of political levitators. While others inhaled heady drafts of utopia, Kung exhaled currency. To Ai-ling, idealism was frosting on the cake, the cake could only be baked with power, and power could only be purchased with money. She had seen it at work long enough to understand very well.   (Seagrave, 1985, 135)

The couple were married several months later in 1915, in Yokohama in a rain of cherry blossom, in a Christian church with Kung cousins and the Soong family in attendance. It was to prove a deal made in heaven: the two had a common interest in money and power, and they complemented one another's talents. Kung was the frontman with the charm, connections, and commercial ability. Ai-ling would be Kung's tireless supporter, his tactician, and his tough enforcer for the next half century. In contrast to his first wife, she was a woman whom Kung could admire and do business with, Kung presenting as the smiling front to Ai-ling's steely determination.

As Kung was well aware, he had married into a very powerful family, one that was to dominate China financially and politically for nearly half a century. They were Christian and religious in outlook, but astute and ruthless in practice. The father Charlie Soong was a very rich self-made businessman. The children had mainly been educated in the United States. Kung's new wife, Ai-ling was the eldest, and with a reputation as a very clever operator: a scheming backroom manipulator, holding the funds, quietly pulling the strings on businessmen, warlords, and the family, both as a tactician and an enforcer. She did not hold back from any business practice, and had no compunction in having any problematic rivals assassinated. Later her enemies would label her 'the most evil woman in China'.

Sun Yat-sen was now in his fifties, and busy with repeated attempts at coups, trying to change Chinese politics from the safe distance of Tokyo. After Ai-ling's marriage to Kung, Sun needed another secretary. Luckily there were plenty of other talented siblings in the Soong family: her middle sister Ching-ling, aged only 20, back from her United States study, took on the secretarial role. In contrast to her coldly commercial sister, Ching-ling was passionate, idealistic, romantic, and revolutionary. Ching-ling and Dr Sun had an intense relationship that developed into an affair. But Sun Yat-sen was already married. As a strong Christian, father Charlie Soong took an unforgiving view of this, cut his friendship with Sun Yat-sen, moving the family back to China, where they settled in Shanghai, despite the ongoing unrest there. But Ching-ling was very determined, despite the strong Chinese expectations of filial obedience: she absconded from the family home and secretly fled back to Tokyo, where she speedily 'wed' Dr Sun, who claimed (inaccurately) to have divorced his previous wife. Charlie was angry and disowned Ching-ling, who remained with Dr Sun until he died. She retained her radical stance, and later became a Communist icon.

In 1916 Kung took his new wife back to his ancestral hometown in the northern province of Shanxi. Political conditions were dangerous, but remote Taigu was relatively safe because of the family's power. There they lived a luxurious life in an ugly but enormous home, a palace set in splendid gardens, with a staff of 500 (today the building is preserved as a museum). Ai-ling gave birth to their first children there. Kung's local school (called Ming-hsien based on his memories of Oberlin in the US) was still operating, and eventually he would devote a considerable sum of money to create a chain of 'Oberlin in China' schools.

Ai-ling's first younger brother T. V. Soong was raised as the scion of the family. He was clever and intellectual. After attending university in Shanghai, he studied economics at Harvard University and later worked in banking in New York. Displaying the family's financial acumen, TV returned to China where he worked for several family business enterprises. By 1919 Sun Yat-sen had returned to China and established a provisional government in Canton in the south. T. V. Soong joined his brother-in-law to work for him as a financial advisor and to help the new government establish a financial base, soon proving to have a talent for public policy.

But it was another brother-in-law who would have the dominant role in forming the early Nationalist Government in China. Chiang Kai-shek was a young man with a poor upbringing who had been educated on the streets as a gangster then learned military tactics in Tokyo. He combined a rare talent for manipulation and personal advancement with insightful military tactics, a fearsome temper, and a predilection for violence. He had been an enforcer for the Green Gang, one of the very powerful Shanghai mobsters that controlled most legal and illegal commerce on that part of the coast. Chiang Kai-shek gradually grew powerful in his own right and joined the fledgling government of Sun Yat-sen.

At this time there was another Soong sister on the scene. The youngest daughter Mei-ling had returned from her Wesleyan College education in the US. She was pert, clever, persuasive, and engaging, and she quickly caught the eye of the upwardly mobile Chiang Kai-shek, by now established as the governor of the Whampoa Military Academy. He ruthlessly divorced his previous two wives and abandoned his sons, so that he might marry this entrancing and politically-connected Soong sister. At first the Soong family opposed the wedding to a much-married street gangster. But Kung and Ai-ling sensed a deal: they could see the advantages that could come from this union, and in 1927 they brokered the wedding. Kung arranged for Chiang Kai-shek to become a Christian of convenience, and escorted him to the wedding altar in an elaborate ceremony that was stage-managed by Ai-ling.

Kung now found himself a member of the most powerful family in China. Rich himself, his wealth was also bolstered by father-in-law Charlie Soong's fortunes and contacts, he was married to a talented business woman, he was brother-in-law to the first President of China Dr Sun Yat-sen, he was brother-in-law to the head of the Kuomintang Generalissimo Chiang Kai-shek, and he was brother-in-law to T. V. Soong who would become one of the richest and most powerful men in China. Two younger Soong brothers would also become money men. Sister-in-law Ching-ling would become a martyr for China, and youngest sister-in-law Mei-ling would become one of America's most influential women. It would be said of the three sisters that Ai-ling loved money, Mei-ling loved power, and Ching-ling loved China.

Kung now held a position that could be leveraged, with that early twentieth-century Chinese mix of family fortune and contacts, street toughness, warlord interests, military adventurism, and international pressures. It was a volatile environment where he would use the disruptions to help himself, his family, his political allies, and his country, in that order.

Kung had kept in contact with Sun Yat-sen, and he was proud to receive an autographed copy of the latter's *Programme of National Reconstruction*, which was to become one of the founding documents of the new China. Dr Sun had established the first enduring Chinese Republican Government based in the southern city of Canton and later Wuhan, exerting intermittent control over much of Southern China with a shifting pattern of political and warlord alliances. Sun needed to build up the government's military capacity, but there was no modern revenue system to fund the operations. The main source of government funding had been a ramshackle system of city taxes and countryside rice taxes which were administered by corrupt officials and gangs. Local warlords and magistrates collected internal tariffs called 'likin' on behalf of the government and kept a percentage for themselves. A much-hated salt monopoly also squeezed money from peasants. Everywhere were bribes called 'tea money'—a deeply corrupt system, despised by rich merchants and poor peasants alike.

Dr Sun had turned to Kung's younger brother-in-law T. V. Soong, who had been working in a Shanghai industrial complex owned jointly by Soong family and Japanese interests. It did not seem to matter that the Japanese were military aggressors in the north: the Soongs did business with whoever could bring advantage. (Ironically before he was assassinated such Japanese investments in China had also been promoted by Takahashi who saw them as a way to access resources without the dangers, costs, and damage of invasion.) The Kung pawn-broking, banking, and merchant empire, the Soong family connections, Japanese investment, and the brutal power of the Green Gang together constituted a very powerful commercial combination in the disrupted China of the 1920s and 30s.

Sun Yat-sen commissioned T. V. Soong to reorganize the Kuomintang finances: there followed a special import tax on key products, a consumption tax on certain items, and a call for all Canton merchants to 'lend' the government sums of money. The Canton-based government negotiated a loan from Lenin's Soviet Communist Government of $10 million, which was used to provide a balance sheet for the establishment of a central bank, to provide asset backing for new banknotes. (Ironically Lenin had famously declared 'the best way to destroy the capitalist system is to debauch the currency'.) TV commissioned a force to police tax collection. Tax collectors found to be involved in major corrupt practices were summarily punished, sometimes by execution. This dire approach seemed to be successful at raising revenue in the southern provinces.

Dr Sun Yat-sen died in 1925, and now Chiang Kai-shek wrestled power from the southern capital. In his early life Chiang had studied the Chinese military classic *The Art of War* where Sun Tzu wrote that 'the supreme art of war is to subdue the enemy without fighting'. Chiang Kai-shek lived his life by this edict, favouring tactical cleverness and intrigue over brute force. This was a philosophy that Kung could understand and support.

Chiang Kai-shek needed funding to feed his power base, based around the Whampoa Military Academy in Guangzhou, and the growing Kuomintang Army. He issued his own short-term 'government bonds', and used soldiers and gang thugs to force merchants to buy them: refusal resulted in kidnappings and violence. Chiang Kai-shek adopted T. V. Soong as his Finance Minister and Central Bank Governor. Following in the footsteps of Takahashi, the latter proposed limits on military spending, adoption of a national budget, the establishment of a mint to standardize coin production and reduce counterfeits, and the abolition of the hated feudal tax, together with some basic labour laws. He repeatedly warned the Kuomintang Central Committee that their undisciplined spending could bring bankruptcy.

Chiang Kai-shek would typically agree with TV, then cynically break his promises. He would make huge financial demands to fund his military force, diverting much of the funds for himself, using money to pay off rivals, untroubled by any moral or legal obligation to account for the spending or apologize for the extortion. When Soong raised objections, Kung's wife Ai-ling pressured him to accede to Chiang's ongoing demands, even going so far as to threaten her own brother with Green Gang thugs. Kung supported his wife; a deep split was developing within the family.

T. V. Soong had been a loyal advisor to brother-in-law Sun Yat-sen, but he had a difficult relationship with brother-in-law Chiang Kai-shek and they argued increasingly. After one violent quarrel, Chiang Kai-shek slapped T. V. Soong's face. This was an insult that could not be ignored: TV walked away, resigning from his offices of Minister of Finance and Central Bank Governor. He had done his best to use his Western-educated policy techniques for economic management, but it seemed that Western economic policies could not work in this chaotic environment. He left to make money on his own account.

1936: Collecting Revenue Chinese-Style

The shadows of war were falling across Europe. In Germany Hitler had consolidated totalitarian powers, reoccupied the demilitarized zone in the Rhineland in violation of the Versailles Treaty, appointed Hjalmar Schacht as Plenipotentiary for the War Economy, and staged the triumphalist 1936 Berlin Olympic Games. A coup by the right-wing Spanish Army of Africa sparked off the Spanish Civil War which was to be a test bed for competing German and Soviet arms. Fascist Italian troops invaded Abyssinia, and Germany signed an Axis pact with Italy and an Anti-Comintern pact with Japan. Rearmament in the Soviet Union was under way but slowed by the start of Stalin's Great Purge.

In 1936 China was a nation that could not be unified: the Nationalist Kuomintang Government had a tenuous hold on the east and the south, with an urban base around the wealthier central and southern coastal cities and a capital in Nanjing. The Chinese Communist Party, now backed by Russia, was building up a support base in the south-west and pushing north. Tension mounted between them. Local generals, warlords, and gangs roamed between these two political movements, with sporadic violence erupting eventually into a fully-fledged civil war. This was worsened with widespread famine from agricultural failures, causing the death of up to five million Chinese peasants.

By this time the Japanese military controlled all Manchuria in the north. The mineral resources and industrial factories of the region were very attractive to their industrialists, offering key resources for the homeland. China had appealed to the League of Nations and to Western powers, without success. Soon the Japanese were pushing south, exploiting the divisive factions to manipulate control and to launch further attacks on Chiang Kai-shek and Chinese territory. The chaotic conditions gave the Japanese many opportunities to exploit. By 1935 they had extended their influence over warlords in the northern and Beijing-Tianjin regions. The Chinese had even been forced to agree they would not use their own troops in the 'international city' of Shanghai, and they had essentially lost control over Northern China, though there was still resistance.

Meanwhile, Chiang Kai-shek had been building the Kuomintang Army, presenting his government as the bulwark against the Japanese. But he had been very reluctant to engage the Japanese on the ground, instead negotiating with and manipulating warlord forces and private armies, and opposing the growing Communist Party forces. This tactic encouraged the Japanese, allowed the Communist Party to score propaganda victories with the peasants, and it aroused considerable popular opposition. The Kuomintang were fighting their brother Chinese, and warlords were fighting warlords. In the midst of this the Kung-Soong family were whispered to have secret links with Japanese cartels in Shanghai.

Desperate for more resources and having fallen out with T. V. Soong, Chiang Kai-shek now turned to his more Chinese brother-in-law, the wheeling and dealing H. H. Kung. He was appointed first Minister of Finance and then Governor of the Central Bank.

Kung was a rather short man who had lost the slimness of youth and was now thick-set and prosperous-looking, known to colleagues as 'Daddy Kung'. He had a receding hairline, small toothbrush moustache, round glasses, and an easy smile. He dressed formally in Western suit and tie, even on trips to the remote countryside. At home with the Soong Sisters he was fond of wearing more traditional Mandarin robes. He liked his luxuries—*TIME Magazine* reported that he smoked 15 Havana cigars each day. Theodore White described him as: 'a round man with a soft face draped with pendulous flabby chins...A cartoonist's delight...An amiable man, he disliked quarrels or crises and he could be coaxed into almost anything with a smile or a sob story....His one great desire was to be loved, and those who knew him well found him so lovable that they called him Daddy.' Less kindly, Edgar Snow wrote: 'He is not only corrupt and incompetent. He is without any will and is pushed around like a flabby sack of meal by any force with which he comes into contact' (Hamilton, 2003, 114).

But these Western commentators underestimated the man, with his complex make-up—a Western sense of Christianity, and a Chinese sense of family interests. Compared with Soong, he took a quite different approach in his dealings, with his focus on relationships rather than policies, his ability to work with ambiguity, his liking for deals, and his comfort operating in the grey zone between public and private interests. He used the cronies and hangers-on of the extended Soong family to do his bidding. He liked old Chinese traditions and traditional Chinese language. While claiming to be a direct descendant of Confucius, he showed little of that sage's deep thinking and he was hardly Confucian himself. In his negotiations he found it profitable to present a benign visage, whether he was doing business with politicians, merchants, soldiers, or warlords. He had a writing desk full of rubber stamps and shiny seals and bonhomie.

After the Kung family had their first daughter, named Rosamond, they left their northern refuge of Taigu, and the family moved to the bustle of Shanghai. Three more children were born there: David, Jeanette, and Louis. The children were raised spoilt and manipulative. Jeanette would grow up particularly overbearing and arrogant, preferring to wear men's clothing with a male haircut, later becoming very influential over her uncle Chiang Kai-shek and her aunt Mei-ling.

Life in 1920s and 30s China was anything but secure and the Kung family did not always keep good company. Kung had bought a palatial modern house in the French Quarter of Shanghai. For a rich Chinese man at that time nowhere was completely safe, although Shanghai offered some protection due to the international concessions there. The district where Kung lived was in Green Gang territory, and hence considered reasonably secure, provided dues were paid to the gang leader Big-Eared Tu. It was not just Kung's personal safety in question but his family members who were at risk of kidnapping, and his household servants who could be assassinated as an example.

Ai-ling formed a particularly close relationship with the gangster chief. On Sundays she would go to church, then afterwards Tu would visit Kung's house while his bodyguards kept watch outside. They had a common interest in controlling business and making money. The gangs controlled some local businesses, extracted extortion money from others, and ran the vice trades: opium and prostitutes. At the time it was estimated that as many as one in 100 houses in Shanghai was a brothel. The gangs, with their sizeable armies of thugs, were beyond the control of the local police forces and gangland killings were common. Intimidation took various forms, but Tu's favourite way was to send a victim an ornate Chinese coffin. He was not above doing this with accomplices, even the powerful Soong family. One time his henchmen gunned down T. V. Soong's secretary in the street as a gentle warning to the latter to remember the Green Gang's interests.

For good reasons Kung was continually concerned about his family's safety in Shanghai. He kept the ancestral home in Shanxi, and also maintained family houses in Peking in the north, Canton in the south, Nanking in the new Kuomintang capital up the Yang-tse River, and Hong Kong under British rule in case they needed to escape the mainland completely.

In the late 1920s Kung had acted as a go-between for Chiang Kai-shek when the Nanking Regime had been inaugurated. Initially he had been appointed Minister of Industry, Commerce, and Labour. However his industrial policies had not been particularly coherent, and the state of Chinese industry suggested that he had not been very successful with his portfolios. He was better at making a corrupt system work than reforming it. Businesses complained bitterly about the high domestic tax structure. If they imported materials they had to pay a heavy import tariff. They also complained that Japanese importers seemed to be able to evade this tariff, and consequently could outperform domestic competitors, despite many Chinese consumers preferring not to buy from the invading foreigners.

By the late 1930s relative stability from the Nanjing Government was at last bringing economic growth to some parts of China, particularly the main coastal cities. There was infrastructure investment, with several thousand miles of railway track under construction, thousands of units of rolling stock imported, and the first locomotives being assembled. There were also some industrial joint ventures with German firms to build trucks and aircraft.

Kung was always available to Chiang Kai-shek as an intermediary between warring parties. He was a fixer who knew how much it should cost to settle a matter, who to pay off, and where to find the funds to do it. He had assisted Chiang to negotiate the 1927 Northern Expedition by paying off the northern warlords. Then he had used these negotiations to build up financial leverage where debts could be banked and favours could be called on. Kung interpreted Sun Tzu's edict about subduing without fighting as a matter of bribing, blackmailing, buying off, or even taking a stake in protagonists. As well as dealing with rougher elements, he could be a diplomat, smoothing relations between the Kuomintang Government and the international community. Many photographs of him exist hosting convivial dinners for US Navy commanders and other eminent foreign visitors.

While Kung continued his public life, Ai-ling worked in the shadows, administering the family fortune, directing teams of secretaries and accountants in her houses. Quite unscrupulous, she would use her husband's position to obtain confidential financial information that she could then trade with. According to Seagrave the FBI kept a file on her: it contained assertions that she hired assassins to kill rivals—she was quite capable of such behaviour with her links to the Green Gang, Big-Eared Tu, and the secret societies. A contemporary observer complained that Mrs Kung was a 'hard world creature, possessed of demonic energy and great will to power, violently able, cunning and ambitious, she is as powerful a personality as any in China' (Seagrave, 1985, 261). It is difficult to judge such comments in the light of 1930s China where she had many detractors including Communist propagandists, but her tough reputation stands.

Kung's instinct was for short-term fixes, and he made little effort to continue TV's attempts to reform the financial base for the Chinese economy. He soon realized that Chiang was running into major debt, but he loyally declared that the drive to suppress 'bandits' (i.e. Communists) was more important than a balanced budget. When he took over as Finance Minister in 1933, Kung had stated that a balanced budget would be desirable but funding the anti-Communist campaign was more urgent. His strategy was to look for new ways to fund ever-increasing military expenditure.

Kung's first job in his new role was to finance the 1933 budget. He had increased cigarette taxes by 50 per cent, and many tobacco factories closed down as a result. He threatened to increase the notorious salt tax. He issued yet more government bonds, which soon weighed down one third of the Shanghai banks' balance sheets. The banks paid for the bonds with their silver reserves. The effect was to choke off banks' loans to agriculture and commerce; the yield on the bonds was very attractive and instead of productive investments, investors were effectively putting their money into Chiang Kai-shek's army. It soon appeared that the lending capacity of the banking system had been exhausted. But Kung proved ever resourceful: later that year he raised more bank loans, including a $C44 million loan from a 16-bank consortium, creatively secured on income from the Italian Boxer indemnity.

The world economy was now in the grips of the Great Depression, and international trade had contracted considerably. In June the US left the gold standard in an attempt to reduce its exchange rate, to increase the money supply, and to lower interest rates. This had a perverse effect on China: the US were building US Treasury silver reserves mainly for domestic political reasons, arbitrarily setting the silver price at US$.50 per ounce. Shanghai investors soon realized they could sell their own silver holdings to the US and get a better return than from Nanking bonds—there was a large exodus of Chinese silver. Without this backing, Chinese government bond sales plummeted, the money market tightened, and bank interest rates rose strongly. At Yale Kung had learned how international capital flows could impact domestic markets, but he now seemed powerless to prevent the silver leakage. He announced an embargo on silver exports, but it was widely ignored by the banks. If silver exports could not be blocked, could they be taxed? In late 1934 the government imposed a 10 per cent export tax on silver, which principle could negate the price advantage to selling in US and British markets. Despite significant smuggling, this tax slowed the outflow. But now China's silver reserves had significantly reduced, Chinese industry could not be refinanced by the banks, and growth was suffering.

Mao's People's Liberation Army had been able to break through the Kuomintang blockade and begin its famous Long March to a new safe base in Yunnan Province. Chiang Kai-shek blamed his inability to contain the Communists on a lack of funds, although he consistently avoided confronting them head on. Needing more funds and with the private banking sector depleted, Kung turned to the Central Bank which had limited its own holdings of Nanking government bonds. He increased this limit by a huge amount, and used the government bank to buy government bonds to purchase government notes and extend loans to the government. Takahashi had done something similar in Japan, but in a far more disciplined and transparent way.

By now China and Hong Kong were the only regions in the world still linking their currency to silver, and as the silver price rose, the Chinese currency rose too, making its exports very uncompetitive. 1934 had been a very difficult year with a big increase in bankruptcies, Shanghai foreign enclave property values halved, and exports fell by 20 per cent. The government responded by nationalizing all existing silver assets, which helped delink the currency from the silver price, and had a positive but temporary effect. Despite these moves, the illegal silver trade continued, some of it smuggled out with the covert assistance of the Japanese in Manchukuo.

Finding silver trading unattractive, speculators shifted to gold, which leapt in price. Kung declared the Central Bank to be the exclusive agent for all gold trading in China, to ensure the government could profit from this new market. His approach had been to try to control private trade, and then failing that, to push private traders out of the way and take the speculative profits for the Kuomintang Government. While continuing to restrict others, the government itself now exported large quantities of silver at significant profit. These profits primarily ended up in Chiang Kai-shek's military budget, but there were rumours that the Kung-Soong family interests were also being advanced.

Amiable Kung was ever ready to act as a go-between, especially where there was profit involved. He encouraged the Shanghai banks to raise more funds for the government. When the banks resisted, Kung called on his enforcers, Big-Eared Tu and the Green Gang, to help persuade them. (Tu arranged a 'banking symposium' at which he explained the consequences of non-compliance to the intimidated bankers present.) The government passed a savings bank law requiring the banks to invest one quarter of their assets in government bonds and securities which would be held by the Central Bank 'in trust' for them. The banks were all aware of the risks involved in this, and there were many protests, but to little avail.

By 1935 there was another banking crisis. The two biggest institutions, the original Bank of China and the Bank of Communications, which were themselves much bigger than the Central Bank and also issued currency, tried to fight back against these rapacious government policies by dumping their Nanking government bonds. This was effectively a declaration of war against the government. Kung decided that if he could not otherwise control the banks, he needed to take ownership over them. But he did not want to do it in a way that the public would lose confidence in the banknotes being circulated by these two institutions. His approach was typically Machiavellian: he launched a whispering campaign against the big banks, blaming them for not lending to industry and increasing the woes of the Depression. He promised that businesses would be in a much stronger position if a three-bank consortium could be formed of the two big Shanghai private banks together with the Central Bank. Kung and his wife personally entertained important local businessmen to help convince them, while at the same time he arranged for Big-Eared Tu to make his own threatening inducements.

Satisfied with the preparations, a month later Kung announced that the government was to take over the Bank of China and the Bank of Communications. Ostensibly this was done to increase the ability of the banks to make emergency relief loans to small businesses and to fight the Depression. Yet the loans to business never eventuated and the Depression continued. To ensure family interests were looked after, and to limit the influence of Chiang Kai-shek and his army colleagues, Kung now appointed brother-in-law T. V. Soong as chair of the nationalized consortium Bank of China. With his usual mix of charm, pressure, and intimidation, compromising as necessary, Kung engineered the election of directors to include the two younger American-educated Soong brothers and also Big-Eared Tu as enforcer.

Pleased with the results of this banking coup, Kung then arranged for the systematic takeover of three other important Shanghai commercial banks that suddenly found their credit lines with the big banks had collapsed. All three were placed under the supervision of Kung's own family holding, the Manufacturers Bank, which now had three Soong brothers on the board. The same fate was dealt to four other private banks in the south of China, and eventually many more banks and companies came under the control of the clan. By now Kung, the family, and the Kuomintang Government controlled over 80 per cent of the country's formal banking system.

Next Kung placed youngest brother-in-law T. A. Soong, another Harvard graduate, in charge of the government's salt monopoly company. The salt company was important and powerful: it controlled and taxed the trade in salt, an item needed by every peasant. The organization had a huge army of tax enforcers, and these were soon to be controlled by TV's wife Laura, who was mainly known for being a socialite. Another brother-in-law, T. L. Soong, who had graduated from Vanderbilt University, was made head of the family bank and also of Shanghai Harbour, a strategic asset that controlled much of China's external trade, and where again authority went hand in hand with the Green Gang.

Concerned by the disruptions and potential damage to their interests, in 1935 the British Government sent Sir Frederick Leith-Ross, a UK Treasury colleague of Keynes, to China to advise Kung. As a consequence in November 1935 the Chinese Government decided to break from the silver standard, and the exchange rate was instead pegged against sterling.

Kung next declared that the government would issue new notes to become the legal tender ('fa-pi'). This gave him scope to print more money. In November 1935 a decree required that all silver still held by banks or individuals must be exchanged for the paper, which would be issued by four banks, all controlled by Kung's fiefdom. To bolster confidence in the new currency, it would be supervised by a Currency Reserve Board, which would guarantee its silver reserves as a hedge against inflation. Kung's idea of bolstering confidence was to establish a board which was dominated by Kung, Tu, and two Soong brothers. When British advisor Leith-Ross objected to the appointment of a gangster to this official organization, Kung pragmatically pointed out that while Big-Eared Tu was indeed a gang leader, he had a force of 100,000 men in Shanghai who could create disturbances to order, and therefore he was simply too powerful to leave out.

It came as no surprise that the Board exercised little restraint on the printing of money. From 1935 to 1937 the amount of fa-pi in circulation increased three-fold, and only half of this was properly backed by silver. At first this printing of money helped to stimulate the economy. Then the inevitable happened—price rises loomed. The rampant inflation that followed would accelerate through World War II, and is now seen as one of the causes of the ultimate defeat of the Kuomintang. Precise data is unavailable because after the 1935 fiscal year the government no longer published a national budget, nor even fully documented its expenditures. In 1936 1.4 billion Chinese yuan were issued to circulation, and by the end of the war this had risen to over a trillion. In 1937 a US dollar would buy 3.4 yuan, which depreciated to 19 yuan by 1941, and then slid completely out of control to 23 million yuan by 1949.

When Kung first took office the Nanking Government was deeply in debt. By 1936 the loan issuance had risen more than ten times, and debt more than doubled. As economic conditions worsened, merchants and industrialists complained they could not get funding because of public sector crowd-out. In 1936 new 'Consolidation Bonds' were offered on very unattractive terms to banks that did not want to buy them, banks which once again had to be persuaded about their public duties by gang leader Tu. Now two-thirds of the government bonds issued were held by the Shanghai banks, which in turn were mainly owned by the government.

Despite such chaotic outcomes, in his own paper written later in 1945 for the *Foreign Affairs* journal, Kung actually praised his own efforts in developing China's new monetary system based on a managed currency. He claimed that without that China could not have continued to resist the Japanese.

The other major source of revenue for Chiang Kai-shek's military machine was opium. Ever since the British opium trade in the nineteenth century, opium had been a significant revenue earner for whoever could dominate this trade. At this time the Green Gang controlled the Shanghai and Yangtze Valley opium trade and the prostitution that accompanied it. Rather than try to reform this evil trade, Kung now worked to ensure that opium revenues would be more equally divided between the Shanghai gangs and the Nanking Government.

Much of the Nationalist Chinese economy was now controlled directly or indirectly by Kung and the Soong brothers with Ai-ling quietly directing behind the scenes. It was a dog-eat-dog world. Some of the silver policy discussions had taken place in the Kung mansion with Ai-ling participating. Ai-ling made it very clear that she was influencing the policy decisions, and she alerted Big-Eared Tu in advance to the planned changes. Tu misunderstood what was planned and his own bank invested on the wrong side of the deal, losing heavily. The gangster then complained to Kung and demanded that the Central Bank should compensate him for his own mistake based on leaked information. Kung refused. That evening he was surprised to find a 'number one style' ornate coffin delivered to his doorstop by half a dozen uniformed funeral attendants. The message from the ruthless gang leader could hardly have been clearer. Kung hastily convened the Central Bank Board, who now voted to compensate this 'patriotic citizen'.

There were growing accusations that Kung, his wife Ai-ling, and son David were all involved in trading on insider information about government policy intentions. It is difficult to be completely sure of the extent because the accusations were promoted as propaganda by the Communists. Ai-ling's Seven Star Company was particularly suspect in the conversion of old bonds to newly issued bonds. In addition the China Development Finance Corporation (chaired by Kung) arranged advantageous loans which assisted many of the enterprises where the Kung-Soong family held interests. Kung himself held directorships in a range of private industrial and mineral companies, and he was also suspected of taking kickbacks from the various arms deals he negotiated with foreign governments.

Despite his Western university education, there was little economic theory behind Kung's practical economic policies. Some Chinese scholars, especially at Yenching University in Peking, had studied in the UK and were aware of Keynes's evolving ideas; however most Chinese academics were more interested in Marxist economics. Kung may have heard about Keynes from brother-in-law T. V. Soong who met him in 1935, and they would later enjoy convivial chats at Bretton Woods, but he was unlikely to have thought much about the potential application of Keynesian reflationary policies to China.

Keynes himself had little knowledge of China, although that had not prevented him, aged 17, loftily informing his father that he was 'in favour of the Boxer Rebellion'. He might later have changed his mind when he had heard from Kung of his own actual childhood experiences. In 1912 Keynes had written a lengthy *Economic Journal* review of a book entitled *The Economic Principles of Confucius and his School* (by Huen-Chang Chen). In China Keynes was best known for his *Economic Consequences of the Peace*, which had been translated into Chinese in

1920. The Versailles Peace Settlement had been of great interest to China because of its treatment of the former German enclaves and its grants of territories to Japan, sparking protests by young Chinese students. The Kuomintang Government had proposed inviting Keynes to China to become their economic advisor in 1932, but this never happened.

Late in 1936 the Kuomintang suffered the Xian Incident. While inspecting troops in the ancient inland city of Xian, Chang Kai-shek was kidnapped by a group of renegade Manchurian troops backed by students who had been protesting at the way the Nationalist Government had been attacking the Communist Chinese rather than fighting the Japanese invaders. With Chiang Kai-shek locked up and out of contact, Kung stepped in as Acting Premier for the government. Though it was clearly dangerous, he decided to travel to Xian. In the heated political conditions there, he negotiated with the rabble of student and soldier kidnappers. It was unclear whether the price of reaching agreement might have to be to sacrifice Chiang Kai-shek, but finally under much pressure Kung negotiated a price for the Generalissimo's freedom. All the parties eventually agreed to the 'Eight Demands' of the Manchurian kidnapping soldiers and to the payment of a ransom: for Kung everything had its price. He then arranged for the money to be sent to certain foreign bank accounts to finance this settlement. True to his own style, Chiang Kai-shek agreed to all the demands pressed on him, then once released he reneged on them all.

1937: Raising Foreign Aid

1937 was to be another year of turbulence around the world. While the French were focused on domestic political instability and the British on the abdication of their King, there was slaughter by the Italians in Abyssinia, terrible anti-Soviet purges in the USSR, and great loss of life in the Spanish Civil War. In the East the Japanese had started their full-scale invasion plans of China. Once again the League of Nations stood powerless.

Takahashi's death had sent a fearful message to China, who well understood the dangers of out-of-control armies, and about the appetite of the Japanese Army for invasion. In Japan the generals took advantage to escalate their budget demands. 1937 military expenditure was three times the average of the previous three years, and by 1939 it had doubled again. The war machine had been unleashed, and in 1937 Japanese troops poured into coastal China.

The Japanese economy had built up a strong industrial base with advanced factory processes, machine tools, railways, and shipping. From 1937 there was a significant increase in Japanese domestic production of ships and planes, the pace of rearmament being limited only by foreign exchange reserves and the availability of energy and raw materials. They had coal resources, but lacked almost all petroleum, fertilisers, timber, nickel, asbestos, fibres, and many other minerals and chemicals that were needed for warfare. Initially resources were stripped by the invading military from the occupied 'yen bloc' (Korea, Taiwan, Manchuria, and coastal China). Worried by this expansionism, the United States imposed an oil embargo and an asset freeze on Japan. This convinced the Japanese that they needed to invade Southeast Asia for its resources, and ultimately led to the Pearl Harbor attack.

Despite his poor record in confronting the Japanese, Chang Kai-shek was still making demands for more war finance. But with the loss of China's commercial heartland in the coastal cities, there was little scope for Kung to raise more money domestically. In particular, Japanese control of Shanghai was a big blow to Kuomintang revenues. It was time to look further afield for assistance.

Initially this meant looking to Germany. To Hitler China was an undeveloped and disorderly country of non-Aryans. But Russia had started sending aid to the Chinese Communists, and the Kuomintang were their natural enemies. Hitler appreciated the Generalissimo's preference to fight Communists rather than Japanese. China was also strategically important to Germany because it abutted the eastern border of the Soviet Union, the regime that Germany feared most, and because it contained some important mineral resources.

Chiang Kai-shek admired Hitler's and Mussolini's National Socialism movement, especially the power, unity, and organization of this creed, while the violence also fitted his norms. He looked to the Nazis as models of police and military organization, and also the Italian fascists who had unified an undisciplined nation. Chang Kai-shek had previously established his 'New Life Movement' which tried to impose strict rules over the population. Following the examples of Hitler's Brown shirts and Mussolini's Black shirts, he now set up his own Blue Shirts Secret Service.

Looking to exploit their common interests, Chang Kai-shek appealed to Germany for military advice, economic assistance, and equipment. Germany established a Commercial Corporation for Industrial Products in China, headed by an arms merchant. Chinese agricultural products and minerals (especially key minerals like tungsten and antimony needed for arms production) were traded for German industrial products, weapons, and assistance to establish aircraft factories and steel plants. In 1935 Chiang Kai-shek had written to German Minister Hjalmar Schacht who indicated great interest in further economic cooperation. In 1936, he wrote directly to Hitler saying: 'If the economic capacities of our two countries are linked together and if by means of our mutual exchange of goods we remedy the economic weaknesses of our two nations, then we will have truly attained our objectives in undertaking cooperation' (Chen Hongmin, 2001, 285). Hitler responded: 'The mutual exchange of goods between our two countries will give benefits of great substance to the economic development of our nations...' These two letters may have been drafted by Schacht and Kung. Following the exchange of letters, the two governments signed a commodities exchange agreement and China undertook to supply raw materials up to a value of $US10 million within the year.

There was also direct military assistance. German army advisors came to China as 'retired officers' without official standing, and they were involved in many political and economic matters, including advice on how to attack the Communist movement in Kiangsi. The technique was to build roads, rail, fortifications, and bunkers through the mountainous provinces, and to bring in trucks and armoured cars, using scorched-earth policies on surrounding villages. The cost was huge and the effect was brutal. Perhaps 150,000 Communist guerrillas were killed and up to one million civilians killed or starved in this German-directed exercise.

Chiang Kai-shek's first son had been sent to Moscow to study, and there he had become a keen Russian supporter. Chiang decided to send his younger (adopted) son Wei-kuo (Kung's nephew) to Germany for schooling. Wei-kuo took to German military life with enthusiasm, embraced Nazism, enlisted in an elitist light infantry unit, and even took part in the Nazi invasion of Austria in 1938.

Several years previously Kung had been appointed as a special commissioner to study Western industry in order to learn how to modernize Chinese industry. Together with his wife and oldest son David he had travelled to the United States. He had called on President Herbert Hoover in Washington DC in 1932. Ai-ling visited her old Wesleyan University in Georgia, where she endowed a scholarship, in line with the Kung-Soong family policy of spreading largesse for future insurance.

The family then sailed on to Europe. Guided by the German generals in China, Kung entrained to Berlin to discuss the German arms industry. Using his warm personality to charm his Nazi hosts, he went on a buying spree on behalf of the Kuomintang Government, spending $US25 million on German weapons that were mainly intended for fighting the Chinese Communists rather than the Japanese.

National Socialism had become internationally fashionable, and Italy, Germany, and the National Government of China were its key exponents. Kung next visited Venice where Mussolini greeted the party. Kung was on familiar territory, charming his hosts, building business relationships, and looking for good deals. Talking with Count Ciano, Italy's Foreign Minister and Mussolini's son-in-law, Kung constructed a creative deal: he used the US$2 million owed to Italy as an indemnity imposed following the Boxer Rebellion decades earlier, as a counter-deal to buy Fiat air force planes. In return Italy agreed to set up a pilot training school in Loyang and a Fiat aircraft assembly plant in Nanking.

The Nanking Government's Air Force was put in the hands of Colonel Chennault, an abrasive renegade American mercenary flyer whose 'Flying Tigers' Corps was the only serious aerial attack force that the Chinese could muster against the Japanese invaders as the latter swept south. Chennault disparaged the Italian training programme arranged and financed by Kung: the pilot selection was nepotistic, the training was poor, the assembly plant was inefficient, the Fiat fighters were a fire trap, and the Savoia-Marchetti bombers were obsolete. There were meant to be 500 planes, but only 100 were airworthy, and the purchases carried a strong whiff of corruption. Looking to build up the fledgling Nationalist Chinese Air Force, Kung next signed a contract with the

US Curtis Wright company for 120 air force planes, which would have cost around US$8 million. These were apparently funded from opium revenues. Kung saw nothing unusual in dealing with Germans, Japanese, and Americans at the same time.

By 1937 the Nationalist Government could no longer ignore the build-up of Japanese invasion forces. It was time to send Kung travelling again. Following the exchange of letters between Chang Kai-shek and Hitler, it was decided that he should travel to Germany to discuss more economic and arms deals. By now Kung had been appointed Vice-Premier of the Yuan, the executive arm of government, as well as Finance Minister and Central Bank Governor.

In May 1937 he travelled as head of a Chinese delegation with his family, initially to London, to attend the coronation of George VI. While there he held talks with the Chancellor of the Exchequer, the UK Treasury, the Foreign Office, Governor Montagu Norman of the Bank of England, Lord Mountbatten, and the Hong Kong–Shanghai Bank. Ever the opportunist, he requested a war loan to finance the expansion of the rail system in China. Back in 1930 Maynard Keynes had proposed to the British Economic Advisory Council that more railways should be built in China to help boost UK–Chinese trade, to be funded by the Boxer Compensation Fund. But this time, advised by Keynes and fearing that the Chinese might use the funds to source rail equipment from Germany, the UK Treasury urged turning down the loan request and suggested instead that China should carry out its own domestic currency reforms. Eventually the UK Government agreed in principle to a loan, subject to several conditions including China reforming its central bank, but no money was ever paid out.

Kung and his team crossed the English Channel and travelled by train to Berlin. On 8 June 1937 in the tense atmosphere of Berlin he was greeted at the Friedrichstrasse Railway Station by a delegation led by German Finance Minister Hjalmar Schacht. The intense, austere, intellectual Schacht was quite the opposite of the genial Kung. Other visiting dignitaries had reported negatively on the clever Schacht, but the latter's difficult personality was no problem for Kung, who sensed a deal in the offing. He spoke of Germany as China's 'closest friend', who might assist in reorganizing China's finances. He was given a very cordial reception, and there was supportive newspaper commentary. Despite its growing coalition with Japan, Germany did not want to jeopardize its important Chinese trade and resources, especially when its own rearming was limited by export embargos on key materials imposed by the Allies. Schacht had developed a framework for doing bilateral trade deals with third countries to evade the trade restrictions. Kung wanted more planes and armaments and could offer important supplies of minerals in return. He was introduced to other leaders of the Nazi Party, including General von Blomberg, the Minister of War, from whom he purchased more arms (to be paid for with exports of tungsten and antimony under the 1936 HAPRO Agreement). Kung also made representations to the Germans about the ongoing threat from Japan, and received some assurances from them, including from Hermann Goering.

The highlight of the trip was on 13 June when Kung met with the German Chancellor Adolf Hitler. The disciplined if ruthless achievements of the National Socialist movement impressed Kung, in contrast to the somewhat ramshackle New Life Movement at home. Kung was received on the terrace at Hitler's Obersalzberges home near Berchtesgaden in Bavaria. They talked in general terms, Hitler saying that he hoped that Japan and China would not fight, and that his real concern was the spread of Communism. Hitler told Kung: 'Germany is anxious carefully to foster and deepen the friendly relations which have long existed between our countries.' He later went on: 'I understand that people in China think the Soviet Union is their friend. But from our talk I understand that you, Herr Doktor, realize the danger of Communist doctrines' (H. H. Kung).

Kung was persuasive as ever: he convinced Hitler to cancel a scheduled speech at a Nazi conference by the Japanese Emperor's brother. Kung said: 'I was able to make Hitler understand that Japan wanted to dominate the world...I was able to make Hitler think twice before getting too close to Japan.' Once again he met Schacht and other top officials, asking them to mediate in the Sino-Japanese War. Hitler, Hermann Goering, and Schacht bestowed an honorary degree upon Kung, and they earmarked a fund for Chinese students to travel and study in Germany. Hitler also offered an international loan which Kung declined in favour of commercial credits. To Schacht, Kung said: 'China considers Germany its best friend...I hope and wish that Germany will participate in supporting the further development of China, the opening up of its sources of raw materials, the upbringing of its industries and its means of transportation' (ibid).

Despite these mutual protestations of economic friendship, ultimately the Germans would not form a long-term supply relationship with China. They were desperately short of overseas funds themselves, they did not completely trust the non-transparent Chinese, and they were already considering a pivot to the militaristic and disciplined Japanese who seemed likely to be a better non-Aryan partner to counter the Soviet Union in the region. Later in the year Hitler yielded to Japanese demands and ceased all weapons and munitions supplies to China.

Following the meeting with the Germans, on 14 June Kung left Berlin to visit the United States, and renew his ongoing funding requests to the US Administration. As he travelled, he heard the news they had all been fearing: following an exchange of fire at the 'Marco Polo Bridge Incident' near Beijing on 27 July 1937, the Japanese launched a full scale invasion of coastal China, soon occupying key northern cities, and pushing relentlessly southwards. It was not unexpected, but it meant full-scale war. Kung decided to return to Berlin where he talked to Schacht, once more asking the Germans to mediate in the war with the Japanese.

Kung and family returned home to China where he sensed the danger from the Japanese. The Kuomintang now moved its seat of government from Nanking (where it had been since the capital had moved from Canton in 1928) a thousand miles upriver to the large but poor industrial city of Chungking, which was to remain as capital until the defeat of the Japanese in 1945. Sensing the closeness of war, Kung had first closed the family home in Shanghai and moved the family to Nanking, and then further up the Yangtze River to safety at Chungking.

This time the Japanese advance forced the Kuomintang Army to confront them head-on at the Battle of Shanghai, which the Japanese eventually won, though at high cost. Japanese military action there resulted in nearly 1,000 factories destroyed, trade blockaded, vast economic damage, and six million refugees left homeless. The Japanese then pushed on to Nanking; the invasion of that city was brutal, with the notorious Nanking Massacre leaving around 300,000 Chinese casualties.

China was very poor, with GDP per capita approximately one third of Japan's (which in turn was only one half of Germany's). The Kuomintang

Armies were far larger than the Japanese, but poorly equipped, lacking basic mechanization and armaments, and sometimes poorly trained and led, especially where they incorporated warlord armies. Some soldiers were conscripted forcibly, others were mercenaries, and when they were not paid their loyalty was in doubt. Both sides were eventually mired in a stalemate war of attrition.

As the Japanese advanced the Chinese economy disintegrated. It was ultimately saved from total destruction only because the country was too huge for Japan to swallow whole. The economy of the occupied region was in tatters as the Chinese had carried out a scorched-earth retreat, and Japanese bombing of cities and railways caused massive industrial damage. By now the government had lost its main source of revenue in the financial base of Shanghai, and the Japanese invaders could control the lucrative trade in opium. The Kuomintang Government's economic modernization programme ceased under the pressures of war.

When the Kuomintang Government abandoned the Nanking capital to the Japanese, they shipped as much industrial equipment as possible upriver to the industrial city of Chungking. The Japanese continued to fight their way until the city came within range of a brutal bombing campaign. Edgar Snow gave an eyewitness account of how terrible life was in that city at the time. Yet Kung seemed able to maintain his opulent life style in this city overrun by refugees. The family was said to own a warehouse there that held food, medicines, and cloth valued at around $US10 million. He was accused of taking up critical space on a daily supply plane from Hong Kong by insisting it should fly in a daily case of fresh fruit from the US for his family (White and Jacoby, 1947).

While confronted with the existential threat to China and its economy and with increasing reason to worry about his own survival, Kung still found time to pursue his private interests in Chungking, establishing the Fuxing Company, a major trading operation used to channel many commodity transactions. Businessmen looking to relocate their factories upriver away from Japanese domination on the coast soon learned that to operate successfully in the hinterlands they had to include a Soong or a Kung in the business, which they much resented. If they tried to compete on their own they were soon dissuaded by threats. By this time Kung was running his own Secret Service, and its role involved reporting on the Japanese advance, spying on the economic state of the Communist Party, and generally protecting family interests.

Kung was now appointed Premier of the Republic of China. He presented a brave face before the Peoples Political Council in early 1939: but the terrible conditions being endured by most Chinese were not evident in Kung's speech—he spoke confidently about how the government had changed its economic policy since the Japanese war had begun, moving coastal factories to the interior out of range of Japanese bombing, developing new industrial regions including coal, petroleum, and gas exploration, in a rigorous exercise of regional economic planning. He asserted there would be more building of the railway network, some of it in joint ventures with foreign investors. He talked about the suppression of the opium traffic, and the need to reduce the monopoly power of important industries as he claimed he had achieved in banking, and he said small rural credit banks had been established to fund agricultural development (Kung, 1939).

It is unclear whether Kung believed all this himself, but for all his confidence, few in the audience are likely to have been persuaded.

3

The Self-Proclaimed Economic Wizard

Hjalmar Schacht in Germany, 1938–9

'One of Germany's Strong Men'

In 1937 Finance Minister Hjalmar Schacht received a visitor in Berlin. It was the rotund beaming H. H. Kung, the Chinese Minister of Finance and Central Bank Governor, come to do a deal, offering Chinese resources and discussing the purchase of German arms. Both Germany and China were rearming at pace, and both were finding it difficult to finance this. As personalities the two finance ministers could hardly have been more different, but they were facing similar pressures from their autocratic leaders and their fast rearming forces. Schacht was naturally austere and severe, but he was soon charmed by the convivial Chinese minister, and before long they were looking to do business together. Neither had much in the way of foreign reserves, but China had raw materials while Germany had industrial expertise, and that was an opportunity for trade.

The photographs of Schacht always show him as formal and austere. He dressed in an old fashioned three piece suit with a high winged collar. He would glare disapprovingly at the photographer, small beady eyes squinting through prince-nez spectacles. The severe appearance reflected his cold unemotional personality—calculating and shrewd, traits that he admitted himself. He was an obsessive chain smoker. With his razor-cut hair, rigid bearing, and characteristic scowl, political cartoons frequently portrayed him as a Prussian Junker. He was also egotistical and vain, boasting about his own achievements, sometimes with a cynical wit. One of his books began: 'I have often been called a financial wizard' (Schacht, 1967, 7).

Schacht felt that his ancestors had predetermined much of his behaviour. He wrote: 'I have been described in public as hard and callous, invariably by those who knew me only superficially. They simply could not conceive that a man outwardly as "buttoned-up" as I am can possess such a thing as a heart. I regret this impression but am unable to change it. A man is not only what he makes of himself—he carries with him the invisible heritage of a long line of forebears' (Schacht, 1956,7).

He led a long and difficult life, and he was a man full of conflicts. Outwardly he displayed considerable self-confidence, a sense of personal superiority, attributing his success to his own intelligence and hard work. He was a solitary character, with few real friends, few followers, and no apparent desire to be liked. He possessed self-discipline, authority and unrelenting drive. Schacht wrote prolifically, including several autobiographies which are his own interpretation of his controversial life: proud of his considerable achievements, self-centred, determined, tough, and defensive against his many critics. Ultimately he would face a tribunal bent on deciding whether or not the work of an economist could be judged evil.

Schacht was born shortly after the end of the Franco-Prussian War, and his upbringing and education were in the new unified Germany, a country surrounded by unreliable neighbours, armies, and conflicts, as nationalist forces rose up across Eastern Europe against the declining Ottoman, Austro-Hungarian, and Russian Empires.

His mother's family was from Hamburg where they were an old established family: one of those members had been a well-known baron. His father's forebears had been peasants, though his grandfather had become a doctor. Schacht's father was an itinerant journalist/bookkeeper/general manager, an interesting and intellectual man who loved discussing important world affairs, but had trouble holding down an ordinary job and supporting his family. He was something of a wanderer, migrating to the United States, part of that large flow of European migrants in the mid-nineteenth century. There he called for his German fiancée to join him. After a few years, having never really settled down, the family headed back to Germany, his wife pregnant with the child who would be Hjalmar Schacht.

Schacht was born in 1877 in Tingleft, a small country town in Prussia (now in Denmark). As his father lost and found jobs, the family moved around other towns in the vicinity, ending up in Hamburg. The family was middle-class but life was not easy—there never seemed to be enough money to pay for food, home, and schooling, a struggle which left its mark on Schacht. In the evenings his father would talk to the children about inventions, scientists, history, literature, politics, commerce, and economics. Schacht remembered the books they owned: Shakespeare, Dickens, Goethe, Schiller, and Heine. He attended a local preparatory school, then to his parents' delight when aged only nine, he passed a difficult entrance exam for the famous Johanneum Grammar School. This was an excellent Hamburg educational institution; the family always struggled to pay the fees, doing without any luxuries to raise the money. At school young Hjalmar worked hard. He was never a popular classmate—life there was full of petty humiliations due to his poverty which meant poor clothing, cheap accommodation, and limited food. He hid his humiliation behind solitary obsessive hard work, and his social insecurity behind a stiff formal exterior. When his father's next job loss forced the family to move to Berlin, Schacht was left to board in Hamburg on his own, still young. He became a temporary refugee at age 15 during the three-month-long Hamburg cholera epidemic that killed around 10,000 people in 1892 and caused chaos, forcing him to flee the city.

While still a pupil, Schacht gave private academic lessons to other pupils to raise money, and he was jubilant when at last he had saved enough to buy a bicycle. He particularly recalled from this time attending a ceremony where he saw the famous Iron Prince Otto von Bismarck. All his life Schacht recalled the values of discipline, purpose, and determination that Bismarck instilled. In his own professed values, Schacht was at heart a nineteenth-century Prussian. But he had also inherited the Hamburg traditions of the Hanseatic League, values of commerce and free trade.

Schacht was talented but unclear what career he wanted to pursue. Following his older brother, he first enrolled at the University of Kiel as a student of medicine, but he did not enjoy the subject. Subsequently he tried studying German philology, then literature, next journalism, and at last political economy. Like his father he found it difficult to settle: within a five-year period he had attended five different universities, experimenting with many different courses of study. Schacht particularly recalled a term that he spent at the University in Munich, attending a course of lectures in political economy given by famous economist Lujo Brentano (about the same time as Takahashi's colleague, Tokuzo Fukuda, attended). Schacht described these lectures as enthralling, and they persuaded him to devote himself to political economy even though in those days in Germany it was regarded as a second-rate subject.

Schacht also had a creative side: he nurtured dreams of becoming a poet, and he enjoyed writing articles and poems for literary magazines. He wrote art criticism reviews, and even a libretto for a German fairy-tale operetta.

Once he had earned his economics degree, Schacht obtained a position as an unpaid intern on the newspaper *Kleines Journal* in Berlin. There he learned the basic tenants of journalism. His favourite job was to do theatre reviews, where he had the opportunity to see famous Berlin performers such as Max Reinhardt. After a year he resigned to continue his peripatetic university education: a term in Leipzig, a winter in Paris, while formally enrolled at Berlin University. Returning to Kiel he enrolled for an economics doctorate, writing a thesis on *The Theoretical Quality of English Commerce* under Professor Wilhelm Hasbach, an economic historian. This was the reason for his first trip to London in 1899, where he read the works of John Hale, John Stuart Mill, and David Hume, and studied records in the reading room of the British Museum (the favourite working place of another famous German economist Karl Marx half a century earlier).

The Japanese had shown the benefits of a modernized navy in the wars with China and Russia. At this time Schacht recalled seeing the opening of the Kiel Canal and the building of the new German pre-dreadnought battleships, symbols of an internationally energized country, but also signalling an arms race with Britain, which would be a harbinger of World War I.

In 1900 Schacht was appointed a clerk in the Central Office for the Preparation of Trade Agreements in Berlin, which as he proudly noted was the only position he ever had to apply for. He continued to contribute reviews and articles for the technical press. The new position gave him experience of economic policy and he started to form views on economic issues such as tariffs, trade, wages, and production. 'The development of the highest and most efficiently organised productivity seemed to me then, as now, the best – indeed the only – means of bringing the greatest possible improvement in the welfare of the masses. To achieve this it is necessary that an economy be kept free from political disturbances. External arbitrary action on matters of commercial policy, and devaluation of currency are as disruptive as internal strikes and lockouts. War and class hatred have always seemed to me the scourge of economic life' (Schacht, 1956, 7).

As his career progressed Schacht was becoming more experienced in policy matters and establishing useful business contacts. Business people found him credible and useful. He had a good education, fluent English, and worked very hard. In 1901 he was invited to stand for the Reichstag, but declined, saying he was more interested in economics than politics.

Schacht was a keen hiker. As a student he had walked across the Alps from southern Germany to Italy. In 1902 he undertook a serious trip from Vladikavkaz in Ossetia across the Caucasus to Tiflis in Georgia, and on to Vagharshapat in Armenia, then back again over the mountains to the Black Sea port of Novorossiysk, a long and difficult journey through an unsettled region. There were to be several other walking trips to the east in the next few years, travelling with groups of young colleagues. Several years later Schacht hiked by himself in Turkey where he met fellow Freemasons, though he also caught very debilitating malaria there.

In 1903 Schacht was invited to join Dresdner Bank. The big three German 'D Banks' covered a wide range of private and business activity, including industrial financing, shares, and bonds, and were responsible for much of the revival of the German economy. It was a fertile place for Schacht to learn about banking, business, and economics. He contributed widely, establishing economic surveys, market reports, and improving the analytical side of banking, always looking for new ways to do business and new skills to acquire.

Schacht had met a young German woman named Luise Sowa at the local tennis club some years earlier while still a student. A tennis-playing, skating athlete, she was attractive and self-assured, traits Schacht admired. Schacht took a very long time to propose, but Luise persisted until he did: they at last became engaged and married in 1903. Luise was the daughter of a senior Prussian police officer and they were a good social fit. She had very strong views that would later prove uncomfortable, but in the meantime they enjoyed what Schacht described as a 'marriage of comradeship' (Weitz, 1997, 31). The couple lived a prosperous suburban life in a comfortable villa in Zehlendorf, a new Berlin suburb, from where Schacht travelled daily by the new electric train to Potsdammerplatz. At the end of the year their first child, a daughter, Inge, was born. Within a few years they had a son, Jens. At work Schacht had been promoted to branch manager, and to all appearances they were a prosperous bourgeois family.

Schacht noted that he was always very busy at work, and admitted that he was never an easy husband to live with. Deciding he had a good understanding of banking theory, but wanting to learn more about the practical side, he simply doubled his working hours. This meant he saw little of his family and had to cut down on sleep, but that was to become his uncompromising approach to life. The comfortable family life did not last. Luise had always possessed extreme right-wing views, and increasingly she became critical of Schacht who liked to think of himself at this time as left-centrist. But Schacht's refuge was his work: he felt especially rewarded when he was given the opportunity to trade on the historic Berlin Bourse.

In 1905 Japan destroyed the Russian fleet, sparking the first Russian Revolution, an event watched with some trepidation from Germany. Schacht had heard about Takahashi's fundraising in Germany that financed this war. In this year he had an exciting opportunity: he was able to travel with a Dresdner Board member to the US. There he talked to many contacts and even met President Theodore Roosevelt. But he was more impressed by his meeting with the aged John Pierpont Morgan, the magnate of JP Morgan Bank, who Schacht regarded as the leading banker in the world. (About the same time Takahashi had been having a tougher time with JP Morgan, whom he regarded as anti-Japanese.)

There were other business ventures: in 1913 Schacht was invited to invest in an emerald mine in Colombia. If he had been aware of Takahashi's very difficult experiences with a silver mine in Peru a quarter of a century earlier, he might have thought more carefully about such a risky project. As it was, the idea attracted him and he prepared to invest. But while he was doing so, World War I broke out, and foreign exchange became impossible to obtain, so the opportunity to become a Latin American mining magnate was lost.

Like both Takahashi and Kung, Schacht had had an unconventional upbringing, a varied education, wide work experiences, and was settling down to a life of bourgeois prosperity and stability. Like Takahashi in Japan and Kung in China, this prosperity and stability would not last forever.

For someone who prided himself on his business intelligence, World War I came as a surprise to Schacht, who had judged it less in human terms but rather as a failure of the Bismarck edict never to seek to fight on two fronts. Schacht himself suffered from acute myopia, and always wore thick glasses, so was not conscripted into the armed forces. However, everyone was affected in some way by the onset of war. He was learning how wartime conditions affected the economy: the raw material short-ages, the limited food supplies, and the rising financial demands of an economy which had to switch suddenly to a war footing.

In late 1914 Schacht was appointed Administrator of the Dresdner Bank in Occupied Belgium. He was assigned to the staff of the German General appointed as Banking Commissioner to organize the financing of Germany's purchases in Belgium. Schacht claimed he did his best to help smooth the introduction of the enforced occupation currency (a job that Takahashi refused to do in Manchuria). He achieved this by raising an innovative bond issue to fund the new currency. But he very quickly ran into disputes with the German military who simply com-mandeered whatever supplies they wanted. Schacht argued that he was the only senior German official sympathetic to the Belgian peoples' plight, by which he meant operating a rules- and market-based economy. He had occasional adventures during his time in Belgium such as help-ing German intelligence identify and arrest in a restaurant a glamorous 'Princess X'—a socialite who seems also to have been a Belgian spy (though he did not seem concerned that she would probably be executed by her captors). Eventually he was dismissed from his post by the army in an argument about how to finance Germany's compulsory purchases.

In 1915 he left Dresdner Bank after an argument with the board. This was becoming typical of Schacht: strong critical views, a point of theor-etical principle, an argument, an uncompromising response, and then he would storm out. Wanting to contribute to the war, he joined the Home Guard. But almost immediately he was offered a new banking job as one of the governors in the smaller Nationalbank für Deutschland.

Life in Berlin was growing tougher because of the raging conflict and the embargo on food supplies. Schacht could now see what war would mean on the home front. He had to dig a vegetable garden at his Berlin home and he acquired a nanny goat to ensure fresh vegetables and milk for the family. At Potsdam Station every morning he passed long lines of people queueing for food and fuel. He blamed Germany's austere fiscal policy that pushed citizens to invest in war bonds for making conditions worse. He blamed this poor domestic economic management and also the British economic blockade for Germany's ultimate defeat.

Germany capitulated in 1918. There was an upwelling of anger, and revolution was in the air. Russia was in the throes of the Bolshevik Revolution, about to assassinate the Czar. Some of the same forces were at play in Germany, and the German Emperor abdicated and fled Berlin. Schacht was in Berlin on that day and he recalled the city was like an armed camp, with overturned vehicles blocking the streets and barbed wire barricades. Leaving the Hotel Esplanade near Potsdammerplatz he was confronted by a troop of German Communist soldiers in trucks, and at the rail station a machine-gun company was ready for action. Sailors had started to mutiny, and Spartacists were raising the red flag in the streets. Schacht and a colleague changed their path to avoid the violence and headed for the Reichstag building to find someone who could tell them what was happening. The place was almost deserted, an emptiness that reflected the vacuum at the heart of German leadership.

Before the war Schacht had been a member of the Young Liberal Association, a nationalist party that supported the Kaiser's expansionist policies. At that time political advancement was reserved for the Prussian nobility, but now the old caste system was disintegrating, and there were opportunities for young blood: the Army and the Empire had collapsed, and the power of the dominating Junker class was being swept away. Schacht felt he needed to become politically involved. The next day he met with colleagues and they formed a political party, the German Democratic Party (DDP), aiming to promote liberal democratic government.

A general strike had been declared and there were mobs in the street. Workers' and soldiers' councils were springing up and taking over local authorities. There was looting and murder. Berlin was preparing for civil war, with barbed wire and barricades, and shots being fired. It looked like there could be a repeat of the bloody Russian Revolution. To someone schooled in the Bismarck tradition of proper law and order this was a very worrying time.

The next few weeks were full of turmoil. By early January Berlin was racked by strikes, street violence, demonstrations, and fighting between

Spartacist revolutionaries and soldiers. Schacht tried to go about his daily work, but on his way home he could hear the noise of machine guns firing. He narrowly missed disaster when a hand grenade was thrown amongst a crowd of Spartacists nearby. It was a very dangerous time— over the next few months 1,200 lives were lost in the uprisings and the very future of Germany seemed to be in doubt.

The German political system was splintering. Initially Schacht's German Democratic Party seemed to be very successful, securing 74 seats in the 1919 elections for the National Assembly and producing two ministers in the new government. It was a party of journalists, businessmen, and academics, attracting such Jewish luminaries as Albert Einstein and Max Weber. Schacht says he was a keen member but he declined to stand as a candidate himself, realizing that he lacked the common touch to appeal to voters, and not being completely trusted by the leadership. However he actively supported the German Democratic Party for the next decade, helping raise funds and writing party policies, before later altering his allegiance completely.

World War I and the 1918 influenza epidemic had brought terrible costs in lives, especially in Germany. However there was relatively limited material damage caused to the country, as fighting had been concentrated on a narrow front-line mainly running through Belgium. Like other protagonist economies, the German economy contracted by a third during the war, though the cost of industrial rebuild was quite limited. (Only the US and Japan did well economically from World War I.) There was a significant build-up of debt, and across Western Europe governments were printing extra money to cover this.

What now absorbed Schacht was the question of reparations that were being imposed on Germany by the victors. Like most Germans he thought the Versailles peace negotiations were completely unrealistic and unfair. In 1919 he was asked to join a private sector group in The Hague negotiating the delivery of consumer goods during the interim settlement period. There the German negotiating team was subjected to many petty humiliations during the discussions such as being forced to remain standing, in order to remind them that they were the defeated nation. These humiliations rankled deeply with Schacht and left an ongoing residue of resentment. It would also bring him into contact with a young British economist named John Maynard Keynes.

The years from 1922 to 1924 were a time of chaos in post-war Germany, an economic manifestation of the terrible social and political instability in the aftermath of World War I. Schacht remembered hunger and surrender, with populations fleeing and speculators making money. In government there was growing corruption and crime. A gold mark was worth two paper marks at the end of World War I, while it was worth one trillion marks by 1923. This was extreme and dangerous hyper-inflation.

Schacht looked on with disgust at this travesty of an economic policy. He had been working very hard at the NfD Bank, which had amalgamated with other banks and grown. Always a workaholic, he claimed to have been on the boards of 70 corresponding companies, and estimated that in a year he had spent 100 nights travelling on the train. But once again he had argued with his fellow directors, and in early 1923 he resigned his position. As the economic situation worsened in Germany, riots were breaking out in several provinces, the National Socialist Party was forming in the south, and at the same time there was the danger of a general Communist uprising. Worried for their safety, Schacht evacuated his family from Berlin to Lausanne in Switzerland.

Hyper-inflation continued: at this time a single tram ticket could cost a billion marks. The demand for high denomination notes was so great that the Reichsbank could not print them fast enough, and private presses began printing what was known as 'emergency currency'. Both the Reichsbank and the government seemed powerless to stabilize the mark, despite the huge political disruption it was causing, and notes were sent in gigantic bundles by truck and train throughout the country. There were many unlikely ideas put forward to anchor the currency. The government even considered tying the mark to a physical quantity of rye seed. Already businesses were doing barter deals to avoid using the German mark altogether.

After exhausting other possibilities, the desperate Social Democrat Government approached Schacht to become Commissioner of National Currency in charge of currency reform. When Schacht assumed this new role in late 1923 the official exchange rate was approaching four trillion marks per dollar. Over the following week the mark plummeted further to 12 trillion on the black market. There were now three currencies existing side by side, but problems with all of them: the paper mark, the rentenmark, and theoretically the old gold mark. There were also difficulties with the black market and with the emergency currency issued by businesses.

Schacht took immediate and decisive action. His first step was to announce that no more payments of emergency money would be accepted by the Reichsbank. This move meant many currency speculators suddenly faced huge losses, and it was initially very unpopular in the country. But it allowed for the orderly introduction of the new rentenmark, and soon Schacht had established a reputation for tough and uncompromising credibility.

Characteristically Schacht had transferred his old secretary to the new position, and on hearing the government would only pay a very low stipend, he offered to divert all his own salary to augment this. Later his secretary was asked what Schacht did during this tense time. She replied: 'What did he do? He sat on his chair and smoked in his little dark room at the Ministry of Finance, which still smelled of old floor cloths. Did he read letters? No, he read no letters. Did he write letters? No, he wrote no letters. He telephoned a great deal—he telephoned in every direction and to every German and International place that had anything to do with money and foreign exchange as well as with the Reichsbank and the finance minister. And he smoked. We did not eat much during that time. We usually went home late, often by the last suburban train, travelling third class. Apart from that, he did nothing' (Schacht, 1956, 171).

'Nothing' meant following classical economic principles and not giving in to market distortions, short-term political pressures, or other vested interests. Schacht's tough uncompromising stance against hyperinflation won him admirers, if not friends. At the end of 1923 after the death of the incumbent, Schacht was offered a new position: President of the Reichsbank—unexpectedly and against the specific opposition of much of the Reichsbank board, who cited his wartime problems in Belgium. This was a very powerful position—he was appointed for life, and sat in cabinet without being bound by cabinet decisions. Accepting the appointment, he saw his first mission as establishing a secure gold backing for the fragile rentenmark. He immediately embarked on a boat and travelled to London to consult with the unofficial doyen of the club of central bankers, the Governor of the Bank of England, Montagu Norman. Norman was an institution in himself, knowledgeable, powerful, and eccentric, an ongoing intellectual rival to Keynes. To Schacht's obvious pleasure, Norman personally met Schacht at Liverpool Street Station on New Year's Eve, and he listened very sympathetically to Schacht's plans to set German industry growing again.

The proposal was to establish a government-owned credit bank based on gold reserves, funded by capital in foreign currency and a loan from the Bank of England, with its foreign currency bills tradable on the British market. This idea of issuing notes in Germany in a foreign currency was audacious and radical. Somewhat surprisingly, Norman admired the bold move and declared himself in favour, offering a Bank of England loan at the then very advantageous rate of 5 per cent, and encouraging London bankers to accept the bills without any mention of guarantees or security. Norman's 'encouragement' was sufficient to ensure that the scheme could work. Norman also agreed with Schacht to jointly sabotage a French attempt to set up a separate Rhineland Central Bank, which Norman agreed would be tantamount to secession of German territory. Over the years Norman became a close personal friend of Schacht despite the war, despite Norman's eccentricities, and despite Schacht's difficult and undiplomatic temperament.

On occasions as recurrent crises worried the world's central banks, Schacht would board a transatlantic cruise liner and sail to the United States. The purpose was to visit the New York Federal Reserve for meetings organized by (New York Federal Reserve President) Benjamin Strong who also invited central bank governors from London and Paris. This cosy club of central bankers seemed to enjoy one another's company and shared their concerns about financial markets, as well as their disparaging views about how to resist politicians who were inappropriately focused on short-term political advantage (Ahamed, 2009).

In the midst of the negotiations there was still a social life for the Reichsbank President to keep up. Schacht remembers social engagements most evenings with friends and politicians. He left the organization of this to his wife. His professional networks were very wide, yet his real personal friendships were very narrow.

In 1924 the Allies established the Dawes Committee to reconsider German reparation obligations in the light of Germany's evident inability to pay in such difficult post-war conditions. Schacht was called to Paris to testify and there he encountered the outright hostility of the French.

He achieved some notoriety by refusing to be summoned to a meeting by French President Raymond Poincaré, then reluctantly agreeing, only to storm out of the presidential waiting room after the president had kept him waiting for 15 minutes. Pulled back by horrified French officials, he had an icy meeting with a hostile president and halfway through terminated the discussions by walking out. Schacht's inter-personal relations were never good, and his bloody-minded approach to crises was becoming a problem.

Acting under French pressure, the Dawes Committee argued that the Reichsbank must be restructured with some foreign directors. A reduced repayment schedule was negotiated in return for these concessions and a 'Dawes Loan' was issued by the Allied countries, allowing 800 million gold marks to flow into the Reichsbank, a reserve base that at last allowed for a sound issuance of currency. In turn there was a gradual restoration of confidence in the German economy and growth of credit to business. But Schacht was not happy at the negotiations: colleagues described him at the time as moody, temperamental, and mercurial. His central bank colleagues feared for his mental stability and were worried about his inability to separate out financial policies from political arguments. Schacht was accused of wanting to walk away from the Dawes Plan for his own self-aggrandizement.

While price inflation had now stabilized in Germany, there were still problems with volatile stock prices and exchange rates. German companies had flocked to borrow from foreign bankers in foreign currencies, and this caused them problems as the exchange rate dropped. The German economy had been limping along; foreign banks which had lent money in foreign currencies were incurring losses and complaining bitterly about it. Schacht's response to these bankers and industrialists was once again typically uncompromising: it had been their decision to lend or borrow, and now they must live with the consequences.

With his tough stance Schacht was becoming increasingly unpopular. In 1928 when the question of his suitability as Reichsbank President arose, malicious rumours started circulating about his poor health. Aged 51 and determined to prove these rumours wrong, he set off on an expedition with his daughter to the Eiger Mountain in Switzerland, climbing the challenging Jungfraujoch summit to demonstrate his fitness. About this time he also acquired a country property in a wooded lake district 70 miles north of Berlin, which he foresaw as a rural fortress to retreat to if his enemies gathered.

Somehow Schacht found the time to document his experiences, no doubt to ensure his own view of his contributions prevailed. In 1927 he published a book: *The Stabilisation of the Mark*, recounting his experiences as Currency Commissioner. Keynes reviewed the book for the *New Republic* magazine the next year. He recounted: 'Dr Schacht has shown himself one of Germany's strongmen. He has won his victories by determination and strength of character, by great obstinacy and courage in the face of opposition, and by holding tenaciously to a few simple principles, rather than by any special subtlety of intellect or method. He can be proud of the results' (*Sydney Morning Herald*, 20.2.28, 13).

Keynes had earlier sparked a huge debate on German reparations with his *Economic Consequences of the Peace*. Now he encouraged a discussion on the technical problems of transferring reparations payments over foreign exchanges, culminating in an article entitled 'The German Transfer Problem'. He circulated advance proofs to Schacht and others, before publishing in the *Economic Journal* in 1929.

The Allied countries were starting to realize that despite the Dawes Loan, Germany's reparations payment timetable was still quite unrealistic. In 1929 the Young Plan Conference under US Chairman Owen Young met in the luxury hotel George V in Paris to reconsider the arrangements. The French delegation demanded payments of $600 million per annum for 62 years. Schacht led the German delegation, and he proposed a much reduced German reparation amount of $250 million per annum for the next 37 years. The US tried to find a compromise package, being more concerned about the repayment of Allied debts than German reparations. The French were particularly hostile to Schacht's position, but were now themselves in a bind because so many German companies were in danger of defaulting to French banks. Schacht felt he was under particular pressure from the French Government, and he reported that their security service was tapping his phone in Paris.

At international meetings Schacht was distinctive: he was a tall man with the upright stance, and extra hide starched collar, smoking a cigar. In winter he wore a fur-collared Chesterfield coat and a Homburg hat. To some he could be a forbidding figure, and he was becoming very difficult to negotiate with, constantly storming out of meetings threatening to abort the talks. A journalist described him as him as 'a vehement, intolerant man; excitable and dogmatic;…the most tactless, the most aggressive and the most irascible person I have ever seen in public life' (Ahamed, 2009, 332). He could change the German negotiating position abruptly, and several times the conference table dissolved into angry disapproval. Eventually the German Cabinet lost confidence in Schacht and recalled him. He responded by heading off on a tour of the Loire Valley castles with his wife.

Despite his histrionics, Schacht saw some advantages in the Young Agreement which withdrew the foreign presence in the German Reichsbank and the German Railways, agreed rescheduled payments of around $500 million per annum, left the repayments mechanism up to the German authorities, and cleared the way for the French to depart the occupied Ruhr territories. On Germany's behalf, Schacht signed the Young Agreement in June 1929, and returned to Germany thinking that it represented a good compromise for the country. However on his return to Berlin he was surprised to find himself under bitter attack from the left, the right, and even from his wife for selling out to France.

In an addendum to the Young Committee, Schacht had presented the 'Schacht Plan' for a clearing union. This proposed to promote sound and stable currency exchange in Europe via a clearing house with capital from central banks in Germany, Britain, France, Italy, US, and Japan. Acting on some of his proposals, the Young Committee agreed to establish a bank to handle the reparations payments; this was to be the Bank for International Settlements headquartered in neutral territory in Basel, Switzerland, tactically positioned on a tongue of land between France and Germany. Schacht recommended to the Committee that they should go further and help stimulate development in former colonies by increasing the Bank's focus to include international development. (When at last in 1944, the World Bank was established, based significantly on a plan from Keynes, Schacht was not shy about claiming its intellectual parentage for himself. In contrast to Keynes, Schacht's 1930 Plan proposed to clear not just trade transactions but also capital movements, at the charge of both creditors and debtors.)

The details about the Bank for International Settlements were hammered out at a further conference in the Black Forest resort of

Baden-Baden where Schacht and other delegates enjoyed the beautiful autumnal tree colours. The mood was becoming more optimistic at the conference, when they received the first dispatches from New York reporting the 1929 Wall Street stock market crash that would plunge the world into the Great Depression, and Germany into a totalitarian dictatorship.

There were soon problems back in Berlin. The German Government had begun to do side deals with Poland which breached the terms of the Young Agreement. In his usual uncompromising fashion, Schacht complained loudly and publicly about his own government's actions. Privately and then publicly Schacht began to repudiate the very plan that he had signed. Keynes agreed with some of his criticisms and argued that Germany needed assistance. Then a further complication arose: the German Minister of Finance Hilferding arranged an American short-term loan to tide over the fiscal situation. Schacht criticized the terms, and tried to impose much tougher conditions on the loan, accusing the German government of failing to control its expenditure. This criticism was sufficient to sabotage the prospects for the American loan altogether. Minister Hilferding resigned. Schacht had alienated the Right by signing the Young Plan and now also the Centre-Left by challenging the Coalition Government's economic policies.

Pressure was building on him, and again there were complaints about his personal behaviour as he started to display paranoia about corrupt politicians. He looked close to a nervous breakdown. His colleagues speculated whether he was nursing unrealistic political ambitions of replacing the ageing von Hindenburg as German President. It was too much this time: Schacht was asked to leave the Reichsbank. He vacillated, and then eventually lost his temper at a press conference, finally submitting his resignation to President von Hindenburg. Angry but still self-interested, he negotiated a very large severance lump-sum pay-out from his pension, one quarter of a million dollars.

In 1930, and now out of the Reichsbank, the 53-year-old Schacht felt lonely and directionless. He had excess time on his hands and he spent it at his country estate. This land had been deforested to provide army supplies in World War I. Now Schacht replanted about three million trees on the poor soil. He also ran a small farm, winning village prizes for milk and raising pigs. Just like Keynes, he took a keen, albeit somewhat academic view of farming, and (like Keynes) soon considered himself an expert on agrarian matters and able to lecture locals on improving techniques. He maintained a brickworks on an island in an adjourning lake. He claimed to have derived much pleasure in long solitary walks, taking a telescope to spot the deer, foxes, badgers, rabbits, wild boar, and birdlife, and sometimes shooting for food. Schacht said that he found a meditative peace there, but his daughter said it was quite the opposite: that he used to pace up and down the garden like a caged lion, consuming an endless succession of cigars.

Later that year Schacht travelled with his wife and son to the United States on a private lecture tour. As he passed through London to catch his steamer, he heard the news of the 14 September Reichstag elections. Following surging nationalism, ugly rallies, and aggressive rhetoric, the centrist parties had lost support. The small National Socialist Party had suddenly gained 107 seats in the Reichstag, and the Communist Party had increased to 77 seats. The moderates in Germany were burning out. It would mark the end of the Weimar era.

Schacht travelled widely on his US tour. Within 50 days he gave nearly 50 lectures and recorded that he had slept in 42 different beds, and he complained about a monstrous American diet of chicken and ice cream. He could speak fluently in English and had many interesting conversations, though the questions from the Americans were usually limited to the subject of German reparations. He took the opportunity to call privately on a number of politicians, including President Herbert Hoover, while continuing to claim he had no political intentions himself. Schacht felt that Hoover agreed with his arguments about the need to cease reparation payments, though Schacht was never a good listener to others' viewpoints. He also stated his position about German economic policies publicly and loudly, which considerably irked the German Government in Berlin. His tour received wide media coverage, *TIME magazine* calling him 'the Ironman of Germany'. Returning to Germany, he found himself the object of intense criticism.

That winter he was involved in a bad motor accident on ice, leaving him unconscious. He had to be hospitalized and went through a long, serious, and painful rehabilitation, which left him crippled for some time. Perhaps it was fortunate that he was not currently in office. But it was typical of his dogged determination that being derided, being sacked, and being knocked down did not change his highly critical views about strong reparations and weak government. He wrote a book based on his US lectures entitled *The End of Reparations,* which sold well and evoked Keynes's earlier volume *The Economic Consequences of the Peace.*

Economic conditions were still very volatile. In 1931 the Austrian bank Creditanstalt failed, setting off runs on other banks. The German Reichsbank tried to present a confident front, but soon there was a run on German foreign exchange reserves. Ultimately an important German institution, the Danat Bank, failed. To Schacht's evident satisfaction, Chancellor Bruning begged him to travel to Berlin to advise on actions. Once there Bruning invited him to retake the position of Reich's Commissioner of National Currency but, his pride pricked by criticisms, Schacht refused, even when President Hindenburg sent his own emissary to try to persuade him.

Despite being out of government, Schacht never stopped giving economic and political advice, often unsolicited and unwelcome. He had argued with his bank employers. He had argued with the Reichsbank Board. He had abandoned the German Democratic Party. He had become disillusioned with the Weimar Government because he objected to the inclusion of Socialist Party policies into government, especially some which he thought undermined the anti-inflation struggle. He was particularly hostile to the Communists. He wanted to see a stronger nationalistic government which could help rebuild Germany and put it back on the world stage. On the sea voyage to America in 1930 he had read an interesting book called *Mein Kampf* by a young rabble-rouser called Adolf Hitler. Schacht was gradually drawing nearer to the new German National Socialist Party.

At the end of 1931 a banker colleague invited Schacht to a dinner where he met an upcoming Nazi leader named Herman Goering, who Schacht described as pleasant and urbane though not very knowledgeable. Shortly afterwards Goering put on a dinner party for Schacht and the steel magnate Fritz Thyssen at his Berlin apartment where he met another senior Nazi, Joseph Goebbels, over a simple German meal of pea soup and bacon. Later in the evening another guest arrived, wearing dark trousers and a yellowish-brown jacket, familiar face adorned by a moustache. This was Adolf Hitler in person. A discussion on economics and politics followed, dominated by Hitler, who Schacht reported was a convincing speaker. He seemed absolutely convinced by his own outlook, and determined to convert this into practical action. Schacht recorded: 'after the many rumours that we had heard about Hitler and the published criticism we had read about him, we were pleasantly impressed. His appearance was neither pretentious nor affected. Our talk quickly turned to political and economic problems. His skill and exposition was most striking. Everything he said, he stated as an incontrovertible truth: nevertheless his ideas were not unreasonable. He was obviously anxious to avoid anything that might shock us in our capacity as representatives of a more traditional society' (Schacht, 1956, 257). It was the start of the relationship.

The bitter debate about German reparations continued. In the end, of the 120 billion marks that Germany was meant to pay in reparations, only about 20 million was actually paid, and this was financed not from German exports but from loans from other countries. In the 1932 Lausanne Conference, the remaining reparation commitments were eventually written off. But the end to reparation payments came too late: populist anger had been building up and now it exploded. The country suffered badly in the Great Depression and unemployment had reached six million. At the election later that year the Nazis received 37 per cent of the vote and the Communists also increased their support. Hitler won 230 seats, more than a third of the Reichstag, and now he led the largest party. The country was split, and people began to talk about a choice between civil war or military dictatorship.

Schacht wrote to Hitler congratulating him on his election victory. 'Your movement is carried internally by so strong a truth and necessity that victory in one form or another cannot elude you for long. During the time of the rise of your movement you did not let yourself be led astray by false gods....If you remain the man that you are, success cannot elude you for long' (Ahamed, 2009, 480). He also took it on himself to organize a petition of business leaders and, unsuccessfully, urge President von Hindenburg and other senior politicians to invite the Nazis into a coalition, claiming this might keep them within reasonable bounds. Efforts at establishing a coalition government failed.

Later in the year, in a desperate move to form a government, Hitler was appointed Chancellor. From time to time several Nazis, including Hitler's own economic advisor, sought out advice from Schacht. Schacht himself viewed Hitler with some suspicion but continued to think '...

it would be possible to guide this man into the path of righteousness' (Schacht, 1956, 274). This shows what a poor judge of personality Schacht was. He never accepted that he might have been completely unrealistic about the Nazis' ambitions.

Schacht never actually joined the Nazi Party but he was close and did not hesitate to use the association when it suited him. He occasionally addressed Nazi rallies, generally criticizing the Coalition Government for misleading the population on foreign debts. Some in the government regarded this as very vindictive, even calling for him to be charged with treason. He was invited to discussions being held by the National Socialist Party, and he helped to raise three million marks for it. Schacht was asked by Hitler to administer the fund, which he agreed to do. A few days later the German Reichstag building was burned down, an event that made it obvious to many people that the country was heading down a dangerous path to totalitarianism. For all his intelligence, Schacht himself did not seem to possess the insight to understand this.

Hitler's views on economics have been much debated. He criticized both communism and capitalism (each of which in his warped perception was dominated by Jews). He was inconsistent about the meaning of socialism. He seemed not particularly interested in economic theory: to him economics was only there to provide whatever resources were necessary to make Germany great again. 'The nation does not live for the economy, for economic leaders, or for economic or financial theories; on the contrary, it is finance and the economy, economic leaders and theories, which all owe unqualified service in this struggle for the self-assertion of our nation' (Tooze, 2007, 220).

In 1934 the 'Night of the Long Knives' brought brutal street warfare between Hitler's SS men and the SA under Rohm. Schacht heard the reports and recalled that he shuddered at their implications. He claimed to have confronted Hitler with the immorality of the actions, and reported Hitler took the criticisms seriously. Schacht seemed to relish his new self-assumed role as providing good economic and moral advice for the new administration, dressing down Hitler personally when any of his officials was lambasted by Nazis.

Not surprisingly Schacht did not enjoy good relations with many of the other senior Nazis. He says that he had to work with 'the little doctor' (Goebbels) who hated him. He soon ran into more overt opposition from

Heinrich Himmler, who openly confronted him, and increasingly also from other Nazi officials. The working relationship with Goering had started off cordially but it soon deteriorated. For several years Schacht relied on his personal relationship with Hitler to protect him from antagonistic senior Nazis.

While Schacht saw National Socialism as a pragmatic way to advance economic policies for national recovery, his wife Luise was a devoted camp follower, hero-worshipping Hitler. Schacht might occasionally pin a swastika on his suit. But Luise made a point of wearing an expensive jewelled swastika made up of rubies and diamonds to all receptions. In public she began to criticize Schacht whenever he did not follow the Nazi line, even passing on disparaging comments that he had made at home. Relations between them worsened, and Schacht felt she might even be endangering his life by behaving like this. He decided to leave her, and later in 1938 he obtained a judicial separation. Luise became sick and she would die early in the war.

1938: Filling the Credit Shortage—MEFO Bills

By 1938 Germany was moving from covert rearmament to more overt preparations for war. Hitler, Mussolini, Franco, and Stalin were all working to eliminate domestic opposition and consolidate their own power. In March Germany announced the Anschluss with Austria, and Nazi troops marched into Vienna. (Among the troops was one who stood out for his decidedly non-Aryan looks—the nephew of H. H. Kung from China.) In September Hitler met Chamberlain and Daladier at Munich, and the British Prime Minister short-sightedly proclaimed 'peace in our time'. A fortnight later German troops marched into Sudetenland in Czechoslovakia and were soon making claims on Poland. The next month there was a Nazi rampage against Jewish shopkeepers across Germany, the 'Kristallnacht'. Refugees were massing on European borders. In East Asia the war news was bad in China, and the British were starting to rearm against the Japanese threat in Southeast Asia. It was becoming increasingly obvious where this militarization was heading.

Back in 1933 Hitler had asked Schacht to resume his role as President of the Reichsbank. This time Schacht accepted without question. Hitler had wanted to reduce unemployment and raise funds for rearmament. The first job was to fund Hitler's work creation (Operation Reinhardt) programme aimed at the reconstruction of houses, factories, and machinery. Schacht directed the Reichsbank to contribute one billion marks to this work. Then followed construction of the national autobahn network, for which Schacht sanctioned Reichsbank loans of 600 million marks. The large public works were to be supported by deficit spending, privatization of major banks and other companies, and replacement of trades unions and chambers of commerce with supervised workers councils. The inflation effects of excess demand were to be managed by controls on prices and wages.

The same year Schacht led a German delegation to the US in preparation for the upcoming World Economic Conference due to be held in London. The US had just surprised financial markets by abandoning the gold standard, and devaluing the US dollar by 40 per cent, apparently to counter the earlier British devaluations. Schacht met President Roosevelt several times and had much pleasure telling him how he had met his uncle Theodore in the same room a generation previously. Schacht also told Roosevelt that Germany would need to cease paying interest on American loans, and to his surprise the President laughed and said that would serve Wall Street right. With his usual lack of perception Schacht thought he had made a good impression on Roosevelt, but the latter later described him as 'extremely arrogant'.

One evening Secretary of State Cordell Hull gave a dinner in Washington in honour of Schacht and another delegation that was visiting at the same time. This was the Chinese delegation to the conference, led by H. H. Kung the Chinese minister. In their first meeting Kung quickly charmed the austere Prussian. Schacht recorded that he very much enjoyed talking to him, and they would later meet again, this time to do business.

Schacht then travelled back to London for the World Economic Conference itself. He reported proudly that he met the King of England there. The vital question was how to return the big economies to stable currency conditions, and how to set world trade going again. Keynes was covering this conference as a journalist for the *Daily Mail*, and though not an official delegate somehow managed to put forward his own plan for the conference. Eventually the much-heralded meeting broke up without achievement, a failure that was subsequently blamed on Roosevelt's prevarication on the gold standard.

The following year Schacht had been summoned again by Hitler. Despite Schacht's blunt and confrontational style, Hitler seemed to recognize and value his technical competence amongst a group of sycophantic political leaders who were not well versed in economics. He also approvingly commented that Schacht was very talented at negotiating, and was later quoted as saying that for all his anti-Nazi snobbery, 'Schacht was one Aryan who could out-swindle the Jews' (Weitz, 1997, 152).

Hitler asked Schacht to become his Minister of Economic Affairs, in addition to continuing to run the Reichsbank. Schacht said he agreed to become Minister provided Hitler gave him an assurance that German Jews would not be affected by his policies. Hitler allegedly assured him of this. Schacht recorded: 'as long as I remained head of the Ministry for Economic Affairs I protected every Jew against illegal economic injury at the hands of the party' (Schacht, 1956, 292). In the light of what we now know really happened this assurance was either naïve or quite untrue.

After several years in his joint roles as Reichsbank President and Economy Minister, Schacht would have been justified in feeling some self-satisfaction. The economy had picked up and was growing rapidly: following negative growth rates during the period 1929 to 1932, Germany spent the next seven years growing annually between 8 and 10 per cent. Industrial production doubled. Unemployment which had been nearly a third of the male workforce dropped quickly to one quarter of that level, partly as a result of the increased economic activity, but also for other reasons—some women, youth, agricultural workers, and Jews were removed from the unemployment register, and increasingly conscription removed young males. The size of the armed forces increased more than ten times in half a decade. The work creation programme, the spending on autobahns and other infrastructure, and the rearmament all involved a huge increase in public expenditure which would be financed by debt.

Despite his pro-market stance, as Minister of the Economy Schacht had also imposed a range of controls over German production and on raw materials allocation, regulating production capacity, encouraging synthetic substitutes for scarce materials, and increasing capacity for essential production. Government agencies under his control issued hundreds of decrees, permits, prohibitions, and instructions. He also promoted the formation of a number of large firms including I.G. Farben, from a cartel of six chemical companies. (IGF would later be accused of using slave labour in World War II and producing poison gas used in concentration camps. Its directors faced prosecution at the Nuremberg war trials.) There was a further increase in public spending on roads and vehicle production, and on heavy industry and arms investment that gradually began to crowd out household consumption.

Some historians have interpreted this as an example of reflationary Keynesian economics, though it only partially rested on Keynes's ideas. (Keynes had published a German version of his essay on *National Self-sufficiency* in 1933, though he allowed translators to censor passages that might offend the Nazis.) The German recovery was somewhat lopsided: there was a big increase in construction, the arms industry, and heavy industry, but at the expense of consumer goods. Exports stagnated under the high exchange rate, forcing Schacht to develop an elaborate system of import controls and foreign barter trade. Schacht estimated that 83 per cent of foreign trade was by then being carried out by barter not using foreign exchange, a primitive set of arrangements. By 1936 military expenditure was more than 10 per cent of German GNP, and military investment had surpassed civilian investment.

As economic growth accelerated, Schacht felt the need to slow spending. As early as 1935 at the Nuremberg Party Convention, the scene of Goebbels's great Nazi rallies, Schacht had tried to deflate the nationalistic fervour by warning that the Reichsbank would need to reduce its loans to the government, and that further purchases of armaments would need to be financed out of taxes or private borrowing.

Two economic policy factions were developing within the National Socialist Government. First the free-market technocrats, such as Schacht and Price Commissioner Carl Goerdeler, called for free international trade, restraints on military spending, and reduced state intervention, who were supported by many leading business executives. The second faction was the more politicized military group under Goering who called for state planning, economic self-sufficiency, and increased military spending. This was similar to the tension being faced by Takahashi in Japan. During the 1935–6 economic crisis, Schacht had led the free-market faction in urging less military spending, less protectionism, and less state control over the economy. Typically Hitler had hesitated between the two factions, then sided against Schacht, calling for a Four-Year Plan to prepare the German economy for war within four years. He appointed Herman Goering 'Plenipotentiary for the Four-Year Plan' with broad powers that ultimately would conflict with Schacht's policy role.

Now Hitler ominously declared that Germany could only produce sufficient food with more lebensraum (living space), stating 'war is inevitable'. The German Army and the German economy were directed to be ready for war within four years. It was at this stage that serious rearmament commenced.

Arms production was now being given particular priority. Schacht noted that arms orders could be distributed among many underused factories across the whole country, and that proved a way to ramp up production and provide local employment. Hitler's war economy was readying itself. Germany was by this stage much more prepared for war in terms of mobilization and military production than other eventual antagonist countries. In Schacht's accounts written after the war, he claimed that he did not help fund the war machine, and that arms financing at this stage was in accord with the support of all the political parties in the Reichstag, was aimed primarily at defence, and was in line with the Versailles Treaty—all positions disputed by historians.

As Germany's aggressive intentions became clearer, other countries imposed new trade sanctions, and the country was soon suffering from punitive tariffs in 80 per cent of her export markets and in some cases from import quotas as well. As exports declined the government's reserves of foreign exchange and gold dropped. There were further proposals to limit German reparation payments and once again Germany found itself struggling with a collection of ersatz currencies—travel marks, renten-marks, and aski marks.

Back in 1934 Schacht had devised a new financial instrument, the MEFO bill. Its purpose was to provide funds for armaments. MEFO bills were used by armaments suppliers and accepted by an operation called Metall-Forschung A.G., a shell company founded under government direction by four large industrial combines. The drawer could present the MEFO bill for discount to a German bank, and these banks could re-discount them to the Reichsbank prior to maturity. That meant military contractors were paid in bills issued by a shell company and could exchange them for cash at a German bank, which would on-sell the bills to the central bank, which in turn converted it to cash by issuing money. The government was effectively printing money for the specific purpose of rearming.

Over the last half of the 1930s decade, Germany's arms expenditure increased four-fold, jumping to 17 per cent of GNP by 1938 and 53 per cent by 1940. Initially this was funded by Reichsbank loans expanded through the MEFO instruments. Official lending by the Reichsbank had been limited by law to 100 million reichsmarks. This financing method enabled the government to go beyond these limits to obtain new credit from the Reichsbank which it could not otherwise have done. By 1939 no more Reichsbank loans were used for arms expenditure.

For several years Schacht had been pushing back at the Nazi Administration which was urging him to provide more foreign reserves for armaments. Like other economic leaders in this book, Schacht felt that he was on a treadmill to feed the insatiable military machine, although for him the principal evil was not military aggression but infla-tion. In 1937 Schacht's appointment to the Reichsbank was due to end, and he said he would only accept reappointment if the loans by the bank to the Reich were limited, eventually agreeing to implement further MEFO bills of exchange up to a strict limit of 12 billion reichsmarks. He accepted a one-year extension of appointment, and warned he would resign if Hitler failed to abide by the agreement. To the surprise of some, Hitler agreed with Schacht and he followed the agreement to the letter. According to Schacht, after 1938 the Reichsbank did not loan or contrib-ute further to arms expenditure.

Adolf Hitler seems to have kept his faith in Schacht for a time, regard-ing him as an economic wizard in an area where he had little interest but where he knew he needed his expertise and his market reputation. Consequently Hitler protected him from his Nazi colleagues for as long as he was useful, while Schacht could keep providing the foreign exchange needed for the rearmament programme. To show his appreciation for this work, on his sixtieth birthday in 1937 Hitler presented Schacht with a 1870s Spitzweg oil painting. Nobody had told Schacht not to look a gift horse in the mouth, especially if it was from Adolf Hitler. Ever the contrarian, Schacht took a perverse delight in proving that the painting was actually a modern fake, and confronting Hitler (himself an ex-artist) with this finding. Hitler still argued it was genuine, but was unable to convince Schacht.

Up until this time Schacht seems to have genuinely believed he could moderate the worst of Hitler's military aggression and racialist outrages, while Hitler seems to have valued keeping Schacht in his cabinet, despite the latter's stalling, arguments, and criticism. However Schacht was completely unrealistic about Hitler's eventual intentions, and this relationship was soon to founder badly.

1939: Trade Deals to Save Foreign Exchange

1939 was a dark year for Europe: after more war-like speeches from Hitler, France and Britain ramped up their rearmament programmes and there was urgent diplomatic activity under way. Germany invaded the entirety of Czechoslovakia. In August the signing of the Molotov-Ribbentrop Pact caught the West by surprise, a nonaggression pact between traditional enemies Germany and USSR, which to the horror of their neighbours divided up Baltic and Eastern European states between them. On 1 September 1939 Germany invaded Poland, the Allies declared war, and almost all of Europe and much of the rest of the world was caught up in the fighting.

Hitler had been focused on creating a wehrwirtschaft (defence economy), an idea widely supported in nationalist circles and by the army. It was felt that one reason Germany had lost World War I was because of poor economic organization and vulnerability to an economic blockade. As the clouds of war loomed, the German economic position became much more urgent. More foreign exchange was having to be diverted to pay for food imports. Sanctions and the world economic crisis had seriously hurt German exports and there was very little export revenue available.

Schacht wanted to access resources from former German colonies. With Hitler's agreement he had earlier visited the French Prime Minister Leon Blum, to explore the possibility of transferring back to Germany the League of Nations-mandated territory of the Cameroons in Africa, for the purposes of using its resources to help rebuild the German economy. Schacht argued that this initiative might have proceeded but for the

Almeria Incident (when German planes bombed that town during the Spanish Civil War). Not to be dissuaded, Schacht also visited the King of the Belgians who he claims was sympathetic to the idea.

Schacht claimed to not be a politician. But he had always been a German nationalist: he opposed the Versailles reparations, and argued that he consistently based his economic policy on the need for Germany to earn enough revenue from its own production and from the overseas colonies that it had lost after World War I. He cited the British Empire as the classic example of how this might work. But he argued that the pure theory of free trade, originated by British Jew David Ricardo, was basically a conspiracy of classical British 'scientific economists' which 'bemused the brains of the continent' (Schacht, 1956, 346).

To try to address Germany's foreign exchange problem, Schacht had in 1934 put in place the 'New Plan'. This mandated the negotiation of a number of trade agreements to guarantee export access. By 1938 there were trade access arrangements in place with 25 countries. This most favoured nation treatment attracted considerable international criticism. Schacht retorted: 'what mattered to me however was not the classical tradition of any economic theory but that the German people should be provided with the necessities of life' (Schacht, 1956, 302).

The New Plan restricted the use of foreign exchange markets for non-military purposes and arranged payment-clearing devices that avoided the need for foreign exchange. This involved the importer depositing the purchase price in his own currency at his own national clearing agency, which placed the same amount to the credit of a clearing agency in another country, which in turn paid the exporter in their own currency. Any imbalance in trade would result in a credit or a debit, to be reimbursed from future trade.

Under Schacht's plan the German Administration authorized imports on condition that foreign sellers agreed to accept payment in the form of credits from special accounts called 'ASKI' (an abbreviation of Auslander Sonderkonten fuer Inlandszahlungen—foreigners' special accounts for domestic payments). These ASKI marks could only be used to purchase German goods for export to the country of the holder of the account, that is they avoided the need to be converted into foreign currency. Each group of ASKI accounts related to one country's bilateral trade with Germany, and the terms depended on Germany's bargaining position in each case.

Trade agreements had mainly been signed with countries in southern and south-eastern Europe. The German Government strongly encouraged trade with them and strongly discouraged trade with others, except where there were key materials sought. To promote his bilateral trade deals and extend them eastwards Schacht travelled to the Balkans and also met Turkish leader Kemal Ataturk, then on to Syria, and finally to visit the Shah of Iran. Everywhere he worked to arrange further trade deals. Germany needed soybeans from Bulgaria, oil from Romania, bauxite from Hungary, and magnesium from Yugoslavia, tungsten from Spain, with payment offered in German goods. He also received visits from countries looking for bilateral trade opportunities (including Kung from China). At first these bilateral trade agreements seem to work well. From 1939 Germany increasingly depended also on imports from the Soviet Union, especially oil, grain, and alloys.

Schacht had originally been on good social terms with Herman Goering, who he had described as intelligent and interesting, but who later became very rapacious and ostentatious. Schacht complained to Hitler that he had found Nazi Party officials abusing the foreign exchange control regulations—Goering was appointed to help regulate this. Goering's Four-Year Plan contained some specific import substitution measures, such as a project to extract benzene from coal, the equipping of a German whaling fleet, and the extension of mining operations in Germany. There was an increase in self-sufficiency in food production (increasingly using controlled labour), but the country was always very short of fats and oils. By the outbreak of war there were only a few months' supplies of crucial materials such as petroleum, iron ore, magnesium, and rubber.

Germany was putting much effort into developing ersatz substitute products, such as producing artificial rubber from acetylene and oil from coal. However these operations were quite inefficient (e.g. six tons of coal were required to produce one ton of oil). Schacht was becoming increasingly critical of Goering's initiatives such as the highly expensive Herman Goering Works to exploit saltpetre ore. Goering was not economically sophisticated, and his policies were naïve: he wanted German industry to maximize production, without worrying about measures of profitability, funding, or value.

Schacht was increasingly concerned about rising public deficits. He supported the short-term use of deficit financing, but advocated long-run conservative financial policies, especially with the memory of the 1920s hyper-inflation. By now he felt that growth was strong and it was time to reduce government expenditure which had increased 300 per cent from 1933 to 1938. By 1938 credit was scarce and it was difficult for the government to borrow, other than very short-term, and more money had to be printed by the Reichsbank. The money supply was growing much faster than industrial output.

But like Takahashi and Kung before him he found it was not easy to cut spending. Schacht initially supported Goering's appointment as Commissioner for Raw Materials and Foreign Exchange, believing he could take unpopular decisions and Schacht would still be able to control him. But Goering refused to worry about a shortage of funds, only a shortage of weapons.

Schacht was particularly concerned as firms started to cash in their MEFO bills. He began to criticize German industrial policies in public. He pointed out that during his own time as minister, imports of raw and semi-process materials had doubled, and this represented more efficient procurement than some of the home-grown schemes. Furthermore the way the military were requisitioning materials and labour was damaging German export potential at a time when export revenue was crucial. Goering's instructions to seize foreign securities held in Germany only worsened the position. Schacht stated his views very directly to Hitler in September 1937, and asked to be relieved from his office as Minister for Economic Affairs.

These disagreements embarrassed Hitler. In a meeting at Hitler's Bavarian home, he asked Schacht to reconsider and to come to terms with Goering, but Schacht would not change his mind. After commenting on the beautiful house and the lovely summer's day, Schacht says 'I remained unmoved even when Hitler finally assured me, with real tears in his eyes: "but Schacht—I am fond of you"' (Schacht, 1956, 342). Hitler began to accuse the Economics Ministry of not understanding the requirements of economic mobilization, an indirect criticism of Schacht himself. Schacht objected that he could not implement economic policy with Goering interfering. At last in November 1937, Hitler sacked Schacht from the Ministry of Economic Affairs.

Needing more funds Hitler turned instead to his new Minister of Economic Affairs, Walther Funk. Funk was a short stout man, and unusually for a senior Nazi, a musician, a homosexual, and an alcoholic.

But he was an unequivocal and compliant Nazi, with none of Schacht's showy cleverness or irritating superiority, a man who would obey Hitler's orders without quoting economic theory at him. Funk's ministry issued two large public loans instead of the MEFO bills. A third loan issue failed, making it clear the domestic loan market was now saturated. Funk would serve out the war as minister, and then be convicted of war crimes at the Nuremburg trials.

By this stage Schacht's blunt speaking and superior attitude was starting to irritate all the administration's officials and, most dangerously, the Nazi hierarchy including Hitler himself. Schacht was still Reichsbank President, but he would not limit his public views to banking policy. When official attempts were made to stop him speaking out, Schacht went public with his accusations. Himmler managed to prevent newspapers publishing one very critical speech that Schacht had tried to publicize. Not to be gagged, Schacht presented Hitler with a memo criticizing Nazi treatment of the church and the Jews, as he put it: 'pointing out the errors and blunders of his system'.

Schacht expanded on his views publicly in a brave speech at Konigsberg in 1939. Only someone with his determined pig-headed vanity would compare himself with Martin Luther attacking the system. This time Goebbels made quite sure that the criticisms of the Nazi Administration would not get aired in the public press. In response Schacht ordered the Reichsbank to print 10,000 copies of the speech and distributed them around the country. This bravery was driven by ego, but it still has to be admired, and at this stage Hitler took no action against him. Several other speeches critical of the Nazi Administration followed.

Schacht later said he opposed Nazi war aims partly on material grounds, arguing that Germany did not have the resources to achieve the invasions it was planning. Schacht continued his approach of supporting the objectives of Nazi economic nationalism, while criticizing their policies for their poor economics. To him purity of economic thought seemed to be more important than nationalist, ideological, or racial purity.

Schacht always argued that he had opposed Nazi anti-Semitism, limited the expulsion of Jewish economic interests from the German economy, and helped provide a refuge in the business sector for them. Nevertheless, many private Jewish banks were closed at the time when he was bank regulator. Schacht claimed that he had opposed Nazi attempts to stop

Jewish financial firms operating, despite the dangers in doing this, and that he had preached these views in public whenever there was an opportunity. During this time he became a regular churchgoer, attending the church of Pastor Neimuller, later to become a famous Nazi victim himself. It may be that Schacht attended church so ostentatiously specifically in order to irritate the Nazi authorities.

Recent research has argued that though Schacht started his career as pro-Jewish and liberal, this changed: he was no innocent and his behaviour went beyond the common anti-Semitism of the period. The argument is that he did not oppose Jewish expulsions, he implemented the racial exclusion laws at the Ministry of Economy and the Reichsbank, and he justified these policies in public. In an earlier speech Schacht had said he welcomed the Nuremberg exclusion laws, and in terms that would have horrified Kung, who was shortly to visit, he said: '...If we had 600,000 Chinese people in Germany today who pressured to occupy our theatres, our press, our culture, we wouldn't tolerate it and would put them into a Chinese ghetto...' (Shoah Resource Centre, 2000, 4). Like some other prominent Germans of the period, he did however seek to help individual Jewish friends.

In November 1938, the destruction of Jewish synagogues and the terror of Kristallnacht dismayed Schacht, and in his usual forthright manner he told Hitler this was barbaric. He told Hitler he should allow German Jews to emigrate, even proposing a scheme that would make money for the country: Jewish property would be placed in a trust which would issue international long-term loans in US dollars, using their property as security, with payments to be guaranteed by the German Government which would take the exchange rate risk. Jews across the world could subscribe to this scheme. A proportion of the loan would be passed to migrating Jews to help them settle overseas. To Schacht's surprise Hitler raised no apparent objections. Schacht then travelled to London to get support from leading Jewish financial figures and bankers there, and also from Montagu Norman at the Bank of England. However his plan never saw the light of day, being viewed internationally as a form of blackmail. Hitler later implied that he had deferred the forced transport of Jews to concentration camps to see if Schacht's emigration scheme would work (Weitz, 1997, 243).

German expansionism had reached a new phase with the 1938 Anschluss. After the Germans had annexed Austria, the Reichsbank was charged with integrating the Austrian economy into the German monetary system. This harked back to Schacht's experience in Belgium during World War I and to Takahashi's experience with yen in Manchuria. Hitler wanted to abolish the Austrian schilling and integrate the economies. Schacht criticized this idea and took a vicarious pleasure in telling the Germans what a good central bank the Austrian National Bank was. Schacht had enjoyed visiting Vienna, and now he took the opportunity to travel all around Austria.

Initially the Nazis continued with the macroeconomic policies that had underpinned Schacht's 'New Plan'—intended to be anti-inflationary, with tight controls on prices, wages, and the exchange rate. There was a focus on food self-sufficiency and foreign trade was directed to war priorities. Most major industrialists cooperated with Nazi economic directives, and more production was handled through giant operatives like *Reichswerke Hermann Goering* and by forced labour plants. But by 1938 Goering's extravagant spending was clashing openly with Schacht's tighter credit conditions. Schacht was exasperated by Goering who fully supported Hitler's policy on military spending and told Schacht: 'if the Fuehrer wishes it, then two times two are five.' Unable to raise any more funds through the banking system, the government demanded financial relief from the Reichsbank. Schacht refused to supply the government with a new tranche of credit: his eventual dismissal now looked inevitable.

On the second day of 1939 Schacht was summoned to Hitler's home at Obersalzberg, the same terrace where he had met with Kung in happier times. Hitler wanted to discuss the fiscal situation, and how to raise more money. Schacht disappointed him once again: he argued that the capital markets were now exhausted. An attempt to raise money from Jewish indemnities had ended up with the Nazi Government stealing a mixture of real estate and securities, and Hitler was now keen to issue notes against the stolen assets. Schacht handed Hitler a statement signed by all the Reichsbank Board of Directors which strongly criticized Nazi economic policy, arguing in very direct language that the currency was threatened by reckless expenditure, national finances were on the verge of bankruptcy, and the operations of the central bank were being undermined. Schacht referred to the 'great objectives' of the country in invading Austria and the Sudetenland, but reported that uncontrolled military expenditure had continued even after these actions. He added there were no available economic or financial policies which could cushion the military expenditure's devastating costs, meaning inflation, deficits, and rationing. Schacht reiterated that Hitler had little idea of the economic preparations that were necessary for war: 'guns, planes and tanks alone are not enough' (Schacht, 1956, 101).

The Reichsbank memo to Hitler proved to be the final straw. Schacht was summoned to the Chancery where Hitler, now in a furious and emotional state, dismissed him from the Reichsbank. Hitler realized however that Schacht's reputation in the markets was still an important asset, and he left him as a minister without portfolio, a powerless position he would occupy for the next few years. The *Manchester Guardian* reported Schacht's dismissal as 'a victory for the more extreme sections of the Nazi Party'.

This time Schacht realized he had gone too far. He decided it was time to withdraw from public life for his own safety. He thought it might be an opportune time to travel overseas. In particular he had in mind to visit China and Japan: he already had a friendship with Kung, and Japan offered a similarly interesting set of economic challenges to Germany's. But Von Ribbentrop the Foreign Minister forbade him to go—Japan had invaded China implicitly backed by Germany, the region was unsafe, and political relations were sensitive. Schacht instead travelled to India where he commented enviously on the material strength of the British Empire and was especially impressed by the internationalization of the cotton industry.

Schacht was back in Berlin by mid-1939. The military situation had worsened, and Schacht sensed a widespread invasion was now imminent. (He claimed later that he had tried to pass German intelligence about the impending invasion to various friendly Allied contacts.) Germany stormed into Poland, rousing Britain, France, and others to declare war.

After the German Army invaded Northern France the following year, Hitler returned triumphant from his conqueror's entry to Paris. All ministers were summoned to the Berlin Railway Station to greet him in a public ceremony. Schacht had no alternative but to attend, this time wearing a Nazi badge, an action that would later cost him dearly. Hitler accosted him triumphantly and said: 'Well, Herr Schacht, what do you say now?'

Schacht claims that he replied: 'May God protect you.'

4

'No One in Our Age was Cleverer...'

Maynard Keynes in Britain, 1939–41

'I Work for a Government I Deplore...'

Hjalmar Schacht had made a last attempt to dissuade the Germans from their intention to invade Poland during August 1939. But the German army was mobilized and massing menacingly near the borders. The Germans delayed their original plans, but by the end of the month their intentions were clear. France called up its army in haste.

In the Royal Palace Hotel at Royat, a spar in central France, famous British economist John Maynard Keynes was taking the waters with his wife, retired Russian ballerina Lydia Lopokova. For the previous year and a half Keynes, now in his mid-fifties, had been in very poor health following an ongoing heart infection and a series of minor heart attacks. As a result he had been forced to cut back his customary hectic schedule of travel, journalism, research, teaching, policy advice, university administration, personal and corporate investing, farming, and arts and theatre support. Following a spell recuperating for some months in Ruthin Castle, a nursing home in Wales, he moved back to his farmhouse at Tilton, West Sussex, where his doctors and his protective wife insisted on seclusion and rest. Never able to completely stop working, Keynes spent his time writing to friends, many of them famous and influential people, sending letters to *The Times* newspaper, and composing for the weekly *New Statesman*.

Keynes was tall, self-assured, arrogant, and very clever, a cleverness that he felt he should put at the disposal of the nation. This was a man who had supported conscientious objector friends during World War I, who had argued against unrealistic reparations from Germany in the Versailles Peace Treaty, and who had favoured world disarmament in the 1930s. But he was now changing his views as he watched the rise of fascist dictators. Keynes favoured diplomacy over war, but he recognized that it could only be credible if Britain was militarily strong. That meant rearming, and rearming required funding. With typical self-confidence and some of his customary arrogance he now fired off letters and articles urging active rearmament and suggesting creative ways to finance it.

By mid-1939 Keynes's health had recovered somewhat, and he was judged fit to travel: the trip to Royat was his reward. For a week he and Lydia followed the specified health regime at the spa: they drank the mineral waters, completed an hour or two of correspondence, and then immersed themselves in the steam baths. Following that they relaxed with a massage, did meditation, and the afternoon was spent on auto-mobile excursions in the surrounding rural countryside. In the evenings they listened to the hotel orchestra which, as Keynes wrote rather dis-paragingly to his mother in Cambridge, 'plays the sort of music father would like' (Skidelsky, 2000, 44).

Over the following week Keynes's correspondence shows him becoming increasingly concerned as he listened to Hitler's posturing and heard rumours of the German Army's movements on the borders of Poland. Fearing the worst, the French Government announced a general mobil-ization of its army. Keynes wrote home that this meant that the hotel lost its restaurant waiter, then several musicians, and a little later the chefs and the concierge, as they all signed up for the army. The realities of war were becoming evident. Keynes decided it was time for him and his wife to beat a tactical retreat home. They endured a slow journey back through northern France: the roads were crowded with troop move-ments and with scared refugees. There was an atmosphere of foreboding as they approached Paris. But the train and ferry services were still run-ning, and eventually after several long days of travel, on 29 August they thankfully regained the reassuring calm of the English countryside.

It was none too soon. Two days later Germany invaded Poland. France declared war. Prime Minister Neville Chamberlain waited two further days before announcing that Britain too was at war with Germany. World War II in Europe had begun in earnest.

The memory of World War I, the so-called 'war to end all wars', was still strong in Britain. It had wrecked lives and caused economic disrup-tion. However it had made one man's reputation: in 1919 Keynes had been present at the Versailles Treaty negotiations and had argued that the reparations demanded of Germany and its Axis partners had been set at impossibly high levels, his views being published in *The Economic Consequences of the Peace*—a bestselling and prophetic book.

John Maynard Keynes was born in Cambridge in 1883 to upper-middle-class parents, his mother a social reformer turned mayor and his father a university professor. In one sense he never left Cambridge and its university throughout his life. His parents were loving, attentive, and admiring (and both outlived him). Precocious and extremely gifted, Keynes won a scholarship to Eton College, which at the time was caught up in the militaristic fever of the Boer War. He studied mathematics and philosophy at Cambridge University, graduating in 1904. He attended economics lectures informally as a student for only one term, and that was to constitute the entirety of his formal education in the subject.

In October 1906 Keynes became a clerk in Britain's Colonial India Office where his first posting was to the Military Department. He initially enjoyed the practical focus of the work, but gradually became bored and returned to Cambridge University. Here he relied on his family contacts, his research position initially being funded by his father and a family friend. He soon repaid this by displaying startling promise. His first serious economic article ('Effect of the Global Slowdown in India') was published in the top academic publication, the *Economic Journal*. Keynes founded the Political Economy Club, a weekly discussion group for graduate students and staff, and he would chair it for his whole life. He soon became Editor of the *Economic Journal*, itself another life-long position. In 1909 Keynes was appointed Lecturer in Economics at Cambridge University, a new position personally funded for him by Professor Alfred Marshall, the father of the neoclassical economics revolution at Cambridge and a friend of his father.

Within a few years Keynes had published his first book *Indian Currency and Finance* and he was appointed by the government to a Royal Commission on that subject. This approach marked out his future life—keen to address real-world issues, active in his research, very prolific in his writing, an appetite for influencing government policy, the con-tacts to help him do so, and strong self-assurance in his (sometimes changeable) views.

Keynes lived the fullest of lives. He enjoyed a very active social life around Cambridge and London. Initially at Cambridge University he was a key member of the elitist and secretive university Apostles Group, and he was involved in a number of romantic and sexual engagements with men. Despite the restrictive norms of British society at the time, Keynes was open about these relationships, even keeping a diary of his sexual encounters. He became closely involved with the Bloomsbury Group, a unique early twentieth-century collection of artistically-talented if rather self-absorbed young people. The artist Duncan Grant was a great love of his life. Keynes also had enduring friendships with other Bloomsbury members including painter Vanessa Bell, writers Virginia Woolf, and E. M. Forster, publisher Leonard Woolf, biographer Lytton Strachey, and critic Roger Fry. Keynes helped and supported many of them financially through his life, while in turn they regarded him as their window into the Establishment.

When war broke out in 1914 Keynes was aged 31. A number of his friends registered as conscientious objectors. Keynes himself was not an objector, however he supported them. He did not seem to have thought of joining the armed forces himself, no doubt feeling his talents would be wasted in the trenches. Instead his contacts soon resulted in him being invited to advise Treasury on wartime economic management, an informal and unpaid position. He advised on sterling convertibility, Britain's wartime credit alternatives, the acquisition of foreign currencies, and the problems of funding British and Russian war purchases from the US. These were all new problems for a government under wartime conditions, issues he was to face later under harsher conditions during World War II. Rather cynically, he wrote to Duncan Grant at the time: 'I work for a government I deplore, for ends I think criminal.' Yet Keynes found this work too fascinating to keep his distance, became very involved, and his advice soon became indispensable to the government.

When the war finally ground to a halt in 1918, Keynes was appointed Financial Representative for the Treasury to the 1919 Versailles Peace Conference. He travelled to Versailles outside Paris in the British delegation headed by Lloyd George. His role there was important, and he was witness to one of the key moments in European history.

Popular opinion against Germany, especially in France, was extremely hostile, and as a result the Allied nations were determined to impose heavy reparations on the defeated country. Keynes argued that these proposed reparations were unrealistically high, could not be met, and would suck revenue from Germany, limiting her exports, preventing her from rebuilding, and causing a balance of payments problem that would result in recession and potential inflation. All this would make it even harder for Germany to service its debt. Lloyd George the British Prime Minister understood Keynes's views, but was pressured by political opinion in Britain. One politician, Sir Eric Geddes, said of Germany: 'we will get out of her all you can squeeze out of a lemon and a bit more… I will squeeze her until you can hear the pips squeak.' The French premier Georges Clemenceau was even more obdurate in wishing to reduce Germany to a pastoral economy that could never again threaten France, and he influenced US President Woodrow Wilson in this. Keynes was depressed, writing to Vanessa Bell: '…you would really be amused by the amazing complications of psychology and personality and intrigue which make such magnificent sport of the impending catastrophe of Europe' (Moggridge, 1992, 296–8).

Keynes was an internationalist. He had read about the Bolshevik Revolution in Russia. Now hearing of the riots in Berlin and Budapest he feared similar disruption in the German and Austro-Hungarian Empires. The Allies had calculated the cost of Axis-inflicted war damage and insisted this be repaid in war reparations, oblivious to the angry and despairing mood in the Axis powers. Keynes developed an alternative plan to write down some of the German debt which would have had the effect of stimulating international trade and economic recovery. But the British could not convince the Americans who held much of the German debt. The resulting Peace Treaty disgusted Keynes, and he resigned from the UK Treasury in protest.

As he would often do later in life, he turned to print, pouring his arguments into *The Economic Consequences of the Peace*, which was published in 1919. This treatise was a mixture of economics, logic, and polemic, blending technical skill and passion. After being heavily promoted by Keynes, who had struck a special deal with his publisher, it proved hugely popular with the public. Selling over one hundred thousand copies within a year, it was translated into 11 languages, and it earned Keynes high royalties and a reputation as an *enfant terrible*. Keynes was dismissive of the reparations payments: 'reparations and inter-Allied debts are mainly being settled in paper and not in goods. The US lends money to Germany, Germany transfers its equivalent to the Allies, the

Allies pay it back to the US Government. Nothing real passes—no one is a penny the worse' (Moggridge, 1992, 475).

The Versailles Commission had settled on a reparations figure of £6,600 million. Keynes's early estimate of what Germany might be able to repay was about £1,000 million sterling, half in immediate transfers in kind and half to be paid in cash over future years. He later doubled this estimate, which ultimately turned out to be more realistic: in the end Germany paid very little of the imposed reparations, and actually received a net capital inflow from US loans.

Having resigned from the UK Treasury, for several years Keynes gave informal advice on the reparations to the post-war German Government. At Versailles he had met a sympathetic German negotiator named Carl Melchior, and they met together a number of times afterwards. Melchior had been acting as a German Government advisor and then became a banker. The two got on very well together, and the homosexual Keynes noted in a letter he had 'feelings' for Melchior. Melchior was later to act as an advisor to Hjalmar Schacht, and he helped the latter to connect with Keynes and put the German viewpoint.

Ultimately Keynes' book was to prove prescient: 'If we aimed deliberately at the impoverishment of Central Europe, vengeance I dare predict, will not limp. Nothing can delay for very long that final war between the forces of reaction and the despairing convulsions of revolution before which the horrors of the late German War will fade into nothing' (Keynes, 1920, 268).

Keynes was well travelled from an early age. With his parents he often holidayed on the Continent, and during his lifetime he visited Germany a number of times. He had made contact with senior German officials, and was knowledgeable about the economy. In 1922 he had been asked by the German Government to give advice on the stabilization of the mark. He addressed a World Economic Congress in Hamburg and reported on the severe hyper-inflation then under way.

That year he edited a 'Reconstruction Supplement' for the *Manchester Guardian* newspaper, and arranged for a series of articles from leading Europeans. On the advice of his friend Carl Melchior he commissioned Dr Schacht to write for him. The following year he travelled to Berlin where he met several German ministers, and advised on the payment of reparations. A few years later he travelled to Germany to give a lecture at the University of Berlin, which contained some (today highly controversial) views about the potential for eugenics and population control in an economy. In 1928 he visited yet again, and with Melchior he met Schacht, then Reichsbank President, to discuss the German economy, the state of reparations, and the risk that Wall Street might stop lending to Germany.

The 1920s were an unsettled period for the world's economies, and so too for Keynes personally. After World War I he had returned to Cambridge University and published his earlier mathematical work on probability. He also commenced writing as an economic journalist, selling his work internationally, and he spent some time in the City of London as a financial consultant. He was becoming well known amongst politicians and business people. He wrote articles and several books attacking the post-war policies of deflation and exchange rates. When Britain re-entered the gold standard in 1925 under Chancellor Winston Churchill, Keynes wrote a critical tract, *The Consequences of Mr Churchill*, which once again would prove prescient. He was proving an astute communicator—his voice was high, his speech upper-class, clipped, very clear, and above all authoritative.

Politically Keynes was a lifelong member of the Liberal Party, but he always refused to stand for office himself. In the 1920s Keynes advised extensively on the Liberal Party's economic policy, but he had to watch his political colleagues gradually slip into third-party status. He never connected with the new and growing Labour Party, he detested Communism, and he was too radical for Tory Conservatives.

Keynes had long been interested in ballet. In 1918 he first saw Lydia Lopokova, a Russian star of Diaghilev's visiting *Ballet Russes* Company. She had been born in Leningrad to a family whose lives were in the theatre. Her father had been a chief usher at the famous Imperial Alexandrinsky theatre. Consequently all the children had been able to attend the Imperial Ballet School in St Petersburg, and all became dancers. Lydia had a very colourful early life: she joined the famous *Ballet Russes*, toured Europe, lived in the US for some years as a cabaret artist, model, and vaudeville performer, married the Italian business manager of the Diaghilev Ballet Company at an early age, had various short-term affairs including with Russian composer Igor Stravinsky, ultimately disappearing back into the USSR with a mysterious White Russian general. In 1921 she returned to London and danced with Diaghilev's troop in *The Sleeping Beauty* in London. She was hailed as one of a new breed of dancers, and known as 'Loppie', she was a favourite with British audiences.

Keynes was entranced. He courted her avidly, watching performances every night from the stalls, while still continuing his homosexual affairs. Lydia responded with equal interest, and soon they began living together. Keynes was 42 and a pillar of the intellectual Establishment, Lydia was 31 and a foot-loose bohemian artiste. This infatuation and unlikely coupling caused widespread surprise, especially from his intellectually arrogant Bloomsbury friends, who saw Lydia as amusing but unintelligent. Lytton Strachey called her 'a half-witted canary.' E. M. Forster later wrote 'how we all used to underestimate her' (Light, 2008, 9). While Bloomsbury found it hard to warm to her, Lydia was friends with many of the cultural elite of the time, including T. S. Eliot, H. G. Wells, and Pablo Picasso, who drew her many times.

Despite the objections of friends, in 1925 the couple were married in a registry office, and the newlyweds went on honeymoon, travelling by train to Petrograd, newly-renamed Leningrad, to visit Lydia's family for a week. Keynes met mother Constanza and the siblings. Her brother Fyodor Lopukhov was now a famous dancer and choreographer. Keynes also represented Cambridge University at a meeting of the Soviet Academy of Sciences while in Leningrad.

The couple then travelled on to Moscow where Keynes held meetings with the Gosplan planning agency, the State Bank, and other organs of economic policy. And he presented a report on the economic situation in Britain to the plenum of the National Economic Council of the Supreme Soviet of the National Economy. Leon Trotsky was there and also a Japanese economist, Tokuzo Fukuda, who would later influence Takahashi. A few years earlier Keynes had written a tract on the financial system of the Bolsheviks; he had previously corresponded with Vladimir Lenin, and there had been some mutual respect between them. However, now Keynes reported that he did not approve of much that he was seeing, and on his return he recorded his opinions in *A Short View of Russia*, a searing attack on Soviet Communism. This took a highly critical view of both the economic ideology of Marxism and the practical New Economic Policy of post-Leninist Soviet Union, views that have once again been confirmed by history. Virginia Woolf recounted a conversation with Keynes about his trip with him complaining: '... spies everywhere, no liberty of speech, greed for money eradicated, people living in common' (Skidelsky, 1992, 209).

Keynes and Lydia would enjoy an unusual but long and enduring marriage, with Lydia taking on the management of Keynes the famous economist as a vocation, and documenting it all in her pointed and funny letters to Keynes and his mother. For example she described Keynes's economist colleagues as 'tiresome, no wide outlooks, no touch with life, inferiority complexes and no great ideas' (Light, 2008, 9). She became pregnant in 1927 but miscarried, and they were never successful in having children.

In April 1928 there was a further visit to Leningrad, and two years later Lydia visited on her own with a friend. Each time she found her Leningrad family in declining circumstances as Soviet economic conditions worsened. By 1932 her aged mother was living in a cramped single room, and the family was surviving on parcels of food and clothing sent by the Keyneses. Even worse, her family seemed to have fallen under suspicion by the secret police, possibly because of their Western connections.

In 1936 the Keyneses travelled to the USSR once more, this time via Stockholm where Keynes met the promising young macroeconomist Bert Ohlin, and then on to Leningrad to visit the Russian family again. On the train Keynes read material from a Cambridge colleague, Joan Robinson, on Marxian economics. Robinson was a strong supporter of Stalin's USSR, and a number of other academics at the time agreed with her, a view that Keynes could not stomach. Despite his antagonism to the Soviet regime, Keynes had been friends at Cambridge with fellow Apostles Anthony Blunt, Guy Burgess, and Michael Straight, all of them to become notorious when exposed as KGB spies. Records show that Burgess gave Keynes's name to his Moscow handlers as someone they should try to influence. That year Keynes recorded a talk on the BBC reviewing Sidney and Beatrice Webb's *Soviet Communism*, which he viewed as an apologist tract. This was the same book that Takahashi had been photographed holding in the Japanese Diet the previous year.

Keynes had never particularly looked to settle to a fixed career, and his volatile financial position reflected that. His interests were too broad and always changing. Initially he had been funded by his family, and he never seemed particularly worried about earning a steady salary. Gradually he was able to live off his earnings as a journalist, a business consultant, and from a very early age a financial investor. Having lost money in card games as a student, Schacht had vowed never to gamble or play the stock markets on his own account. Keynes had no such concerns.

He willingly took on the extra duties of Bursar of King's College at Cambridge for many years, and in this position he set up an actively-managed stock portfolio that fluctuated considerably but ultimately far outperformed the British equities index and left Kings College rich. In 1920 he organized a syndicate of friends to speculate on foreign exchange. Unanticipated events meant the fund was wiped out after a few months and left with liabilities of £20,000. Keynes did not seem to be particularly perturbed, and within two years had repaid the debt and rebuilt the fund. He became Chairman of the Board of the National Mutual Insurance Company, and also ran several investment companies with friends. He managed his own money very actively, usually while still lying in bed in the morning, leveraging his position substantially through margin trading. He devised his own investment theories, enjoyed combining theory and market reality, and was supremely self-confident in backing his own instincts against others. And when shown to be mistaken he had no compunctions about changing his mind.

Though often prescient, he certainly was not infallible—two years before the 1929 US stock market crash he famously wrote: 'we will not have any more crashes in our time'. This view of the future was proven far too optimistic. Keynes made some substantial investments in the shares of a number of British companies, together with some long positions in commodities. The portfolio unravelled through 1928 as he failed to take into account the deflationary forces that were sweeping the world. By the middle of 1929 he had lost three-quarters of his assets in the Wall Street Crash. However once again he was not put off: reassessing his theories about equities and bonds, he soon regained his positions.

Keynes was an astute collector, building up a fine collection of art including works by Cézanne, Degas, Modigliani, Braque, Picasso, and Seurat. He started buying in Paris in 1918, taking advantage of war-depressed prices. Over three decades he spent around £600,000 amassing a collection valued at around £70 million today (*Wall Street Journal*,

30.3.18). He collected antiquarian books and became an authority on the papers of Isaac Newton. At his death his net financial worth was about £500,000, approximately £20 million in today's terms.

Keynes always seemed to be at the centre of things. He did not attend the Dawes Committee, but he nevertheless wrote a report on the Dawes Plan for the UK Treasury. His friend Carl Melchior kept him in touch with Dr Schacht's angst at the proceedings. Five years later when the Young Committee re-examined the problem of reparations, Keynes wrote a paper 'The German Transfer Problem' on the practical problems involved in transferring large-scale German reparations in marks into foreign currency. The paper was published in the *Economic Journal*.

The turbulent macroeconomic conditions of the 1920s had brought volatile exchange rates, rampant inflation, plummeting equity prices, and terrible unemployment, a major challenge for any policy economist. In 1930 Keynes published his two-volume *Treatise on Money*. In it he argued that if a country's savings are higher than its investment (for example if interest rates have been too high), then the economy will suffer from slack and unemployment will rise. He also warned of the unreliability of the exchange rate for signalling a true picture of a country's competitiveness: once again these arguments were proved prescient.

In 1931 Keynes visited New York, Washington, and Boston, and delivered lectures at the University of Chicago. He took the opportunity to learn about economic conditions there, to talk to academics, and to give advice to the New York Federal Reserve on the financial crisis under way in Germany. In January 1932, a time when Schacht was out of favour and out of office, Keynes travelled to Hamburg to give a lecture, and was hosted again by Melcher, following this with a meeting in Berlin with Chancellor Bruning, who had just announced that Germany would not resume its payments following the moratorium. Keynes suggested to him that Germany should leave the gold standard and negotiate a final settlement to reparations. Keynes returned depressed about conditions in Germany, noting the poor living standards, massive unemployment, and contracting exports. His close friend Carl Melcher died of a heart attack soon after, leaving Keynes very upset.

As the 1930s Great Depression gathered pace, the British Government was faced with falling revenue, but it felt it must still hold to the classical policy of good governance by cutting expenditure to balance its budget.

Keynes was deeply critical of this move, pointing out that the government was contracting the economy just at the time that it needed to stimulate it. He developed this thinking further in his 1933 pamphlet, *The Means to Prosperity*, which contained specific policy prescriptions for tackling unemployment through countercyclical spending, outlining the concept of a spending multiplier. This work was published in four articles in *The Times* newspaper.

Never reticent about his writings, Keynes arranged for copies to be sent to world leaders including President Roosevelt. This developed into the Keynes–Henderson Plan suggesting that an international institution could be used to finance reflationary programmes. Some of the ideas were discussed in the 1933 World Economic Conference in London, though ultimately they were rejected as being impractical. Keynes reported on the conference as a journalist for the *Daily Mail* and as a radio commentator, and continued to be full of innovative ideas. Schacht attended the conference in London and put forward his own competing but similar plan. Keynes had followed the Schacht Plan, and that year gave a lecture at University College in Dublin in which he cited Schacht's achievements.

The key economist on the US team attending the World Economic Conference was Professor Oliver Sprague, who had been President Roosevelt's old economics teacher. He was a long-standing Harvard professor, and had been at the University of Tokyo early in the century (where he was a colleague of Professor Fukuda). He had been based in Britain as an advisor at the Bank of England, where he argued with Keynes on the risks of leaving the gold standard and also about his broader macroeconomic ideas.

The Economic Conference was dominated by the US announcing their departure from the gold standard with a temporary bridging arrangement to be in place for the duration of the meeting. Sprague's advice had been key to this policy. Then to the surprise of many, President Roosevelt rejected this interim arrangement, and the conference had to be suspended. Keynes said he was 'magnificently right' to reject the proposals. Few others agreed, but the conference finally petered out without resolution in July 1933. Late that year Keynes wrote an open letter to the US President with more suggestions for economic policy. In the New Year Keynes followed this with a lecture at Columbia University in New York, and also visited economists, business people, and officials. In Washington he met the US President himself for an hour to argue his views. Keynes described the meeting as fascinating but said he was surprised at Roosevelt's economic illiteracy. He also had some comments on the shape of the President's hands, a topic which was something of a personal obsession for Keynes. Roosevelt, who had already put up with a similar lecture from Schacht only a few months earlier, was reportedly less excited by the Keynes visit.

Following Hitler's Anschluss entry into Austria, Keynes wrote 'A Positive Peace Programme' in *The New Statesman*, arguing there was now a choice between directly resisting the dictators or a policy of 'positive pacifism' based on a new European pact amongst Allied countries (an idea that saw light after the war with the founding of the European Economic Community). The article was republished in Germany with the criticisms of dictators removed (apparently with Keynes's reluctant agreement). As Keynes developed his macroeconomic ideas further, a summary of these were published in Germany in 1933, and they had created much debate there.

Several years later in 1936, Keynes published the magnum opus for which he will always be famous. This was the book that combined the theoretical and policy ideas he had been developing for a decade entitled, *A General Theory of Employment, Interest and Money*. In it Keynes argued that the classical economic theories of his mentors Marshall and Pigou were special cases which applied only in conditions where workers would be willing to absorb demand shocks by flexibly reducing their wage rates to maintain full employment. Partly due to price stickiness, the interaction of overall supply and demand could lead to enduring unemployment and unnecessary economic contraction. Keynes's new approach turned the policy focus from production to consumption as a key variable in economic activity.

The book took the academic community by storm. Academics were quick to respond, both positively and negatively. The *Quarterly Journal of Economics* contained four early reviews of the *General Theory* in November 1936. One was by a young Russian-American Harvard economist Wassily Leontief and it was rather dismissive of the work, claiming it represented another special case rather than a truly general theory. Keynes wrote a reply, himself dismissing Leontief in his first paragraph in a rather haughty tone and suggesting how 'his idea might be applied more fruitfully'. Leontief was never to be a keen supporter of Keynesian economics.

The General Theory of Employment, Interest and Money was also published in German. However it was poorly translated and rather difficult to understand. Keynes wrote a special preface for the German edition, and some historians have argued that this showed Keynes as sympathizing with the National Socialist regime, yet it seems clear that Keynes abhorred fascism as much as communism.

Ironically the two major countries that actually adopted Keynesian-style reflationary policy in time to cushion them from the worst of depression were the dictatorships, Japan with Takahashi Korekiyo and Germany under Dr Schacht. And Benito Mussolini had earlier written: 'Fascism entirely agrees with Mr Maynard Keynes.' In the UK and the US, traditional economic opinions were too entrenched to adopt such a radical approach early enough to make a difference, and the democratic processes made it more difficult to rapidly adopt such a radical new approach.

1939–40: How to Pay for the War

The latter part of 1939 was known as the 'phoney war' in Britain. After the major Allied powers had declared war, there was relatively little military action, except for the invasion and dismemberment of Poland by Germany and the Soviet Union. And by the year's end the Soviet Union had invaded Finland. But in April of the following year the extent of German territorial ambitions became very clear: they invaded Denmark and Norway, then in the following month swept into the Low Countries and France. Very quickly the occupied Allied countries sur-rendered, and the Germans began to pillage their arms and resources for their own war effort.

During the years of fascist build-up, Britain had put in place contin-gency defence plans. But by 1939 the country was not well prepared for the huge economic costs that the war would impose. The government formed a War Cabinet with several part-time economic advisors to form departmental war plans. After several months it had become clear that Britain's initial approach to economic planning for the war was proving rather haphazard, and the Central Economic Information Service was established to centralize and professionalize the efforts.

Keynes was now 56, apparently recovered from his poor health, and he was feeling frustrated; he wanted to be more involved in the war effort. After the publication of the *General Theory* he could claim to be the world's best-known economist and he was brimming with ideas. But his strong personal and free-wheeling public views on economics, foreign policy, and politics meant the UK Government hesitated to appoint him to an official position.

For all his cleverness and insight Keynes had been somewhat inaccurate in his forecasts of foreign affairs. He had originally thought war would never happen. Now he thought that such a war would be concluded within a few months. However he reasoned that even a short war would cause economic problems, and he felt this needed a new approach. As in peacetime, Keynes's thinking in wartime was guided by his desire to apply theory to practical concerns, being prepared to question long-held assumptions, aiming intuitively at the fundamentals of a problem, applying conventional tools until they proved inadequate, and then fashioning new approaches where necessary.

The initial impulse of the British Government was to place controls on everything practicable—transport, imports, prices, and even factory costs. There was particular concern for the island nation about ensuring food supply during the war. After the experience of World War I, Keynes protested that now more than ever the British economy needed price signals rather than direct clumsy regulation. He ran a small farm estate in West Sussex and (just like that other part-time gentleman farmer Schacht) he felt that entitled him to speak with authority on this topic, as on much else. He illustrated his argument by pointing out his breeding sows' value had dropped because the Ministry of Agriculture had set bacon prices too low and consequently his incentive was to produce less not more. Eventually this advice was followed with guaranteed prices, crop subsidies, assisted mechanization, and schemes such as the Women's Land Army to promote agricultural production despite the loss of many workers to mobilization.

It was becoming clear that there would be major war shortages. Keynes's new insight was to ask whether a better outcome might be achieved by rationing demand rather than rationing supplies. Few people had framed the rationing problem in this way before. For most the war was a time to forget the ivory tower and focus on the real world; for Keynes, wartime was more than ever the time to exploit the power of ideas.

He was soon feeling his old active self again, travelling busily between London and Cambridge for discussions, seminars, arguments, and meetings, then retreating to his farmhouse at Tilton when he had the time to write. In April he composed a two-part article for *The Times* entitled 'Crisis Finance: An Outline of Policy'. The following month he broadcast a talk on the BBC about whether rearmament could at least have one positive outcome, curing unemployment. But before long he was feeling frustrated again. His memos and letters to various arms of government, politicians, and the media were being ignored or overlooked. He formed a discussion group with several other retired administrators from World War I whom he nicknamed 'the Old Dogs'. They met at his house and produced memoranda on the war effort to try to influence government. Keynes complained that the efficiency implications and financial costs of pricing policy, rationing policy, wages policy, budget policy, export policy, and manpower policy were all being dealt with in isolation and needed to be treated as part of a consistent macro-economic policy approach. Nothing limited the scope of his interests.

At last Keynes was invited to contribute to the Government Committee on Economic Information, producing a report clumsily entitled 'Defence Expenditure and the Economic and Financial Problems Concerned Therewith'. During the two years preceding the war, the UK Treasury had borrowed heavily in order to spend on armaments, fearing the contractionary effect of increasing taxes to pay for it. In September 1939, as they realized the likely magnitude of the war effort, the British Government announced an emergency budget. This increased defence spending by £600 million over the year, a huge amount for the time, to be funded by a small tax increase and with a large projected budget deficit amounting to 25 per cent of public expenditure. This alarmingly high deficit would have to be financed by borrowing. The Treasury thought they were following modern Keynesian reflationary thinking by stimulating the economy in this way, so that it would grow faster and increase productive capacity.

But they were soon to be disabused of this misconception by Keynes himself. He did not see a case for reflation in these circumstances, but worried instead about excess demand. He felt the government must find a way to stop the public consuming the extra resources flowing from the extra public spending, to ensure that these resources could be available for the war effort. The main method of funding World War I had been through inflation involving the government printing extra money. It would be undesirable and perhaps impossible to do the same this time.

Economists were dividing into two camps on the topic of wartime economics, the planning method that LSE's Lionel Robbins (ironically an Austrian free-market economist) felt would be inevitable for a major conflict, and the fiscal controls method that Keynes favoured. One reason for the difference between them was that Keynes had expected this to be a brief war (as also had Schacht), but it now looked more long-term.

Keynes had a new approach in mind. In a speech to Cambridge University's Marshall Society in October 1939 he tried out his ideas. He was evidently pleased with the response, because over the next week he wrote a long article which he sent to *The Times* newspaper, but also circulated to others for comment. *The Times* cut it into two articles and published these on 14 and 15 November. Bizarrely however, due to a leak from a neutral correspondent, the first publication of Keynes's full text was to be found a week earlier in the German paper *Frankfurter Allgemeine Zeitung*, where no doubt it would have been read with much interest by Schacht and others.

Keynes recognized that a long large-scale war must involve major shifts of resources away from peacetime uses. Domestic output would likely rise, but the increase in government consumption would swamp this. The problem was how to divert resources from peacetime to wartime needs, and how to reduce private consumption as incomes rose. Keynes saw four possible methods: voluntary lending to the government; reducing consumption by rationing; bidding for the necessary resources through inflationary financing policies; or using increased taxation to transfer public resources to the authorities.

Rationing might be required when some essential good was found to be in structural short supply, but that would not be a defence against a general increase in purchasing power. Some price rises reflecting real cost increases would be inevitable, and might even be desirable as signals of scarcity. But to avoid general inflation, taxation would need to be increased across the employed classes in order to suck up the excess liquidity in the system. Keynes proposed implementing this, partly via a direct tax (income tax and surtax), and partly as compulsory savings through the Post Office Savings Bank. This could prevent excess consumption and delay other low-priority spending. The scheme would involve employers deducting amounts from employees' wages and lodging them in savings accounts which could not be drawn on until after the war, on conditions to be determined by government. The proposal was for a progressive saving scheme whereby higher-paid workers would contribute a greater fraction.

His radical idea was to reject traditional inflationary financing and rationing as a way to pay for war. You could not, Keynes said, forbid prices to rise. He hoped his approach would maintain a natural system of price signalling as far as possible, revoking many of the policy controls that had already been put in place. He thought a more controlled system might work in a totalitarian regime, but not in Britain with its open markets, and looked instead to replace controls and officials by macroeconomic management through monetary and fiscal policy.

The Keynes Plan received enormous press coverage and public debate. Perhaps surprisingly, most economists, both Keynesian and non-Keynesian, seemed to agree with it. A fortnight after *The Times* article had appeared, Keynes suggested to MP Harold Macmillan that the articles be turned into a short book to be published by his family's firm: this was to become *How to Pay for the War*.

Economists may have been impressed, but not all politicians were. One immediate problem was that the labour movement saw this as an attack on the working classes. Keynes sent a flurry of letters to Clement Attlee of the Labour Party and to other Labour politicians arguing his case, generally unsuccessfully. Labour's Deputy Leader even wrote in the Labour press that the Keynes Plan smacked of 'Hitlerism' (Skidelsky, 2000, 59). Ernest Bevin, who was the dominant trade union figure, argued that government had a duty to directly control prices and preserve workers' real wages. In his view the war should be financed by the rich where possible, and otherwise by borrowing. Keynes was particularly disappointed by this partisan response at a time of crisis.

Keynes rewrote his plan over Christmas 1939 at his Tilton farmhouse. The work took place in between visits to his old Bloomsbury friends:

firstly ex-lover artist Duncan Grant and the Bells, and then the literary Woolfs who were increasingly tart about Keynes—his busyness, his war focus, and his continuing devotion to Lydia, to whom they condescended. They were particularly sarcastic about Keynes's general attitude of omniscience on all topics, though he did not seem particularly hurt by this. His biographer Professor Roy Harrod wrote: 'No one in our age was cleverer than Keynes nor made less attempt to conceal it' (Harrod, 1951).

As he redrafted his book, the hardest problem was how to manage the question of deferred pay. It was unclear whether there would be a consumer boom or a demobilizing slump after the war—Keynes thought the post-war world would likely need more consumption not more savings. He knew he had to win over the support of the Labour politicians who were influential in the new wartime government coalition. He altered his original tax scheme to include a family allowance to deal with overall cost of living increases, and wrote that basic foods could be subsidized if necessary. He put his revised views to several politicians, but he still found it hard to persuade them. A number of them regarded Keynes, a Liberal, as too arrogant and upper-class, though he tried hard to present his amended plan as a 'socialist solution'.

By now Keynes's health had improved so that his life once again became a busy whirlwind of meetings, talks, concerts, ballets and plays, dinner parties and late nights, all the time working on his manuscript *How to Pay for the War*, travelling between Cambridge, London, and Sussex, which had become more difficult under war conditions. He finished the draft in early February 1940. His publisher proposed printing 5,000 copies. Typically arrogant, Keynes responded that he had never written any economic book which had sold so few copies. The publisher capitulated and doubled the printing, despite wartime paper shortages. The book was published at the end of February 1940. Keynes immediately embarked on a speaking crusade, addressing Westminster MPs, the Trade Union Council, the Treasury, and the Bank of England. As usual Keynes was right about the publication: 38,000 copies were eventually sold, a bestseller for the period, aided by Keynes's own active marketing and lobbying. He received a huge post bag from supporters and critics, and tried to reply directly to many of them.

The work has since excited much interest amongst economists. Some have argued it was a particular application of the argument in the

General Theory. Others have seen it as a shift from 'the age of plenty' to 'the age of scarcity'. Skidelsky wrote: 'a case can be made for *How to Pay for the War* as the quintessence of Keynes's achievement. It engaged all the qualities of his complex nature: the union of theory and practice, the linking of economic doctrine to political philosophy here achieved its most compelling artistic expression' (Skidelsky, 2000, 67).

The Chancellor of the Exchequer seemed initially supportive of Keynes's ideas. But Treasury had for a long time regarded Keynes as someone who enjoyed proposing radical ideas that turned out to be impractical or unfeasible. Before Keynes, the prevailing view had been that government borrowing to supplement taxes should not be inflationary if it were matched by an increase in private savings. Keynes was the first economist to articulate two unpleasant facts: that paying for the war must mean reducing civilian consumption, and that the reduction could not be met without inflation simply by government taxing or borrowing.

Britain's pre-military preparation had initially been limited, but from 1939 military production ramped up rapidly. Industrial mobilization brought some regulation of prices but not wages (a lesson learned from World War I), with financial assistance to key firms, and a 100 per cent excess profits tax to mop up rents. Without a full pricing system to allocate resources, Britain used what Harrison (1988, 11) has labelled war production allocation by committee.

Initially the British war economy was in poor shape. For a year unemployment remained high despite mobilization, civilian consumption remained strong, there was a major balance of payments problem, and foreign exchange was becoming very scarce. There was a shortage of ships and transport bottlenecks, stocks had been run down, metal and engineering skills were hard to find, and wages were rising.

One practical problem facing all the warring powers was that governments had only a hazy idea of how large financing gaps might be because they could not properly measure production, let alone 'aggregate purchasing power', while GDP data did not exist. A practical anti-inflationary budget policy needed quantifiable national accounts, and Keynes had been making this point since writing the *General Theory*. The calculations for the Keynes Plan relied on pioneering work done by ex-student Colin Clark and later by Erwin Rothbarth at Cambridge University, a German émigré economist whom Keynes had helped release from enemy internment. They estimated gross national income and savings for the year 1938–9 in an innovative paper which was published in the *Economic Journal* under Keynes's editorship. The work was based around his *General Theory* concepts of aggregate demand and supply, measured via prices, disaggregated by sectors. For the first time the principles of double-entry bookkeeping were applied to an economy. Using basic calculations, Keynes estimated that government spending in 1939–40 would likely rise by almost £2 billion out of a total national income of just under £5 billion. He concluded that about half of this would be seen in increased investment, but the rest would lead to increased incomes. How could the government stop the public from spending these extra incomes? Extra taxes would absorb half this amount, but there would still be a need for a compulsory saving scheme if inflation was to be avoided.

Unconvinced by this pioneering national accounting data, the UK Treasury raised a number of practical objections. Keynes urged the Chancellor to announce in the upcoming budget that he would set up the institutional machinery to implement the Plan. Then the urgency increased: on 10 May 1940, the Germans invaded Belgium, the Netherlands, and France. The same day the British Government fell and Chamberlain's Government was replaced by a wartime coalition under Winston Churchill, followed by a humiliating army retreat from Dunkirk. The aggressive Churchill had no particular interest in economics, other than using it as another weapon of war. It helped that Keynes moved in elevated circles and he knew Winston well. In addition his publisher Harold Macmillan was now Churchill's Parliamentary Secretary, so Keynes had the contacts to make his case again.

But it did not all proceed smoothly. Several days later Keynes suffered a minor heart attack while at work at Cambridge University, and a few days afterwards there was another attack. He recovered, but it was a further reminder of his very weak health and over-commitment to work and other interests, with the stress of the war effort only adding to this. Under the strict supervision of wife Lydia, Keynes submitted himself to the idiosyncratic health regime of his favoured doctor Janos Plesch (nicknamed 'the Ogre' for his harsh regimes and prescriptions).

In June 1940 Keynes was invited to join a Treasury committee to review special problems of the war. The *enfant terrible* was at last becoming a little more acceptable to the Establishment. For Keynes the committee was a channel for his apparently inexhaustible flow of new ideas about how to advance the war effort. Within the month Keynes was sending the committee memoranda on the operations of the stock exchange, a further note on exchange controls and payments agreements, and many other communications. He also began a series of *Notes to the Chancellor* emphasizing the fiscal burden ahead that would be involved in paying for a war which was now looking likely to continue much longer than expected.

In August 1940 Treasury allowed Keynes to come a little closer to policy decisions. He was given an office in the main building in Great George Street. He installed a secretary and a bed for resting, and during daylight bombing raids he would descend to the deep Treasury basement. Without being assigned formal duties or granted any pay he was now given what he described as 'a sort of roving commission' and placed on several other senior Treasury committees. This meant he was now ensconced in Whitehall, where he had access to confidential government information, and had the ear of the Treasury Permanent Secretary and the Chancellor. He urged Treasury to search for new ways to address the mounting fiscal deficit, and in particular to consider a graduated surcharge on incomes coupled with deferred pay. He joined Treasury's Budget Committee to argue for this against competing departmental counterproposals. As ever he continued to raise eyebrows and hackles.

The worst of the Battle of Britain was now under way with nightly bombing raids over London. Keynes was in the thick of it. He slept at his Bedford Square house, moving into a bunk in the basement to seek shelter from the frequent air raids aimed at nearby rail yards. As he observed the bombing, he was scathing about the inability of the Germans to achieve much real economic damage. However on 18 September 1940 his views suddenly changed.

At this time the German U-boat blockade was significantly restricting available food supplies in Britain. The Ministry of Food had put in place 'Dig for Britain', pig-raising clubs, and other initiatives to stimulate home production. With his farm and his private income Keynes did not seem to be suffering shortages: he had bought a duck from Fortnum and Mason, and the household was enjoying supper at home, when their meal was rudely interrupted. The small group was sitting in the basement kitchen of the Bedford Square house when there was a huge blast, the house rocked and all the windows and doors on one side were smashed. The front door was blown from its hinges. A landmine had been dropped by the Luftwaffe at the opposite end of the square, probably aimed at nearby Euston Station or the Ministry of Information tower. The Keynes household were very lucky to be spared injury: the shutters on the windows saved the occupants from flying glass, but they had to evacuate the house for some weeks because another unexploded bomb was found nearby soon afterwards. World War II and the Battle of Britain had now intruded into everybody's life.

Keynesian demand management policy required empirical estimates of economic slack or pressure. Keynes helped Cambridge colleagues James Meade and Richard Stone, who had worked on earlier measures of the economy, to prepare a paper entitled 'National Income, Savings and Consumption' to get better estimates of its size and its imbalances. Initially the paper raised alarm bells because it suggested the economy had almost doubled in money terms since the war started, and thus that inflation could be spinning out of control. It was reworked and published as a White Paper. The budget was read on 7 April 1941, the first that Keynes had ever contributed to, and the first to be based on more reliable national accounting figures. It revealed a large 'inflationary gap' (i.e. the amount of excess purchasing power which could not be supplied at current prices) estimated at £500 million (about 5 per cent of GDP). This was to be covered half by an expected increase in savings, half by new taxation.

The 1941 Budget was not exactly as prescribed in *How to Pay for the War*, having evolved considerably during the drafts, committees, and new arguments (not least new suggestions put forward by Keynes himself). But it did adopt the broad approach that Keynes had recommended, packaged in a more socialist-acceptable form, and in future years other aspects of the Keynes scheme were adopted, although less than a quarter of the targeted savings sum was ever raised. Keynes's scheme certainly focused the argument about who should bear the burden of lower living standards to pay for the war, a tension between different groupings of wage-earners, taxpayers, foreigners, and future generations.

As the year passed Keynes continued to contribute budgetary counsel, advising how to increase taxes on nonessentials, and helping to design a new Treasury bond to soak up excess savings. Skidelsky listed five unique contributions that Keynes made to wartime finances, showing how governments could borrow and repay in cheap money, using the budget as an anti-inflationary weapon, showing that demand management was not impacted by foreign financing, clarifying the vital budgetary link between taxes and subsidies, and articulating the social compact by clarifying who would bear the burden of paying for the war.

As the Battle of Britain raged and the Germans advanced through the Balkans and North Africa, it was becoming clear that this war was going to be very long and very expensive, and that it could not be financed by Britain alone. British Commonwealth and other Allies were providing considerable troops and material. But international financial markets were not operating as in peacetime and appealing to the US for direct financial support seemed the only option.

However the UK soon found this to be rather more difficult than expected. The British saw themselves as holding the front line in a war for civilization. To their surprise, the US viewed them as a fading imperialist power who had enriched themselves off the back of native peoples who should be looking to the model of US independence. Washington resented the continued existence of the British Empire, and had seen the 1932 Imperial Conference as entrenching it. In addition, the British had seriously underestimated the hostility from German and Irish immigrants in the US, they did not realize the popular appeal of isolationism there, they were confused by the political checks and balances in the complex US federal system, they had been misled by presidential assurances from Roosevelt who was very non-transparent, and they appeared to the Americans as arrogant and cunning. American financiers were less politically blinkered than the politicians, but they still resented the British repudiation of World War I US debts in 1933, which had been partly blamed on Keynes himself. He also underestimated the negative impact of his own intellectualism on key US players.

Whereas the British had spent the previous half-century promoting internationalist policies, the US approach had been more isolationist. With the outbreak of World War II in Europe the US Congress had passed the Neutrality Act preventing the sale of arms to belligerents. Crucially for Britain it was eventually amended to allow belligerents to buy arms which they could pay for and transport themselves. This 'cash and carry' arrangement suited Britain at first. However soon there was a cash problem: as British export capacity declined, the country was forced to pay for its imports of food and war materials from the US by shipping gold and selling securities to the Americans, which was in the latter's interests. Churchill did not try to limit arms purchases, ordering as much war material as his Chiefs of Staff claimed they needed. In addition Britain spent almost £2 billion on construction within the US, building aircraft factories which were later handed over to the Americans without compensation.

By mid-1940 as the Battle of Britain raged, Keynes and other well-connected British were starting to realize that the risks of military defeat were real: there was no certainty that Britain could hold back the Nazis. Worried by the impending prospect of British military defeat, in June 1940 President Roosevelt at last found a way around the US neutrality legislation prohibiting government-to-government weapons sales, by consigning rifles to Britain via a third party. Later he agreed to add the transfer of heavy equipment including US destroyers. By the end of the year the British military situation had slightly consolidated, but the economy was suffering from a large outflow of capital, and US suppliers were insisting on ever-tougher payment conditions as a result.

It was now an acute problem how to finance purchases from the US to keep the war machine operating. The British had ordered a programme of 3,000 aircraft per month from the US, but increasingly American businesses doubted Britain's ability to pay, leading to demands for cash advances. At this rate Britain's reserves could be exhausted by early 1941, which in turn would worsen the acceptability of the sterling debts that had been used to finance British war effort in other countries. The US Treasury led by Henry Morgenthau was opportunistically pressuring the British to sell off their holdings in big companies in the US (Shell Oil, Lever Brothers, tobacco companies, and others) in order to raise credit, but the British were understandably concerned that this would leave them without assets after the war.

Eventually, just before Christmas 1940, President Roosevelt used one of his homely fire-side chats to announce the 'Lend-Lease' program—employing the folksy image of lending a neighbour a hose to put out a fire. The US would lend or lease defence equipment to Britain to be returned after the war, conveniently ignoring the fact that equipment used in wartime has little return value. Morgenthau still had to sell this concept to a hostile Congress. They finally passed it in March 1941, and then only grudgingly and with conditions attached.

Keynes had been observing these developments closely. He had already made some creative suggestions to extend British funding. He had become friendly with John Winant, the US Ambassador to London, and they would dine at one another's homes. Winant suggested Keynes should travel to Washington DC as the Chancellor of the Exchequer's representative to put the British Treasury position to the US Government. The Treasury wanted to find a way to replenish Britain's dangerously draining reserves up to at least £600 million. In May 1941 it was agreed that Keynes needed to visit the United States again. He wrote to his mother that he vowed not to talk too much, not to drink cocktails, not to speak his mind, and always to obey Lydia who would travel with him. This was to be the first of Keynes's half-dozen wartime Treasury missions to the United States.

Travelling across the Atlantic Sea at a time of German U-boat menace was judged too dangerous. Even by air it was a long and potentially hazardous wartime journey for Keynes, his wife Lydia, his secretary, and his assistant. They endured a train to Bournemouth, a British flying boat to Costa dol Sol in Portugal where they overnighted, then an American clipper to the Azores. They took off the next day only to have to return with engine trouble. Eventually they landed in Bermuda, and then embarked on the final leg to New York. The whole trans-Atlantic journey took a week, and was not much faster than by sea. In New York the press was waiting for the party. They entrained to Washington the following day and installed themselves in the Mayflower Hotel. Keynes was exhausted.

Once again he had to learn about the differences, misunderstandings, and suspicions between the two countries. The trans-Atlantic positions on economics, strategy, and world outlook were quite different, and Keynes could not always comprehend this. Keynes's own position at the Versailles Settlement, his rudeness to the Americans at the time, his attacks on Woodrow Wilson, and his upper-class intellectual arrogance had not been forgotten or forgiven. In his favour however, there was now an enthusiastic band of young Keynesian macroeconomists at work in the New Deal government agencies. Keynes soon found he particularly disliked many of the administration's lawyers and officials, and did not appreciate the way they operated. He tended to try and score intellectual points off them, and was not a natural negotiator in style. His first encounter with Henry Morgenthau, Roosevelt's dour and political Treasury Secretary did not go at all well. Morgenthau always felt that Keynes was putting him down. For his part, Keynes thought that Morgenthau was dull, and did not always bother to hide this view.

At issue was a very difficult problem: both players had an eye to post-war recovery; but Keynes wanted to reduce Britain's dependence on Lend-Lease, and thus to reduce American control over the British balance of payments. Morgenthau wanted the opposite, partly to aid Britain's war efforts, partly to minimize British opposition to rebuilding its reserves. He saw Britain as a client state. To make the negotiation even more complex, American interests and tactics differed within the Administration: the US Treasury Department wanted to keep Britain fighting but keep them financially dependent on the USA, while the State Department wanted to dismantle Britain's Imperial Preference trading system.

Keynes began with his usual approach: discussion and negotiation by memo and argument. His strategy was for the US to refund $700 million of British money already committed to Lend-Lease, which the UK would then use to rebuild resources and import more from the United States. This proposal was immediately rejected by the US, and that put a long and tedious round of negotiations on to a difficult footing.

Weeks of arguments followed, with Keynes wandering through a series of smoke-filled rooms making little progress. He thought he was negotiating on behalf of a great internationalist nation. Instead the Americans saw a tired country near defeat: the British had been driven out of Greece and Crete, Rommel was ascendant in North Africa, German air raids and U-boat raids were causing huge losses in the Atlantic. Keynes was further bamboozled by the complex US administrative system, and completely at a loss over the spoiling role of Congress. In contrast to Britain, everyday life was relatively easy with few shortages and less sense of urgency.

Keynes called on President Roosevelt again, and passed on his views about wartime and post-war time economic management. The British Foreign Minister had just given a speech about post-war economic settlement based on one of Keynes's proposals, and Keynes was keen to elucidate. Rather like Schacht, Keynes thought his presidential conversation had gone down particularly well, but also like Schacht, Keynes was not the best judge of his own persuasiveness. The British Ambassador Lord Halifax, also present, said Roosevelt did not seem particularly receptive to yet another lecture from Keynes.

As usual Keynes was working very hard—meetings and writings were occupying 12 to 17 hours per day. A month into the trip was his birthday, and he was invited to a grand birthday party by Chinese lobbyist T. V. Soong (brother-in-law of Kung). There was a Chinese banquet with 16 courses and a birthday song composed in Keynes's honour and sung by Soong's daughter. No doubt with each course Keynes would have received advice to encourage the US to keep funding the Chinese war effort.

Keynes took the opportunity to talk to American economists whenever possible. In late June he visited Princeton University to confer with academics there including at the Institute of Advanced Studies, reporting later that he found the mathematicians more interesting than the economists. On the staff was John von Neumann (though it is unclear whether he was present at the meetings). Keynes did however get the opportunity to talk to Albert Einstein, who received him in bed; Lydia commented on his bare toes poking through the sheets.

At this time Britain's official foreign sterling reserves were falling precipitously. Worth over £500 million at the beginning of the war, they had dropped to almost £100 million by the end of 1940, and while Keynes was busy negotiating in Washington, had plummeted further to a very worrying £65 million, a dangerously inadequate buffer for the economy. Had Britain survived Goering's Luftwaffe only to fall prey to the financial markets?

Keynes tried again: he could understand that the US Government was determined Britain should pay a price for assistance. He proposed that the US Reconstruction Finance Corporation could make loans available to the British Government, with British overseas assets put up as collateral. The US Treasury was prepared to accept in principle that Britain needed around $600 million in liquid reserves, though they proposed to charge penal interest rates for the loans. Keynes also now saw the need to offload as many imports as possible from the US into the Lend-Lease scheme;

extending Lend-Lease commitments to the British Dominions could save up to $250 million of reserves a year.

It seemed that progress was being made at last, and Keynes was pleased. He felt that Lend-Lease extensions with the addition of further loans would permit a gradual build-up of a trade surplus with the US. This turned out to be correct: by the end of the year Britain's foreign reserves had risen to £564 million. Keynes had been instrumental in the negotiation, though overall he may not have improved British–US relations much. As it ultimately turned out, 40 per cent of Britain's wartime imports would be paid for by exports and reserves, 30 per cent by American aid, and 10 per cent by selling off overseas assets.

The final negotiations for the deal had turned out to be frustratingly long and protracted, revealing the internal competition between US Treasury and US State Departments. There was much in the redrafted texts that Keynes objected to and tried to renegotiate. At last the deal was near and he was able to return to the UK at the end of July 1941. He was very relieved to be back in war-torn Britain. However on reading the final drafts of the agreement back in London he became depressed at the way that the US Administration seemed to be systematically eroding Britain's competitive and financial position, and he was now having to confront the reality of his country's diminished economic standing.

1941: The International Clearing Union

In the second half of 1941 the war prospects of the Allies worsened. Allied troops retreated from Crete, were besieged in Malta, were pushed back by Rommel in North Africa, and suffered naval defeats in the Mediterranean. The whole war changed when Germany turned on the Soviet Union and launched a three-pronged attack towards Leningrad, Moscow, and the Caucasus oilfields, dragging the Balkans into the conflict. By later that year the German Army was tied up in titanic struggles besieging Leningrad, Moscow, Stalingrad, and Kiev, the US had extended Lend-Lease assistance to the Soviet Union, and Britain, now facing desperate shortages from the Atlantic U-Boat blockade, had increased male conscription.

The news from the East continued to be bad. The Japanese had invaded French Indo-China, and were bombing the Nationalist Chinese war capital at Chungking. There was growing resistance to British rule in India, and political upheaval in Japan had brought the warlike General Tojo to power, spelling the end to any prospect for a negotiated settlement. Reacting to Japanese aggression, the US imposed an oil embargo which exposed Japan's extreme vulnerability to imported resources. On 7 December Japanese planes attacked Pearl Harbor, and within days the biggest blitzkrieg in history saw them storm down Southeast Asia through Thailand, Malaya, Hong Kong, the Philippines, Singapore, and Micronesia. The US declared war. It was now clear to all this would be a long, costly, bloody global conflict.

In 1941 Keynes was grateful to be home from the US and very keen to resume his now highly influential role in Treasury. Officially he remained unpaid part-time advisor to the Chancellor. He was said to be 'in Treasury', but not 'of it'. His ideas on paying for the war, on financing equipment purchases, and on international clearing arrangements would lead the great Treasury wartime debates. When he chose to get involved in any other topic his influence was usually decisive. Senior official Lord Salter recalled: 'he was the strangest civil servant Whitehall has ever seen, less the servant and more the master of those he served than any I have seen' (Moggridge, 1992, 639).

For some time Keynes had been concerned about exchange control. The UK budget could harness domestic resources, but foreign items had to be paid for by exports or by the sale of British assets overseas. Keynes felt that the exchange control system set up at the outbreak of war had been leaking badly. The system required British exporters to channel earnings of hard currency (primarily dollars) through a Treasury account, selling sterling at a fixed exchange rate to the dollar. Free sterling transactions were allowed within most of the British Empire, but not outside.

Initially Keynes's attention had been triggered by his personal interests: the government nationalized some corporate stock which had left him with some money to invest for himself, for King's College, and for a corporation of which he was a director. Keynes examined the existing regulatory arrangements and decided this needed his superior attention. He would 'follow in Dr Schacht's footsteps and block foreign balances as a whole' (Skidelsky, 2000, 75). Once again reliable statistics on the linkages were very difficult to come by. Helped by Thomas Balogh, a young Hungarian economist, and others, Keynes estimated foreign exchange leakages of around £100 million since the war had commenced. Keynes wrote several drafts of memoranda that he fired around Treasury to highlight this problem, and found an unexpected ally in the Governor of the Bank of England, Schacht's friend, the imperious Montagu Norman, with whom he had more often been locked in disagreement.

As the war prospects continued to worsen, the UK Treasury took further action to block all sales of sterling by non-residents. Keynes redrafted his plans to prevent further leakages with a proposed new foreign exchange and import control authority. Being Keynes he went further: could there be a policy to pool the foreign financial reserves of all four Allied empires now under attack from the Germans (i.e. the British, French, Dutch, and Belgian empires) in order to exploit their combined bargaining strength to renegotiate credits with the US? This vision proved too fanciful for the UK Treasury.

With the main framework for wartime finance having been put into place, Keynes now turned to one of the looming post-war problems: the world's new financial clearing arrangement. Driving his intense interest were his stark experiences of international economic failure that he had predicted and experienced after World War I.

The views of Churchill and his War Cabinet about wartime economics were unsophisticated. They disliked the gold standard as it had been associated with high unemployment. They liked the sterling area as it symbolized Britain's imperial power. They wanted money to fight the war. Such simplicity of objectives meant it was left to greater minds such as Keynes to consider the economic possibilities. Churchill liked and respected Keynes, even if he did not always understand him. In turn Keynes presented a continued challenge for the Treasury, an institution that had traditionally managed the government finances, whereas Keynes felt it should be managing the national economy, an altogether bigger and more complex task.

Keynes felt Treasury was at its intellectual peak when Sir Richard Hopkins was Permanent Secretary, a man he described as having 'a general appearance rather like that of an extremely intelligent monkey' (Skidelsky, 2000, 145). Over time Keynes drew closer to two key economists working in the Economic Section: one was Lionel Robbins who before the war had been a trenchant critic of Keynes, and who went on to be Director of the London School of Economics. One of Robbins's main achievements (against considerable opposition) was to establish a price rationing system for foodstuffs. The other was James Meade, a visionary economic thinker and future Nobel Prize winner who helped integrate Keynes's unemployment analysis into classical free-trade theory. Keynes was at his strongest in Treasury during the early wartime period. There were many opportunities to challenge traditional approaches, and he used his reputation with other economists and the genius of his high-octane mind to challenge them. He worked ceaselessly all day until late in the evening, fuelled by ideas and arguments. He showed no particular respect for hierarchies. He was an intuitive thinker, a generalist, and an optimist, confident about his views, even when he had to change his mind. Despite the gloomy wartime news Keynes was fundamentally positive that there would be eventual victory.

In 1940 the Central Economic Information Service started work on the Stamp Survey to improve its economic data. By the beginning of 1941 the survey had split into an Economic Section and the Central Statistical Office in the Cabinet Office. The first British national accounts framed the 1942 Beveridge Report. But it was not for several years that Keynes declared such numerical economic analysis had, in his opinion, reached the point where it was fit to be applied to policy. By this time there had been an influx of younger economists to Whitehall: into the newer ministries involved in planning and supply, into the Prime Minister's Statistical Branch under Lord Cherwell, and into the Economic Section and the Central Statistical Office in the War Cabinet. Perhaps surprisingly, economists were not so evident in the Treasury Department. The Economic Section and the Central Statistical Office provided the nucleus of a more modern economic staff, though in the British administrative style, they serviced rather than directed the departments.

Keynes acted as a link between these economists and the Treasury, aided by the fact that many of them had been his colleagues or students. The economic heart of wartime Whitehall was physically compact, a complex of government buildings between St James's Park and the Palace of Westminster. The Treasury building suffered a direct bombing hit in 1940 and had to be evacuated. As well as being risky, this was not profitable work. A senior economist at the time would earn less than £1,000 in a year (perhaps £50,000 at today's prices), this amount being pegged for the duration of the war. Keynes himself remained unpaid. This did not seem to worry him—he was responding to a greater calling than his colleagues, and anyway he was by now independently well off: his annual income during the war years was around £12,500, much of it earned through his own investments, as well as some farming revenue.

The War Cabinet had a Production Committee headed by a senior minister, issuing directions to supply departments and the Ministry of Labour, which in turn devised directives for individual firms. Economist Alec Cairncross, who worked in the civil service through the war, explained the attempts to plan production by ensuring a just-in-time inventory of components. In practice this was often unsuccessful, for example with bombers being grounded because spare propellers were not available and many other examples of misallocation. Manpower planning was attempted but also appeared ad hoc.

Keynes was less involved with the brutal war in the East. He had written to *The Times* following the Japanese invasion of China back in 1937, advocating economic sanctions against Japan (advice eventually taken by the Americans some years later). But he argued with Kingsley Martin, editor of *The New Statesman*, who urged China to fight a war to the death. Like the Russians, H. H. Kung and brother-in-law T. V. Soong had already targeted Keynes as a person of influence. In early 1942 they requested a British loan to help counter the Japanese and Southeast Asia. Keynes analysed the proposal and advised dispassionately and strongly against it.

Though already overburdened with wartime work, Keynes could rarely resist the opportunity to get involved in other unrelated wartime economic problems that his deep reading, wide contacts, and own investments alerted him to. Was the problem of getting supplies to the UK in the winter of 1940–41 due to insufficient shipping, or was the problem actually related to congestion in discharging due to labour shortages at the ports? Were the Bolivians reneging on their tin agreement with Britain in favour of higher US wartime prices? Could the Middle East's Allied transport system be improved? All these and others attracted his eager though sometimes unfocused mind.

Despite the pressures of war and as far as his health allowed, Keynes retained his many other interests and he continued to throw himself into these. During the week he would usually work at his Treasury office in Whitehall, staying at Gordon Square in London's Bloomsbury until Friday evening, then entrain to Cambridge with Lydia. There he would catch up with academic colleagues, and deal with Kings College and other Cambridge business on Saturday. In the evening they might attend a play or ballet at the Arts Theatre that he had helped to establish, and on Sundays they would take lunch with his parents and enjoy a concert in Kings College Chapel. When he could, he travelled down to his farmhouse in West Sussex near his Bloomsbury friends, but even in the countryside there was little time to relax as he dealt with his farm manager and farming business. As if he did not have enough to do, he took over management of one of the neighbouring farms belonging to less competent friends, and directed production decisions there as well. On 28 March 1941 he received the tragic news that Virginia Woolf, always emotionally fragile, had drowned herself. He described her and husband Leonard Woolf as 'our dearest friends'.

During this time he also kept up his active editorship of the *Economic Journal*, was Chairman of the *New Statesman* weekly, and he became a trustee of the National Gallery on Trafalgar Square. By December 1941 he was devoting much time and energy as Foundation Chair of the Council for the Encouragement of Music and the Arts (CMA), later to become the Arts Council. Keynes believed strongly that wartime British workers needed culture. In addition he was an active fellow on the governing body of Eton, his old college: he believed that the upper classes needed his assistance as much as the workers.

Keynes had last visited Russia in 1936, travelling with Lydia to visit her family in Leningrad. By 1940 with Britain at War and the Soviet Union in a pact with Germany, communications were severely disrupted. Despite the Soviet–German Pact Keynes made a point of keeping in touch with the Soviet Ambassador in London, Ivan Maisky. In June 1940 he had lunch with him, and the Maisky couple also dined with the Keyneses in the kitchen at Gordon Square. Keynes predicted accurately to the Ambassador that Britain and the USSR would eventually be fighting Hitler together. At this time Keynes had been re-reading *An Essay on Marxian Economics* by Joan Robinson. Keynes described Marx as penetrating and original but a very poor thinker. In July 1943 Maisky sent Keynes an article by academician M. Mitin on 'Twenty-five Years of Philosophy in the USSR', asking Keynes's help to publish it in the West. Keynes described it privately as 'pathetic' but nevertheless tried to assist with its publication.

In September 1941 Keynes was invited to join the Bank of England Court, where he soon locked swords intellectually with Montagu Norman, the powerful Bank Governor. Norman later said 'Keynes on a committee is rather like yeast' (Skidelsky, 2000, 203). After his death Norman described Keynes as a great economist but a bad banker.

The Lend-Lease Agreement with the US contained a draft clause prohibiting Britain from discriminating against US goods after the war. This was a direct attack against the British Imperial Preference system that the Americans wanted to dismantle both for financial and political reasons. Keynes thought he might find a solution to this impasse: if all countries could be guaranteed access to sufficient foreign reserves, that might make it possible to dismantle the trade barriers of the 1930s, restoring a pre-1914 world but without the old gold standard. Back at Tilton farm in August 1941, he started working on this international problem. It would occupy him for the rest of his life, and would bring him into direct conflict with the US Treasury.

There were some big differences in policy positions to address: Britain could now see it might end the war stripped of assets and heavily in debt. In contrast the US expected to be the world's creditor nation. The British were planning from a banking tradition based on financial stability. The US approach was based on legal rules of engagement. The British felt they had suffered from the gold standard in the past, while the US felt it had benefited them. The central bankers of the major economies after World War I had seen the international payment system as self-equilibrating. Keynes however had built his *General Theory* on the hypothesis that markets could be persistently illiquid or inflexible, and he saw currency misalignments as another example of this.

In his ideas for international clearing, Keynes looked for inspiration to a scheme designed by Germany's ex-Minister Schacht. The Schacht Plan that had been submitted to the Young Committee had been designed to get around international restrictions on Germany. Keynes now wanted to find a way to adapt these bilateral arrangements into a multilateral clearing system. With Hubert Henderson, Keynes had speculated about the role that an international body might play as early as 1930 in his *Treatise on Money*, and had then produced a related plan to increase international reserves for the inconclusive 1933 World Economic Conference in London. Keynes's own views then and later had been widely reported in Germany and read by Schacht. Through the 1940s Keynes labelled those who wanted to base clearing on bilateral barter deals from a fortress economy as the 'Schachtians'. Ironically this was now closer to Soviet policy with its state monopoly of imports and exports.

The Germans themselves were planning for a new post-war economic world. Schacht's successor as economics minister, Walther Funk, had produced a plan for a 'New World Order', in which German marks would be the centre of a Europe-wide international clearing-house. Keynes first saw this document in November 1940, when the British Government suggested that he do a propaganda broadcast to discredit it. The problem was that when he read it, Keynes inconveniently found that he agreed with much of it. He went further, publishing a French economist's analysis of the German 'New World Order' in the *Economic Journal*. In fact the German plan helped Keynes develop his own ideas over the next few months, and he prepared a set of 'Proposals to Counter the German "New Order"'. At this stage he was thinking of multilateral clearing within a sterling area, with an external exchange rate fixed to the US dollar. This idea was developed in a Treasury document in mid-1940, and generated considerable debate inside Whitehall.

Keynes returned to his Sussex farmhouse in September 1941 to settle down to do some serious writing about post-war international currency plans. Despite an interrupted week, he drafted two papers: *Post-war Currency Policy*, and *Proposals for an International Currency Union*. These were analytical papers focused on the past problems of the gold standard and the problems ahead for post-war clearing. It was now clear that Britain's ability to earn export revenue was much reduced, and the country would likely end the fighting with a huge overseas debt that would be difficult to service. Keynes believed comprehensive exchange controls would initially be necessary, but in the long run a multilateral scheme would be a preferable arrangement to avoid trade wars.

How could Britain re-establish monetary equilibrium in the face of a huge post-war deficit? Keynes now proposed moving from a sterling area clearing body to a truly international currency union, an argument that would combine Schacht's and Funk's clearing ideas with his own perception of international banking principles. The underlying idea was that a country's net international transactions (balance of payments surpluses and deficits) would be settled by member central banks through an international clearing bank, with each member having some overdraft rights. Never one to do things by halves, Keynes also proposed a supranational police force, a reconstruction and relief organization, and buffer stocks to be funded by the clearing bank. Eventually these ideas would contribute to the formation of the World Bank and the International Monetary Fund, with its Bretton Woods system of exchange rates. Keynes was also involved in the British policy of buying up commodities from neutral countries in order to deny supplies to the enemy. Now he proposed using the stocks to feed and clothe Europeans post-war, a forerunner of what would eventually be the US Marshall Plan.

This policy package became known as the Keynes Plan, and it attracted positive interest from all corners of the Whitehall economics machine—from colleagues such as Ralph Hawtrey at the Treasury, Roy Harrod in the PM's Statistical Branch, and Lionel Robbins and James Meade in the Economic Section of the War Cabinet. Montagu Norman and Henry Clay at the Bank of England were less enthusiastic, being more inclined to the type of controls and payments agreements pioneered by Norman's friend Schacht. Keynes redrafted the plans in November. The next months were extremely busy for him as he tried to incorporate some US comments, aiming to position the international clearing bank as an Anglo-American club. A third draft was finished by Christmas 1941.

The situation was changed by the war in the East. Although the British were not yet aware of it, one week after the Pearl Harbor attack the US Treasury Secretary directed his assistant Harry Dexter White to prepare a memo on an inter-Allied stabilization fund as a basis for post-war monetary arrangements. The US was taking its own path.

Keynes had another problem closer to home: the German Operation Barbarossa had unleashed a vicious attack on the Soviet Union. By late 1941 the German Army Group North and the Finnish Army were hammering at the gates of Leningrad. For the Keynes family this was terrible news because Lydia's mother and family were caught in the vicious pincer movement. Since the start of the war it had been increasingly hard for the Keynes couple in London to communicate with Lydia's family in Leningrad. Keynes cultivated his friend Soviet Ambassador Maisky in London, to try to get the two Lopukhov brothers out of the Soviet Union on the pretext of a travelling ballet tour. Despite his persuasiveness he was unsuccessful.

As the Keynes couple heard news of the German siege they became increasingly worried. They knew the geographical layout of the city, and understood that a siege would be disastrous. In Leningrad there were no drugs and almost no food to be had. By Christmas 1941 3,000 people were dying of malnutrition and cold on the streets each day. Lydia's famous brother Fyodor had fallen from grace after directing a new Shostakovich ballet which had been condemned for 'aesthetic formalism', and he had been interned in a camp. Lydia's mother Constanza was now aged 80 and ill, and her sister was also unwell. Keynes could advise the British about supporting the Russian war effort to relieve Leningrad by shipping war supplies via the northern Murmansk route. But he was powerless to get help to Lydia's family.

5

The Calculating Iceman

Leonid Kantorovich in the USSR, 1941–2

The Boy from Petrograd

Maynard and Lydia Keynes were anxiously following the war reports. The reason was that Lydia's mother and her brothers and sisters were caught up in the siege of Leningrad. All mail had ceased, the Germans were tightening their grip, and the Soviets gave out very little information about conditions. BBC wireless reported that Britain was diverting some scarce planes and supplies to help the Soviets defend the city, but it was hard to understand just how grim life had become there.

Hitler had turned on his unlikely ally the Soviet Union, and unleashed the full fury of Operation Barbarossa. It was a brutal triple-pronged blitzkrieg involving three German army groups aimed at the western defences of Russia and Byelorussia. Army Group North headed straight for the key strategic city of Leningrad. There the Germans joined with Finnish military forces coming from the north in a pincer movement. By September of that year they had cut off all road access to the city, and were blocking all supplies of food and arms. The Siege of Leningrad, one of the most horrific in history, had begun.

Late in 1941 a muffled figure wearing a great coat and boots could be seen shuffling across the ice, keeping a wary watch on the grey winter skies above. Every now and again he bent down and prodded into the snow and ice underfoot. Beside him a convoy of trucks slowly ground past, engines revving noisily and smoke belching from their poor-quality fuel. The man made a note and looked at his probe again. It was 30° below and his breath was crystallizing. He heard a truck tyre spin, its engine roaring, and he looked up anxiously.

Lake Ladoga on the edge of Leningrad was covered with thick ice. The temperature was very low. The trucks were instructed to load lightly, drive very slowly, and keep a specified distance, as they cautiously traversed the ice 'road'. Big ploughs of snow on each side provided a little shelter from the icy wind, but there was nowhere to hide from enemy planes above. So far the man felt relieved. By his calculations this convoy should survive, delivering its precious cargo down the Road of Life across the lake to a small rail spur, then into the besieged city of Leningrad.

The citizens of Leningrad were caught in a terrible existence. The Germans and Finns had closed off all road and rail access. The German Army occupied the suburbs and was advancing, shelling the city centre, soldiers and civilians alike. It was freezing cold but there was no fuel available for heat. There was no medicine. Worst of all was the lack of food: rations were down to 125 grams of bread per person per day, bread made partly from sawdust, and every day as many as 3,000 people were dying on the streets from malnutrition and the extreme cold. Each morning sleds full of corpses were dragged away. Some people resorted to cannibalism to stay alive. One and a half million citizens would eventually die.

The Germans did not merely want to capture the city—they wanted to totally destroy it. They had calculated that the three million population of Leningrad could be starved into submission within six weeks. But they had not managed to cut off the lake access, and in winter when the ice was thick enough and the temperature low enough, trucks might cautiously be driven across. Their precious cargoes were the only way to keep the city alive.

The Road of Life (*Doroga Zhizni* in Russian) had been built to careful mathematical calculations, yet it proved very dangerous. In early December 1941 when the ice thickened, trucks started traversing the route, but in the first week alone more than forty trucks broke through the ice and sank to the bottom of the deep lake, drowning the drivers and losing the precious supplies. The authorities called in a mathematician named Dr Leonid Kantorovich, a renowned academic from the University of Leningrad, to calculate what temperature and ice thickness would be required to support trucks of a certain weight and speed, and he was frequently to be seen out on the lake testing the conditions, sometimes walking between the vehicles. The vehicles were instructed to keep a specified distance apart

1. Takahashi Korekiyo: Reading his daily English-language newspapers

2. H. H. Kung: Meeting with Adolf Hitler in Bavaria to discuss barter trade

3. H. S. Schacht: In the dock at the International Military Tribunal at Nuremberg

4. J. M. Keynes: With Henry Morgenthau, US Treasury Secretary, at Bretton Woods

5. L. V. Kantorovich: Receiving the Nobel Prize from the Swedish King in Stockholm

6. Wassily Leontief: In full flight at a seminar

7. John von Neumann: with J. Robert Oppenheimer in front of the IAS Computer

and steering was difficult because most of the time they were driving through surface water which camouflaged the ice.

Like most of his academic colleagues, with the outbreak of war Kantorovich had been drafted into the military, initially as a private (where it was noted he 'met some difficulties with military discipline.') An unusual man with an extremely clever theoretical brain, his talents were soon recognized and he was re-assigned the military rank of major. Kantorovich had been a brilliant young professor at the Military Engineering –Technical University which had been set up on the site of the old Petersburg Polytechnic Institute in the city. As the German blitzkrieg advanced towards Leningrad the task of all citizens was obvious: defeat the Germans, break the siege, and survive. The institute played a key part in engineering defensive positions against the besieging Germans, and the university students helped man the military installations. Major Kantorovich was put in charge of calculating safe cargo limits on the Road of Life. For his courage and achievements he was subsequently awarded the Order of the Patriotic War.

Dr Kantorovich constructed an algorithm: he calculated that a 10 cm thickness of ice was necessary to bear the weight of a horse, that a minimum of 17 cm of ice was necessary to support a horse-drawn sleigh with a ton of cargo, while 20 cm thickness could support a one ton cargo truck. The calculations had to take into account varying ice thicknesses along the 220 km route. The mathematician derived other formulae to calculate the rate of ice formation at various temperatures, but this was further complicated by the region's erratic winds which could change the water level and the ice thickness very quickly. It made a difference what time of day the convoy operated, and the warming effect of the truck tyres melting surface ice. Finally he had to factor in the mathematical probability of air attacks along the unprotected route. Kantorovich was very aware that his calculations could spell the difference between life and death.

German surveillance soon discovered the route, and their planes attacked it repeatedly, countered by inadequate Soviet anti-aircraft guns placed along the road and Soviet pilots flying British Hurricane and US Tomahawk planes. In the white-out conditions there was nowhere for this lone mathematician to hide as he carried out his calculations.

Many vehicles laden with food were destroyed by the Luftwaffe, drivers were killed, and the route also became known as 'the Road of Death'.

While patrolling the Lake Ladoga ice road, Kantorovich no doubt had time to contemplate that the German front lines were only a few kilometres away. He would have heard of the cruel roundups and deportations of Jews from the overrun lands of Poland, Lithuania, and Byelorussia to the south-west. The war held a special danger for Russian Jews like him from anti-Semitic Soviets on one side and Nazis on the other.

In Britain Keynes had been working with others on extending the Lend-Lease programme. It had become clear that this would be the only way to save Leningrad. In late 1941 under an agreement with the Soviet Government, Britain started shipping tanks, aircraft, and other supplies using perilous naval convoys from Britain through the Barents Sea to Archangel and Murmansk, from where they could be transported to Leningrad on the Road of Life to help keep the city alive.

In February 1942, the worst month of the siege, 67,000 tons of food and 20,000 tons of petrol, lubricants, and ammunition were transported over the lake. After the ice trucks had unloaded their precious supplies, they reloaded for a return trip with women and children evacuees. Over half a million civilians and wounded were evacuated this way. In addition, industrial equipment was dismantled from key factories in Leningrad, to be reassembled elsewhere in the country. During the first winter the ice road operated for 152 days. By the following year the road had been made more efficient with a railway and an oil pipeline also being constructed across the frozen lake.

On 23 April 1942 with the ice now too thin for trucks, three cars carried a cargo of onions across the dangerously melting route, the last ice road supplies for that year. But it was too late for some. In that terrible winter Keynes's ailing mother-in-law Constanza died in the siege. The following year, with the city still encircled and still held at starvation levels, his sister-in-law Eugenie also died.

Leonid Vitalyevich Kantorovich had been born in St Petersburg in 1911, was raised in Petrograd, and lived in Leningrad, the turbulence around him indicated by the name changes of the city following the outbreak of World War I, and again with Soviet rule. The family had been comfortably middle-class. Kantorovich's father Vitalyi was a popular medical doctor, specializing in sexually transmitted diseases, which at that time presented a major problem in the city. The family already consisted of two girls and two boys (both later to become doctors) when the new baby named Leonid was born. This city in foment was the world of Leonid Kantorovich's infancy. For the first decade of his life he encountered political disarray, criminal dangers, and military violence. Though very young, Kantorovich would always remember the unrest in the city during his childhood, and it would drive his search for security and stability throughout his life.

The Russian Czar had granted limited civil liberties following the 1905 Revolution. A decade later Russia entered World War I and was soon committing huge troop numbers to the Eastern Front. Military stalemate and massive troop losses spawned the successive 1917 crises and revolutions. Aged only six, precocious young Kantorovich would have been very aware of the strikes, demonstrations, and protests in Petrograd, sparked off in February by mutinying sailors. The Czar abdicated and a provisional government was formed, led by Alexander Kerensky. The next few months were highly dangerous, with spontaneous protests against the provisional government, the return from exile of Vladimir Lenin, a failed coup by the Russian Army, dissident groups fighting for power in the Duma, and the October Revolution when the Bolsheviks took control by force.

The 1917 Revolutions did not provide political stability. Instead they marked a period of conflict among the revolutionary and reactionary parties, leading to civil war in which the Bolsheviks and others fought bitterly with the Royalists. Taking advantage of the instability, German troops invaded Estonia and threatened nearby Petrograd with bombardment and invasion. Life became very dangerous in the city. The Czar's family was assassinated in 1918. The following year British forces attempted to besiege Petrograd and capture the city. They were unsuccessful, but they managed to block the shipment of food supplies to the population, and anti-Soviet White armies roamed the surrounding area, with intermittent fighting continuing for some years. In the city street crime was rife, the post-war Spanish influenza epidemic was raging, food was scarce, and life was unsafe.

The family was Jewish, although they were not actively observant. (The name Kantorovich descended from a Cantor, a synagogue official who led prayers.) Ashkenazy Jewish families had lived in the region for centuries, but they had suffered waves of pogroms and restrictions. The chaotic years of World War I and the Russian Civil War had intensified the anti-Semitism, and now there were new rumours of Jewish massacres. Aware of the dangerous past and worried for his family's safety in this unsettled city, father Vitalyi decided they must flee. He took the family including seven-year-old Leonid by train on a long and dangerous 1,000 km journey southwards to Byelorussia (now Belarus), where they stayed in exile for over a year. But this was not safe either. It has been estimated that some 25,000 Jews were massacred in Byelorussia between 1918 and 1922. As the pogroms struck nearby the family was forced to flee again, returning home to Petrograd.

One of the more positive outcomes of the revolutionary period was that more Jews were able to attain senior positions in the academy, government, and army, and it became easier for Vitalyi to practise again. Nevertheless those of Jewish ancestry were always very aware of their fragile history, and this contributed to Kantorovich's strong sense of caution throughout his professional life.

Back in Petrograd it was becoming clear to the family that their 10-year-old Leonid was a child prodigy. Despite the dangers in the streets, he could now at least go to school. Kantorovich later recalled that despite all the political turbulence around him, it was at this stage of his life that he became very interested in academic ideas.

In 1922 personal tragedy struck the family: father Vitalyi died while still young. Mother Paulina took on the tough task of raising and providing for the family in these difficult times. The young Leonid's talent was shining through, and he was naturally inquisitive and interested in science, politics, and history. Paulina realized his potential and took his education very seriously despite the desperate lack of money in the family.

In 1924 Lenin died and Kantorovich's city was renamed in his honour. The Bolshevik Government was gradually stabilizing municipal life. Paulina managed to enrol young Leonid in the Mathematics Department of Leningrad State University at the tender age of 14. This was the pre-eminent university in the city, and the department was well known for its research on real analysis, the mathematical study of series of numbers. Because of his youth, Kantorovich needed special permission to attend and that was not granted till late in the year, so he spent much of his first year in private study covering a wide range of subjects. Thanks to stimulating tutors he became more interested in political economy and modern history. Once he had received formal permission to attend lectures, Kantorovich studied with famous Soviet mathematics professors Grigorii Fichtengolz and Boris Delone.

Kantorovich excelled at mathematics, surpassing his much older classmates. By his second year he was already working on complex and abstract topics. He was soon given the very unusual distinction of being invited to join the professorial 'Descriptive Function Theory' seminar while still an undergraduate. In their third year students were required to gain work experience during the university breaks. Despite the dangers involved in these turbulent years, Kantorovich opted to travel to Tashkent, thousands of miles away in the Uzbek Socialist Soviet Republic where enforced collectivization was in process, to work for the Central Asian Water Board, studying irrigation and the optimal use of water for large-scale cotton farming.

Back in Leningrad by 1930, and still in his teens, Kantorovich graduated very early with the equivalent of a doctorate degree. (The Bolsheviks had abolished the awarding of formal doctorate degrees and only reinstated them in 1935.) Kantorovich was immediately appointed to the academic staff of Leningrad University, an unheard-of honour, and he began to lecture other students, most of them much older than himself. Photographs show him with a very young boyish face, and Kantorovich recalled that his first lectures were difficult: the class refused to believe this young man was old enough to teach them, until he had the chance to demonstrate his unusual mathematical talents. At last he was earning an income: the small academic salary was a relief for the family which had been nearly destitute.

After the Bolshevik Government stabilized, the 1920s were initially a fertile time for research on the new socialist economy. Two key texts available to Kantorovich at the time were the *Balance of the National Economy* by Pavel Popov (1926) and *Towards the Theory of National Income Growth* by Grigory Feldman (1928). But after the death of Lenin in 1924 and the strangling consolidation of power by Stalin, narrow ideological views were imposed by the state, and this restricted independent economic research. The freewheeling academic debate and criticism of government policies enjoyed in the UK by Keynes and by US academics at the time was not to be possible in the new Soviet Union.

Lenin had read and agreed with much of Keynes's *The Economic Consequences of the Peace,* and he had several of Keynes's works translated into Russian. Trotsky had also been positive about some Keynesian economic ideas. But in 1929, midway through the highly disruptive first Five Year Plan, Stalin addressed the need to move from 'bourgeois' to 'red' specialisms, and he directed his criticism specifically to the unlikely subject of mathematics and probability. Now the Soviet view of Keynes and Keynesianism turned negative: Stalin used terms like 'social fascism' to denigrate Western theories. After some years the *General Theory* was eventually translated into Russian, apparently on the direct orders of Stalin, but it had very restricted access and that probably excluded Kantorovich.

In 1930 Kantorovich was invited to attend the prestigious Mathematical Congress in Kharkov, Northern Ukraine. Kharkov was growing into a modern industrial centre, though the region was not stable. Stalin was forcing the kulaks into collective agriculture with a tragic loss of harvests and widespread hunger, and Kharkov was becoming a refuge for villagers fleeing early signs of famine brought on by Stalin's forced agricultural collectivization. Peasants could be seen dying on the streets. Kantorovich had seen some signs of collectivization chaos in Tashkent, but this was far worse—over the next few years it is estimated that four million peasants died in the deliberately-engineered Holodomor Famine. Kharkov was also the site of ongoing Soviet executions of Ukrainian nationalists.

Despite all the disruptions of the time, as many as 500 participants attended the congress, including some outstanding Soviet mathematicians and a dozen eminent foreigners: this was Kantorovich's first real exposure to foreign intellectual ideas. He presented a paper entitled 'On Projective Sets', though later he was embarrassed to realize it was not up to the very high standard of other speakers. Somewhat menacingly, Lazar Kaganovich, Secretary General of the Ukrainian Communist Party and a Stalinist henchman, gave a speech to the congress where he warned about 'ideological inadequacies' in mathematics. Following this lead several Marxist ideologues at the conference began to criticize 'bourgeois reactionary' mathematicians that they sometimes grouped with other miscreants such as Ukrainian nationalists and covert Trotskyites. Kantorovich watched several eminent mathematicians being criticized for their thinking, though luckily for him he was still too junior to attract much attention.

These ideologues were politically well connected and they were to be an enduring problem for Soviet academic thinkers for several decades. Stalin was building a cult of the personality, ruling through show trials, pogroms, executions, and exile. This period of intense suspicion and paranoia was not a fertile environment for new ideas to bloom. Kantorovich was very young, but he learned quickly that fraternizing with foreigners and their theories could be dangerous: it was a risk Kantorovich would have to manage for most of his life.

Later that year Kantorovich was appointed to the Leningrad Naval Engineering School, a famous old military college, though one that, for historical reasons, Stalin distrusted. Kantorovich kept his links with this school, while also being appointed Research Associate in the Research Institute of Mathematics and Mechanics at the University. The following year he also became an Associate Professor in the Department of Numerical Mathematics. Aged only 20 he now simultaneously held three prestigious positions in the top branches of Leningrad academies.

Over the next few years Kantorovich built an academic reputation for doing complex mathematics, in particular solving some protracted puzzles on projective sets (solving data series by projecting them on to other forms). He began publishing mathematics papers, and by the age of 23 his first book was co-authored with colleagues, entitled *Calculus of Variations*. The next All-Union Mathematical Congress was held in Leningrad the following year, and Kantorovich presented not one but two mathematical papers. He was now appointed full Professor.

The following year he was allowed to travel to Moscow, where the Soviets had moved their capital, to take part in the Moscow Topological Congress. In Moscow he met several Western mathematicians, including one whose work would later cross paths with his own, the brilliant Hungarian mathematician John von Neumann, and also his Princeton colleague, the Canadian A. W. Tucker. In discussion with some of these mathematicians, Kantorovich moved his efforts in a new theoretical direction, to the study of functional spaces, dealing with the measurement of variables driven by much more complex series than in linear algebra. Kantorovich later corresponded directly with von Neumann on 'a circle of problems related to partially ordered spaces' (Vershik, 2001, 19). That year Kantorovich achieved a significant mathematical breakthrough with his work on a particular type of series, which are now known as 'K spaces' in his honour. As he gained experience, his interests broadened, and he began to apply his mind to researching real world problems: he could see new opportunities to apply mathematical techniques to economic problems as the country began to industrialize. But his reading of Western economic sources remained very limited.

At this time the Leningrad Mathematical School had attracted some famous participants: mathematician Vladimir Smirnov was teaching the new subject of functional analysis, and Kantorovich together with his Leningrad colleague Sergei Sobolev attended his seminar. One of their texts was the classic 1932 book written by von Neumann, *The Mathematical Foundations of Quantum Mechanics* (in German). In the next few years Kantorovich published several articles in Russian extending von Neumann's analysis to generalized functions which the latter had named Hilbert spaces. But the heavy hand of Stalin hung over the department: Director Kulisher of the Institute of Mathematics and Mechanics was arrested. Then department chair Nikolai Gunther was denounced as a 'reactionary in social life' and forced to resign and repent. The denunciation was signed by several of his colleagues including Kantorovich, which does not reflect well on him. However he subsequently refused to sign further denunciations of colleagues.

The later 1930s were turning very dangerous for academics and policymakers in the Soviet Union. The Moscow Show Trials and widespread purges took place as the Communist Party turned inward on itself, and Stalin consolidated supreme power. Many apparatchiks were executed or condemned to the Siberian gulags. The study of economics in the Soviet Union had become difficult and potentially dangerous. The best-known Soviet economist of the time was Nikolai Kondratiev, a much respected academic who had founded the Institute of Conjuncture in Moscow, which grew into an important institution. There he had published his famous work on the long cycles undergone by capitalist economies, known internationally as Kondratiev Waves. Kondratiev travelled widely abroad, including to the United States, and he also became active in advising the newly-formed Soviet Government on agricultural policy and on Lenin's New Economic Policy promoting market-led industrial strategy initially to be financed through the export of agricultural production. His advice had been welcomed by the Lenin Government. However when Stalin came to power he wanted complete government control of the planned economy, and any alternative views were seen as seditious. Kondratiev had tried to apply mathematical techniques to early drafts of the first Soviet Five-Year Plan, and he advised Stalin that he had concluded that its goals were unrealistic. Stalin angrily rejected the advice and explicitly banned mathematical and technical analysis from early Soviet planning. Kondratiev was summarily sacked in 1928, and arrested shortly afterwards. He was labelled a 'kulak professor', and put on trial. He was eventually sentenced to six years in prison where he struggled to continue his research. Unfortunately Stalin saw him as a continuing threat, and in 1938 he was put on trial once again, found guilty, and executed the same day.

By this time other well-known economists, such as Grigory Feldman who had written the standard Soviet text on economic growth, had been consigned to the gulag. The other internationally recognized Soviet economist of the day, Evgeny Slutsky, had been a colleague of Kondratiev working at the same institute. He took a much more cautious path, confined his work to probability and consumer theory, and remained close-mouthed about his personal views. As a result, he survived the Stalin era. In later years Kantorovich recalled that early Soviet economic research had relied heavily on the demand models of Slutsky and on the growth models of Feldman. He said he later saw similarities in the independent work of Western economists including von Neumann. Faced with the bold Kondratiev approach to public economic advice or the cautious Slutsky approach to academic economic research, Kantorovich took the cautious path and survived.

The country faced massive economic challenges: a poor semi-feudal agricultural state being converted into a modern industrial economy at a fast pace, in the face of a hostile Western world. The ideological guidebook was *Das Kapital*, later described by Wassily Leontief as a 'really rich' economic text (DeBresson, 2004, loc.1930). Production decisions were to be taken through a centralized planning process, based on the untried economic dogma of Marxist-Leninism. This was radically different to Western market allocation systems, and attracted the ire of

Western economists such as Keynes: 'How can I accept a doctrine which sets up as its Bible, above and beyond criticism, an obsolete economic textbook (i.e. Marx's *Das Kapital*) which I know to be not only scientifically erroneous but without interest or application for the modern world?' (Skidelsky, 2000, 258).

Although Stalin was highly suspicious about economists, he was well informed about economic events. He had few trusted economic confidants. There were economic advisors in government, but they were selected for their political beliefs and personal loyalty rather than for their economic insight and technical expertise.

During the 1930s official Soviet annual GDP growth was claimed to average 14 per cent per annum, but modern estimates suggest the real growth rate was far lower, probably only around 3 per cent. Stalin's paranoia increased as he watched the rearmament of Nazi Germany and the vacillations of Britain and France. The Soviet Union had been rearming for some time. But now Stalin realized he had to urgently divert resources to the military build-up. There was a shock in the East in 1938 when the militarist Japanese Government in Manchuria attacked the Soviet military at Lake Khasan, though they were eventually repelled. In China Kung had sought assistance from the Soviets, but now they were shifting their support to the Chinese Communist Party. The traditional Russian foe had been Germany which had been rearming under the fiscal direction of Schacht; however in 1939 the fragile balance of European power was upended when Molotov and Ribbentrop surprisingly signed a German-Soviet Non-Aggression Pact.

1941: Solving Linear Programming

By 1941 the Soviet Union had invaded eastern Poland and had been caught up in the costly Winter War with the Finns. Significant rearmament had taken place, conscription had begun, and the labour force was harshly regulated, but the war had only just started to affect consumption. That was all to change with Operation Barbarossa in mid-1941, which unleashed a brutal and unexpected German attack on the industrial heartlands to the north, the capital to the east, and the agricultural and petroleum resources of the south. At first the Germans carried out their mobile blitzkrieg very successfully, encircling and razing cities as they moved, with terrible losses of Soviet soldiers, civilians, and infrastructure. Early the following year the general advance had slowed, but by then the Germans controlled half of European Russia, and they had encircled the key cities of Leningrad, Moscow, and Stalingrad.

Kantorovich was now 30 years old, a short balding man with a broad face, already losing his hair, usually dressed in an ill-fitting Soviet suit. It had been a memorable year for Kantorovich personally: he met Natalya Ilyina, a medical doctor (like his father and both his brothers), and they were married in 1942. In the next few years they would have a daughter, Irina, and a son, Vsevolod, who they would raise under very difficult conditions.

A local plywood manufacturing trust had earlier approached Leningrad University with a practical production problem. Lathes were used to peel veneer from Russian birch trees, to be manufactured into laminated plywood. There was increasing demand for high-quality plywood in order to build cheap Soviet planes for crop dusting and wartime use, and the trust was under considerable political pressure to produce more efficiently. There were five different plywood specifications to assign to eight different lathes. The trust's laboratory had tried and failed to work out a schedule to maximize efficiency. Could the clever young mathematical professor assist?

Kantorovich put the question to a group of mathematicians in his department. When no one could volunteer an answer he took on the practical challenge himself. Initially it seemed straightforward, but this proved to be no simple matter: to calculate every possible solution to this particular problem with eight machines and five products, Kantorovich estimated it would be necessary to sift through nearly one billion linear equations with 12 variables.

Kantorovich kept pondering the question while he was on summer vacation with his new bride. He soon realized this was a generalizable problem: there could be many other managerial and engineering applications if only he could find a way to solve it. He began by working through a very simple example where a single product has to be milled and lathed by a number of different machines, articulating the objective as maximizing a linear function, subject to a number of constraints which could also be written as linear equations. Assuming linear relationships vastly simplified the calculation. He manually calculated the numbers for this simplified version of the problem. Following this he incrementally generalized the exercise to include many machines and many products. Eventually he managed to devise a general mathematical solution that could maximize the output of the different plywood products in the ratios that were required by customers. This represented the world's first example of a calculation formulated as linear programming—a way to answer a problem expressed as optimizing a mathematical function subject to a set of linear constraints, which is now standard and widely used in economics and engineering.

Recognizing that this technique had applicability far beyond the Soviet plywood industry, Kantorovich considered further practical applications: at first he had wanted to minimize scrap wood. Next he devised a method that would optimize the rotation of agricultural crops in the fields, a way to minimize the wastage of raw materials cut from standard forms, and a cost-minimizing route to transport goods making best use of limited fuel. With such applications spanning agricultural, manufacturing, and service industries, Kantorovich could point to the wide practical applicability of the linear programming technique. In fact many economic problems relate to some form of optimization subject to constraints, and when they can be mathematically approximated in linear form, this can be a very general and powerful optimization technique. In this case, the 1930s Soviet economy was focused on maximizing production from scarce resources, and therefore the technique seemed to be extremely promising.

The professor wrote the results into a paper which was presented to a meeting of the Institute of Mathematics and Mechanics of the Leningrad State University, and it was much praised by mathematicians present who recognized the ingenuity of the solution. Then there was another test: the paper was presented again at a special meeting of industrial workers called by the university to discuss its practical applications, and they also showed great interest.

The paper noted that more complex problems would soon present computational problems and would need simplification. Kantorovich also discussed how to represent the value of components, which he was at pains to explain was different from capitalist market prices. He called these variables 'revolving multipliers' as they mathematically resembled

Lagrange multipliers. In later years as their significance was gradually realized, Soviet economists renamed them 'objectively determined valuations'. T.C. Koopmans was to call them shadow prices. They are also similar to Kuhn-Tucker multipliers in mathematical terms. Under Kantorovich's methodology the revolving multipliers were adjusted until an optimal plan could be reached. He was keen to point out these are not problems that arise in capitalist economies where capitalists make individual investment decisions, driven by their appetite for profit. The Soviet Union was different, for individual enterprises were all subordinated to the overall state plan.

This paper pointed out that in principle it should be possible to apply the technique much more widely than a single industrial problem like plywood cutting. Would it be possible to address it to the whole economy's usage of materials, labour, and equipment, as laid out in the Third Five-Year Plan? The paper proposed that in principle this could achieve significant improvements through better use of labour for tasks, better distribution of work amongst machines, better assignment of orders amongst enterprises, and better use of fuels and war materials.

Kantorovich wrote that these general objectives had been outlined in the resolutions of the Eighteenth Party Congress. 'There it is stated that the most important thing for the fulfilment of the goals of the program for the growth of production in the Third Five-Year Plan period is...the widespread development of work to propagate the most up-to-date technology and scientific organisation of the production...I discovered that a whole range of problems of the most diverse character relating to the scientific organisation of production (questions of the optimum distribution of the work of machines and mechanisms, the minimisation of scrap, the best utilisation of raw materials and local materials, fuel, transportation, and so on) lead to the formulation of a single group of mathematical problems' (Kantorovich, 1960, 367–8).

His brief paper was entitled *Mathematical Methods of Organising and Planning Production*, published in 1939 as a pamphlet by the Leningrad State University. One thousand copies were printed and it was distributed to Peoples' Commissariats and academics in the Soviet Union. The Peoples' Commissariat of Transportation reported back that they had a related problem of minimizing the mileage of wagons in wartime, but there was little other response. Later Kantorovich published a purely mathematical version of the problem in the academic Soviet journal *Doklady AN SSSR*, entitled 'On the Translocation of Masses'. Because of wartime confidentiality it was written in theoretical language, though the background applications involved optimizing rail scheduling and levelling airfield surfaces. It was published in Russian and English, the first source for foreigners to learn about linear programming.

But there were problems ahead. In 1938 the Chairman of the People's Commissars Council, Vyacheslav Molotov, had simply banned any discussion by economists of prices, and soon there was a brutal official response to Kantorovich's 1939 booklet. Colleague Vershik wrote that the government very quickly forbade discussion of Kantorovich's brilliant breakthrough: 'this turn of events threatened to bury the whole research direction, as well as to bury its author, in the most direct sense. Only many years later it became known how serious were the accusations and threats of high scientific and ideological officials. This veto existed for several decades. And it applied not only to economic matters, but even to mathematical aspects of Leonid Vitaliyevich's works' (Vershik, 2001, 2). For this Kantorovich was lucky not to be sent away or worse.

Among his many paranoias, Stalin distrusted economists and particularly mathematical ones. He had said the planned economy of the USSR was 'dizzy with success', and therefore any criticism would be seen as being anti-Soviet. Instead he called for what he labelled 'political economy', which should provide ideological support for party policies. Mathematical economics could be seen as removing the need for ideology and supporting self-regulating market mechanisms, which was a very dangerous direction. It was also dangerous because optimizing technical solutions could threaten the authority of Communist Party and state officials to make judgements. In addition any work that used the term 'prices' was challenging the fundamental Marxist-Leninist dogma where labour was seen as the only true source of value. Kantorovich's *Mathematical Methods of Organising and Planning Production* was full of these potential faults and it was now condemned as 'capitalistic apologetics'.

As Kantorovich later recounted: 'in the spring of 1939 I gave some more reports—at the Polytechnic Institute and the House of Scientists, but several times met with the objection that the work used mathematical methods, and in the West the mathematical school in economics was an anti-Marxist School and mathematics in economics was a means for apologists of capitalism. This forced me when writing a pamphlet to avoid the term "economic" as much as possible and talk about the organisation and planning of production' (Kantorovich, 1975, 3–4).

It seemed safer for Kantorovich to limit his work to practical industrial problems. An ex-student now managing the Egorov Railroad Car Factory was keen to introduce optimal cutting techniques. He turned to the University for advice, and Kantorovich put a team together that recommended linear programming techniques to improve the wasteful metal-cutting procedures at the plant. The recommended new procedures worked well. However the plant had been the largest supplier of scrap iron for steel mills, and the reduced wastage meant there was little scrap available for steel production. (This type of inter-industry problem was one that Leontief was on the way to solving through his intra-industry techniques, but the Soviets had no knowledge of this.) In the highly accusatory Stalin era, Kantorovich was blamed for causing a shortage of material for steel production and summoned to appear at the Leningrad Regional Party Headquarters on charges of 'complicity'. Luckily by now he had some powerful friends in the military. When another arm of the Soviet Government revealed that Kantorovich was deeply engaged in a hush-hush military project (building tanks and working out patterns for laying mines), the charges were quietly dropped.

But the problems were not over: the Egorov plant (itself named after another famous Soviet mathematician) had improved its operations significantly as a result of Kantorovich's advice, achieving something like 94 per cent efficiency performance. Now it ran into another problem of Soviet planning. The Soviet Ministry used a ratchet principle: the plant must add 7 per cent to its efficiency level each year. Kantorovich's Institute had to write to the ministry pointing out that a 101 per cent level of efficiency would never be possible.

In this suspicious wartime period there were no opportunities to connect with international academics, so Kantorovich's major breakthrough remained largely unknown in the West until some years later. The linear programming techniques were to be rediscovered by Dutch economist T. C. Koopmans after the war, when he was working on transportation programming involving moving troops and materials in the US Navy. Koopmans later independently developed a somewhat similar methodology. But most Western economists would remain ignorant of the technique until the work of economist George Dantzig (the son of yet another émigré Russian mathematician), who independently developed a general linear programming method for planning purposes in the US Air Force by the end of the War. Dantzig recalled that in the early war years, as a statistician in the US Air Force's Combat Analysis Branch, he helped prepare detailed plans for urgent aircraft manufacture, trying to optimize hundreds of thousands of products and up to 50,000 special skill requirements. He was assisted in this by yet another émigré economist who had first met Kantorovich in Moscow in 1935, namely John von Neumann, who helped develop duality theory in linear programming. Dantzig's work was part of a major war effort by British and American mathematicians calculating optimal stocking, routing, bombing, and other military routines. This became known as operations research, and its post-war application to business is known as management science. Although not known until later, Kantorovich's linear programming breakthroughs were core to this, and later in Moscow he would help develop a Soviet version of management science.

By the winter of 1942, life in Leningrad had become awful, with starvation, sickness, and constant bombing. As the lake froze over, some women and children were able to be evacuated, and the main destination for these refugees was the historic Russian city of Yaroslavl, 300 km away to the north of Moscow. Fearing that Leningrad would eventually fall to the Germans, a strategic decision was made to also evacuate some key personnel, including certain professors of the Higher Technical School of Military Engineering, for fear that they could be captured and interrogated by the Germans. Professor Kantorovich was named among this group, and he set off on the cold and dangerous journey by truck over the same ice road that he had helped construct. Once across the lake he spent several uncomfortable days on trains that slowly made their way on the damaged rail tracks northward to Yaroslavl, the whole journey vulnerable to the sights of German fighter bombers.

Yaroslavl was even colder than Leningrad. There was less starvation, but food was still very scarce as industry and people were evacuated. It had been an historic city on the Volga, and it remained an important transport hub. Key strategic industrial plants had been relocated there, a location that the Russians had expected to be beyond the range of

German bombers. However if Kantorovich expected a quiet haven to do his work, he was to be disappointed. As the Nazi invaders pushed eastwards, they captured airfields that put Yaroslavl within long-distance bombing range, and the city suffered heavy persistent air attacks during 1942–3 with huge casualties, resulting in an estimated 200,000 Russian deaths. At the outbreak of war the rubber tyre and textile plants had been converted to military needs. The German tactic was to bomb the electrical plants that supplied heavy industry in the city, and also aviation fuel production. For part of the year many roads were impassable due to mud and for that reason bombing the rail lines was also a priority. However at least this city still felt safe from the advancing German armies.

1942: The Best Use of Economic Resources

Prior to World War II the Soviet Union economy had been in poor shape to resist a military invasion, due to the disruptions of the 1920s civil war, the forced collectivization and famines of the 1930s, the purges of military leaders, and industrialization plans that focused only on West Russian economic development. The German invasion was earth-scorching, and by 1942 the Soviets were in retreat, defending desperately, with resources pillaged and factories razed to the ground. The Germans occupied over half of the Soviet Union's cultivated land, and controlled 70 per cent of pig iron, 60 per cent of steel, and 40 per cent of electricity production. Life was very tough, the military had suffered many defeats, supplies and armaments were near exhaustion, the economy running down: there was no assurance that the Soviets could continue to fight.

The Soviet Government responded by ruthlessly diverting their remaining resources to military purposes; by the end of 1942 rifle production had quadrupled, while tanks, artillery, and plane production had increased even more. Directives from Moscow ordered the mass relocation of industry to the safer eastern regions of the Soviet Union, increased compulsory mobilization of people, and requisitioned all factories. There was severe rationing and major restrictions on consumption (pre-1940 levels of household spending were almost halved during the war). In addition, the Soviet Union received assistance from the West: a trickle of military aid at first, then from 1943 motor vehicles, high-grade fuel, communications equipment, industrial machinery, naval vessels, and processed foods. Direct controls resulted in defence spending doubling its share of the government's budget to a massive 60 per cent by 1942. By this time three-quarters of national income and most of the working population were devoted to war.

Economic planning in the Soviet Union since the 1930s had borne some similarity to planning in Nazi Germany, both using fixed prices, military mobilization, economic coercion, forms of market socialism, and consumption being sacrificed to investment and heavy industry. Germany under-priced capital but the Soviet Union made it available to enterprises without any cost. The Soviet Union's five-year plans were more specific, but central planning there was not as coherent as this might have suggested: the economy was more agrarian and primitive, prices were not used or were arbitrarily set to equal costs, and hence offered poor signals, and there was use of terror and show trials to discipline poor managers. There was extreme centralization and vertical decision-making, with decisions being delegated upwards by the managers who actually knew the issues, for decision by their superiors, due to the atmosphere of fear and suspicion. Decisions on the allocation of resources were made by individual members of Stalin's cabinet directly led by the dictator himself.

In the midst of this wartime drama and disruption, an important meeting of top Soviet economists took place in Stalin's office in the Kremlin on 29 January 1941 for an hour and a half. At Stalin's direction the Soviet Union Central Committee had commissioned a textbook on the Soviet political economy. A draft had been sent to Stalin who read and edited it in detail. He was not satisfied with the draft, and he demonstrated this in his inimitable way, by arresting one of the original authors. More drafts would follow.

Attending the 1941 meeting were several Politburo members and half a dozen state economists. Stalin's approach was to encourage the economists present to speak freely, but then to criticize them harshly when he disagreed, which was terrifying for the recipients who were well aware that the consequences could be imprisonment or execution. The record of discussion makes it clear that Stalin wanted to prepare a manual which would be an authoritative guide to the correct thinking and teaching of political economy in the context of Marxist-Leninist theory. It included positions on political economy, markets, value, planning, wages, and other economic concepts, in the light of what had been learned from two decades of Soviet economic experience.

Though more commonly seen as a totalitarian tyrant locked in mortal combat, Stalin was also something of a scholar with a huge library. Despite war, famine, and disruption, he would spend hours reading, annotating, and redrafting. But to him economics was a way of framing an ideology rather than a technique of management. The discussion in his office that day reveals much about his thinking on economics, a subject which he followed closely but also regarded as potentially subversive. He later said he saw the main task of state planning as being to win the battle with world capitalism. On the difficult question of how to allocate with no market pricing he said: 'without the cost of production it would be impossible to do calculations, impossible to carry out distribution according to labour, and impossible to set prices. As yet the law of value has not been overcome. It is not true that we are in control of prices. We want to be, but have not yet achieved this. In order to be in control of prices you need tremendous reserves, an abundance of goods, and only then can we dictate our prices' (Pizano, 2009, 17).

Stalin was deeply and continually immersed in all economic decision-making. He had been very focused on this economics text; after the war he was to take it up again, and there would be several more meetings with economists on the subject. It was not until 1951 that the text was completed and distributed to a number of teachers for guidance. But Stalin was not yet finished with the exercise; towards the end of his life, he took the time to rewrite 50 pages of comments about it. In late 1952 just before his death, these comments were assembled and published as a small book entitled *Economic Problems of Socialism in the USSR*.

Kantorovich had not been directly involved in these discussions, but he was aware of Stalin's approach to economics, and unlike Keynes who was free to disparage Marxist-Leninism, he had to work within this frame. He later said: 'the economic theory of Karl Marx became the methodological background of the new created Soviet economic science and of the new control system. A number of its important and fundamental statements on general economical situations turned out to be applicable immediately to a socialist economy. However a practical use of Marx's ideas needed serious theoretical research. There was no practical economic experience under the new conditions' (Kantorovich, 1975, 3).

He had arrived in Yaroslavl, aware of the intense problems of economic allocation in the wartime Soviet Union. As he saw the political machinations behind the economic policy process he became deeply depressed: he had important insights about how to improve the Soviet economy, but he realized it would be very difficult to continue such work and to persuade policymakers to take it seriously (Gardner, 1990, 640). In such an environment it was no surprise that a researcher like himself would regard mathematics as a safer discipline than economics.

Somehow in the midst of the Nazi dangers, wartime disruption, internal security surveillance, and authoritarian dictatorship, Major Kantorovich continued his teaching and work in his new field of resource allocation. His paper on linear programming had developed an optimization technique for particular production decisions. Now he wanted to achieve something much bigger: to optimize planning decisions for a complete economy. Colleague Aron Katsenelinboigen wrote: 'in 1939–41, he realised that the socialist economy as a whole could be perceived as an optimisation problem. The logic of the Soviet planned economy naturally impelled Kantorovich towards this notion...In investigating (optimisation relations), he was also able to penetrate deeper into the role of prices than had Soviet economists before him' (Katsenelinboigen, 1979, 136; Klein, Daza, and Mead, 2013, 385).

In 1942 despite the hunger, the bombing, the shortages everywhere, even a lack of paper, Kantorovich managed to complete the draft of a short but important book to expand on his new ideas: *The Best Use of Economic Resources*. This work was completed during the desperate attempt to ramp up Soviet war production, but it also foresaw the huge challenge that lay ahead for efficient post-war production in an economy which lacked Western market allocating mechanisms.

Kantorovich proposed a framework where production requirements would be optimally distributed amongst firms in line with the lowest possible production cost. Each factory would be assigned the production of those goods which had the highest net product. In a mathematical appendix, Kantorovich argued the 'objectively determined values' that were necessary to guide the allocation were compatible with the

Marxist labour theory of value, as they would be proportional to the required labour in the original plan. Later he expanded this to a more general approach to planning, distinguishing between short-term planning (with current methods of production) and long-term planning (where there was scope to build new factories, infrastructure, and skills). Solving a short-term plan was a technical task, but outlining the goals of a long-term plan would require political decision-making.

In contrast to Keynes's focus on aggregate demand, Kantorovich's approach, as in his linear programming work, was on supply-side analysis. His *Economic Resources* work aggregated his sector-specific approach in linear programming to identify optimal production. But to achieve best outcomes for the economy as a whole involved knowledge of how the sectors interacted with one another, an approach that became known as input-output analysis.

There had been continual reorganization of Soviet planning bureaucracies during this period, leaving them in a chaotic state. Different agencies had different sectoral responsibilities and conflicting governance. Gosplan, the central planning agency, had been established in 1921 to coordinate the unified state plan, but the organization itself was very political and frequently purged, with technical specialists replaced by Communist Party members. They lacked data for the whole economy, and planning was highly aggregated (with only about 100 commodities) and incomplete. It was later estimated that there were 12 million identifiably different products in the Soviet Union, for which targets were to be set (Nove, 1991, 36). There was no data or comparable time series on costs or investment for which capital was effectively free. The plans prioritized rapid industrialized growth over efficiency, and used material balance planning as their principal tool: major sources of supply and demand would be drawn up in tabular form and a rough balance achieved through iterations. Production might be accounted for in natural units not in roubles.

In his 1942 work Kantorovich recognized significant shortcomings in the Soviet economic performance as a result of underused labour workforces, underused equipment, wastage of raw materials and fuel, rushing projects to meet deadlines, delays in deliveries, unnecessarily holding surplus materials in stock, and long-drawn-out construction jobs. He complained about the inaccurate allocation mechanisms and the mismatch in orders and requirements, blaming these on imperfect planning and accounting. He avoided pointing directly to the obvious governance problems inherent in the socialist system, but nevertheless this was brave stuff, though Kantorovich's intention was incremental improvement within the current system. His hope for the future was for better social-ism assisted by better mathematical tools.

Kantorovich felt that his new work could help the progress of the war economy in practical ways. In 1942 with the support of his old colleague Sergei Sobolev, who had become an influential academician, he pre-sented his text, which had been written in a very accessible style, to Gosplan. the Soviet economic planning agency. He proposed applying linear programming techniques at the level of state planning, afterwards describing this as his most important economic contribution. In a later work ('A Dynamic Model of Optimum Planning') he extended his work for long-run planning, with time-bound shadow prices and time-discounted future variables.

The response to Kantorovich's proposals was very negative. Partly this was due to the general atmosphere of repression and fear propagated by Stalin and worsened by the onslaught of the Nazis. Partly it was for tech-nical reasons—the Marxist planners objected to Kantorovich's develop-ment of what he called 'revolving multipliers', which in the West became known as shadow prices. To Kantorovich they were valuations of scarce resources which allowed production decisions to be decentralized and guided without loss of efficiency. However to the Communist author-ities this was tantamount to allowing market relationships to drive deci-sions, a backdoor to the capitalist economy. The Soviet planning system clearly needed some mechanism to signal consumer needs to producers, but it could not accept a capitalist concept like prices, which presented both technical and ideological problems. The Marxist labour theory of value was a non-negotiable tenant of Soviet planning, and therefore all value must be assumed to originate from its labour input. Yet in the real world production required different combinations of labour and other factors—this inconsistency caused an ongoing fundamental tension between centralized direction and market information.

In his seminars and publications Kantorovich tried to promote his micro-optimization techniques while still claiming they were consistent with the Marxian theory of labour value. But this was a dangerous era where economist ideologues or incompetent planners could accuse an academic like Kantorovich of anti-Marxism in order to cover their own failings. That was how a number of economists of the period had been exiled, imprisoned, or executed. In one seminar Kantorovich was accused of being a follower of Eugen von Bohm-Bawerk, an early Austrian pioneer of utility theory. Having heard this accuzation, Kantorovich had to consult a number of friends to try to find out who Bohm-Bawerk actually was.

Talk of integrating markets and socialist planning to form a kind of market socialism was thought seditious by the ideologues. But to economists the underlying question remained—could a central planner coordinate all of the production and consumption decisions necessary to run a complex economy efficiently? Economists had argued over this for years. At the turn of the century Italian military strategist Enrico Barone turned his attention from artillery targeting to how a planning agency in a collectivist state might calculate prices. His colleague Vilfredo Pareto argued that the conditions for optimizing production could be the same for a centrally-planned and a free market economy. The Austrian economists Ludwig Von Mises and Friedrich Hayek had argued that this was logically and practically impossible. But in 1936 Polish-American economist Oskar Lange showed that it could be done if the economy could be described as a series of simultaneous equations for supply and demand. Stalin was intrigued enough to invite Lange to the Soviet Union during the war. His suggested approach involved using an auction-like process that would demand a huge amount of data, but computers showed this might be practical: as he later wrote: 'let us put the simultaneous equations on an electronic computer and we shall obtain the solution in less than a second' (Lange, 1979, 126).

Kantorovich also ran into particular opposition from the Vice-President of the Academy of Sciences, Konstantin Ostrovitianov, an old Bolshevik political economist who was seen as an authority on Marxist-Leninism. He blocked the publication of Kantorovich's work and supported other critics who attacked Kantorovich, including promoting articles in *Kommunist* that warned that 'false science only becomes science when it takes control of mathematics'.

Kantorovich recalled later that his book had been criticized by another comrade (Boris Yastremskii) who said: 'you are talking here about optima. But do you know who is talking about optima? The fascist (Italian classical economist) Pareto is talking about them.' This was also very damning criticism. Chief of the Department of Prices, Shamai Turetskii, took Kantorovich aside and warned that such arguments could cost him dearly. Kantorovich was probably only protected from the gulags because he was already a famous Soviet mathematician who had been decorated in the war, and because he had been commissioned by the Soviet military to work on urgent wartime problems. Kantorovich was not skilled in political intrigue, being very direct and not tactical at getting support from his colleagues. For the rest of the war he was aware of mounting ideological opposition and political risk; temporarily he terminated his economic work, saying that he felt depressed and might need to give up economics altogether.

His colleagues described Kantorovich as full of contradictions: kind and mild, yet tenacious and forceful. Physically he was short, balding, bespectacled, rotund, and unimpressive in appearance. He enjoyed playing practical jokes. An unusual combination, he was privately introverted and not good at social conversation, yet he could also come across as publicly extroverted. He was poor at articulating his arguments privately, yet students reported him a brilliant lecturer. His colleagues recalled his unusual style in seminars. He would sit in the front row and apparently fall asleep, then at the end would suddenly awaken and ask probing questions, animating the whole seminar room. Colleagues talked with admiration about his ability to listen to an argument, walk to the backboard, wipe out all the equations, and write up a new proof on the spot. His explanation might confound his colleagues, yet the result was inevitably innovative and accurate.

Kantorovich was said by those who knew him well to be a kind, generous, witty man, known to his friends as 'Lenechka'. But, repressed by political dangers, his personality was never easy to define. His colleague Semen Kutateladze noted: 'the contradistinction between the brilliant achievements and the instances of poor adaptation to the practical seamy side of life is listed among the dramatic enigma that is Kantorovich. His life became a fabulous and puzzling humanitarian phenomenon. Kantorovich's introversion, obvious in personal communications, was unexpectedly accompanied by outright public extroversion. The absence of any orator's abilities neighboured his deep logic and special mastery in polemics. His innate freedom and self-sufficiency coexisted with the purposeful and indefatigable endurance that reach the power of an "iron grip" in the case of necessity' (Kutateladze, 2007, 1–2).

Most of Kantorovich's work was done with little communication or knowledge of work under way outside the Soviet Union. He had access to the standard works of Marxian economics, but for much of his career little else. He had met von Neumann and other mathematicians but had not been able to correspond with them for years. A number of Western economists (e.g. the Cambridge colleague of Keynes, Joan Robinson) had travelled extensively to the USSR in the 1930s, seeing it as the brave new way forward. But there is no indication of Kantorovich having any connections with any of them.

Ultimately Kantorovich felt his work could improve the economic life of the Soviet people. He wrote carefully on politically contentious issues and tried to avoid giving ideological offence. As he was rebuffed Kantorovich, who had spent all his life in an atmosphere of economic disruption, military violence, religious persecution, and political repression, knew when to withdraw and stay quiet. His pioneering 1942 book would not be widely distributed until 1959 in the post-Stalin thaw, and even then the authorities insisted on including a preface criticizing Kantorovich for his ideological errors. Cut off by ideology, language, and war, researchers in the West remained ignorant of many Soviet developments. This book was not translated into English until 1965 (with the assistance of T. C. Koopmans), though it has now been re-published in many languages.

Back in 1925 a brief article on the newly compiled *Balance of the Russian Economy* had been published in Germany, and shortly afterwards translated and published in Russian. This work might have provided the framework for Kantorovich to build a full production model of the Soviet economy, but there is no evidence that he knew of it at that stage. The author was another young Petrograd economist called Wassily Leontief.

6

The Peacenik who Helped Bombing Tactics

Wassily Leontief in the USA, 1943–4

That Other Boy from Petrograd

In a complex of offices in old buildings on the corner of 23rd and E streets in Washington DC an investigation was under way, a study of Russian defence expenditure and the economy. Hard at work was a trio of talented economists with Russian connections: the Head of Unit, Abram Bergson, was the son of Russian immigrants, Simon Kuznets was a Russian migrant, and the principal author was a promising young Russian-speaking economist from Harvard University, Wassily Leontief.

The Office of Strategic Services, forerunner of today's Central Intelligence Agency, had been set up by President Roosevelt in 1941 under Colonel William J. Donovan to coordinate US military intelligence. As the war developed, the OSS expanded its operations from collecting intelligence to spying, performing sabotage operations, waging propaganda, and organizing anti-Nazi resistance groups in Europe and anti-Japanese guerrilla groups in Asia. It developed spy gadgets and assassination devices, both conventional and bizarre.

The OSS was initially focused on covert military action. But William Donovan also comprehended the need to recruit experts who could understand foreign languages and customs, and analyse intelligence data. For this reason, in 1942 he set up a Research and Analysis Branch to recruit university-trained personnel to carry out more sophisticated analysis of statistics, economic capacity, and tactics of the enemy. By 1943 the OSS had been farsighted enough to recognize that the US had a huge pool of talent amongst its academic refugee community.

They hired prominent scholars in anthropology, classics, history, geography, politics, psychology, and sociology. In addition they put together an impressive group of economists, both conventional and Marxist. Among these economists was Wassily Leontief.

The Russian Revolution that had turned Kantorovich's childhood upside down also scarred Leontief's life. Named Wassily Wassilyevich Leontief, he always assumed he had been born in Russia in 1906 to peasant stock. This turned out to be incorrect (Bjerkholt, 2016, 11). He had actually been born in Germany a year earlier to a merchant family, facts that he only realized later in life. His grandfather had been a very successful trader who established a factory producing printed cotton fabric. This was a family of 'Old Believers', an early branch of the Orthodox Church. Unusually for the time, his father had studied as a student in Germany at the turn of the century, and he may have been exiled from Czarist Russia for political reasons. During a gap year 1904–5 in Paris he met Zleta Bekker, a well-educated beautiful Jewish art student from Odessa. She became pregnant, and they travelled to London for a hasty marriage away from the family. They then moved back to Munich, where Leontief was born.

In Tokyo Takahashi Korekiyo had been present at the celebrations for the defeat of the Russians by the Japanese Navy in 1905. News of the disaster trickled back to Petrograd and on Bloody Sunday there was an explosion of violence. As citizens heard of the defeat, a group of workers marched on the Winter Palace in St Petersburg and many were shot dead.

It was the start of a very dangerous time in Russia. Several of Zleta's relations had been arrested for political activity in Odessa, and her brother had been shot dead there. To make things even worse there was a cruel Jewish pogrom under way. In exile in Munich, Leontief senior completed his doctorate in labour economics, supervised by famous Italian economist Lujo Brentano (who had lectured both Schacht and Takahashi's colleague Tokuzo Fukuda there several years previously). In 1906 the family returned to St Petersburg, and the Jewish mother converted to Orthodoxy. The family was progressive and politically active, and they were caught up in the waves of unrest shaking Petrograd. The father joined the Socialist Revolutionary Party, and he even encouraged the labour union to strike in his own father's factory.

The family lived in an apartment on Petrovskii Island on the Neva River, together with the extended Leontief family. Leontief remembered playing with bear cubs in the garden and visiting the family's grand old mansion nearby. They also owned a dacha on an estate with forests and lakes in Finland. Occasionally fleeing Russian revolutionaries were offered refuge there.

Leontief had had a similar upbringing to that other St Petersburg Jewish economist Leonid Kantorovich, both of them precocious and clever children raised by liberal parents in a very unsettled environment. Wassily was an only child and he was doted on by his parents. He spoke Russian at home, and was educated by private tutors in French and German which he soon spoke fluently (but his fourth language English was always rather accented). Amongst his earliest memories as a child was the country plunging into mourning for the death of writer and visionary Leo Tolstoy. Similar to the Keynes family, the Leontief family was internationalist in outlook: in his youth young Wassily was taken on many European trips by his parents, travelling through Germany, Austria, and Switzerland to Italy.

Leontief was brought up at the epicentre of the biggest revolution in the world. At school he shared his class with a son of Alexander Kerensky, the leader of the Russian Provisional Government, and also a daughter of Leon Trotsky, the radical Bolshevik. He could recall the murder of charismatic monk Rasputin taking place very near his home. Aged seven, young Wassily heard Russia enter World War I on the side of the Allies, and then he watched it suffer major economic and military setbacks. There was considerable war weariness in the city, now renamed Petrograd: by 1917 hyper-inflation had raised prices to 400 times the level of 1914, there were food shortages, widespread strikes, considerable unrest, and heavy military losses. The Dumas parliament demanded more democratic government, but the Czar rejected this. Petrograd became the focus for many groups of protesters.

In February 1917 Czar Nicholas tried to put down the spreading strikes, remove demonstrators, and disband the Dumas. He was soon forced to abdicate and an unstable Provisional Government took over. This government was more progressive than its predecessors, but still not radical enough for the protesters on the streets.

Leontief remembered the state of near-anarchy: demonstrations and riots as workers and soldiers thronged the squares. The troops disobeyed orders and refused to fire on the protesters. The Provisional Government established worker and soldier soviet councils, and the Socialist Revolutionaries, Bolsheviks, and Mensheviks all battled for leadership. Leontief recalled stray bullets whistling by in the streets, and he heard speeches by Vladimir Lenin, Grigory Zinoviev, and other Russian revolutionary leaders outside the Winter Palace. Social Revolutionary party leader Kerensky became Prime Minister in July 1917, and at the following election Leontief's own father was elected to the assembly. But this administration was short-lived, with the return of Lenin from abroad and the Bolshevik Revolution abruptly ending the prospects for a democratic Russia. In October 1917 workers stormed the Winter Palace and the Socialist Revolutionary Government was deposed by the Bolsheviks.

Following the Bolshevik seizure of power, the family feared political retribution, and they thought it would be safer to go into hiding in the countryside. After some months it appeared that life had settled down in Petrograd, and they returned to their home. But there was a surprise in store: they were confronted by revolutionary sailors acting as Lenin's shock troops. The sailors took over the comfortable Leontief apartment, confiscated all their furniture and clothing, and evicted the family. The family also lost all its business assets and was left in a state of penury. Leontief recalled his youthful hunger (he got three slices of bread a day, and suspected that some of that was from his parents' ration) and there was no wood for heating. But he later said that living through a revolution was a very good lesson, and his parents never once complained about their treatment, optimistically expecting that the new regime would be a more just one.

In World War I Russian forces had suffered nearly two million deaths, and as if this were not enough, returning troops had brought back with them the terrible Spanish influenza epidemic. During the time of the Russian Revolution life became especially difficult: there was little to eat and no way to heat homes. For the next six years, as Leontief grew up, Russia was racked by a bitter civil war. In 1919 the troops of the White Army besieged Petrograd causing food shortages again, but eventually they were beaten back by the Red Army forces organized by Trotsky.

As civil war continued Petrograd lost two-thirds of its pre-war population. The local and national economies were both very fragile at this time. By 1921 agricultural production had dropped by a third and industrial output was at only a fraction of pre-war levels. Severe inflation caused a reversion to a barter economy for many.

Leontief's father held a position as economics professor at Petrograd University teaching foreign trade economic policy (similar to Keynes's economics professor father). By 1921 he felt that Leontief was ready for university, although he was still very young. Like Keynes, Leontief was able to take advantage of his father's position at the top university to gain a place there. But like Kantorovich he then found he needed special permission, because it was thought he was only 15 at the time. Like Schacht he took some time to settle to a subject, starting with philosophy, then moving to sociology, and only picking up on economics when he found there were many practical ideas he wanted to pursue. He studied economics and history with some enlightened Russian professors. Leontief claimed he had systematically read the classical economists of the seventeenth, eighteenth, and nineteenth centuries in Russian, French, German, and English, starting with François Quesnay in the court of Louis XIV, who had constructed the famous *Tableau Economique*, the first such mapping of an economy. Of all these economists he felt Marx was the 'richest'.

Like his parents, Leontief soon also grew politically active, and as a student he was arrested several times after disruptions at the university. He came under the influence of Pitrim Sorokin, a well-known sociology professor. Sorokin had worked for the Kerensky Socialist Revolutionary Government (which despite its name was relatively moderate) and was strongly anti-Communist. With the Bolsheviks coming to power he had been arrested by the Cheka secret police. Fired with student passion, Leontief and other students protested in support of academic freedom, demanding Sorokin's release. Leontief now described himself as 'a socialist of independent views', a description he adhered to through life.

The naïvely enthusiastic young Leontief set out one night to stick propaganda posters around the streets. But the city was full of informers, and Leontief was followed and arrested in the early hours of the morning outside a military establishment, carrying glue and posters that called for freedom of the press, freedom of expression, and freedom of government.

He had been detained before (he said they used to arrest him once a year just to keep him in order), but this time was much more serious. He was imprisoned in the basement of the Cheka (the predecessor of the KGB) and held there for three months. For some of the time he was locked in solitary confinement in a dark cold cell. After being marched to interrogation in the early hours of the morning, his jailers threatened to shoot him. By any standards this was dangerous, but later Leontief downplayed this episode in his life; he reported that he had had many stimulating arguments with his jailors about philosophy and politics. As with Schacht, argument was to become a way of life for Leontief.

When his parents managed to visit him in prison he requested some reading material, and in particular a book on nineteenth-century German economist Johann Robertus who had written about the labour theory of value some time before Karl Marx. To read the book he had to stand balanced on the cell bench to get enough light from the very weak bulb high above. His parents were very scared about the situation, but Leontief—only 16 at the time—was still rather naïve and dismissive about the dangers he faced. He was fortunate in that this was a time of reform amongst the Cheka. Ultimately he was warned and released. He returned to his studies and in 1924 he was able to graduate as 'Learned Economist in the Social Sciences'.

From almost his first year at university, Leontief started to write research papers. In 1923 he translated from the German a study on currency stabilization in Germany by C. A. Schaefer, a work that no doubt Schacht was aware of. Then, like Kantorovich in Tashkent, he had a quite different experience, working as a summer intern at a Soviet astronomical observatory.

In 1925 he wrote a research paper entitled 'Laws in the Social Sciences—the Experience of Abstract Logical Analysis', about causal and normative approaches to the philosophy of science. It was accepted for publication in a top journal, but a censor ruled that it was too controversial with its references to Kant and Hegel, and prohibited its publication. This act of censorship had a deep effect on Leontief, who now realized that if such an innocuous theoretical article was prohibited, it would not be possible for him to work effectively as a scientist in Russia. He made the fateful decision that he must leave the country, and thus he would be able to lead quite a different life as an economist compared with his compatriot Kantorovich who stayed.

The way Leontief left the country was unusual: he discovered he had developed a deformity on his jawbone and it was diagnosed as a malignant sarcoma. An operation followed and ultimately the tumour was found to be benign. However Leontief claimed that he had a fatal prognosis, and acquired a certificate stating he was unfit for Soviet military service. He managed to use this as an excuse to acquire an exit visa. In March 1925, aged 20, he left his homeland and travelled by train to Berlin.

At this time Berlin was the largest industrial city on the Continent. After the post-war unemployment and hyper-inflation, life had settled down under the Weimar Republic and the city had become a cosmopolitan centre of cultural and academic life. Leontief's Leningrad family was now poor and could not send him any money, so Leontief's lifestyle in Berlin was very precarious, subletting a single room and living on potato pancakes and sour milk. For several years he pieced together a scanty income by writing coal and iron market reports for a Russian weekly commercial journal (an experience that exposed him to the world of industry, similar to the commercial journalism of Keynes and Schacht).

Leontief had enrolled for a PhD in economics at the well-regarded University of Berlin. (Schacht had studied there himself many years before, and von Neumann had also spent time there as a student and would return as a summer lecturer several years later.) There Leontief studied under Ladislaus Bortkiewicz, a famous statistical/mathematical economist, and also under Werner Sombart, a prominent Marxist economist/sociologist later to be accused of Nazism. Leontief said they offered a good combination of quantitative skills and original approach. Professor Sombart was a particular admirer of Schacht at that time. Keynes visited Berlin and Leontief attended a lecture that he presented. In 1927 life improved for the Leontief family when Wassily's parents moved to Germany where his father got a job at the Berlin office of the Soviet Ministry of Finance. Leontief now had more funds to enjoy the stimulating Weimar Republic era, attending cheap theatre, concerts, and opera in cosmopolitan Berlin.

In 1928, even before he had finished his doctorate, Professor Sombart recommended Leontief to a post in Kiel at the Institute for the Study of the World Economy specializing in statistical economics and business cycle research, probably the only such centre in the world. Business cycles were a new topic of interest to post-war economists, and the Kiel Institute led the way in their study, viewing the cycles as best explained by interactions between production sectors under conditions of technical change and unbalanced growth. There Leontief was able to grow his skills as a mathematical economist and develop his interest in economic dynamics. He worked on supply and demand analysis based on Alfred Marshall's approach to static partial equilibria, estimating elasticities in markets, dividing shocks into price shifts and structural changes. This work was published as a major statistical paper that helped to establish his name.

Kiel had been a centre of the arms race leading up to World War I, and it was also the site of the German naval mutiny of 1918 that had led to the German surrender. The Institute was sited at the western end of the Baltic Sea opposite Petrograd, and Leontief could look eastwards and reflect on how far he had come. He enjoyed living in Kiel (as had Schacht three decades previously) and was able to pursue similar hobbies: sailing, tennis, and hiking.

His time there was interrupted by an unusual Chinese sojourn. In China the railways had been an important economic and political issue for a long time: most had been built and operated with foreign concessions and they bore the taint of colonialism. The fall of the Qing Dynasty in 1911 had been associated with the Railway Rights Protection Movement that protested against the government allowing foreign banks to take control of railways.

A modern railway system was at the heart of the Kuomintang's vision for modern industrial China, joining up the economy and uniting disparate provinces politically. The chief enthusiast behind these ideas had been Kung's brother-in-law, the first Republican President Dr Sun Yat-sen. He had served as Director of China's National Railroads, appointing Charlie Soong, Kung's father-in-law, as the Treasurer and Kung's wife Ai-ling as Secretary. He had seen the opening-up of the USA through rail (much of it built by Chinese labourers) and envisaged something similar to modernize China. In 1921 Dr Sun had developed a railway plan, and he himself painted a grandiose map with 50,000 km of rail that he proposed should be built; this plan was to guide economic development in the country for the next half century.

After Dr Sun's death, the Nationalist Government had seen the advanced industrial structure of Germany as a development model to follow. By now Sun Yat-sen's son was Railways Minister. The Minister of Industry and Commerce was his uncle H. H. Kung. In 1928 a Chinese delegation travelled to Germany to seek financial and technical assistance. There, by complete chance, the delegation enlisted the help of a young Russian graduate who knew something about how sectors of the economy could fit together: Leontief had been sitting with colleagues in a restaurant near the Kiel Institute when he joined a conversation with a group of Chinese travellers sitting at the next table. They turned out to be from the Nanjing Kuomintang Government led by the Chinese Ambassador to Germany, and they were looking for a foreign expert to help with Chinese development planning.

The conversation turned into a technical discussion, and the discussion resulted in a telegram from the Chinese Government inviting Leontief to visit China for a year to advise on economic issues, particularly on planning a new rail system. Now aged 22, Leontief accepted with alacrity, and was soon travelling by train to Marseille, where he picked up a slow ship and sailed through the Suez Canal via India to Shanghai. It was his first long journey and he enjoyed learning about countries along the way. Arriving in Shanghai he took an apartment at the Burlington House Hotel in the International Quarter of this bustling chaotic city, a city inhabited by Kung and where Takahashi had visited 30 years previously. There he began his work on economic and technical problems with rail routes.

Leontief spoke no Chinese, knew nothing about China, and little about railways. But he was confident that he understood this work was all about connecting up economic sectors and regions. There was no available survey information to work with and the maps were unreliable, so he hired an aircraft to photograph the landscapes, mapping farming zones and urban settlements for his work. His was an economic task to help bring China's fragmented industrial production into a more modern age. But like everything to do with the Chinese economy at the time, it also had a military and geopolitical purpose—to help tie warring regions together, and specifically to help the Kuomintang Government to carry out its pacification of warlords and counter the strengthening Communist forces. Within a decade the invading Japanese Government would also be a beneficiary of Leontief's mapping and planning, as they waged war along the railway tracks.

Schacht, Keynes, and von Neumann had all at varying times hoped to visit China, but Leontief was the only one to actually make the trip.

After his Chinese sojourn, Leontief returned to Kiel to find that the mood in Germany had changed, and changed for the worse. It was 1929: the Weimar Government was increasingly unstable and the Great Depression had begun. Joseph Goebbels was National Socialist Party chief in Berlin, Nazi propaganda was everywhere, and Leontief's own landlord was an active Nazi. With his Jewish mother, his Russian background, and his liberal cosmopolitan outlook, Leontief was starting to feel rather unwelcome. It was time to look to a new world which could offer refuge for him to continue his work.

With the support of Austrian economist Joseph Schumpeter at Harvard and Russian economist Simon Kuznets at the National Bureau of Economic Research, Leontief was offered a National Bureau of Economic Research fellowship in New York to carry out supply and demand studies in markets. He accepted, leaving old Europe and arriving at Ellis Island in September 1931. Simon Kuznets met him at the dock and took him straight to the NBER. He arrived only to find the institution was plunged into a funding crisis caused by the Depression, cutting its staff and budget by two-thirds. He was hired but there were very limited resources available for research.

The NBER focused on measuring time series. Leontief wanted to think more widely about how economic change impacted on economic systems, isolating first-round changes from subsequent ones and tracing the impacts through neighbouring parts of the system. The New York bureau was directed by Wesley Mitchell, an empiricist who was not much interested in theoretical foundations. Leontief was interested in empirical issues, but he also wanted to ground them in good theory. There was still something of the subversive student about him: within months he was arguing with his new American colleagues. He organized an 'underground theoretical seminar' that challenged established NBER ways of operating. There were more arguments and before a year had passed, despite the risk of unemployment in the Depression, Leontief resigned (DeBresson, 2004).

While in New York he met a young piano teacher, Estelle Marks. He was staying at an international student house, and had been living a solo and lonely life, when one day he saw a young woman in the cafeteria. He stared at her until she invited him over to drink chocolate with her. In 1932 they married. Leontief made a journey back to Europe to visit his parents, and found a continent facing totalitarian dictatorship. On his return to the US he took up an offer of a teaching position at Harvard University with the promise of a statistical assistant, for he was now clear that his radical new ideas of mapping the economy would require a considerable amount of data. His new colleagues were at first taken aback by his unusual approach and his combative manner, but were soon won over by his economic insights and what this pioneering work on input-output analysis appeared to offer.

By June 1933 he had written a key paper, 'Economic Changes and General Equilibria', taking a new approach from his earlier price equation work. He submitted it to the *Economic Journal* in London. Very soon he received a letter from Keynes the editor, somewhat cursorily rejecting the paper. (Keynes later told Frisch that it had a well-written introduction but poor mathematics.) This would be the start of an ongoing stand-off with Keynes (Hagemann, 2010, 15). Leontief resubmitted the paper to the *Econometrica* journal and received many comments back from Ragnar Frisch, the argumentative young editor. Typical of his own combative personality Leontief refused to rewrite it.

In 1934 Leontief and his wife embarked on another trip to Paris, Berlin, and Spain, but reported that dictators were everywhere in power and Europe was looking increasingly dangerous. Back in the US in 1935 he commenced teaching a specialist course on price analysis, which was to become the incubator for mathematical economics at Harvard. (At the same time Kantorovich was struggling with an economic paradigm that effectively outlawed price analysis.) Despite his heavily accented English, Leontief would become an active, clear, and engaging lecturer at Harvard, inspiring the best from his students: later several of them would win Nobel prizes in economics. Paul Samuelson (2004) described him as soft-spoken, but interestingly cosmopolitan and a very stimulating lecturer, 'brown-suited, dark, scarred and handsome', retaining his handsome appearance even as an elderly man.

Early in 1936 a daughter was born to Leontief and Estelle, and filled with Russian nostalgia she was named Svetlana. As he settled down Leontief purchased a dacha on Lake Willoughby in Vermont countryside reminiscent of his family's Finnish retreat. Here he enjoyed trout fishing, local history, mushrooming, pastel painting, and wine tasting. Like Keynes he was also a lover of ballet. He began sketching during university meetings, simple yet accomplished pencil portraits of colleagues. He was also fond of sketching animals, landscapes, and of course ballerinas. By 1939 he had been promoted to associate professor at Harvard (with help from Joseph Schumpeter who wrote to Keynes asking for his support), and that meant he now had enough funds to purchase a home in Cambridge.

War had broken out in Europe. His parents were stranded in Berlin, where life looked increasingly dangerous for his Jewish mother. His father was ordered to return to the Soviet Union to answer some trumped-up charges, but Wassily senior knew that suspects did not return from Stalin's courts. Intensely concerned, at last by the end of 1939 Leontief managed to arrange passage for them to New York. The Vermont home was a refuge, where Leontief enjoyed long days by himself fly-fishing, a skill learnt from his father at their Finnish home, and the parents settled nearby.

1943: Reports on the Russian Economy

The last months of 1942 saw the German offensive at its peak, besieging major Russian cities, razing towns rather than occupying them, confiscating or destroying civilian supplies. In early 1943 the brutal siege of Stalingrad marked a turning point when the German Sixth Army was forced to surrender to a Soviet counter-attack. The year brought a series of major Soviet offensives at Kursk, Kharkov, and in the Caucasus, blocking the German push to seize the oilfields, and beginning the long counter-offensive, slowly driving the Germans back westward. Combined Allied forces began the push north through the Italian Peninsula.

Resistance was strong and all these engagements were bloody, showing that the Axis powers still commanded considerable economic resources and had the military ability to use them. In the East the Americans had been bogged down against the Japanese in the Western Pacific, but by mid-1943 the tide was starting to turn there too: US troops landed in the Solomon Islands and began cutting the Japanese supply lines and pushing them northwards.

In November 1943 Roosevelt and Churchill met with H. H. Kung's brother and sister-in-law Chiang Kai-shek and Soong Mai-ling in Cairo to discuss progress in the war in the East. It was agreed they would keep fighting until Japan unconditionally surrendered, then all Chinese territories invaded by Japan including Manchuria and Formosa would be restored to China. Stalin had also been invited to attend but he had refused to leave the Soviet Union, and he did not want to assist the Nationalist Government while he was covertly supplying the Chinese Communist Party.

With these assurances, Chiang was dispatched home to his beleaguered Nationalist capital of Chungking. The two remaining Allied leaders travelled to Teheran in Persia where Stalin had at last agreed to meet them at the Soviet Embassy. For the first time the three key political leaders had come together. They realized that German defeat would require breakthroughs on both Eastern and Western Fronts, but there was considerable suspicion between Western and Soviet Governments about wartime tactics and post-war economic domination. At the conference dinner Stalin proposed executing 50,000 to 100,000 top German officers so the country could never fight again. Roosevelt thought he was joking. Churchill knew he was not, and stormed outraged from the room. When the conference eventually resumed, written agreement was reached about how to halt the German industrial war machine, about the Soviet Union's goals in Eastern Europe, and about the timing of a new front in North-West Europe.

Measured by fatalities, the European war on the Eastern Front was ten times as costly as that in the West, and the forces in the East were much more evenly matched. At this time, it was not only the Russians who were worried about their economy and their potential to beat back the Nazi forces. Their worries were shared by the US Government. If the Soviet economy ruptured, their defences were breached, and the Nazis gained access to the oil production of the south, wheat from the Ukraine, and Russian industrial production, then the future for Europe looked very bleak. If the Soviets could not hold back the Germans, the balance of power in Western Europe might not be sustainable and Japan would not have to worry about defending a second front. If the Soviets did defeat the Germans but the struggle left that country exhausted for decades, then there would be pressure on the Americans to fill that power gap. Either way, the US Government needed to have a much better understanding of both the German and Soviet economies.

There had been some pre-war experience of using economists in official American agencies, especially the Department of Agriculture and the Department of Foreign and Domestic Commerce (where economists had helped develop the US National Accounting system). Now the new Research and Analysis Branch of the OSS was charged with wartime problems brought to it by government agencies, including the Board of Economic Warfare. The Research and Analysis Branch could access all sorts of public, commercial, and intelligence data: during the period of the war they produced over 3,000 reports, many of them on economic topics. While looked down upon as being desk-wallahs (they were known as the 'Chairborne Division'), the Branch soon built up a high reputation for useful intelligence.

In late 1941 an Economics Division was established in the Research and Analysis Branch, headed by another Harvard economics professor, Edward Mason. Mason brought in some top economists, and ultimately there would be five future presidents of the American Economics Association on staff, including Leontief. The economists worked across different geographical regions, with an emphasis on Germany and Japan.

The Far East Division of the Research and Analysis Branch focused on the economic conditions in Japan during the war. On the very day that Japanese bombers were taking off to bomb Pearl Harbor, OSS researchers led by Harvard economist Emile Despres, completed a report entitled *Evidence of Economic Pressure in Japan*. It reported that Japanese imports and exports had both contracted significantly due to US sanctions, and that since the death of Takahashi in 1936, the Japanese public debt had increased five times.

The European theatre was different, but again the supply chains were key. When the Germans first stormed into the Soviet Union, they had captured ten major Soviet rail lines which were the key to transport forces and supplies as their war effort moved eastwards. The US Research and Analysis Branch economists were now tasked to estimate how long it would take to resupply the advancing German army following the defence of Leningrad and Moscow. This involved gathering data on train performance, track capacity, temperatures, rations, clothing, and the weights and volumes of armaments. They concluded that before the invasion Germany had built up a large stock of supplies, but that each additional 200 km of military advance would require a huge 35,000 freight car equivalent of deliveries, which would ultimately limit their progress. This analysis proved correct: indeed the Germans concluded they would need to attack the oilfields of the Caucasus to access fuel directly, rather than freight it in.

Economists in the Research and Analysis Branch had first put together their views in a report entitled *The German Military and Economic Position*. This report reached conclusions that challenged conventional military thinking, but from hindsight turned out to be largely accurate. Prevailing military intelligence was that Germany was on the edge of an acute food shortage. The new report found, to the contrary, that frontline military rations had increased since 1936–7 for the major food groups. Civilians had less access to food, but there was a 50 per cent increase in potato consumption in Germany. Similarly, the authors argued that the supply of oil, armaments, and other strategic materials were not currently an impediment to the German war production effort. The real constraint was a lack of manpower resulting from low birth rates due to World War I and the demands of the military. It had been assumed that the German economy was fully mobilized for war and was at full operating capacity by 1941. In fact the report concluded that this was not the case until 1944, partly a result of German self-belief in early and fast victory. At this stage most of Germany's factories were still running only one shift, and housewives were not being actively encouraged to enter the labour force. (This was all confirmed after the war by the investigations of the US Strategic Bombing Survey headed by Harvard economist J. K. Galbraith.)

The Allies were particularly interested in any analysis that could help them identify and strike at the Axis powers' economies more effectively. Initially this meant understanding Germany's ability to fight in all theatres, pointing to the pressure points in the economy, and later analysing how heavy bombing could best shorten the war (Guglielmo, 2008).

Another branch study on agricultural production and consumption concluded that (unlike in World War I) the British blockade of Germany would not be able to hold provisions down to a starvation level. A further study on industrial production, inventories, and military–civilian requirements showed that basic raw materials such as minerals and oil presented a key bottleneck. Labour sector studies accurately predicted that Germany's critical investment bottleneck would be manpower not materials. Military supply studies estimated German armaments and its vulnerability to bombing. In addition the branch made an estimate of German national income.

The economic capabilities and intentions of the Soviet Union in war and afterwards were also very much on the minds of the Allies. In some ways the Soviet economy was proving harder for its wartime allies to understand than the German economy. This was due to the small amount of published data, language problems, a lack of on the ground intelligence, the restricted role of Soviet economists, and Stalin's paranoia about releasing information. The Soviet economy was different from others in Western Europe: geographically massive, centrally controlled, lumbering. The USSR had been an ally since 1941, but the Allies' relationships were not easy: there was ignorance and distrust on all sides. In particular it was unclear how much damage the Nazis' Operation Barbarossa had imposed on the Soviet economy and how they might recover from it.

With its Harvard-dominated faculty, it was little surprise that the OSS now turned to another professor from Harvard University: between 1943 and 1945 Wassily Leontief put his Cambridge academic career on hold, took a two-year leave of absence. There he was appointed Head of the USSR Division of the Research and Analysis Branch. He was perfectly suited to the role: he had the advantage of speaking Russian and understanding the Cyrillic alphabet, he had worked on the Soviet economy in the past, he was a brilliant mathematical economist, and he had already developed a pioneering approach to sectoral analysis. He commuted to Washington DC during the week, but said that he never felt part of the place; Estelle recalled that this was a very difficult time for them both. Leontief was commissioned by Dean Acheson (Assistant

Secretary of State) and Donald Nelson (Head of the War Production Board) to report on the probable course of the USSR's economic survival during and recovery following the war.

One reason why there was little data on the Soviet economy was that Stalin closely guarded his economic information, distrusted his economists, and disbelieved his Western intelligence. The US had one particular advantage: access to a cadre of first-rate Soviet émigré economists, many of them like Leontief with a Jewish background. They had highly-developed analytical skills, though their view of the Soviet economy was frequently coloured by the difficult personal experiences they and their families had encountered, their distrust of Soviet hegemony, and their distaste for Marxist-Leninist economics. In addition many of the Western estimates of Soviet economic capacity were based on presumptions about the inherent superiority of the free market system over a planned economy and about the superiority of democracy over dictatorship. In reality during the war Russian manpower commitment, Russian military production, and Russian morale all appeared to have remained high.

Initially the US military had many questions: they wanted to establish whether the Soviet Union could continue to withstand the Nazi invasion, whether they would have the resources to counter-attack, how effective military assistance to the Soviets might be, the extent of war damage to the economy, the likely Soviet post-war reparation demands, how fast the USSR might recover after the war, and what its military capacity would be that stage.

US military intelligence had initially been concerned that the German invasion would give the Axis powers access to the huge agricultural and petroleum resources in Russia, Byelorussia, and the Ukraine. The economists of OSS concluded differently: the invasion had imposed heavy economic losses on Russia but the gains to Germany were limited, mainly because the railway system had been so disrupted, and that made it hard to move arms and resources. In addition, because the Soviet system was so highly centralized, it was harder for the invaders to exploit occupied lands, and the Germans found it difficult to extract the surpluses from the occupied Soviet agricultural collectives.

In 1943 Leontief set to work in his Washington office. By September he had produced the first estimate of the size of the Soviet economy. Branch publication number 1004, *Russian National Income and Defence*

Expenditures was a brief ten-page paper. In it Leontief made ingenious use of the wide range of estimates that the OSS had put together on parts of the Soviet economy, constructed a Kuznets Index of industrial production, and fed this into a Cobb-Douglas production function. With this technique he was able to estimate the net output of consumable goods produced by the industrial, agricultural, construction, transportation, and trading sectors together. He had always known that this would be particularly complex for the Soviet Union with its limited market pricing data, with problems estimating the services sector, without reliable inflation data, and having to use an artificial exchange rate. After making several further assumptions, Leontief reached an estimate of the Soviet GNP at 33.8 billion roubles. He considered this might approximately translate to less than 40 per cent of the US economy of the time. He then used the rather basic forecasting techniques of the day to predict Soviet national income in the years following the war.

In November 1943 a conference of Allied foreign ministers met in Moscow to discuss the economic situation: it was clear that German reparations would be a major issue in post-war settlements. The US needed better estimates of Soviet war losses to avoid repeating the mistakes of the 1919 Versailles Settlement so clearly articulated by Keynes. The indefatigable Keynes was once again at work on how to construct a post-war economic settlement, but the US wanted their own estimates. To assist them Leontief completed a more systematic estimate of the Soviet economy using input-output matrices. Though littered with empty cells which it had been impossible to calculate, these tables provided an estimate of the overall wartime losses to the Soviet economy— around $18 billion in fixed capital. This resulted in another Research and Analysis Branch report by Leontief and colleagues, *The Capabilities and Intentions of the USSR in the Post-War Period*, which indicated a more successful wartime planning experience and a stronger Soviet economy than had been believed previously. This report was used in preparation for the upcoming Yalta Conference of the three Allied leaders.

By this time the Soviet Union had regained most of its occupied areas. Industrial output in the eastern regions was strong, though insufficient to offset the scorched-earth losses in the west. National income was significantly below pre-war levels, mainly due to a decline in agricultural production and in household consumption. Leontief concluded that the Soviet Union would have lost about one quarter of its capital stock as a result of the war. He further concluded that German reparations or Allied assistance of $1.5 billion per annum would enable pre-war national income to be reached again within only four years, and that the Russians had sufficient foreign balances to purchase any urgent imports (*Russian Reconstruction and Post-War Foreign Trade Developments*, 1944.) By comparison, post-war calculations by Linz suggested that the replacement costs of all material war losses was approximately eight to ten years' earnings of the post-war labour force. Further foreign contributions (German reparations, foreign aid, and Lend-Lease funds) could potentially compensate for up to half of this loss (Linz, 1984).

Leontief's work challenged the established view of the time that the Soviet economy had been so damaged by war and was so dependent on the West, that it would not be able to pursue an independent economic or foreign policy for some years. By extension it would be subservient to the greater economic power of the US and there should not be a risk of Communist expansionism because they would not be able to afford a Cold War. Leontief's counter-view turned out to be rather more accurate, though such an opinion was not particularly popular in the later war years when there was still popular Western support for 'Uncle Joe' Stalin.

As the balance of war changed Leontief maintained his interest in the Soviet economy. In August 1944 he published a review in the *Review of Economic Statistics* of a book on *Management in Russian Industry*. In his later essay *The Decline and Rise of Soviet Economic Science*, he wrote there was no point trying to discover the principle of Soviet planning because no such principle existed. Leontief argued that the whole basis of Soviet growth had simply been to channel as much income as possible into productive capital investment, while holding back consumption. This centralized Marxist-Leninist approach involved depressing the living standards of the masses, while keeping them all working hard, ironically repressing labour wages while returns to capital remained high. The lack of basic data and computable procedures necessary to balance millions of different goods and services meant this allocation process would be inevitably inefficient. Leontief felt that the economic success of the Soviet Union through the later 1940s was due not to economic sophistication but rather to political determination and control. At this stage he had no way of knowing about the optimization techniques developed by Kantorovich, nor how the Soviets might later use his own work.

1943–4: Input-Output Analysis and Bombing

By the start of 1944, after several years of brutal warfare, the terrible Siege of Leningrad was at last relieved. On the Western Front the Allies were now producing considerable quantities of armaments and their control of the air gave them significant bombing capacity. Yet the German war machine seemed to be capable of ongoing resistance. It was time for the military to review the Allies' offensive strategies. Could economists assist?

Several years previously an interesting report on the US economy had been compiled, one that displayed a new picture of how an economy fits together: it was Leontief's book *The Structure of the American Economy*. He had been working towards this for decades. Some in the military had been dubious about the practical use of economists' work. At last this report provided a map that the military could understand and use.

But this mapping had not originated in the US. In the early years in the Soviet Union, the establishment of the Central Statistical Administration and the Gosplan Planning Agency had brought an innovative approach to measuring economic activity. In 1922 P. I. Popov, the Head Statistician had prepared a preliminary *Soviet National Balance* for Gosplan. Popov's work had been partially inspired by François Quesnay's eighteenth-century *Tableau Economique*, a schema that had been reproduced as a model of the capitalist economy in the second volume of Marx's *Das Kapital*. In 1925 Leontief had published an important early paper 'The Balance of the Economy of the USSR', a review of Popov's report. Leontief pointed out many problems with the work: it was biased to material goods with inadequate measurement of the state sector, the services sector, and subsistence agriculture, with double counting of inputs and outputs, and with various other technical discrepancies. Nevertheless he recognized this report as a pioneering attempt at national accounting, and it sparked a lifelong interest in the Russian economy. Later Kantorovich was to recognize the importance of this first Soviet development which he described as: 'the "chess-table balance analysis" done in the Central Statistical Department, which was later developed mathematically and economically using the data of the US economy by W. Leontiev' (Kantorovich, 1975, 4). Oskar Lange, who later came to know Leontief well at Harvard, claimed that at the time Leontief did some work for Gosplan, though this has not been confirmed.

This early statistical progress in the Soviet Union had ground to a sudden halt in 1929 when Stalin criticized the work as pointless, and the studies were abruptly terminated. In 1932 the official *Materials Balance of the Soviet National Economy 1928 to 1930* was published, but this was merely an accounting record of six sectors of the economy that had no technical coefficients, and by itself did not constitute a model of the economy. Several years later a more detailed *Materials Balance* would be compiled.

By that time Leontief had left the Soviet Union and moved to Berlin to work on his doctorate. There he eagerly embraced the classical German tradition: the accepted general equilibrium approach was the mathematical tradition of Gustav Cassel, published in 1918 in the text-book *Social Economic Theory*. Leontief was able to draw on the work of Cassel and Leon Walras which appeared to offer more exciting alternatives than his Soviet education for the underpinnings to his pioneering input-output approach. Leontief later recalled that his original approach had been neoclassical, but that he soon became dissatisfied with aggregate demand and supply equilibria, and therefore invented a new 'framework for the study of interdependence of individual cells in the economy' (DeBresson, 2004). His university thesis used a simple classical model with two interconnected sectors, constant returns to scale, scarce resources, technical coefficients, and a circular flow of income. A few years later John von Neumann was to draw on the same German foundations in his work on a dynamic equilibrium model, finally published in English in 1945.

Leontief's thesis offered an original way of viewing the economic system. The challenge now was to construct a map and to show how the sectors of an economy fitted together and fed into one another. He had concluded that partial analysis focused on individual markets could not provide an understanding of how a whole economy functioned, and hence he set out to design what we now know as a general equilibrium framework, but one capable of empirical estimation. Unlike Popov's work, the origins were not in Marxist-Leninist economics, but derived from early work on national income accounting. Leontief considered Malthus, Newton, and Darwin, not Marx, as his intellectual forebears, and like many émigré economists was dismissive about Soviet economics: 'so far as the Russian technique of economic planning is concerned, one can apply to it in paraphrase what was said about a talking horse: the remarkable thing about it is not what it says, but that it speaks at all. Western economists have often tried to discover "the principle" of the Soviet technique of planning. They never succeeded, since, up to now, there has been no such thing' (Leontief, 1960, 225).

No one had previously tried to demonstrate just how the economy interacted in this way, and Leontief wanted to do this for the US. He always insisted that the job of the economic theorist should be to propose a well-formulated theory, then to show how to apply it to real economies, making predictions and confirming their accuracy by statistical analysis. He was definite about the need for economists to get their hands dirty, constructing adequate data for real-world analysis.

An advantage of his work in New York and Cambridge, Massachusetts was that he could access the US Census, the best statistical record of an economy anywhere, and with the help of an assistant he began work on sectoral analysis using real data. Obtaining up-to-date data presented an immediate problem. For practical reasons Leontief settled on using the 1919 census data first, then later 1929 as his two base years. Where official figures were not available, he would pick up the telephone and call companies in specific industries to seek data from them directly. His first attempt at a US input-output table was relatively simple with many data shortcomings.

Traditionally economists had viewed an economy as being constructed from inputs of capital, labour, land, and innovation. Leontief now proposed a more sophisticated approach, measuring the production of intermediate goods and services, and showing their allocation among sectors. Firms in agriculture, industry, and services produced goods and services and on-sold them to other industrial sectors as inputs, or sold them to final consumers called households. Adding in the government sector's role in production and intermediate consumption, and also the role of exports and imports, completed the framework.

Through this tableau of inputs and outputs Leontief could illustrate the market interactions in an economy in a way that demonstrated their interaction. He could trace for example the effects of investment on other sectors, the impact of a bottleneck in production, or the change in demand for imports resulting from extra production of a good. The interactions could be complex: the rubber industry produced tyres for the auto industry, while some of the autos produced were bought by the rubber industry. An outside shock such as a tax on oil would have an impact on the auto industry and ultimately on the rubber industry too. Input-output gradually became a tool for business and government alike to understand and predict ripple effects through the economy of changes in demand, supply, or policy.

Robert Dorfman has noted that Leontief was the first to see the possibilities of constructing a numerical model of the whole economy. But he faced three obstacles: firstly he had to develop production functions to avoid the assumptions of perfect substitutability in classical production theory; secondly he had to go beyond national income accounts which lack sectoral coefficients, instead adapting data from the US Census of Manufactures and other sources; thirdly he had to find a new way to calculate the model (Dorfman, 1995, 306).

Input-output computation depended on calculating large inverted matrices: too many variables made estimation impossible. (In those days such calculation was typically carried out by banks of women 'computers' working with electro-mechanical desktop calculators.) Realizing that it was not practical to carry out full calculation for the 40 industries in his 1936 work, he contacted John Wilbur along the road at the Massachusetts Institute of Technology to use his 'simultaneous calculator' (a ton of mechanical moving parts that had already been copied by the Japanese for their own wartime research) to solve a vastly simplified nine linear equation version of his model.

The following year he made use of OSS colleague Simon Kuznets's national accounts estimates for 1929 to build a new input-output model. Leontief's model assumed that each good would take a standard time to produce, that outputs would be used as investment goods or inputs, that each production process could be described by a technical coefficient, and that each industry would operate according to a linear production function. This work became the foundation of modern input-output analysis.

Leontief produced a 44-sector table, with about 2,000 coefficients. The solution of 44 simultaneous equations was clearly going to be quite impossible to calculate, so Leontief then consolidated these equations into the ten largest sectors for computational purposes.

This work was put together in a pioneering book entitled *The Structure of the American Economy 1919–29*, which was published by Harvard University Press just before the US entered the war. Although now recognized as a classic, initially it did not sell well. When Leontief updated the work Harvard University Press refused to publish the second edition saying it was 'obsolete and of little scientific interest'. Oxford University Press bought the rights for one dollar (and ultimately they made money from it).

There is not much evidence that input-output techniques were formally used to plan US war production. It is however ironic that in 1939 the German Imperial Office for Military-Economic Planning (RWP) published *The Outcome of Official Census of Production—German Industry*, based on their 1936 industrial census. This provided the first measure of value-added following Leontief's framework and containing a comprehensive account of input-output data for all branches of German industry. Certain strategic industries such as aircraft production were hidden by aggregation or mislabelled. Surprisingly frank, the forward to the publication noted that the data was for the explicit purpose of planning for war: '...there is no doubt that due to our endowment with natural resources a war economy in Germany will be by and large a planned one by its nature. Thus its preparation essentially has to be based on thorough statistical planning' (Fremdling and Staglin, 2014, 9). It has been demonstrated that this data could have been used by the Allies to produce a relatively complete input-output table for Germany, something Leontief had presumably not known.

The Keynesian revolution had arrived in Cambridge, Massachusetts in the 1930s, borne by students who had heard Keynes teach at Cambridge, England, and who had been impressed by the publication of the *General Theory* in 1936. One of these students was J. K. Galbraith who was in charge of controlling US prices during the war and worked on the Strategic Bombing Survey in Germany at the end. Later Alvin Hansen of Harvard wrote a seminal textbook introducing Keynes's *General Theory* to American economists and policymakers.

Leontief had been quite aware of Keynes's work: he had written one of the first critical reviews of the *General Theory* in 1936, and he wrote several others in subsequent years. But unlike Galbraith, Leontief did not swallow the arguments uncritically. He claimed in an article in the *Quarterly Journal of Economics* that the theory was not more 'general' than classical theory as Keynes had asserted, because there were some key limiting assumptions such as money wages being rigid downwards, and interest rates being insensitive to increases in the money supply. The following year Keynes responded haughtily to Leontief in the same journal: 'I should have thought, however, that there was abundant evidence from experience to contradict this postulant; and that, in any case, it is for those who make a highly special assumption, rather than for one who dispenses with that, to prove a general negative' (Keynes, 1937, 209).

Leontief continued through life to be unimpressed by Keynes's *General Theory*, and said he would never describe himself as a Keynesian. 'I criticised Keynes very early because he was too pragmatic...No doubt he was an extremely intelligent man' (DeBresson, 2004, loc. 1960). When Keynes visited the US he met with several of Leontief's past and current colleagues (including Wesley Mitchell, Joseph Schumpeter, and Alvin Hanson) but apparently not with Leontief, who no doubt heard of the great man's visit. Leontief saw him as more of a politician than an analyst, one who had devised an economic theory primarily in order to fit his economic preconceptions. (Despite this, two of Leontief's doctoral students, Paul Samuelson and Robert Solow, became leading Keynesian economists for which they won Nobel prizes.) For his part Keynes showed little interest in the supply-side models of Leontief and Kantorovich.

One strong Keynes supporter, Frances Perkins, was President Roosevelt's progressive Secretary of Labour. During the New Deal era she had been influential in encouraging the US Administration to adopt some Keynesian ideas. In 1935 she had orchestrated a meeting between Roosevelt and Keynes. Now in April 1941 before the US entered World War II, she wrote to Leontief at Harvard saying the President had asked her to explain what would happen to the US economy after the war, and she had not known how to respond. Donald Davenport who had left Harvard for the Bureau of Labour Statistics had told her that Leontief's pioneering input-output approach might provide some answers. Leontief agreed but pointed out it would be expensive and time-consuming. With Perkins's urging, the US Government agreed to the request to fund a new division of the Bureau of Labour Statistics to work on an input-output map of the US economy, using a congressional grant of $96,500, very large at the time, to fund a study on the effects of demobilization.

The bureau opened an office near Harvard University and Leontief hired a team of engineers and economists to construct a full input-output table activity. It was to be a 95-sector model of the US economy using 1939 data. This would be extremely resource-intensive, but at last Leontief had access to the manpower, the resources, and the up-to-date data to attempt it. But he still needed computational capacity. It was completely unrealistic to solve such a model manually, but he had heard there was a new machine being built by a researcher at Harvard, a massive five-ton electro-mechanical calculating computer which became known as the Harvard Mark One. Leontief arranged to get access to carry out what were probably the first modelling calculations of the type by an economist, carrying out what is now an everyday task, but then involving a laborious pioneering exercise involving punching binary instructions into a fragile paper tape and waiting for calculation, which took 56 hours!

By 1943 one version of the table had been produced, and the final report was completed by Leontief a year later, with unpublished transactions tables. The report began with the question: 'how will the cessation of war purchases of planes, guns, tanks and ships—if not compensated by increased demand for other types of commodities—affect the national level of employment?' (Kohli, 2001). Making further assumptions about reducing spending and increasing consumption allowed the bureau to use the model to forecast post-war employment.

To make the work more accessible, Leontief put together a simplified 11-sector version of the tables in 1944. This appeared later in an enlarged and updated book, *The Structure of the American Economy 1919 to 39*, eventually published in 1951, containing a key chapter on 'Output, Employment, Consumption and Investment' written in 1944. The Bureau of Labour Statistics continued their work on an enlarged 43-sector model in an unpublished study apparently completed in 1946. This later version reconciled the transactions table with the national income accounts by adding an investment column (recording the sectoral output resulting from sectoral investment) and an investment row (representing depreciation charges). The bureau's version delivered estimates of each sector's consumption, investment, government, and trade flows. They found some interesting results. For example, they concluded that instead of closing armaments plants after the war, pent-up civilian demand would likely require more steel capacity.

Later the US Defence Department constructed an even more detailed table which Leontief described as being primarily aimed at war production planning, investing considerably more resources to complete it. Leontief admitted to the considerable ongoing problems of resources, of updating the table, and of incorporating the phenomenon of technological change.

The US Administration had been using the technique to predict employment, but the air force had a more practical interest in input-output analysis: bombing tactics. Could this technique be used to identify weaknesses and where to strike at the German economy? A group of OSS economists known as the Enemy Objectives Unit had been established in London in 1942 by Colonel Richard Hughes, who was the Senior Target Planning Officer for the US Air Force in Europe. He had felt he was too dependent on British Intelligence for bomb target selection, and requested assistance from Washington. The unit's first chief was Chandler Morse, yet another Harvard graduate. In fact of the 15 professionals who served in this unit over the next few years, many, if not most, were Harvard PhDs or Harvard instructors. The London-based unit (first at 40 Berkeley Square, then a Georgian mansion at 68 Brook Street near Claridges) was under the direction of economist Charles Kindleberger.

Initially the unit aimed at a strategy for strategic bombardment that would cripple the capacity of Germans to field a highly mechanized fuel-dependent mobile army. The task was to develop and apply criteria for the selection of one target system against others, one specific target versus others, and if the target was large enough and the bombing approach precise enough, one aiming point versus others.

Earlier in the war the RAF had begun a bombing campaign aimed at Germany and its occupied territories. Initially the campaign was focused on disrupting the Axis war effort by selecting key military and commercial targets. However there were many problems with this approach: it was unclear which targets to prioritize; the RAF was losing too many undefended bombers in the day raids; and the safer night-time raids often completely missed the target altogether. Bombing crew reported hitting targets, but independent estimates of damage in the early days showed the bombing was not having much impact. The British changed their strategy to saturation bombing, an approach led by the reviled Commodore 'Bomber' Harris. His strategy was to over-fly the industrial targets and aim bombs on city centres and civilian housing, especially in older cities where fire storms could be created. He argued that the resulting big civilian losses would make the military machine lose heart (something that never happened). Harris organized saturation bombing such as the massive thousand bomber raids on German cities in late 1943. Two of the worst hit were Leontief's old stamping grounds of Berlin and Kiel.

When the Americans entered the bombing war at the end of the year, they resurrected the idea of precision bombing on industrial targets. This was more practical with their bigger long-distance aircraft that were much better defended, allowing them to fly day-time raids, and also with the development of improved radar and other target-locating technology. The Americans' entry brought with it an argument amongst the Allies about bombing strategy and the possibility of much more selective targeting. 'The philosophy of selective attack was that it was believed preferable to cause a high degree of destruction in a few really essential industries than a small degree of destruction in many industries' (Hays Parks, 1995, 145).

At the 1943 Casablanca Conference, Allied leaders Roosevelt and Churchill had agreed to continue with both approaches: the British would keep on saturation bombing while the Americans would do precision bombing. The conference agreed guidelines for the selection of bomb target categories including the German Navy, the German Air Force, and any other targets considered vital to the economy. Included in these was the transport sector and oil refineries (which later became a substantial factor in the Axis defeat).

Colonel Hughes called for help from the American economists of the Enemy Objectives Unit to advise on industrial targets. They began by identifying a number of equivalent British industrial plants to learn what they could about the practicalities of supplies, location, production, plant layout, and vulnerabilities. By this stage in the war there was considerable intelligence about enemy plant locations available from aerial photography and on-the-ground sources. The economists then analysed specific German industrial plants, trying to establish the most vulnerable points of attack. Altogether they produced several hundred 'aiming point' reports.

The unit focused on principles of target selection where destruction of a minimum number of targets would have the greatest, fastest, and most long-lasting direct effects on the battlefields. A memo written by another Harvard graduate William Salent presented the problem in theoretical terms: target selection should be based on the ability to reach, bomb, and damage the target, in the way that would impair the enemy's war effort most effectively. This came down to three components: degree of impairment to the enemy war effort as a result of physical destruction; degree of physical destruction achieved per cargo of bombs; and extent of losses to own planes and costs of materials.

Salent devised a single equation containing these three elements, and the unit began to objectively identify and rank enemy targets for this purpose. The second component about physical destruction was largely an engineering problem, and the third about bombing risks was an air force operational matter. The economists focused on the first question: maximum impairment to the war effort. Initially this was to be measured by simple metrics such as the assumed extent of plant and equipment damage or the man-hours lost from a raid. But the unit knew there were more complex elements involved, namely how the plant interconnected with the wider economy.

With so many Harvard economists on staff, they were aware of Leontief's input-output work that focused precisely on this question of inter-sectoral linkages. Director of the Unit Charles Kindleberger recalls that they largely had to intuit the idea of input-output analysis (Kindleberger, 1999, 181). He had worked under Harry Dexter White at US Treasury, who in turn was aware of Leontief's research. If they needed advice about the techniques involved, they had Leontief himself in another section of the OSS back in Washington. Leontief himself later recalled 'they also had an input-output table of the German economy because it enabled them to choose targets' (Foley, 1998, 122).

Target selection presented a classic input-output problem—many goods act as both inputs and outputs in the economy, sometimes even for one another. For example, steel was needed to produce coal and vice versa. Some sectors were relatively insulated from impacts on the rest of the economy. Others were the opposite, and if their production could be disrupted, it would have very significant effects through many other industries, causing major bottlenecks. These disrupted sectors were the ones the economists wished to identify and target. If they could put together a rough sectoral mapping of the German economy, then Leontief's work could provide a way to identify the key weak points which could create bottlenecks.

The economists then took the analysis further. They wanted to measure the 'depth' of damage and the 'cushion' to the industry. The 'depth' measured how long damage would take to impact the battlefield. This pointed to finished armaments as targets. The 'cushion' measured how much scope there would be to divert demand or find new substitutes for supply. Shallow damage and shallow cushion presented better targets. These questions instilled a dynamic element into the modelling, and required data on the elasticities of supply and demand, some of which even went beyond the formal Leontief modelling framework.

The Enemy Objectives Unit economists derived their data using military intelligence from pre-war documents, from agents behind the lines, from prisoner of war interrogations, and wherever else they could gain insights. Some of their work was quite innovative, taking advantage of the German habit of systematically recording everything. For example the unit derived considerable information on fatalities from officers' obituaries available in German newspapers, they established petroleum shipments from railway cargo rates published in German papers, they located a number of secret industrial plants from printed German freight schedules, they estimated oil usage from intercepted German communications, and they sourced additional data from pre-war maps, industrial blueprints, books, and trade journals.

Using captured equipment and documents the Economic Warfare Division studied markings on tyres, tanks, trucks, guns, and rockets, markings that might indicate name, location, and date of manufacture, production serial number trademarks, mould type, and other distinguishing data. From this they built up detailed pictures of stocks, usage, location, importance, and substitutability of these items of war. For example information on tyre-making plants in turn could assist Allied forecasts of Axis tank and aircraft production. Military intelligence had estimated German monthly tyre production at around a million units. The economists scotched this estimate, calculating only 186,000 units at this time, which later turned out to be quite accurate. From captured vehicles and their logbooks, they obtained serial numbers and other information that allowed them to identify the relatively small number of tank assemblers, the two producers of tank engines, and the two plants producing tank gearboxes. Such industrial concentration meant down-stream production was vulnerable to bombing, and this information was very useful for tactical assessment. In addition they became skilled at forecasting the production of tanks due for battle readiness in the next few months. In contrast to the concentrated production of tanks, the V1 flying rocket introduced in 1943 was found from its markings to be produced in as many as 50 component manufacturers. This made the V1 a much poorer choice for targeting.

Based on their analyses the unit recommended that Allied forces should particularly target aircraft factories and ball-bearing plants for maximum effectiveness. From hindsight both of these were probably sensible targets, but they both encountered problems. Aircraft factory buildings were damaged extensively, but the equipment in them often proved robust. The small number of key ball-bearing plants meant they were an important tactical target, but the Germans were soon busy designing alternative friction-reduction techniques to reduce their need for ball-bearings.

Some months after the Casablanca Conference the Allies issued the 'Point-Blank Directive' identifying some new high-priority targets to dislocate the German war effort, including fighter aircraft factories and their components. German monthly production of fighter aircraft had increased from 381 in January to 1,050 by July that year. The prospects for a major invasion of the Western Front were threatened by this renewed production. The US Air Force began bombing aircraft production plants in central Germany, and as a result German aircraft factories had to be dispersed, so that by the end of the year monthly production had dropped to 560. In February 1944 the whole of the US Air Force bomber force was dispatched to attack aircraft production across Europe, what was called 'the big week': German fighter production never recovered.

A few months later the D-Day Allied invasion of the Continent was being planned. The Allies plotted their landing locations in secret, forcing the Germans to disperse their defences. The unit's economists were then presented with another problem—how to prevent the Germans rapidly moving reinforcements from other zones to counter the invading force. Their answer was to attack railway marshalling yards where trains were concentrated, and to use more precise bombing techniques on key bridges.

The British wanted the US Air Force to join them in their night-time saturation area bombing raids, but the Enemy Objectives Unit argued that was the wrong approach. A major tactical argument took place between US General Spaatz and RAF Air Marshal Tedder. The US drew up plans to bomb German oil production (which the economists had identified as a way to reduce fighting ability on the ground). Meanwhile Tedder wanted to target Western European marshalling yards, but Spaatz thought they could be too easily repaired. In March 1944 Commander-in-Chief Eisenhower decided to target marshalling yards for a more immediate effect. The US Air Force found another way to win their argument: in a targeting 'error', the US bombed Ploesti in Romania, officially aiming at marshalling yards but deliberately straying and actually hitting oil refineries instead. That proved to have an immediate effect on oil supply, proving the point made by the economists who had identified this as a tactical bottleneck. As if to reinforce the argument, military intelligence soon detected some signs of German panic about limited oil availability. Following that information, American bombers were re-targeted to oil targets in central Germany. In March 1944 German oil production was 98,000 metric tons dropping significantly by the month of September. Soon German activity was limited not by plane availability but by lack of fuel.

Immediately after the German capitulation in 1945 a team of economists and others commenced the US Strategic Survey to assess the effectiveness of Allied bombing tactics. The survey was headed by J. K. Galbraith (a Harvard colleague of Leontief) with other well-known economists such as Nicholas Kaldor (a colleague of Keynes and frequent correspondent of von Neumann). The survey was critical of the impact of bombing, noting that damage to military targets was frequently repaired rapidly, albeit tying up manpower, and that the Allies had not predicted the creative solutions used by the Germans to mitigate damage or shortages.

In July 1944 Leontief was given another quite different assignment: he was asked by US Treasury Secretary Morgenthau to join the US team negotiating the Bretton Woods agreements in New Hampshire. This may have been at the request of Harry Dexter White who would likely have known of Leontief's work, having written his own doctoral thesis on a related subject (the French system of international accounts) at Harvard. At Bretton Woods Leontief was to meet Keynes face to face. He reported him as being very intelligent, very politically connected, but still did not find him as persuasive as some of his fellow Harvard economists. The Bretton Woods Conference was to be one of the most influential gathering of economists ever, with a huge task: to design a new international economic framework to promote post-war stability and peace.

7

'If They Say Bomb at One O'clock...'

John von Neumann in the USA, 1944–5

'Johnny von Neumann and the Rest of Us'

By late 1944 the negotiations at Bretton Woods on new international arrangements for exchange, development and trade were well under way. The United Nations Charter had been signed in San Francisco, and the Potsdam Agreements would define the division of influence amongst the major Allied powers in post-war Europe and Asia. There was much talk about new channels for international cooperation. To pacifists like Albert Einstein and J. Robert Oppenheimer this seemed to offer a newly cooperative world order. To their Princeton colleague John von Neumann, this looked more like a dangerous realignment of world powers, powers that at the Teheran Conference had already been jostling for post-war superiority, powers that would soon be equipped with even deadlier weapons. Von Neumann would be in the middle of this new weapon development and the conundrum it would cause.

In that year the front page of the *New York Times* drew attention to a book about an idea called 'game theory'. It offered a new and scientific way of modelling political and economic conflict and rivalry. Once again John von Neumann had made a pioneering foray into economics, offering a tool that could change great power politics. Who was this portly Princeton professor with the rapier mind and the Hungarian accent? Eugene Wigner, colleague and Nobel physicist, said: 'there are two kinds of people in the world: Johnny von Neumann and the rest of us.'

World War I had pushed the Russian Empire into terminal decline, and Kantorovich and Leontief had lived through the consequences. That war also sparked the end of that other great European empire: Austro-Hungary, with its twin capitals of Vienna and Budapest. Von Neumann had been born in Budapest in 1903, a period of economic and nationalist revival in that city, only a decade before the Austro-Hungarian Empire fell apart. The fin de siècle era encouraged middle-class Catholic and Jewish business and culture, and it spawned many famous scientists, mathematicians, and economists. Johnny von Neumann stood as a genius amongst them.

His father Max was a well-known and well-connected Jewish banker from a northern Hungarian family. His mother, Margit, was from Budapest, part of a large and well-off family. Von Neumann was brought up in a spacious prosperous Pest apartment with a comfortable summer house in the Buda hills, living amongst an extended family of laws and in-laws. Initially he was educated at home: governesses were employed to teach him in German and French, and von Neumann showed a prodigious talent from a very precocious age: at the age of six he could divide eight digit numbers in his head, and as an eight-year-old he was familiar with differential and integral calculus. While still very young he would challenge his father to high-level chess games. He could talk and exchange jokes with his father in classical Greek which he used as a secret code from his siblings. As a child, seeing his mother staring aimlessly at him, he anxiously enquired what problem she was calculating. He seemed to have a uniquely retentive memory: a party trick was to ask a dinner guest to select a column of the Budapest telephone directory which young Johnny would read a few times. He would then be able to answer any questions about names, addresses, or phone numbers occurring on it.

His father purchased a voluminous collection of classical books to establish a library, and the boy read his way through the heavyweight tomes, including the 44 volumes of *Allgemeine Geschichte*, a German universal history, making notes as he went. Decades later he was able to recite whole chapters verbatim. Encouraged by father Max, meal times were an occasion for family seminars: the father would introduce cultural, literary, scientific, investment, or mathematical subjects for family discussion. Over the dinner table Johnny would frequently give the rest of the family, including his younger brothers, a lecture on whatever might have attracted his interest that day, always pondering the underlying science behind his observations—how did reptiles' nervous systems work, was the eye really a camera, his views on business. Max used to bring some of his banking clients home and he would task his young children to listen to them then give their views about appropriate business strategies and financing decisions. His father eventually became an advisor to the Austro-Hungarian Minister of the Economy, and won the right to add the title 'von' to his name.

In 1913 Johnny attended school for the first time aged 10, by now speaking five languages. This school was the Lutheran Gymnasium, one of a remarkable collection of high-quality educational establishments in Budapest at the time. There he received a serious education in Latin and Greek, but also a humanistic syllabus of history, maths and science. Judged by the standards of the day the gymnasia system was experimental and progressive, and there were three such institutions in the city. At approximately the same time, a number of other brilliant young Budapest students of Johnny's age also attended them, including Leo Szilard, a key player in the making of the A-bomb, Eugene Wigner who won the Nobel Prize in physics, famous mathematician Paul Erdos, and Edward Teller one of the leaders of the Manhattan Project. Among other contemporary and later students at the gymnasia also to become famous were economists Nicholas Kaldor, William Fellner, John Harsanyi, and Thomas Balogh. All of these brilliant Hungarians would emigrate.

At school von Neumann seemed to enjoy all his subjects and he was outstanding at them all. He showed an interest in most things, and was never satisfied with a 'truth' unless he could actually prove it. He later said that truth is much too complicated to allow for anything but approximations. He could display other-worldliness when confronted with a difficult problem, mentally removing himself from whatever physical space he was in, and muttering fiercely until he could compute an answer. Colleagues who watched this process said he showed a very rare ability to compute sequentially and logically, in great detail.

Several of von Neumann's schoolmasters were themselves talented mathematicians, and they recognized the boy's unusual talents early, arranging for him to receive special tuition from a number of famous professors. While still at school von Neumann had been accepted by the university's mathematics academics as a worthy colleague. When he was only 17 he wrote and published his first scientific paper in German—it was on a weighty topic: an esoteric investigation into the zeroes of certain minimal polynomials. This was to be the first of a huge publications output in his lifetime, most of it on theoretical mathematical topics that would hardly be comprehensible to a lay person.

As well as displaying these prodigious intellectual powers, von Neumann was quite sociable and he enjoyed his unusual but happy family life. This pleasant and stable family upbringing is remarkable considering the political backdrop at this time. During Johnny's schooldays, Hungary had been on the losing side of a terrible world war, though most of the fighting had taken place at some distance from Budapest. The war broke up the old Austro-Hungarian Empire and led to widespread unrest. Nearly one million people in Hungary died from World War I casualties and the 1918 Spanish influenza epidemic. There were general strikes in 1918, with looting and riots. Unperturbed, 15-year-old von Neumann walked to school through the unrest.

The instability eventually deteriorated into a Communist coup under revolutionary Bela Kun. One of Bela Kun's first acts was to appropriate private property and businesses. Budapest became a dangerous city with political gangs roaming the streets and looking for violence. When gangs of Communist thugs gathered to attack rich bankers in the city, the von Neumann family decided to beat a hasty retreat, travelling late at night by train to a holiday home on the Adriatic (rather as Kantorovich's family had fled to Byelorussia and Leontief's to the Finnish hinterlands to seek safety).

After what von Neumann referred to as 'The 133 Day Red Terror', the revolutionary government was overthrown, and Kun fled to the USSR (where he was later executed). The lesson learned by von Neumann was that Communism is harsh and will not work. In 1920 the family was at first relieved to see a more disciplined right-wing administration come to power under Admiral Horthy. But the von Neumanns soon became distressed when the new dictatorship took brutal vengeance against the Communists, killing 5,000 of them in the period of the 'White Terror'. The harsh new government felt the Kun Administration had been too Jewish-influenced, and Horthy turned out to be very anti-Semitic, imposing quotas on Jews in the education system, an ominous sign for the education-hungry Jewish von Neumann family. Hungary was forced to sign the 1920 Treaty of Trianon; intended as a World War I peace treaty, it confiscated two-thirds of Hungary's territory, and ultimately it caused disruption in Eastern Europe similar to that caused by the Treaty of Versailles in the West.

With all these disruptions, violence, and instability, the Jewish family's banking fortunes were badly disrupted. After he had graduated from school, Johnny's father urged him to focus on a subject where he excelled (which was more or less everything) and where he might find good job prospects. Following his father's advice he decided to study chemical engineering, though this did not interest him for long. Then followed a very peripatetic university education; he enrolled at Budapest University, though he did not see the irksome need to attend lectures. Although straight from school, he also enrolled at the same time to become a candidate for a doctorate degree in mathematics; at almost the same time, he enrolled at Berlin University in an undergraduate programme in chemical engineering. (Two others who similarly could not decide what they wanted to study were Schacht, who had attended Berlin University two decades earlier, and Leontief, who would attend several years later). This unusual combination of basic engineering and very advanced mathematics all being studied at the same time did not seem at all unusual to the young von Neumann.

It soon became clear that von Neumann's real talent was not in practical engineering but in theoretical mathematics, and he spent most of his time in Berlin studying at the feet of senior mathematicians. Within only a year he had a draft of his doctorate thesis with the title (in German) *The Axiomatization of Set Theory*. If his parents had hoped he would escape the political instability and anti-Semitism of Budapest, von Neumann now found that Berlin in the early 1920s was also a hive of unrest and anti-Semitism, starting to suffer from the scars of World War I with post-war hyper-inflation, protests, putsches, and threats of civil war.

In 1923 the 20-year-old von Neumann moved on from Berlin, with a new goal: to attend the famous Swiss Federal Institute of Technology, known as the ETH in Zürich. The entrance test was notoriously difficult—it had been failed by Albert Einstein. Von Neumann passed easily. In von Neumann's first seminar he gained perfect marks in every subject, and he was soon helping the professors to teach. Within a few years he graduated with honours. From time to time he returned to Budapest University where he was now simultaneously doing his advanced PhD in mathematics. This degree was granted in 1926 with the highest honours. He was still only 22 and had the equivalent of three doctorates from top European institutions.

But this was not enough—now von Neumann had a chance to realize his dream of working at the epicentre of theoretical mathematics. This was the University of Göttingen in Saxony, a famous old academy with alumni that had included statesman Otto von Bismarck, mathematician Carl Friedrich Gauss, scientist Alexander von Humboldt, philosopher Arthur Schopenhauer, and poet Heinrich Heine. In the 1920s it was the world centre for research into the exciting new subject of quantum mathematics. Here there were fierce arguments among a brilliant faculty with such famous professors as Norbert Weiner, David Hilbert, Wolfgang Pauli, Max Delbruck, Robert Oppenheimer, Enrico Fermi, and Werner Heisenberg, and with visitors such as Erwin Schrödinger from Switzerland, Niels Bohr from Copenhagen, Kurt Gödel from Vienna, and Paul Dirac from Cambridge. Together these dozen men revolutionized quantum mechanics and launched the nuclear age.

Von Neumann fitted perfectly into this intellectual hothouse. Within a year at Göttingen, he had published a dozen major papers in mathematics, and he continued to produce approximately one per month for the next few years. They were all written in German, and they explored the new boundaries of mathematics and physics in the light of developments in quantum theory. Von Neumann had a brilliant and daring mind, but a low boredom threshold, and was always ready to move on to solve the next problem that might be articulated to him by a colleague or to build a new theory around a chance remark made by a student. Students did not find him an easy lecturer in English because he was speaking in his fourth language, and because his fluid line of thought was hard to follow. Typically he would dash out equations on a small corner of a blackboard, then erase them before his students had time to absorb their full significance.

By 1928 he was back at the University of Berlin, in the same city as Leontief, employed as a privatdozent (a qualified university teacher), the youngest the university had ever elected. But von Neumann was no ivory tower professor—he could clearly see the fragile politics afoot, the risk that Germany would want to avenge the 1918 settlement that had been so criticized by Keynes, and the alienation of German and

Austro-Hungarian lands. He foresaw the rise of Adolf Hitler and totalitarian Germany, but he hoped they could be played off against the totalitarian Soviet Union. He was starting to realize that the Göttingen-type hothouse might not survive these pressures, and began to look to the US to provide the intellectual environment that he needed. He knew his English was inadequate, so he selected a number of books, both novels and encyclopaedias, and read them with enormous concentration. In later years he was able to quote long passages of these books by heart. It has been suggested that he did not have a 'normal' photographic memory but rather an unusual ability to think and remember in any number of dimensions.

In the late 1920s Princeton University in semi-rural New Jersey was aiming to build up its mathematics faculty, and it was looking to Germany and Central Europe for highly talented professors, especially those who were being alienated by the ultra-right-wing populist policies taking root there. Von Neumann was viewed as an exciting young talent, and in 1929 he was invited to take up a lectureship in mathematical physics at Princeton.

Before departing Europe, he returned to Budapest, and proposed marriage to Mariette Kovesi, a childhood family friend he had grown up with. He suggested marriage in his typically clumsy way: 'you and I could have a lot of fun together, for instance you like to drink wine and so do I' (Macrae, 1992, 157). Mariette was six years younger, smart, witty, vivacious, and party-loving. The nominally Jewish Johnny had been non-observant, and he now promised to convert to Catholicism in order to marry her. (He later drifted from Catholicism to agnosticism, though he once wrote to his mother saying that it is more convenient to assume God does exists, because otherwise it is too hard to explain some important phenomena mathematically. At the end of his life he reverted to Catholicism.)

Mariette apparently understood von Neumann's coded proposal and the couple were quickly married in Budapest. Von Neumann then impressed her on a honeymoon trip to Paris by the (for him) simple act of memorizing all the available guidebooks and instructing her in detail on all the exhibits in every museum that they visited.

The newly-wed couple travelled across the Atlantic in the New Year of 1930, and settled into the small town of Princeton in New Jersey, where they rented a well-appointed house and took on servants. Passing through New York, von Neumann paid an unethical driving instructor ten dollars and received a driver's licence without ever sitting a test. He would drive fast and dangerously down the middle of the road often completely absorbed in other matters. It was said that on average he wrecked one automobile per year.

After his first term in Princeton von Neumann returned briefly to the University of Berlin, where he had arranged to share seminars on quantum mechanics for the summer term with Leo Szilard and Erwin Schrödinger. This was an exciting intellectual prospect, but outside the lecture theatres he saw the same threats on the streets as did Leontief: the political outlook in Berlin was darkening.

In 1931 a large bequest to Princeton University resulted in the establishment of the Institute for Advanced Study (IAS) on a new academic model: it offered a small number of world-leading mathematicians and physicists highly-paid professorships with no laboratories, no set routines, no lecturing, and no student obligations. In 1933 the Institute offered von Neumann a professorship. A fortnight later Adolf Hitler was appointed Chancellor of Germany. It was now obvious that there was little future for an ex-Jewish Hungarian in Berlin, and he accepted the offer. It was a timely move: within three months the Nazi Government had dismissed all non-Aryan civil servants including academics in Germany. In protest von Neumann resigned immediately from all his German academic affiliations, and urged other German professors to oppose the changes. On his return to the US von Neumann cut his European links and applied to become a naturalized US citizen.

John von Neumann's personal relationships were distinctive. He was always the brightest person in the room, but unlike Keynes, he was careful never to insult or put others down. He enjoyed conversation, though such was his reputation that it often took the form of listening to a colleague express a logical problem, then responding by racing on ahead with solutions and a way forward. Many mathematicians published important papers based on breakthroughs after they had had informal discussions with him. Most of his conversations took place in male-dominated academic groups, and here he would also display his memory for an inexhaustible supply of sexist jokes; a colleague said he was the only man known who could simultaneously tell *double entendres* in three languages. For the classically minded he could quote Goethe in German, Voltaire in French, and Thucydides in Greek.

His relationship with women could be clumsy. He seems to have been liked by those women who knew him, but on meeting him for the first time, some thought him rather creepy when he would subconsciously stare at their bodies. He always dressed in a formal European way, wearing a neat business suit; at first this was worn defensively to prevent him being mistaken for a student—as a 26-year-old he still had very young features. When he went on outdoor hikes he would persist in wearing his suit. He once rode a mule down the Grand Canyon in a smart three-piece outfit.

Life in small town Princeton was enlivened by the parties that Mariette organized to counter her feeling of isolation from cosmopolitan Europe; they were gay affairs attended by many refugee European scientists who were fleeing the Nazi threat. Von Neumann enjoyed these occasions, and he could be collected and confident, courteous and jovial, though sometimes he would abruptly retire from the party to his study to jot down some equations. Two years after their marriage the couple had a baby girl, Marina, who grew up to become a well-known economist, serving on President Nixon's Council of Economic Advisors. Von Neumann was a besotted father but not much use in practical parenting or housework—he once had to ask his wife how to get a glass of water.

In 1935 the couple travelled to Europe once again. This time they first visited Cambridge in England, where Keynes still reigned as the most famous economics professor. Next von Neumann travelled to Moscow to attend a famous mathematics seminar where he met a talented young Soviet economist called Leonid Kantorovich. The city of Moscow had suffered from Stalin's collectivization, and to von Neumann it seemed obvious that the economy was in chaos, the allocation system not working, and Soviet repression even worse than in Nazi Germany. Having lived through a Communist coup, von Neumann was always to be highly suspicious of Soviet intentions, and continually surprised that some of his left-leaning colleagues saw Marxism as the way forward. In contrast to Kantorovich's more sympathetic assessment, von Neumann agreed with Keynes who had described *Das Kapital* as an obsolete and erroneous text, and disagreed with Leontief who had described it as very rich.

The following year von Neumann was invited to lecture in Paris. His wife travelled directly to Budapest. It was gradually becoming clear to colleagues that the couple were not happy together and were going through a separation period. Von Neumann returned to Princeton alone. Mariette had formed an attachment to another Princeton academic, and the couple divorced, though remaining close through their lives.

John von Neumann would base himself at the Institute for Advanced Studies for the next 22 years, while often also working elsewhere. During that time he produced 75 academic papers, most of them on the cutting edge of theoretical mathematics, as his active brain never rested. However such was his genius that he also made major contributions to theoretical physics, to computing, to artificial intelligence, to philosophy, and of course to economics. Asked later in life about what he considered his greatest achievements, von Neumann did not mention economics, citing quantum mechanics instead. He effectively established the first rigorous mathematical framework for this, showing how the state of the quantum system can be represented by a point in a complex 'Hilbert space' (a theoretical n-dimensional representation in set theory), a variation of Kantorovich's work on the 'K-space'. He would write only two pure economics papers in his career, yet these are amongst the greatest in the discipline.

Princeton was not Göttingen with its vibrant mathematical discussions. The Institute for Advanced Studies had been rather cut off from the business, political, and social currents of the US. But with Einstein and von Neumann present, it was now becoming a mecca for international visitors such as Paul Dirac and Wolfgang Pauli in quantum physics, Kurt Gödel in logic, and Alan Turing in computing. The peaceful campus provided a haven from dictator-torn Europe, inward-looking UK, and Depression-hit USA.

But for von Neumann, Princeton was no refuge from the world. He maintained his up-to-date international outlook and acute political interest. He was developing a deep loathing for Nazism. In 1935 he wrote 'there will be war in Europe in the next decade' (Macrae, 1992, 185). He hoped the conflict would be between Nazi Germany and the Soviet Union whom he disliked equally, but he feared that European Jews might suffer genocidal slaughter during such a war, somewhat like the Armenians in Turkey in World War I. On this he was to prove tragically perceptive.

In 1937 academic Norbert Weiner tried to encourage von Neumann to make a visit to China, writing to one of the Chinese universities on his behalf. The Japanese invasion several months later put an end to that idea. Nothing came of the proposal (as also with Keynes's planned visit), and consequently he never had the enlivening Eastern experience that Leontief enjoyed.

In the summer of 1938 von Neumann travelled one last time to Europe to conferences in Warsaw and Copenhagen, where he enjoyed himself immensely arguing with the lords of quantum theory: Bohr, Heisenberg, and others. It was the last time these intellectual giants would be able to meet together before war engulfed them all. Von Neumann also had another purpose: he was planning to marry again, this time another Hungarian childhood friend called Klari Dan. She was going through a painful divorce in Budapest at the time, but as soon as this was completed they wed. They were to have a long and intense marriage, though it was often an argumentative relationship. She was a Jewish beauty, bright but flirtatious, and increasingly insecure, with constant demands for his attention. He returned with his second bride to the USA in January 1939, just as Europe teetered on the edge of war. Like Keynes and Leontief, von Neumann now worked on his contacts, trying urgently to get his family and in-laws out of war-doomed Europe. His mother and his in-laws eventually managed to escape just as war was declared, arriving in the US at the same time as the Leontief parents.

1944–5: Bombing, Computing, and Modelling

By the second half of 1944 the World War had been raging for years, and the Allied bombing strategy was gradually altering the economic balance of power in Europe. The successful D-Day landings had pushed the Germans back from the English Channel and the triumphant Soviet Army was advancing from the east. The bombing tactics guided by input-output analysis were helping to disrupt the German war economy. But the Japanese fought on, and their military strategy was quite different, not one that would be ended by traditional bombing of industrial centres: it would take the biggest bomb in history.

That was something that von Neumann was pondering as he sat in the bunker at Los Alamos testing station. When the European war had broken out von Neumann had lobbied the US Government, advising them to join the war: he saw this as necessary to defend the critical principles of civilization. President Roosevelt might have agreed but Congress did not, and the US was to stay neutral for another two years until the Pearl Harbor attacks legitimized US intervention. Like many other Central European émigrés, von Neumann was triumphant at the news of the US joining the war.

Even before the war von Neumann had been considering what role he might play in this struggle. He recognized his talents were in mathematics, and he understood that this discipline would play an important role in modern warfare. Rather naïvely he thought he might best play a part in the conflict by joining the US Army, as that would help him get access to the military data he needed for his calculations. Though a somewhat unlikely applicant, he sat the US Army Officer's examinations, and by the simple method of memorizing all relevant army manuals he gained 100 per cent in most of the tests.

Back in Princeton after his last European trip, he completed his final army exam with yet another 100 per cent mark, only to be turned down for a commission because he had now reached the age of 35. Unperturbed he continued his mathematical research, which was starting to take on a military focus. He wrote a paper on 'Estimating Probable Error from Successive Differences', or in lay terms, 'where to aim bombs if you have already missed the target several times'. He was now becoming an expert on the mathematics of bombing patterns.

He may have been ineligible to join the US Army, but very soon von Neumann was being extensively used as a consultant by the US Military. A long-standing application of mathematics in warfare had been producing accurate firing tables for the military. This quest lay behind very early computation devices such as Charles Babbage's calculating engines. Increasingly bigger more complex artillery had made the mathematics more complex. In World War I the armed forces had to calibrate ground firing from moving tanks, naval firing from rough seas, and firing at altitude from unstable planes. More complicated still was the modelling of shockwaves from an explosion, understanding how the resulting turbulence around a projectile or aerofoil would affect ballistic trajectories. These problems required complex mathematical calculation.

A little over an hour south of Princeton was the US Government's Aberdeen Proving Ground, where test firing was carried out, and von Neumann was asked to help the mathematical research under way there. To his delight he found the work intellectually challenging, and his special talents were soon recognized: he was invited to become a member of the Government's Advisory Board on Ballistics Research, a board which boasted a list of top academics. Several times a year they would run conferences on such military applications as the mathematics and physics of shockwaves, fragmentation, demolition, wind tunnel experiments, and air pressure. This work exposed von Neumann to a range of firing and bombing applications, and he became the acknowledged expert at calculating the impact of complex explosions. Soon he was also co-opted onto the National Defence Research Council to work on the design elements in explosive charges used to concentrate the effect of detonations. One practical result from this research was the anti-tank bazooka. The US war departments' organization of research stands out as particularly effective compared with other countries in wartime.

Von Neumann soon became so valued that US generals and admirals were competing for his time and attention. (He said he preferred the latter because they would drink more at lunchtime.) Soon he was also working for the Navy's Bureau of Ordinance, researching the pioneering field of operations research with applications for mines warfare.

News of von Neumann's talents spread across the Atlantic where his special expertise was soon requested. In the first half of 1943 he was sent to assist the US Government's explosives work in Britain. In preparation he packed and repacked his bags several times; in order to find space for some bulky volumes of the *Oxford History of England* series, he decided to leave out his navy-issue steel helmet because there was no room left. Having done his own estimates on mathematical risk probabilities, he took out a life insurance policy for himself valuing his worth at $20,000 (approximately $300,000 in current prices). He was temporarily assigned a high military rank for the trip so that, if he was captured by the Germans, under the Geneva Convention he should not be subject to interrogation.

In Britain the navy wanted him to work on the mathematics behind the sophisticated German mine-laying patterns which were using complex delayed explosive devices. Von Neumann soon identified the specific algorithm that the methodical Germans were using to plant mines along the convoy sea routes, and he devised a formula to best counter them. Then followed collaboration with many of Britain's wartime boffins, particularly on how to magnify the effect of explosions, using information from wind tunnel experiments and photographic records to monitor explosive outcomes.

While in Britain von Neumann visited the Nautical Almanac Office in Bath. The *Nautical Almanac* was an official publication which pinpointed the position of the sun, moon, and stars for each hour during the year, and was used by navigators for celestial navigation. The office was producing sophisticated maps to assist transatlantic Allied shipping to locate their precise position in order to avoid U-boat blockades or to seek help if attacked. The almanac was produced on an ingeniously modified National Cash Register calculating machine. On his train trip back to London von Neumann wrote a mathematical programme to help the machine work better. This was a very early application of computer programming.

The next part of his work proved complex: he joined the massive effort that was already under way to make the Allied bombing raids over Germany more effective. British night bombing raids were extremely risky (at one stage losing up to 20 per cent of planes each mission) and were bombing very inaccurately with little location guidance and poor monitoring of results. At this time American bomb target selection was being guided by the concepts of input-output analysis, and Leontief was working for the wartime intelligence agency OSS in Washington on the Soviet economy. One of his colleagues there was Nicholas Vonneumann who had become the OSS expert on Hungary. Despite the different spelling, Nicholas was actually Johnny von Neumann's younger brother (not to be confused with the German émigré Franz Neumann who apparently worked with Leontief on Soviet economic issues at the OSS, and was later suspected of being a Soviet spy).

Leontief's approach had been used to target bottlenecks in the economy. Von Neumann was now working to make bombing explosions more destructive. An insight into how his mind operated came from famous scientist Jacob Bronowski who was working with him to interpret photographs of bomb explosions. One day von Neumann said to him: 'Oh no, no, you are not seeing it. Your kind of visualizing mind is not right for seeing this. Think of it abstractly. What is happening is that the first differential coefficient vanishes identically, and that is why what becomes visible is the trace of the second differential coefficient.' Bronowski knew when he was out-classed (Macrae, 1992, 211).

Von Neumann himself was keen to keep working on European conventional bomb targeting, but the US Government now had bigger things in mind for him. At their direction he returned to Princeton in September 1943. In the early 1940s US scientists had been working on the possibility of a completely new and deadly form of explosion. In 1941 President Roosevelt had authorized the world's most expensive scientific project ever: a $2 billion spending decision made under executive order, a month before the US even joined the war. This was the Manhattan Project to devise an atomic bomb, and soon von Neumann was asked to join.

The Manhattan Project was jointly run by its Military Director, General Lesley Groves, and its Scientific Director, J. Robert Oppenheimer. Both were unusual men, very talented though with quite different personalities. They collaborated to run their huge project with its hard-to-manage cast of top theoretical academics, and its awe-inspiring objective of causing more destruction on earth through atomic fission than ever before. The project was centred at a large but secret establishment built in the high New Mexico desert outside Los Alamos. The scientists there were a unique mix of brilliant minds from Europe and the US, most of them somewhat left-wing in their politics. It may have been the greatest collection of scientific talent ever collected for one of the most momentous events in history.

When von Neumann was appointed to the project in September 1943, despite the remoteness and rigour of life in the army barracks, he found this mix of minds and tasks the most exhilarating of his life. Initially the research was dominated by physicists (including many ex-Hungarian ones) rather than mathematicians. There was much intellectual debate and difference of opinion at Los Alamos. Von Neumann seemed to be able to get on well with the directors of the project and also the scientists. This was despite his being decidedly more right-wing in his political views that most of the latter.

As well as the mathematical research, von Neumann also participated in the social life at Los Alamos. Occasionally he would join the Sunday outdoor hikes, albeit reluctantly and usually wearing his business suit. He played a lot of poker: despite having done pioneering work on gaming strategies, von Neumann usually lost his hands, apparently because at the same time as playing, he was continually turning over other problems in his mind, and his was a very complex mind. His second wife Klari said of him: 'the strange contradictory and controversial person; childish and good-humoured, sophisticated and savage, brilliantly clever yet with a very limited, almost primitive lack of ability to handle his emotions—an enigma of nature that will have to remain unresolved.' His daughter remembered his cheerful bonhomie on the surface but that he could be deeply cynical and pessimistic underneath (Whitman, 2012, loc. 778).

At the time he joined the development team, the common view amongst Los Alamos scientists was that there was no alternative but to race the Nazis to build a working A-bomb, even though some saw this as a fundamentally sinful task. After the war some of his colleagues planned to make amends by offering to open-source the technologies. Von Neumann disagreed with this view: in his opinion there was nothing sinful about defeating militaristic totalitarian regimes, and furthermore he felt that this war would not finish with the German defeat. He foresaw that this A-bomb would only be the first of a new generation of super weapons, and Hitler would only be the first of a new generation of evil dictators to defeat. Von Neumann was already clear in his own mind that with the German economy on its knees and the country nearing surrender, first Japan and later Russia would be the next big enemies to defeat.

Two main approaches were taken to A-bomb design at Los Alamos. One used a mass of uranium-235 to be exploded by another piece of U-235 being fired into a cavity. This technique looked likely to be practically possible, but it was taking a very long time to refine enough U-235 from raw uranium. The second technique was to use plutonium which could be produced chemically far more easily. But the existing explosive device would not work with plutonium, and a new implosion method had to be devised. A group of scientists including von Neumann was assigned to this problem, and they argued intensively about different possibilities. Eventually von Neumann was able to design an implosion lens which would solve the problem.

In addition to the problems of detonation, von Neumann was also absorbed in researching the optimal height to drop such bombs, modelling how this impacted on bomb design and on the explosive effects on the target, and even how to minimize the possibility of the bomber plane being destroyed. He calculated all this with mathematical precision using confidence intervals and other measures of probability.

Unfortunately also on the team was the German Klaus Fuchs who was systematically spying on von Neumann, and passing on some of his experimental results to the Soviets. Klaus Fuchs was a German Communist (who had attended the University of Kiel at approximately the same time as both Leontief and von Neumann). Von Neumann and Fuchs even filed a patent application together for the design of a fusion bomb in 1946. Ironically, neither the US nor the Soviets made much use of this information, which could have advanced the H-bomb design by several years. It seems likely that Kantorovich may have worked with some of Fuchs's leaked data. But luckily for the US, Stalin distrusted much of the intelligence he received and the Soviets did not even translate all of it.

In 1933 when von Neumann had first become interested in turbulence in hydrodynamics, it had soon become clear to him that the mathematics of modelling was intensely complicated and that there would need to be a lot more number-crunching than the 1930s desk calculating machines were capable of doing. This computational problem had reoccurred frequently as von Neumann pursued his practical military research, and now it came to a head with the calculations involved in the Manhattan Project. Von Neumann had arrived at Los Alamos at a time when the physicists were hitting blockages and there was an urgent need to integrate mathematical techniques into their research. This team pioneered mathematical modelling techniques to simulate bomb design outcomes. With enough computational ability, physical experiments could be modelled through mathematical equations with likely outcomes calculated.

The mathematics behind the detonation lens designs for the A-bombs was intensely complex. Initially many of the simulations were done on the basis of rough mental estimates to give orders of magnitude, an exercise at which von Neumann was lightning-fast. He gained a reputation at Los Alamos for being able to solve anything mathematical. Formal calculations were carried out on desktop calculators. But the research team was running into calculation problems far beyond their capabilities. In June 1944 the project installed some IBM punch card sorting machines at Los Alamos. Von Neumann was impressed by these, and started to apply his mind to how they might be made more efficient by converting them to heavy-duty routine calculation. Little did he know that Kantorovich was doing something similar in the Soviet Union.

Modern electronic computing still lay ahead. Its origins are complex but the underlying theory would be based on the pioneering breakthroughs in quantum mechanics in the 1920s by the Göttingen University mathematicians. Von Neumann had worked with many of these men who were ushering in the electronic age.

The biggest practical advance in computing so far had come elsewhere in World War II, with the desperate efforts by the Allies to break sophisticated enemy-encrypted communications codes. Most important was the work of Bletchley Park in Britain in decrypting the German Enigma machine and other codes. Such machines could change their settings several times daily and could generate about one trillion combinations, defying any normal calculation. A brilliant team of British mathematicians led by Cambridge's Alan Turing had succeeded by 1943 in linking hundreds of vacuum tubes (the Colossus machines) into which a paper tape could feed thousands of characters a second, until something resembling a German text appeared.

When von Neumann had been working in wartime Britain he had written that he had developed 'an obscene interest' in computing. We do not know if he managed to hear of the highly-guarded Bletchley activity, but it is possible, given that Turing had been his research assistant in pre-war Princeton, and Max Newman, who was a friend from his 1937–8 Princeton days, was now heading research at Bletchley Park.

On his return to the US, von Neumann asked what computing devices might be available for the Los Alamos work. He was told they could use the huge electro-mechanical Harvard Mark One computer in Cambridge, Massachusetts, that had been used by Leontief to solve his giant input-output model of the US economy, and also the Bell Laboratory's electrical computer in New Jersey. In early 1944 von

Neumann tried out both these machines and found them to be of little use. The Harvard machine took five whole weeks to complete the first half of his calculations. The other existing option was the Vannevar Bush differential analysers at the University of Pennsylvania, which each weighed a ton, included 150 motors and complicated machinery based on photoelectric cells. These machines have been described as being like giant mechanical slide rules.

But there was to be a major advance ahead. During the late summer of 1943 von Neumann was waiting for a train on the platform at the Aberdeen station in Pennsylvania, when he was approached by a young mathematician named Lieutenant Goldstine who was working on a new development at the Moore School at the University of Pennsylvania. Goldstine recalled: 'when it became clear to von Neumann that I was concerned with the development of an electronic computer capable of 333 calculations per second, the whole atmosphere of our conversation changed from one of relaxed good humour to one more like the oral examination for the doctor's degree in mathematics' (Macrae, 1992, 281).

Goldstine was talking about the ENIAC (Electronic Numerical Integrator and Computer) machine partly funded by the US Army Ordnance Department, but apparently still unknown to the Los Alamos military staff. It had been developed over the previous year by engineer J. Prosper Eckert and mathematician John William Mauchly. In August 1944 von Neumann visited the laboratory in Philadelphia. He saw a monster machine 100 foot long and 10 foot high, with 17,000 vacuum tubes, 70,000 resistors, 10,000 capacitators and 6,000 switches. Von Neumann was very impressed, but characteristically his mind immediately jumped far ahead to how to improve its logical design.

He pondered how the ENIAC might assist with the calculations of aerodynamic blast. It became clear that it would take a long time to reset the programs with all the data that had to be fed each time into the computer's accumulator. Calculation would be much faster than on the Harvard Mark One, but the set-up would take far longer. They needed some way of storing programs. Events moved fast, and von Neumann was bursting with new ideas about how to do this better. The Aberdeen Ballistics Research Laboratory agreed to look at his suggestions in late August 1944. By the start of 1945 he was asked to report on his practical improvements. In March 1945 he issued *First Draft of a Report on the EDVAC* (Electronic Discrete Variable Automatic Computer). This was a 101-page report written by hand while commuting long-distance by train to Los Alamos, mailing the notes back to the Moore School in Philadelphia as they were written.

This report on EDVAC changed the future of world computing. Von Neumann had been musing for some time about how the human brain worked, and how a machine might operate more like a brain. Now his report explained how to think of a modern computer: it should have three essential components—a central processing unit to do the central arithmetic calculations, a central control part to provide proper sequencing of operations, and a memory for data and instructions. The data could be fed in via teletype tape, magnetic wire, steel tape, or punched cards. He wrote: 'the three specific parts...correspond to the association of neurons in the human nervous system' (Von Neumann, 1945b).

This study pointed to a new form of architecture: a computer with a simple fixed structure that could be programmed to execute any kind of computation without the need for the rewiring of circuitry. Known as the stored program technique, this would become the foundation for future generations of high-speed digital computers. The program sequence could be interrupted and reinitiated at any point, following instruction programs that would be stored in the memory unit with the data. This allowed for subroutines that did not have to be reprogrammed, but could be kept intact to be read into the memory as required: much of any given program could be assembled from a subroutine library. These techniques would soon become standard practice.

The report detailed the design of a 'very high speed automatic digital computing system'. Unlike the decimal ENIAC, numbers were represented in binary notation. The computing architecture was to be kept as simple as possible by avoiding overlapping operations. This advanced programming system to instruct the machine also changed the role of computer programmers—and von Neumann's wife Klari (who had been working on statistics at Princeton) became one of the world's first modern programmers. Coached by von Neumann in assembly language, she took on programming work for the US Military.

An unusual decision was made: the Moore School typed up the EDVAC report for the US Army (which was still at war), and on 30 June

1945 published it as a monograph. This very open approach was taken in the afterglow of the suicide of Adolf Hitler and the surrender of the Axis powers in Europe. The report was released the same week that the UN Charter was signed in San Francisco, which for some optimists presaged a new peaceful world government. Copies of the report circulated widely internationally. With the considerable technical detail contained in it, in principle anyone could now build the EDVAC. This may be seen as being in today's open-source computing tradition. It resulted in many researchers around the world attempting to build their own machines, and various incremental improvements being suggested. The physical machine was eventually constructed by the Moore School several years later. But before that Cambridge University engineers had produced their own version based on the draft report, which they named the EDSAC.

Not everyone welcomed the open publication of the report. At the time of publication, calculations were still under way at Los Alamos on the highly secret A-bomb tests. In addition, the ENIAC pioneers Eckert and Mauchly took exception to von Neumann's report, claiming that it contained confidential intellectual property from their own work, and that it effectively put their own ENIAC machine, which they had been trying to patent and commercialize, into the public arena. Von Neumann himself had no commercial interests in his work, and seems not to have been much interested in its commercial implications.

At about the same time as the computing report in 1945, von Neumann published a revolutionary paper in a top American economics journal. He had just changed the future of computing; this new paper would change the future of dynamic economic modelling. He was a mathematician that few economists had heard of, but this did not hold him back from making a foray into a different field. His mathematical research had given him some sophisticated tools and his work on the mathematics of explosions had given him some new insights. When a bomb hit a target, shockwaves radiated out through the whole system: could there be an analogy in a dynamic economic system?

Back in 1928 on a summer holiday in Budapest, von Neumann had met another brilliant Budapest economist named Nicholas Kaldor. Kaldor was somewhat like von Neumann: sparkling, clever, strong-minded, and divisive, though his left-wing ideas contrasted with von Neumann's right-wing views. Despite their differences the two became close. After his death Kaldor said of his friend: 'he was unquestionably the nearest thing to a genius I have ever encountered.' Von Neumann was interested in economics just as he was interested in many analytical subjects and he had a number of economic discussions with Kaldor. He asked him for advice for reading about the mathematical framework behind modern economics. Kaldor would go on to be a colleague, a supporter, and ultimately a critic of Keynes. He was aware of the role of Hjalmar Schacht, whom he quoted approvingly in the House of Lords, and also claimed to be knowledgeable about Kantorovich's work (Pizano, 2009, loc. 1240).

Kaldor recommended the economic novice von Neumann study a foundation book on mathematical economics written by Leon Walras. Walras had built on classical economics and the concept of marginal utility to derive supply and demand conditions for inputs and outputs in an economy (an intellectual forebear of Leontief's work). With this framework, in principle one should be able to write equations to explain how an economy worked. Von Neumann appears to have read this book at his usual high speed. He reported back to Kaldor that there were several problems with Walras's exposition: in particular, there was no accommodation of problems of social cost from individual actions that were assumed to be optimal. Also Walras's equations made unrealistic assumptions about market clearing. More fundamentally, von Neumann felt it would be more realistic to redesign the whole system so that it maximized welfare subject to constraints (in effect a variation of Kantorovich's linear programming approach), rather than using a simultaneous system of equations.

Around this time in Berlin, von Neumann attended an economic seminar by Jewish Ukrainian economist Jacob Marschak (who in 1928 was at the Kiel Institute, where Leontief was working). Kenneth Arrow reported from another participant at the seminar: 'von Neumann got very excited when Marschak put production functions on the board and jumped up, waving his finger at the blackboard, saying (approximate): "but surely you want inequalities, not equations there?" Jascha (Marschak) said that it became difficult to carry the seminar to its conclusion because von Neumann was on his feet, wandering around the table, et cetera, while making rapid and audible progress on the linear programming theory of production' (Macrae, 1992, 252).

In 1932 back in the US, von Neumann had given an unscripted half-hour lecture to a Princeton mathematics seminar with the unpromising title 'On Certain Equations of Economics and a Generalization of Brouwer's Fixed Point Theorem'. The talk was recalled by colleagues, but no record was taken and no formal paper was presented. In 1936 von Neumann attended a mathematical conference in Vienna. This was the famous University of Vienna Colloquium of Karl Menger, which brought together Europe's top mathematicians and some economists between 1928 and 1936. Menger asked von Neumann to repeat and expand on his 1932 informal Princeton lecture. This time von Neumann wrote a paper, but it was only nine pages long and very terse. It has been speculated that von Neumann may have scribbled it down in a lonely Paris hotel room, very miserable at the Austria Anschluss which threatened his homeland, the increasing restrictions on Jews, and the worsening politics of Europe, together with the unhappy split with his ex-wife at the time (Leonard, 2008, 46).

At the mathematical colloquium he presented a written version of his Princeton talk, aiming to answer 'under what conditions it is possible to find a meaningful solution to the existence of a nonnegative price factor in the Walras/Cassel general equilibrium model'. This represented the proof of a theorem of existence of an equilibrium in an expanding system. (Walras and Cassel had also guided Leontief's pioneering input-output modelling.)

It appears that some conference participants still did not understand von Neumann's pioneering but very terse explanation of an expanding multisector economy, pointing to a solution which was a 'saddle point'. It was the first paper to use duality principles, where if the primal objective is optimal resource allocation, then the dual is a resource valuation problem. This was to be the last mathematical colloquium, as the Nazi invasion of Austria prevented any future meetings (although later Leontief would try to revive something similar post-war). The paper was published in German in 1937 in the colloquium's last volume of proceedings.

Two years later von Neumann wrote to his colleague Kaldor, now at the National Institute of Economic and Social Research in London, sending him an off-print of the paper, marked 'with apologies from the author'. Kaldor admitted that he could not understand it himself, but he thought it could be very valuable, and he wanted to make it more accessible to economists. He arranged for a refugee colleague in Britain to translate it from German. Next he sent it to a brilliant ex-colleague, David Champernowne, a British mathematical economist and associate of Alan Turing who had been a student of Keynes at Kings College Cambridge, and also a collaborator on Keynes's national accounts work. Champernowne was now working in the Statistical Section of the Prime Minister's Office on wartime statistics, programming, and wartime decision-making. He wrote a commentary that helped to unpack this very dense mathematical exposition and explain it to Anglo-Saxon economists. With von Neumann's agreement, Kaldor arranged for the translated original paper and Champernowne's commentary to be published together in the *Review of Economic Statistics* in 1945. The title was much simplified from the original German: it was now called 'A Model of General Economic Equilibrium', known since then as the Expanding Economy Model (EEM). It had taken a decade, but now economists had to take notice.

The model was pioneering because it showed that under certain conditions an economy could settle into an equilibrium, where goods would be produced at the lowest possible cost in the highest possible quantity, while over time outputs could expand. This was a new approach— one of the first to try to model an economy that was not static but undergoing continuous change, and in principle it could be used to work out the conditions for economic expansion.

Nevertheless, there were many unrealistic assumptions: the economy was not restricted by labour supply or resource availability, and the economy would continue to grow in its current configuration. Von Neumann constructed a technical factor, a price vector, and also an intensity vector (like capacity utilization), all somewhat similar to Leontief's input-output formulation. The production processes would exactly return the rate of interest (i.e. there were no profits to be made). With these assumptions, von Neumann then showed that there would be an equilibrium state in which an economy would grow at a rate equal to the cost of capital.

At first economists were somewhat baffled by this paper—it was so brief, so new, so dense, and so hard to understand, written largely in mathematics (von Neumann's favourite language which he preferred over English—his third tongue, especially when there were difficult ideas to explain). Von Neumann never intended his model to be a complete description of a real economy. To mathematicians it was very neat—the first use of a generalized fixed point theorem to prove that equilibrium did exist, there were mini-max and maxi-min solution methods, and saddle point characterizations, with a pioneering dual theorem of mathematical programming.

A number of objections were raised by the economics profession, some of them due to misunderstandings. Some left-wing economists thought that the paper meant von Neumann was advocating an economy where wages would be kept at subsistence level. (This reflected similar problems that Kantorovich was having with his own Marxist-Leninist colleagues.) To the contrary, von Neumann was in fact showing that growth is fastest when labour can be absorbed from low-productivity sectors into high-productivity ones without wage rates increasing too fast. His approach bridged the differences between Kantorovich and Leontief about 'original factors' of production (i.e. labour) by removing the distinction between primary factors and outputs: labour was a factor of production and workers needed to consume commodities in order to produce other commodities. Some thought von Neumann had implied that changing interest rates would immediately impact economic growth rates, an argument taken up later in the bitter Keynesian–Monetarist debates. Rather, von Neumann was showing that long-term growth would be related to the real cost of capital. Others were confused by the circular flow of the model, where all outputs used inputs that were also outputs. Paul Samuelson wrote 'the EEM is a model where everything is potentially produced from everything else' (a circularity which could be clarified by reference to Leontief's input-output framework).

Leontief himself did not accept von Neumann's argument that a solution was not evident for the particular set of equations. At a meeting of the American Philosophical Society, of which they were both members, he challenged von Neumann about the published article, later telling an interviewer: 'it did not make any sense. It was really a big mess. I could not agree with it....I challenged him. I said he was wrong. I could show it; I had an empirical example. He did not object, he did not contradict me. Not every such system can be solved, but my economic system could. He did not disagree' (DeBresson, 2004, loc. 2012).

The EEM model might sit somewhere between pure capitalism (where profits are positive) and pure Communism (with no determined prices and with labour as the source of all value). Eventually it came to be understood as a synthesis that could clarify the distinctions between central planning and market economies. It presented a special case of Kantorovich's linear programming, with linear sectoral characteristics in common with Leontief's input-output framework, it spelt out the concepts of balanced and steady-state growth, and it derived a golden rule: showing interest rates related to growth rates rather than to the quantity of capital (anticipating optimal growth theory). Thus it helped to pioneer dynamic models of economic growth (later to be picked up by Keynesian economists such as Leontief's graduate students Paul Samuelson and Robert Solow and his Russian colleague at Harvard, Evsey Domar). Several of these economists would win Nobel prizes for their efforts. Economists have now recognized that the paper moved economic theory to a new level of sophistication.

Like many people who had been in Germany in the early 1920s, von Neumann was always concerned about instability, inflation, and the interaction of bad policies and bad politics. During the Great Depression he had supported New Deal policies supporting the expansion of demand as a practical matter, but like Leontief he was not a classical Keynesian in his views. However despite his appetite for realpolitik, his economic interests at this stage were theoretical rather than practical: he had not expected to see his model used for practical macroeconomic policy purposes.

Von Neumann's work was too late to have a direct impact on wartime economic management. Half a century later it was rediscovered by Professor E. R. Weintraub, who declared it 'the greatest paper in mathematical economics that was ever written'. As modern readers reviewed the work, Weintraub's view came to be supported by a number of influential economists. In a 1989 book entitled *John von Neumann and Modern Economics*, Dore et al. traced the important impact of this mathematician on the pioneering work of Leontief, Kantorovich, and other Nobel laureates, ultimately allowing for more sophisticated analysis of dynamic macro-management and stabilization (Dore et al., 1989).

1945: Game Theory and Confrontation

By April 1945 the European war was at last drawing to a close: Soviet and US troops met at the river Elbe in Germany. A few days later German forces in Berlin were surrounded by the Soviets, Mussolini was hanged in Italy, the Dachau concentration camp was liberated by the US Army, Hitler committed suicide, and at last on 7 May Germany surrendered. In the Pacific the Japanese were in retreat in China and Southeast Asia, but open hostilities had broken out once again in China between the Nationalist Government and the Chinese Communist Party.

With some traditional powers defeated or exhausted and with new atomic bomb armaments in their arsenal, military, political, and economic strategists were looking for ways to understand the new balance of power. Von Neumann offered them a new tool to use to do this: it was called game theory.

The origins of game theory extended back some years: several of von Neumann's Hungarian teachers had written about the mathematics of games (Leonard, 2008, 27). French mathematician Emile Borel had published an original paper on the mathematics of gaming in 1921, using poker as his example. His ultimate goal was to discover whether there was a single best strategy to play in any game, though he had not been able to take his insights very far.

Von Neumann himself had played chess with his mathematical colleagues in Zurich and Göttingen. He also played poker, although not in a disciplined way, as his mind restlessly wandered on to new problems while he waited for other players to make up their minds. Back in 1926 he had presented an early paper on gaming to the Göttingen Mathematical Society. He showed that there is a rational outcome to a well-defined game between two players whose interests are completely opposed, defining a rational outcome as one where both players understand they cannot do any better given the rules of the game.

Two years later von Neumann developed his theory further in an innovative mathematical paper called 'The Theory of Parlour Games'. It provided decision rules for such competitions, including more sophisticated games where a player needs to take into account complications, such as considering what the second player expects the first to do. In a zero-sum two-person game (i.e. where if one player wins, the other must lose), the paper demonstrated a rational strategy to maximize potential earnings or minimize losses. On average such a strategy will win out in the long-term, what is today known as the minimax theorem. Von Neumann showed that under these conditions the two players' minimax outcomes would be equal in value. This paper single-handedly established the concept of 'gessellschaftsspiel' or game theory.

Von Neumann realized his theory was not yet very sophisticated, and he continued to mull this line of thinking, foreseeing potential financial, economic, and political applications. During the Vienna colloquium in 1936, he had met an Austrian-German political scientist who was professor of economics at the University of Vienna. Oskar Morgenstern had been researching the topic of perfect foresight and incomplete information. In 1938 Morgenstern visited Princeton University, partly driven by the opportunity to work with von Neumann. While he was there Hitler invaded Austria under cover of the Anschluss. Morgenstern took the decision to stay on at Princeton, where he had the chance to collaborate with von Neumann, who in the meantime had written several further pieces on the mathematics of game theory.

Morgenstern debated with von Neumann about what might happen in more realistic gaming situations. He was particularly interested where players had imperfect information about outcomes, and also where there were more players. In 1941 Morgenstern wrote down his observations and showed these to von Neumann. The latter was expert at reading others' work, and instantly suggested how Morgenstern could improve and extend it. Initially this had been intended as an article for the *Journal of Political Economy*. His daughter recalled that the two academics had numerous breakfasts together at the Nassau Club discussing progress. The exchanges between the two were repeated several times, and soon the paper had expanded to a pamphlet and then to a short book of 100 pages. The process of discussion continued and eventually it was agreed that von Neumann had become a co-author. The work continued to grow organically, finally becoming a major text of 641 pages.

The Theory of Games and Economic Behaviour was published in 1944. If von Neumann's EEM model had been obscure, this book attracted immediate considerable interest from economists and others, reflected by the *New York Times* reporting it on its front page. The theory of games was mainly von Neumann's contribution and the section on economic behaviour was mainly authored by Morgenstern. Together they proved a very powerful combination. Harold Kuhn wrote of their roles: 'if von Neumann played both father and mother to the theory in an extraordinary act of parthenogenesis, then Morgenstern was the midwife.' As with Leontief's experience with Harvard University Press, Princeton University Press previewed the book and anticipated it would be a loss-maker. However they found to their surprise that it sold very well and they had to reprint a number of times. In fact it was a turgid text, which has been described as one of the most influential yet least read books of the twentieth century. For the first time interdependent decision-making had been formally modelled in economics.

One of the first reviews of the work was by Arthur Copeland, an American mathematician. He wrote: 'posterity may regard this book as one of the major scientific achievements of the first half of the 20th century. This will undoubtedly be the case if the authors have succeeded in establishing a new exact science—the science of economics. The foundation which they have laid is extremely promising' (Copeland, 1945, 498).

The book set its framework in the give-and-take of competitive business. But the stakes need not be monetary—they might be broadly generalized to 'utility'. In this way von Neumann and Morgenstern reduced the idea of business or economic strategies to the simple format of a parlour game, which could then be modelled mathematically. The authors noted that in games (business games, parlour games, or the game of life itself) players frequently must decide amongst probabilistic rather than certain alternatives. They showed that if these alternatives can be arranged by choice, it should be possible to assign a numerical utility to each, which then would allow a best strategy to be determined.

The authors commenced with a one-person game (e.g. a Robinson Crusoe-type economy), then moving to two-person games where there are fixed winnings to share. For von Neumann this was an opportunity to incorporate behaviour that had fascinated him in games of poker: a formalized theory of bluffing and second guessing. They showed how imperfect information, complex behaviours, and bluffing could all complicate the outcomes. Next they enlarged the gaming environment to cover three or four player games, ultimately extending the analysis to any number of players, and distinguishing between cooperative and non-cooperative actions.

Subsequently economists would build on utility theory and choice theory under uncertainty, based on von Neumann's insights. In reality the semi-competitive, semi-rivalrous, imperfect information, 'mixed strategy' nature of most real-life economic situations increased the degree of complexity so that players could not necessarily determine final solutions. (It would be left to John Nash and other economists such as von Neumann's fellow Budapest student John Harsanyi to develop other equilibrium conditions to help make these games more realistic.)

The original focus had been seen as guiding business behaviour in oligopolistic industries, and to inspire economic strategies in situations like trade negotiations. Subsequent research has extended the application of game theory to psychology, sociology, and many other aspects of gaming. As the post-war situation became tenser, von Neumann became very interested in applying game theory to politics, economics, and warfare. It has been suggested that this interest may have stemmed from his favourite childhood game *Kriegspiel*, a strategy game, which originated from a Prussian military training exercise. After defeat by the Prussian army in 1866, the Austrian army adopted the game for military training, and von Neumann had a childhood version of it. (Takahashi may also have known this game as the Japanese military had also adopted it, and some attributed Japan's defeat of Russia in 1905 to its use. And the ideas would hardly have been a surprise to Kung as the famous Chinese classic *The Art of War* was also written in a gaming context and had links with the game of xian qi or 'Chinese chess'.) Von Neumann had already thought of World War II in game theory terms, confidently projecting the Allies' victory to colleagues, partly because of their industrial advantage. Soon he also would become interested in modelling the possibilities of conflict between the USA and USSR as the Cold War developed. In the meantime he kept working on the Manhattan Project at Los Alamos.

By mid-1945 it had become clear that the first target for an atomic attack would be Japan, where local military leaders were calling for a massive suicidal defence against the likelihood of American occupation. The Los Alamos meetings were now focused on specific Japanese targets for the new A-bomb. A Targets Subcommittee was established and von Neumann was asked to provide advice to it. The US Air Force had suggested six targets for the bomb—Kyoto, Hiroshima, Yokohama, the Tokyo Imperial Palace, the Kokura Arsenal (near Fukuoka in the South), and Niigata. A second group of targets had been suggested by US intelligence, including the Dunlop rubber factory in Tokyo, a steel mill, an airframes plant, a dockyard, and another arsenal. The A-bomb Target Committee intended that the bomb should have a horror demonstration effect on Japan (and potentially also on Russia). Von Neumann opposed all the industrial sites, seeing them as more appropriate targets for the conventional bombing campaign already under way. His first choice for an atomic explosion was Kyoto. This was vetoed by Henry Stimson Secretary of War, who regarded Kyoto as a holy centre of the Buddhist and Shinto religions: it would be uncivilized to select that target (an argument that did not convince von Neumann).

By June Yokohama had been removed from the list as it had already been largely destroyed, and another port Nagasaki was substituted. It appears that von Neumann agreed with the final selection—Hiroshima, Kokura Arsenal, and Nagasaki. On 16 July von Neumann observed the successful Trinity test in the New Mexico desert which showed that his proposed detonation device for the plutonium bomb would work. He coldly calculated that the resulting 20,000 tons of TNT explosion would have the effect of reducing a city of nearly half a million people to ashes. These calculations show that unlike the European bombing, the aim was not to disrupt Japanese economic capability—that had already been effectively destroyed. Von Neumann did not yet know about the lingering effects of radioactivity (though he was to discover this in a very painful way). But his bomb selection was intended to kill as many civilians as possible in an awful demonstration of power. He then constructed a mathematical model based on game theory which was used to plan routes for the US planes carrying the atomic bombs to Japan that would minimize their chances of being shot down.

The rest is history. On 6 August 1945 the ('Little Boy') U-235 atomic bomb was dropped on Hiroshima City. Three days later the plutonium ('Fat Man') bomb, using von Neumann's ignition device, was to have been dropped on Kokura, but encountering cloud cover, the US Air Force pilots flew on, instead dropping the second bomb on the city of Nagasaki. Both bombs exploded as planned, with terrible destruction.

To von Neumann this was a grand success. He watched the outpouring of both triumph and remorse from the scientists led by Einstein and Oppenheimer, commenting somewhat cynically 'some people confess guilt to claim credit for the sun' (Macrae, 1992, 245).

Half a century earlier Takahashi had commenced his economic career in the Western Division of the Bank of Japan, where he frequently visited the city of Hiroshima, which was growing rapidly as a military centre, as the Japanese eyed conquests in Siberia and Manchuria. On 6 August 1945 due to von Neumann's mathematics and site selection, the centre of Hiroshima, as Takahashi would have remembered it, disappeared, and with it went Japan's military adventures.

8

Economists at Armistice

The Economists at War's End, 1946

'...Even if the A-Bomb Had Not Been Dropped'

Hiroshima, that city where Takahashi had first learned his economic policy, had been reduced to rubble. One quarter of the population had been killed immediately and another quarter injured, with huge material damage. Yet the US Bombing Survey of Japan concluded damningly that: 'certainly prior to 31 December 1945, and in all probability prior to 1 November 1945, Japan would have surrendered even if the atomic bombs had not been dropped, even if Russia had not entered the war, even if no invasion had been planned or contemplated' (US Strategic Bombing Survey Summary, 1946, 1). The chief reason was that Japan had run out of supplies.

1946 was meant to be the first year of peace, but instead it would turn out to be the start of a new era of turbulence and disruption, with demilitarization, localized civil wars, pressure to decolonize, mounting tensions between the great powers, atomic weaponry, and ultimately the Cold War.

The surviving remnants of the defeated Japanese Army limped home, hovering on the verge of revolt. As they pulled out of China, bitter conflict erupted again between the Communist and Nationalist forces there. In the meantime civil wars had broken out across the world: in Greece, Iran, Korea, the Philippines, the Dutch East Indies, and Indochina, some fuelled by fervour for independence, some driven by competing ideologies.

As the Allies and the Soviets faced one another across Europe, the Potsdam Agreements were coming under pressure: the Cold War was gathering momentum. On 9 February 1946, Josef Stalin gave a speech claiming that the differences between capitalism and imperialism were irreconcilable and this must mean future wars were inevitable. A fortnight later diplomat George Kennan wrote his influential 'Long Telegram' from the US Embassy in Moscow to the US State Department in Washington, arguing that post-war Soviet Union should be treated with suspicion and containment. Wartime British Prime Minister Winston Churchill had been warning of this for some time. A fortnight after Kennan's telegram, Churchill, now out of office, delivered his famous 'Iron Curtain' speech in Missouri: 'From Stettin in the Baltic to Trieste in the Adriatic an "Iron Curtain" has descended across the continent.' Stalin responded angrily, accusing Churchill of warmongering and interference in Eastern Europe.

Later that year the US Secretary of State announced the American intention to keep troops in Europe indefinitely, while the Soviet Ambassador in Washington responded to Kennan's Long Telegram with his own, in which he claimed that the United States are 'striving for world supremacy'. Shortly afterwards, President Truman announced the 'Truman Doctrine', which offered reconstruction aid to strategic European countries specifically to prevent them falling into the Soviet sphere. The following month US advisor Bernard Baruch gave a speech describing worsening relations between the US and the Soviet Union as the 'Cold War'. The term resonated and stuck.

Economists who had been advising how to make their own wartime economies stronger and how to make enemy economies weaker, now found their world was changing too. No longer were they focused on policies to restrict domestic consumption, boost military production, and fund the necessities of war in disrupted financial markets. Rather, they were now being asked to turn their attention to retooling factories for domestic production, meeting the demands of long-delayed household consumption, and assisting the process of demobilization and labour market adjustment domestically. The military–industrial production complex had to be converted, and workforces re-skilled. Overseas, their attention was more strategic: reconstructing damaged infrastructure, funding development in vulnerable countries, and designing policies to encourage a new stable world order.

1946: Peace in the East

In Memory of Takahashi Korekiyo

26 February was the tenth anniversary of the assassination of Japan's Finance minister Takahashi Korekiyo. On that day his dutiful children and grandchildren would have visited his grave at the Tama Reien Cemetery near the town of Fuchu. Situated 20 miles from downtown Tokyo, the cemetery had escaped the worst of the saturation and fire-bombing of Tokyo. In Tokyo part of Takahashi's beautiful traditional wooden house survived and is now in the Edo Open Air Architectural Museum there.

In 1946 the US carried out a survey on bombing effectiveness in Japan. The survey established that the Japanese military had built their wartime strategy around their need for economic resources, with plans to 'speedily extract bauxite, oil, rubber and metals from Malaya, Burma, the Philippines, and the Dutch East Indies, and ship these materials to Japan for processing' (US Strategic Bombing Survey Summary, 1946, 2). In some ways this was based on the East Asian economic integration strategy that Takahashi had envisaged, but it was to be achieved by conquest and command rather than through trade and investment. In contrast to the German war effort, this strategy depended heavily on maritime supply chains: initially Japan had constructed large tonnages of naval and civilian shipping fleets. However a high proportion of these fleets were eventually sunk, mainly by US submarine torpedoes and by mines dropped from the air. It is estimated that by VJ Day 80 per cent of the Japanese military and commercial shipping fleets had been sunk in the fighting. The Bombing Survey concluded that the inability to trans-port raw materials from conquered countries was the major reason for the collapse of the Japanese war economy.

In contrast the aerial bombing of Japan had been less important. It had initially been quite inaccurate, until US tactics turned to low-level night-time incendiary raids against Japanese cities. The US had criticized British saturation bombing against civilians in Europe but they adopted these same tactics themselves in Japan. This approach reached its greatest intensity on the night of 9 March 1945, when 16 square miles of downtown Tokyo were incinerated in a firestorm ignited by US Air Force B-29 bombs with 100,000 civilian casualties, comparable to the Hiroshima bomb. Arms production and food supplies were severely disrupted, though this interruption proved temporary.

The United States Survey reported that almost all major Japanese cities had been subjected to strategic bombing. Many civilians had been killed but significant production capacity still survived (34 per cent of industrial machinery was destroyed, but only 10 per cent of road and rail vehicles), and it showed that industrial production had been quite resilient to bomb damage. The report concluded that US bombing would have been more effective targeting railways rather than housing.

There were now huge changes afoot in Tokyo, as the International Military Tribunal for the Far East tried many Japanese military officers as war criminals. Amongst these was Okinori Kaya, one of Takahashi's successors as Finance Minister, who would be sentenced to 20 years' imprisonment. In February 1946, General MacArthur's occupying forces released the draft of a new Japanese Constitution. Japanese Emperor Hirohito proclaimed he was no longer to be treated as a god, assuming instead the role of Head of State in a constitutional monarchy based very loosely on the Westminster system. The constitution specified roles for an elected diet and an executive cabinet, with specific limitations to prevent any repeat of the 1930s military domination that had led to the assassination of Takahashi. It expressly renounced the right of the Government to go to war, and it laid out the principles of public finance in nine simple articles that would have made Takahashi proud. The Cabinet (which was now to be composed of civilians only) must prepare an annual budget to submit to the Diet, which would need to approve all spending under strict guidelines, to audit accounts, and to receive any financial information required; no other spending would be permitted. If they had existed previously, these articles might have saved Takahashi's life, and also the lives of millions of Chinese.

H. H. Kung Flees to Safety

It was not only a matter of Chinese deaths: the Chinese economy was also in desperate straits. The Germans had been supporting the Japanese and the Soviets were supporting the Chinese Communist Party. Kung (now Vice-Premier in addition to his other portfolios) had long targeted the US as a wartime ally and a lucrative source of funding. Back in June 1940 he had dispatched brother-in-law T. V. Soong to Washington as the Premier's personal representative to raise war funds, while continuing to look after the family business interests there. He remained in the US for most of the war. Initially he tried to raise a loan of US$50 million against future exports of Chinese tungsten. As Japanese invading forces moved down the Pacific Coast towards Indochina, the US Congress agreed to lend China half this amount.

Since 1940 Kung and family had been mainly living in the safety of Hong Kong where he had been printing huge quantities of 'fa pai' dollars and flying the cash into Chungking. But without any proper asset backing, this cash was simply inflationary, and was useless for foreign purchases of the arms that China desperately needed. Inflation had rocketed in China from 49 per cent in 1938 to 235 per cent in 1942. There was an official exchange rate of 20 Chinese dollars to the US dollar, but the black market rate was as low as 3,000 Chinese dollars. Where possible the Chungking Government used the official rate to inflate the cost of US aid projects, while actually transacting on the black market and pocketing the difference.

Following the Japanese attack on Pearl Harbor the Americans had seen renewed reason to support Chiang Kai-shek with his two fronts against Japanese and Communists. Sensing the opportunity Kung instructed Soong to call on Henry Morgenthau, Secretary of the US Treasury, with a request for a huge $US500 million loan, ten times the size of the original request. Chiang Kai-shek insisted there should be no security, no interest, no repayment terms, and no conditionality on the use of the loan. Amazingly, the US Congress approved this very loose arrangement within a month.

Over the next few wartime years US officials, including the FB, expressed increasing concern about where all the US funds were going, and about the continuing failure of Kung and others to separate family interests from the Nationalist Chinese war effort. President Roosevelt appointed Lauchlin Currie White House Economist, and sent him to Chungking to discuss financial and arms support with Kung and other members of the Chinese Government. (At his request he also covertly met Chou En-lai at the British Embassy.) Currie had been a Harvard economist with Leontief until 1934 when he moved to the US Treasury where he worked with Morgenthau and White promoting Keynesian policies. He reported back from China that the US had far too rosy a view of the prospects for reform there, and did not understand the deep-seated waste, inefficiency, and corruption embedded in the Kuomintang. Currie had been a Soviet sympathizer, which may have coloured his views. However as usual, Kung managed to charm him, and Currie suggested to Chiang Kai-shek that he might appoint Kung as Chinese Ambassador to the US to replace the deeply distrusted brother-in-law T. V. Soong.

The US was still supporting the Kuomintang war effort, but the feeling in China was deeply cynical. In 1942 Kung had been accused of using $200 million in US loans to buy supplies from Japanese-occupied Shanghai, trading through companies controlled by his family and Japanese joint ventures. There was widespread anger at this conduct. On his return from the 1943 Cairo Conference Chiang Kai-shek had to face down an uprising by younger officers aiming to overthrow Kung and others in the corrupt inner circle of the Kuomintang.

Despite these pressures, T. V. Soong and later Soong Mei-ling on behalf of Chiang Kai-shek continued to spend much time profitably lobbying US politicians and the US public, on instructions from Kung. By arguing that Nationalist China was the last bulwark against fascism and communism, they gained financial support and political aid despite the increasingly obvious corruption. Wherever there was official aid, shipments of arms or public subscriptions, there seem to be a way for the Soong-Kung family to pocket a percentage. The data are not reliable, but it has been estimated that around this time, together with wife Ai-ling, Kung had become the third richest person in China. The richest was said to be T. V.Soong, followed by Big-Eared Tu, while Chiang Kai-shek was the fourth—it was all in the family. It is estimated that by 1944 the Kung-Soong family dynasty was worth more than $2 billion, perhaps the largest fortune in the world (Seagrave, 1985, 416).

In Chungking Kung came under new pressure: the gold scandal. The US had been lending gold to China for several years. Theoretically it was to be on-sold by government banks there to stabilize inflation. Now Kung had announced that the banks would sell 'gold certificates' in advance of the gold actually arriving, effectively an early commodity futures market though without any credible regulation. There were rumours that the market was being manipulated, and as usual suspicion fell on the Soong family. An investigation of irregular trading volumes pointed to the activities of two clerks in one of the Soong banks. The unfortunate duo were put on trial, accused of market manipulation. There was no mercy shown: in the brutal way of the times, the two junior employees were sentenced to death for their endeavours, despite their convincing claims that the deals had been ordered from above, perhaps by Kung himself. As usual, he emerged unscathed by the scandal.

But as the family got richer they began to fall out among themselves. T. V. Soong sought revenge against Chiang Kai-shek, and his way to do this was by attacking his chief minister Kung, turning against his own family in order to attract other Chinese cliques to his side. US diplomat Robert Service wrote: 'the most obvious fact at present is that Dr H. H. Kung, the Minister of Finance, is under attack from almost all factions. Joined with him as the targets of the attack are his wife and sister-in-law Mme Chiang' (Seagrave, 1985, 413).

There had commenced an internal power struggle for control of the clan businesses: TV was orchestrating whispered rumours about Kung, his wife, and sister-in-law Mei-ling: 'Daddy Kung is getting too powerful' was the refrain: in volatile wartime China such whispers could be dangerous. In addition there were rumours, circulated by the Communists although quite probably false, that the Kungs were involved in US General Joe Stillwell's alleged OSS contingency plans to assassinate Chiang Kai-shek. This was dangerous stuff indeed.

At short notice in order to avoid any gang or family retribution, Ai-ling and her younger sister Mei-ling judged it would be prudent to leave China for a sojourn in Brazil. The trip was to ensure their own safety, but it was also an opportunity to build the family assets in Latin America. Brazil had been neutral in World War II and was prospering by supplying both sides with commodities. Ai-ling transferred large sums of money, and on her arrival in South America acquired properties and formed a business relationship with a local strongman. With large deposits in banks in Brazil, Venezuela, and Argentina, the family diversified their interests into oil, minerals, shipping, rail, and airlines throughout Latin America.

By the time the war was drawing to its weary end, an estimated four million Chinese soldiers had died from Japanese aggression, factional fighting, or famine, while civilian casualties may have been double that. But Kung's wealth, connections, and native caution meant that he and his family continued to enjoy a comfortable and safe lifestyle. In 1946 he paid his last visit to the main family home in Shanghai. The Communist Party were using their northern base to consolidate their hold over the coastal regions. It would be another year or two before the Communists Chinese would take over Shanghai, but Kung understood that it could only be a matter of time. He closed down the family home there and removed the household treasures. Over the next year he would do the same with the remainder of his family properties, realizing that only British-controlled Hong Kong would be safe.

Some of his assets were shipped to Taiwan where the Kuomintang was consolidating its base. But Taiwan itself was in considerable flux; the Japanese occupiers had retreated and Chiang's forces were filling the gap, but they behaved badly and were not universally welcomed. By the year's end Taiwan, like Japan, had adopted a new constitution, but it did not look like a stable place to retreat to. Kung decided that the more secure future for his family and himself would be the United States. He claimed that Ai-ling was ill and would need treatment there, which may or may not have been true. Looking to the future he invested in a new Soong family base in New York, a mansion in Riverdale, on the northeast corner of Manhattan, overlooking the Hudson River.

The following year Kung visited the old ancestral estate in northern Shanxi Province one last time to close the mansion before the region was finally overrun by the Reds. It was a sentimental visit, for he would never return. He knew that for him there could be no reconciliation with the conquering Communists: that year Mao Tse-tung had announced a number of demands from the Communist Government and among them was one that was very explicit: 'confiscate the property of the four big families of Chiang Kai-shek, H. H. Kung, T. V. Soong...and other war criminals'.

By the end of the Japanese War as the fighting continued against the Communists, huge shipments of goods, food, clothing, and arms were dispatched from the US to China, much of it paid for by the US Government. And everywhere there was corruption, as fundraisers, suppliers, and middlemen all took their cut. By VJ Day in August 1945, a large amount of gold and dollars had been dispatched to China from the US.

Kung had worked very effectively to build a US–China support lobby to ensure the largesse continued. But when President Truman came to office in 1945 there was a much more cynical and realist US Administration. US investigations revealed significant deficits in the aid budgets, and blame was placed on a group of corporations controlled by Kung and his son David, by now the only family member remaining in China. With the Japanese at last retreating the US attempted to broker a truce between the Kuomintang Government and the Chinese Communist Party. Optimistic Americans felt this could end the two-decades-long devastating Chinese Civil War. But the hardened realists on the ground such as Kung simply expected the Communists to substitute for the Japanese as the primary enemy.

Sure enough, on 20 July 1946 Chiang Kai-shek launched a large-scale assault on Communist-held territory. The Communist Party forces used guerrilla tactics to wear down the attacks. Over the year a million Kuomintang troops were killed or deserted. The Communist troops remained strong in the North, and were gathering strength elsewhere. Some of the early fighting took place around Kung's ancestral homeland in Shanxi, which was no longer safe to visit. Chiang would battle on for several years, but Kung was above all a realist as he watched the advance of the triumphant Communist forces. The American aid continued to flow, sometimes through multilateral agencies: the United Nations Relief and Rehabilitation Administration (UNRRA) shipped nearly US$.7 billion worth of goods between 1945 and 1947, much of this arriving in Shanghai at wharves controlled by Big-Eared Tu, and being diverted to the black market (Seagrave, 1985, 424).

Kung was now spending less time on China's economic management, and focused on his pressing personal interests, safeguarding his family and their fortune. He devoted his considerable energy and contacts into moving his fortune beyond the reaches of the Communist (and any other) government, shuttling backward and forward between China, the USA, and the offshore island of Taiwan.

Back in June 1944 the whispering campaign against Kung had convinced Chiang Kai-shek to fire Kung from the Ministry of Finance.

His family had already departed, but ever alert to the developing storm Kung knew he too must now leave China to ensure his own safety. To save face the government gave him a special assignment—to travel to New Hampshire in the USA to attend the Bretton Woods Conference there. This arrangement would suit all sides: the conference was negotiating a set of rules for international finance for the post-war era, Kung knew a thing or two about moving funds across borders, and he could work on his worldwide investments in safety.

1946: Peace in the West

The Legacy of John Maynard Keynes

The Bretton Woods Conference would bring together the biggest group of economists and economic ideas. It had been years in the making. Back in 1941 in Washington Keynes had met Harry Dexter White, a man who was in some ways Keynes's opposite and nemesis. Dexter White was short in stature, balding, working-class, insecure, pugnacious, and Jewish. Keynes had spent the Depression years comfortably as a Cambridge don, whereas the only job that Dexter White could find was as assistant professor at a small college in rural Wisconsin. Keynes wrote about him: 'he is overbearing, a bad colleague, always trying to bounce you, with harsh rasping voice, aesthetically oppressive in mind and manner; he has not the faintest conception of how to behave or observe the rules of civilized intercourse. At the same time, I have a very great respect and even liking for him...His over-powering will combined with the fact that he has constructive ideas mean that he does get things done, which few else here do' (Skidelsky, 2000, 684).

Dexter White turned out later to have been a covert spy, leaking information to the Soviets. He much admired Soviet planning methods, and thought that a Soviet planning approach could assist the New Deal. In addition, he had hoped to persuade the US Government to support the Soviet economy. It is now known that he passed considerable confidential information to Soviet intelligence. A number of members of the US delegation to Bretton Woods, including White and also Lauchlin Currie are now believed to have belonged to the 'Silvermaster Ring' passing secrets to the Soviets, and amongst the papers may have been the Keynes Plan for international reform.

While Keynes had been finalizing his 1941 pre-Christmas draft, so too had White. On New Year's Eve the latter had completed his memo *Suggestions for Inter-Allied Monetary and Banking Action*, proposing two new institutions, an international monetary fund and an international bank. The fund would help stabilize exchange rates, encourage productive capital flows, unblock balances, reduce dysfunctional markets, and promote sound credit policies. This was not to be an international currency, but it would fix exchange rates among its member currencies, only allowing changes to correct fundamental disequilibrium by consent (and effectively with a US veto). By mid-1942 White had redrafted his proposals and suggested a conference of finance ministers of all major Allied nations including Russia and China to consider it. Roosevelt initially rejected such a conference as premature, but it would eventually take place as the famous Bretton Woods Conference in New Hampshire.

One of the first to see the need for such a multilateral agreement had been the internationalist Takahashi, but he was now dead. One of the first to write a specific proposal on the subject had been Schacht, who had published his plan for international exchange, but he was now out of contact in Germany.

In early 1943 the US sent their own proposals to the UK, Russia, and China all at the same time, making it clear this would not be a US–British initiative. Somewhat irritated at this, the British promoted their own version of the Keynes Plan, similar to the Schacht Plan, but with capital assigned to member states on a quota formula, and distinguishing between short-term financing of international trade and long-term financing of capital movements. The British then sent their own plan to Russia and also to China where it would have been reviewed by Kung. Keynes also asked the Russian Ambassador in London to send experts to discuss it. Surprisingly both White's and Keynes's plans received careful coverage in the German press, and the Germans agreed that the latter was superior, being more closely based on the original German Schacht-Funk proposals.

Keynes had already led a large British delegation to Washington for six weeks of difficult talks, unconvincing argument, and frustrating negotiations with Harry Dexter White and the US Administration. It was small comfort to him that while the enemies agreed with him, the Allies did not! He received some recognition when he was made a baron in recognition of his contribution to the war effort, but this honour did not impress the egalitarian Americans.

Talks about international financial arrangements ground on. In April 1944 a document was jointly issued by Washington, London, Moscow, and also by the Kung Ministry in Chungking, setting out a proposal for a major conference to discuss developments.

While the soldiers were fighting the D-Day invasion, Keynes was travelling to the United States once again for an international conference to discuss developments, this time sailing on the ship *Queen Mary*. Led by Kung, the Chinese delegation (the largest at the talks) was also aboard the ship and there was opportunity for discussion between them. Despite the wartime privations at home, Kung travelled in style, leading a huge Chinese team.

In July 1944 the planned international conference finally came together—736 delegates from 44 countries met at the Mount Washington Hotel at Bretton Woods in New Hampshire, to work out a plan for post-war international payments. Throughout the negotiations Keynes had displayed a majestic command of the facts and he could be very articulate and compelling. But he often thought others were stupid to disagree with him, and sometimes he would let these personal views show, appearing arrogant, dominating, intolerant, and overly clever to the Americans. After one such session, colleague James Meade, normally an admirer, wrote in frustration: 'that man is a menace in international negotiations' (Skidelsky, 2000, 319).

On the day of the conference opening, Keynes organized a private dinner party in his drawing-room to commemorate the 500th anniversary of the 'Concordat' between King's College Cambridge and New College Oxford. Kings College also had a more recent concordat link with Yale University. For this reason Keynes invited Dean Acheson, later to become famous as the Cold War US Secretary of State, and his fellow Yale alumnus H. H. Kung. British delegate Lionel Robbins recorded: 'with the delicate skill of a great corporation lawyer, Acheson tried to draw the weather-beaten Kung into some admission of the divided nature of the present Chinese policy. As might have been expected, the old pirate was much too adroit to fall into this trap...deviating into a long historical excursus on the nature of his relations with President Roosevelt and Neville Chamberlain...The duel broke off with honours even' (Steil, 2015, 275).

The next day Kung convened a special meeting to try to galvanize support amongst delegations against Japanese aggression in China, and he called for a vast programme of foreign aid for post-war industrialization (Schenk, 2015, 275). Successful at stirring American nationalist emotions, Kung would however prove less successful at corralling international sources of aid. He met Keynes several times over this period, and using all his natural charm they became friends.

At these Bretton Woods events, Kung also met Harry Dexter White, the US Assistant Treasury Secretary who continued to play a key role in the design of the Bretton Woods institutions. Kung was also unaware that White was a Russian spy and sympathizer. It appears that White was at the time attempting to help the Chinese Communist Party by delaying US aid payments to Chiang Kai-shek's Nationalist Government. This was assisted by the US Treasury advisor resident in China in the 1940s, economist Solomon Adler, who strongly opposed the Kuomintang's proposed gold loans. The Venona Papers later revealed that Adler too was a Soviet spy, and he ended up working for the Chinese Communist Government.

Following further discussions with Keynes, Kung agreed China would support the Keynes Plan at Bretton Woods, but there would be a price: his support was to be in return for China being granted the fourth highest asset quota (after US, UK, and USSR). It had been difficult to make a convincing case based on the size of the Chinese economy because the Chinese data was so approximate: GNP (including Manchuria but not Taiwan) was estimated to be around $8–9 billion. This position gave China extended voting rights and a high borrowing potential. Once again Kung's sharp sense of deal-making had proved profitable.

At Bretton Woods Keynes chaired some of the committees, and in the plenary meeting (where seating was alphabetical) he sat next to the USSR delegation leader Comrade Stepanov (neither of whom could speak the other's language). Ever opportunistic, Keynes tried to take the opportunity to persuade the USSR to send the Bolshoi Ballet to Covent Garden the following year, but the People's Commissar of Foreign Trade was too worried about possible defections.

By this stage it was becoming clearer that the European war would eventually be won by the Allies, and that the USSR was paying the highest price in terms of lives and damage. The Soviets used this moral and military advantage to extract major concessions from the Bretton Woods negotiators. Yet in the end, driven by political suspicion, the Russians would refuse to ratify the Bretton Woods Agreement, an early indication of the Cold War that lay ahead.

In the plenary meeting, led by Keynes himself, the British delegation once again argued strongly for the Keynes Plan. But it was becoming clear that the Americans held all the negotiating advantages and the British none. Ultimately the Keynes Plan was rejected and the Bretton Woods assembly accepted the amended White Plan for the future of international financial regulation. Whereas Kung had been successful in lobbying the US Government, Keynes was less so. Over the next two years Keynes, with Lydia, visited the US several more times to discuss UK financial arrangements. The travel was a huge burden on them both.

He had been looking forward to the end of the war and had positioned himself on an official committee on reparations and economic security. Under his influence the report laid out principles for the payment and use of reparations in the post-war era. Drawing from his experience in World War I, Keynes urged that reparations should be set at a realistic amount and should focus on economic reconstruction. At the Potsdam Conference the three Allied leaders agreed general principles to follow. Later, the British government tried to clarify how to apply these principles. Ex-colleague Alec Cairncross was the UK Treasury representative on an international team that discussed the issue; he knew Keynes's 1918 experiences intimately, and based his arguments on them. However both the US and the UK Governments ultimately decided the agreed principles were unworkable, as they watched the USSR occupy the territories of Eastern Europe and systematically loot them of industrial infrastructure.

Keynes's US visits concluded with a final US/UK Lend-Lease agreement that left Keynes very depressed, labelling it 'a financial Dunkirk'. Once again he was proved right: one week after the atom bomb had been dropped on Hiroshima, the Lend-Lease arrangement was cancelled by the US in a very peremptory way without any consultation. The British were left with huge debts (over $20 billion in US loans). Somewhat ironically given his liberal position following World War I, Keynes estimated that this time the US were giving a much better fiscal deal to its defeated enemy Germany than to Britain its ally. Once again the UK Government had relied on arguments from Keynes to oppose this settlement, but this time they had few cards to play. Furthermore, the new Labour Government that had just been elected in Britain had little understanding of the financial problem they had inherited, they had limited faith in Keynes (even though Hugh Dalton the new Chancellor had been his student), and they came from a different political background from him. Keynes was left feeling ignored, tired, aged, and depressed.

His difficult trip to the US in late 1945 had completely drained Keynes, and he had never fully recovered his health. There was a big Christmas dinner at Tilton for the farm staff and the Bloomsbury friends that year. Keynes knew he should reduce his workload, but there were still economic and cultural projects he felt compelled to complete. He warned the British Government that the expenditure was continuing too high and would need to be urgently reduced. He wrote another paper entitled 'Political and Military Expenditure Overseas' highlighting problems of UK austerity, imports, and international financing.

Though only entering his sixties, Keynes was now visibly ageing, and in persistently poor health. He suffered a series of small heart attacks, and this forced him to spend at least twelve hours a day lying down. This did not however slow his work output. Nor did it reduce his intense interest in the possibility of better international organizations to help rebuild the war-torn world without the negative fallout that had followed World War I and had spawned World War II. Keynes had watched the old League of Nations fail. Now he watched the first meeting of the new United Nations General Assembly in London at the start of 1946, and he desperately hoped for something better.

Despite all the setbacks and all the arguments, Keynes felt that the proposed Bretton Woods institutions still offered the best available prospect for international financial stability. Against all medical advice he travelled one last time to Savannah in Georgia for the opening of the International Monetary Fund and World Bank institutions, of which he had been named British Governor. After years of thought, policy papers, and negotiations, the final design of the IMF and the World Bank had not exactly followed the Keynes template, but nevertheless he had had a huge effect on the outcomes. Keynes was welcomed to Savannah and feted by all in attendance, with speeches and warm applause. He seemed to know it would be his final visit.

In March 1946 he returned to Britain. It was a rough crossing and he was rather sick. Nevertheless he completed a formal report on the Savannah Conference. He was rumoured to have also written another article condemning American Bretton Woods policy and urging the British Government not to ratify it, though this document has never been identified (Moggridge, 1992, 834).

Back in London once more, Keynes was soon busy again, and as ever, he spent his time across his wide range of interests: on committees, contributing to the Treasury's budget discussions, filling his public and private board responsibilities, and attending evening meetings of various clubs. He even drafted articles on George Bernard Shaw, whom he had known, and Isaac Newton, whose work he had been collecting. At last, with Easter approaching, he took a large box of official papers and returned to Tilton, the farm in Sussex for a 'holiday'. There he spent his days working, reading, writing, consulting his farm manager, and visiting Bloomsbury friends at Charleston. Each day with Lydia and his mother he took exercise driving along the Sussex Downs. On 20 April, he and Lydia drove to the top of the Downs on a fine spring day, and enjoying the unusually clement weather, decided to walk the few miles back down to the farmhouse. It was too much: he went to bed feeling particularly fatigued that night. Early the next morning he suffered a final heart attack. He never awoke.

John Maynard Keynes was cremated in Brighton several days later in a small private ceremony with only a few close friends and family attending. His ashes were scattered on the Sussex Downs above Tilton where he used to walk. (Lydia's ashes would also be scattered there when she died 35 years later.) After a week a formal memorial service was held in Westminster Abbey, attended by a huge congregation of eminent mourners and there were many eulogies to this remarkably talented man.

It was hard to believe that the Keynes reign was over at last, for he had dominated economic policy thinking for so long and revolutionized macroeconomics. His Bretton Woods colleague Sir Lionel Robbins wrote in his diaries: 'Keynes must be one of the most remarkable men that have ever lived—the quick logic, the birdlike sweep of intuition, the vivid fancy, the wide vision, above all the incomparable sense of the fitness of words, all combined to make something several degrees over the limit of ordinary human achievement.'

Was Schacht Guilty of Economics?

Despite the wars and conflicts that divided them, many of the eminent economists of Western Europe knew of one another. News of Keynes's death swept the world in 1946, but of those who knew him, one man was slow to learn of it. Hjalmar Schacht was being held in a prison in Nuremberg.

In the intervening years of war, life had changed for Schacht. He was now in his sixties and had been rejected by the Nazi regime. His first wife (long estranged) had fallen sick and died during the early years of the war, and his two children were grown up and had left home. Schacht had been considered a distinguished older statesman but was increasingly seen as remote and severe, although his biographer John Weitz said his cold and aloof exterior hid a man who adored women and who in turn could fascinate some of them. He met an attractive and cultured young lady named Manci, an art expert at the Munich House of Art, 30 years younger than him. He said that like most people she at first thought him 'a starched chilly sober-sides' and was surprised to find that beneath that stern exterior he was more human. She had a 'slender figure, well cut features, curly fair hair and blue eyes which might have served as a model for the Epple angels in Bogenhausen Church' (Schacht, 1956, 370). At first Schacht was worried about associating too closely with her, knowing that in the eyes of some Nazis he had become a figure of political suspicion and now was in danger. However he called on Hitler (for the last time) apparently to inform him that he was getting married again, and the next month he married Manci. They went on honeymoon to Switzerland, visiting Lugano and Gandria. Even on honeymoon and retired, Schacht could not resist giving the Swiss the benefit of his advice on how to deal with German coal policy.

On their return from honeymoon, the couple moved out of Berlin to the remote country house at Guhlen. Through his contacts Schacht had learned of the German intention to attack Russia. Like Takahashi and Keynes, Schacht was an internationalist. And like Kung and Keynes he had no love for the Soviet Union: 'so long as the Russian Government continues its propaganda of world revolution, we are obviously bound to look upon this as a menace to Germany. A highly industrialized country such as Germany cannot tolerate Bolshevism under any circumstances.' Despite this deep dislike, Schacht was convinced that invading the Soviet Union would be sheer madness. (According to Bill Donovan of the OSS, Schacht warned the US Embassy in Berlin about the upcoming Nazi attack.) He was proved correct: as well as national downfall it would also lead to personal tragedy.

Despite being out of the regime he could not forbear from getting involved, letting various Nazis know his (usually disapproving) views on the conduct of the war. Unwilling to believe that his advice was no longer welcome, Schacht even wrote to Hitler, lecturing him that this was the time to sue for a vigorous peace policy. He had corresponded with Hermann Goering: 'the repeated announcements that the Russian resistance was definitely broken have been proved to be untrue. Allied supplies of arms to Russia, and the manpower reserves of Russia have been sufficient to bring continuous counter-attacks against our Eastern Front' (Schacht, 1956, 349). He also noted the increasing problems with supply lines, lack of raw materials for armaments, labour force shortages, and rationing of civilian goods. As usual Schacht was proved correct, but as usual his warnings were unappreciated. Goering replied angrily: 'my answer to your defeatist letter, that undermines the powers of resistance of the German people, is that I expel you herewith from the Prussian State Council.' More importantly, at last Hitler also lost patience. In January 1943 Schacht was dismissed as Minister without Portfolio, and expelled from his (largely ceremonial) post on the Prussian State Council. It was the final end to Schacht's long involvement in German economic policy.

Now Schacht took another and very dangerous step. He had finally reached the view that Hitler was unreformable and damaging to Germany, and that he was pursuing total war. Schacht began thinking about how to overthrow the regime. He talked carefully amongst high officials he knew but encountered deaf ears. He even sounded out his friend Montagu Norman at the Bank of England about supporting a coup, and

Norman passed on the warning to an unappreciative Prime Minister Neville Chamberlain. Eventually Schacht connected with General von Witzleben who was known to be a determined opponent of the regime, and was in touch with like-minded senior army officers. They had hatched a plot to arrest Hitler as early as September 1938, but the Munich Conference intervened and the plot had to be cancelled.

Living in his country estate during the war years Schacht's connections with the plotters continued, and he seemed naïve about the consequences. In the guise of issuing hunting invitations, he entertained visits from a number of friendly officials and officers who he thought were unsympathetic to the Nazi regime. He became aware of several other plots to assassinate Hitler, but he was starting to realize the terrible risks of being involved in this. This time the plotting was led by Commissioner Goerdeler, his old Price Commissioner colleague, who sounded out Schacht about joining a post-Hitler cabinet while walking in the park at Sanssouci in Potsdam. Schacht also talked frequently with another resistance organizer Theodor Strunck and when the latter's house was bombed out, allowed Strunck to live in one of his own homes where clandestine meetings were occasionally held. With another general, Lindemann, Schacht discussed preparations for an attempt on Hitler's life, though proposed dates were continually postponed due to Hitler's unexpected movements.

It seems that Schacht was close to some of the conspirators without ever being directly involved himself. His name had even been mooted as a potential successor to Hitler in the event of a successful coup. But the more serious of the plotters had little faith in his usefulness or reliability. Anybody else would have foreseen the warning signs long ago, but Schacht was obstinate and blinkered: he seemed surprised when one day he noticed that he was being followed by a car full of Gestapo officers.

In July 1944 a failed assassination attempt had been made at Hitler's Wolf's Lair HQ. Schacht had known there would be no mercy shown for anyone associated with the plotters. He knew he was suspected of associating with conspirators, but he only now began to realize the dangers that he and his family were facing. He was most worried about his wife and his two small children, and he took the children to his older daughter in Bavaria for safe-keeping. Back in his country home with his wife early one morning he was rudely awoken by the Gestapo. To his outrage they arrested him while he was still wearing his pyjamas and, refusing to explain, they dragged him off to the dreaded Ravensbruck Concentration Camp.

A long period of harsh imprisonment by the Nazi regime followed. Initially he was classed as a 'prominenten' prisoner and held with a number of similar political miscreants. Sometimes he could trade with his jailers, paying for small favours such as a newspaper (using his small stock of cigars), while other times he was treated very harshly with no washing facilities and insufficient to eat. After a few months conditions changed for the worse: he was ordered to give up his civilian clothing and put on a rough concentration camp tunic with wooden clogs, then thrown into one small cell after another, where he was held in solitary confinement under very unpleasant conditions for over a year.

It was characteristic of Schacht that rather than admitting being scared, he seemed perplexed at his confinement and outraged at his treatment, protesting noisily and trying to explain to unsympathetic warders that he was a 'security prisoner' and not a 'convict'. He was moved around a series of other prisons without explanation. Usually he was confined to solitary cells with the light always illuminated, where the only food was cabbage soup or similar, and where his only pastime was squashing bedbugs on the prison walls. At all hours of the day he would be interrogated about his own role in the assassination attempt on Hitler, about fellow plotters, and about other conspiracies. He claimed that he persistently refused to reveal names of co-conspirators. He regarded his interrogators as idiots, and it showed. The arrogant Schacht temperament prevailed and provided him with strength: despite the torture threats and the occasional violence, he seemed to take a perverse pleasure in lecturing his Gestapo interrogators about the Nazis' mistakes in politics, and in war strategy, and most of all in wartime economics.

As the Russians advanced westward and gradually closed in on the prison, conditions worsened; Schacht was transferred to other prisons further from the front line. Now his jailers told him that as a political prisoner he should expect to be hanged. He was particularly shocked as he was transported through the wrecked streets of bombed-out Berlin, driving through a continuous wall of flame and smoke, with burning ruins all around: the explosive calculations of von Neumann and the targeting calculations of Leontief were evident all around. He ended up in Flosenburg Extermination Camp, a place of horror, where every day he witnessed the executions, at night there was a fearful chorus of screams and shots, and each morning the dead bodies were carried out.

For two months he survived the inadequate food, inhumane treatment and terrible atmosphere there, waiting for his own turn to be executed. He wrote bad gothic poetry to record his feelings: '...The long dark hours on thy soul converging/ Haunt and mock thee throughout the night...' He was also very worried for the safety of his wife and two infant children as he heard of the Russians' advances. On one fearful day he saw four of his closest fellow prisoners being hanged, and it seemed that Schacht would be next in line. Then with the Russians drawing closer, he was transferred yet again, this time to the notorious Dachau Concentration Camp. There, to his considerable surprise, he was treated to better conditions from the camp commandant who seemed to be preparing for the inevitability of capitulation.

After spending what had threatened to be his final days in an extermination camp, at last Schacht felt lucky—the camp was relieved by Allied troops, and these troops were American not Russian. They set him free and for some golden days he enjoyed the almost forgotten luxury of food and cleanliness in a series of local hotels and camps.

Then to his confusion, annoyance, and mounting horror, a contingent of American troops arrived at the hotel and informed Schacht he was on a register of suspected Nazi war criminals, and he was arrested. Once again he was interned, firstly in Italy and eventually returned to Germany where he was held captive in Kransberg. There Schacht heard over the wireless a list of German leaders who were to be placed on trial in front of the International Military Tribunal at Nuremberg. To his great surprise and outrage he heard his own name being read out. He seemed shocked to discover that he was to be put on trial, simply unable to understand why he should be accused for what he saw as his role in classical and successful economic policies. It hardly seems to have occurred to him that, with his years of very close association with Hitler and the Nazis, he might be seen to bear some war guilt.

By the time the tribunal started its hearings, Schacht had spent a long time in captivity, shuttled between a dozen prisons. In late 1945 he was charged by the International Military Tribunal with 'conspiracy for war' and 'preparations for war'. There were two dozen senior Nazis on trial with him at Nuremberg, the others being the top Nazi military, industrial and political leaders. Schacht could understand that they might have been involved in war crimes, but he simply could not believe that his own economic policies should bear any guilt.

He complained constantly to the American prison authorities and noted that they were most discourteous to him. In his own perverse way, Schacht was in his element: he enjoyed being a celebrity, signing autographs for the American guards. Like all the Nuremberg accused he was IQ-tested, and proudly recorded that he received a score of 143, the highest of all the accused war criminals on trial.

The major defendants were put on trial together. For much of the hearing Schacht sat to one side, deliberately apart from his Nazi co-accused, listening disdainfully. For his cross-examination he stood in the dock without headphones, making it clear to all that he understood his English-, French-, and Russian-speaking accusers. He faced a long trial before a hostile American prosecutor who was determined to prove his guilt. The prosecution focused on his MEFO Bills scheme used to extend funding, and on whether these instruments were knowingly used to prepare for war, as well as his role in designing a system of exchange controls and the stockpiling of scarce materials. Schacht took considerable pleasure in bringing forward all sorts of logical yet complex arguments about why his economic policies had been aimed at achieving German prosperity not German war, and how the financing schemes allowed armaments for defence and not for offence.

Schacht claimed he had never been a registered member of the Nazi Party, although he had been close to senior party members including Hitler, and he had at times worn a swastika badge and decoration. He also claimed he had never been anti-Semitic, while at the same time admitting: 'I have always declared myself in favour of limiting Jewish activity to a certain extent in all these fields—a numerical limitation, based not absolutely on population figures, but rather on a certain percentage' (International Military Tribunal, 1946, 4–6).

Much of his defence centred on a remark by Albert Speer to the tribunal that Hitler had complained that Schacht had upset his war economy plans. He told the tribunal: 'that was entirely correct; I did upset Hitler's financial plans, and for a vital reason. I did not wish him to prepare for a war of aggression and I had no intention of helping him to do so. In fact where Hitler was concerned I laid an embargo on Reichsbank funds. He was compelled to apply to the big banks, and it is easy to imagine what he thought of me' (Schacht, 1956, 421). He responded to accusations in German, his voice clear, definitive, authoritative. He took delight in consistently wrong-footing the tribunal prosecution with such logic and continued to lecture them. When his lawyer asked why he had not explained to Adolf Hitler that he was refusing Reichsbank loans because the latter wanted to use them for war, Schacht responded: 'then I could not have the pleasure of this verbal exchange. I would be dead. I would need a preacher not a lawyer' (Weitz, 1997, 315). For him this was an intellectual exercise, but such arrogant cleverness was dangerous, for he was now fighting for his life.

At last in October 1946 the tribunal gave judgement. Of the prisoners on trial, 20 were judged guilty, half of them sentenced to immediate execution. The American prosecutor had urged a conviction of Schacht and the Soviet judges had agreed. Schacht's economic arguments did not save him. However the British judges argued that he had lost his official powers before the outbreak of war, had been in contact with the Resistance, and had been already punished by the Nazis. It was a very close call. When his name was called he found he was acquitted, one of only two defendants found not guilty (International Military Tribunal, 1946).

Once again Schacht was released, full of economic and personal self-justifications. But he was to find that his tribulations were not yet over. To his continued amazement a few days later he was re-arrested, this time by the German Stuttgart Police who were conducting their own de-Nazification exercise. Eventually their charges were dropped and he was released. Yet there was more to come: several months later he was arrested yet again, this time by the Bavarian Police, who after a decade of National Socialism were anxious to prove that they too could be determinedly anti-Nazi. It was not until 1948 that all charges were dropped and Schacht was finally and fully freed. He had been imprisoned by various authorities for almost four years.

It was some time after the war ended before Schacht received the news that his two infant children were still alive, and he only learned later that his wife had evaded the worst of the invading Russian troops, although an armed battle had taken place on their very own estate at Guhlen. He was overjoyed to reconcile with his wife again and to see his two small daughters after so long. His older daughter by his first wife had married a prominent civil servant and had also stayed safe through the war.

Having survived Hitler's concentration camps, the Allies war-crimes tribunals, and Germany's de-Nazification prosecutions, Schacht emerged with no house, no money and his family split up. When he had been at last released from four years in captivity, he found his home was now in Russian hands, three small dwellings he had owned had been bombed, he was massively in debt to his lawyers, he was aged 71, and he had only 2.5 Deutschmarks in his pocket. He found himself hated across much of Europe and especially in his homeland, seen as a surviving relic of the old regime. He was battered but indestructible.

Though his career was finished in Germany, ever resilient, Schacht was determined to rebuild his life. Initially he managed to earn some money by writing a book entitled *Settling Accounts with Hitler*. It proved very popular and sold a quarter of a million copies.

In the post-war world a number of newly independent governments found themselves facing problems of economic management for the first time, generally with poor populations, low levels of education, little economic infrastructure, high expectations about independence, but lower post-war commodity prices. Though he was unappreciated at home, some of these governments asked Schacht for advice. He started his own small investment bank, Deutsche Aubenhandelsbank Schacht & Co., and he re-invented himself as a development economist. As a specialist in economic development for the non-aligned Third World, he was ahead of many of his peers in the World Bank and other multilateral institutions who would try to apply conventional Keynesianism to developing countries even though their markets were not well developed. Schacht's thinking followed von Neumann's economic model: an economy could enjoy balanced growth with the right policies and the right investments. His first assignment was in Indonesia, struggling to recover from the Japanese occupation and a war of independence. Schacht would go on to advise Iran, India, Egypt, Syria, and other countries of the non-aligned movement.

It had taken some years before Schacht learned the details of the wartime fate of his son Jens, a captain in the German Army. It was a tragic story: towards the end of the fighting on the brutal Eastern Front, Jens had been captured by the Russians and interned. He had suffered under terrible starvation conditions in captivity. During the last days of the war he was taken on a forced march out of Germany and into the USSR. After some torturous days of journeying, he died of hunger, sickness, and exhaustion on the side of the road. Schacht described him, in unusually tender words, as a gentle soul. In his own clumsy attempt to express his love, he wrote about his son: 'he was quiet, reserved, very clever, and would have made an outstanding economist' (Schacht, 1956, 110). Until the end of his life in 1970 aged 93, Schacht hated the Russians.

Leonid Kantorovich's Next Challenge

Schacht's son had invaded Russia, retreated with the Wehrmacht to Germany, then been forced as a captive back into Russia. His death was just one of millions of tragic wartime losses that took place within the territory of the USSR. By the time that Kantorovich had returned to his home town of Leningrad, one and a half million residents had died there. The city was in a terrible state with apartments, factories, and utilities wrecked, and with a much reduced, malnourished, and impoverished population. The suburbs outside the siege area had been looted and destroyed. By some estimates this constituted the greatest destruction and the largest loss of life ever known in a modern city.

The wartime devastation continued to take its toll even after the Armistice, and adjustment to the peacetime economy was very difficult. During 1946 and through the following winter the Soviet Union went through a major famine—the grain harvest was only 40 per cent of pre-war levels, there was a shortage of rural manpower and agricultural implements, and the government's compulsory confiscation of grain exacerbated the situation. Millions had died during purges and World War II; in the immediate post-war year a million or more may have starved to death (though the numbers are hotly debated). Early post-war life remained extremely grim.

The Soviets realized they faced a very difficult job of reconstruction. Initially they had confronted this by demanding reparations, looting factory equipment, and requisitioning supplies from the conquered territories. Keynes and his colleagues had watched the Soviet Union refuse to sign the Bretton Woods agreement and start to erect diplomatic barriers. Now the Soviets watched the US Marshall Plan financing reconstruction in Western Europe, and decided they did not trust the intentions of the West either. The Soviet Union responded by funding world Communism including sending aid to Communist China, where Nationalists such as Kung were fleeing the mainland. It was a time of growing political hostility and confrontation.

After the war Stalin named Leningrad a Soviet 'Hero City'. A huge civil reconstruction programme was begun, rebuilding infrastructure, and replacing the 20,000 dwellings that had been destroyed. Some schools and universities were re-opened, and theatres were re-established (among them Keynes's brother-in-law's).

Kantorovich and his family had survived the war. But physical life for him, his wife, and their two young children, Irina and Vsevolod, who had been born during the fighting, was still very tough in the wrecked and impoverished city. Intellectually, things were little better with the dangerous and blinkered ideology of the time. Kantorovich later recorded of 1945: 'I even fell into a state of depression for a while, and was not sure that I would ever be able to return to economics' (Nitusov, 1997, 6).

At Leningrad University classes were restarted; in the Mathematical Institute of the Academy of Sciences, Kantorovich was appointed to head a unit imaginatively called the Department of Approximate Methods, and he taught mathematical programming to economics students, while continuing his military operations research for the military. In 1946 he was writing on 'The Theory of Probability', advocating a probabilistic approach to military applications. This work would be poorly received and deemed 'anti-Marxist'. He wanted to apply his earlier programming methodology to economy-wide planning, but knew that if probability theory could be deemed anti-Marxist, there was little chance to do this.

At this time Kantorovich's old mathematics colleague from Leningrad, Sergei Sobolev, was appointed as a lead scientist in a major top-secret government programme codenamed 'Enormoz'. The Soviets had been tracking progress on the Manhattan Project. The US atomic bombs dropped on Japan left them very worried: could they be the next target?

The Enormoz Project was to help the Soviet Union develop its own atom bomb. Sobolev was working on the mathematics behind the preparation of uranium and plutonium for atomic reactions, and he would soon be looking to his old colleague Leonid Kantorovich for assistance.

Wassily Leontief Goes Back to Work

At the same time as Kantorovich was adjusting to the tough post-war working conditions at the University of Leningrad, that other young genius from Petrograd, Wassily Leontief, was returning to a much more comfortable life at Harvard University where he had now been appointed professor. The operations of the OSS were being terminated and the new Central Intelligence Agency was being established in its place. The OSS had been a World War II agency, but the CIA was designed to fight the new Cold War. At Harvard Leontief was busy absorbing his Washington wartime experiences, helping establish the Harvard Russian Research Centre where he directed economic studies, and teaching a course on the economy of Russia, while tutoring the new influx of post-war GI students in his techniques of input-output analysis, and working on his latest book on the US economy.

By 1946 the first reports of the Strategic Bombing Survey in Europe had become available, and with his eye for input-output technical coefficients, Leontief would no doubt have devoured it. President Roosevelt had directed the US Military to carry out a comprehensive survey of the effects of bombing first in Europe and later in Japan. This European survey had turned into a huge exercise with 100 staff working on it, one third of them civilians and academics. One of the directors of the project was J. K. Galbraith, who had studied at the feet of Keynes in Cambridge and had been a fellow instructor in economics at Harvard alongside Leontief from 1934–7; he also had known von Neumann from his year at Princeton in 1938–9. The survey gathered a considerable amount of evidence from the bombed-out areas of Europe, and produced a huge report with 200 supporting documents.

The survey pointed to some significant economic successes from the bombing in Europe. But it warned against being definitive as to how far strategic bombing of the economy had contributed to the general political and military collapse of Germany. It concluded that for a long time the German economy had been in better shape than had been previously thought: economic activity—both military and civilian—had remained economically buoyant until 1942–3. Food and clothing production remained adequate. When the bombing campaigns began to seriously disrupt production, there was still considerable scope to increase output, double-shift factories, and bring women into the work force. Food had to be more strictly rationed, but there was a nutritionally adequate supply (German wartime rations provided about the same calorie intake as their British equivalents).

The key economic problem for Germany had been the growing imbalance of payment, undisciplined macro-policy and scarcity of key materials. The Allied blockade had restricted its access to world markets. Germany was using coal gasification to supplement shortages of petroleum and relied heavily on Romanian oil production. It had been dependent on Sweden for iron ore, and on Spain and Portugal for tungsten, with grain and other raw materials sourced from the USSR. This dependence on foreign industrial materials had been one reason why the Germans had invaded the Western Soviet Union, but the intensity of their scorched-earth destruction meant there was little plant left standing. The Nazis had plundered material more successfully from occupied Western European countries such as France, Austria, and Norway, where there had been less physical destruction, also taking forced labour and imposing 'quartering fees'.

The later Allied bombing campaign targeting petroleum, oil, and lubrication products, and their synthetic substitutes had been much more successful. Ammunition production had been particularly disrupted by bombing and blockades: by 1944 German arms producers were having to pack bombs and shells with rock salt as the country had exhausted its supplies of nitrate. Truck factories had been heavily bombed: by the Armistice two of the three big producers had been decimated, and production had dropped to one third. Submarine construction had been completely halted. In contrast to these bombing successes, German aircraft production remained high throughout the war, tanks and armoured vehicles continued to be produced, and while the bombing significantly reduced production of steel and ball-bearings, this had only limited impact on wartime output.

These studies provided evidence of major economic disruption in almost all the protagonist economies. There was one exception—the US was in relatively good economic shape at the end of the war, and the only country capable of funding a major programme of international reconstruction. Their position had been different in a number of ways: the economy was richer, it had a sophisticated industrial sector, considerable unused capacity and labour at the start of the war, it was never bombed or besieged, and it had several years to observe the fighting before joining the conflict. Consequently the US managed fast mobilization of labour and resources after declaring war, public and private investment growing rapidly. There had had to be some diversion of resources from household spending to military investment, and some consumption had been rationed, though not to the extent of most other countries. Overall, living standards declined slightly despite an illusion of 'war prosperity'.

US armaments producers had drawn on industrial techniques of mass production from the steel and auto industries, rapidly scaling up production of trucks, tanks, ships, and aircraft. For example, during the war years, the US produced nearly 5,500 naval ships, 80,000 amphibious craft, 2.4 million trucks, and nearly 300,000 planes. Raw materials were readily available, particularly from neutral South America. In order to finance Lend-Lease, British industrialists had been required to hand over some investments to the Americans. One enduring legacy from wartime was a big growth in regulation and the size of the government sector.

At the end of war, increased Soviet–US confrontation in Eastern Europe and American worries about Communism led the incoming President Truman to abruptly terminate US Lend-Lease assistance to the Soviet Union. UNRRA funds, intended as aid to war-devastated areas, were abruptly cancelled in 1946 for fear they were being used for Communist expansion. In its place, based on the OSS reports of Leontief and others, the US proposed a loan of $1 billion for Soviet reconstruction; Molotov summarily rejected this offer.

Colleague Abram Bergson had continued Leontief's work on the Soviet economy. By 1947 the US Air Force R & D (RAND) Corporation had been established to focus on the Soviet economy and it also investigated the techniques of Kantorovich. This work programme was eventually subsumed into the CIA. In Moscow US Ambassador George Kennan used Leontief's OSS report and later updates to support his famous 'long telegram' outlining the Soviet Union's threat to dominate Eastern Europe. By then Leontief was back at Harvard, and that was where General George Marshall gave his famous speech about the US Marshall Plan, outlining what would become a huge programme of financial support for post-war European economic recovery.

Apart from his Russia work, Leontief was building on his inter-sectoral research. His study of post-war employment had led him to investigate questions of wages and labour. This was a productive period for him, and he published a number of important papers in top journals. One of the most important (though overlooked at the time) was his 1946 *Journal of Political Economy* article: 'The Pure Theory of the Guaranteed Annual Wage Contract'. This paper considered the governance problems around the paying and monitoring of work forces, and how to align the interests of the owners and employers of labour. The work made use of von Neumann's game theory, and it pioneered what came later to be called principal–agent theory or contract theory, about the control of factors of production in a market economy. Leontief had come a long way from his hometown upbringing in Petrograd: his approach contrasted sharply with the focus of Soviet economists of the time such as Kantorovich, for whom allocation had to be centrally controlled and only labour could be considered as a source of value under Marxist-Leninist doctrine.

The MAD Strategies of John von Neumann

World War II may have ended with the dropping of the A-bombs, but John von Neumann did not see a peaceful world ahead. He felt sure there would be a future war with Russia unless the US remained on guard. For him the main purpose of the atomic bombs had not been to damage the Japanese economy, which was already on its knees, but rather to demonstrate to Russia the technical capability and political determination of the US Government to exert its will in the upcoming titanic struggle between communism and capitalism.

Von Neumann was frustrated that some of the cleverest men he knew (such as Princeton colleagues Einstein and Oppenheimer) could not recognize this mounting Soviet threat. Einstein wanted the A-bomb secrets to be made available to all the large powers. When other American scientists suggested that nuclear developments should be handed over to international control, Russia scornfully rejected the proposals. This came as no surprise to von Neumann who distrusted Stalin the dictator and also distrusted his proposals for Eastern Europe (including von Neumann's homeland Hungary where a Communist takeover was under way). To von Neumann the post-war world had become a zero-sum game.

The Soviet Union had been badly battered by the war (as Kantorovich had experienced and Leontief had researched), and many strategists thought it would be unable to mount a credible military threat. In contrast von Neumann believed that within five years it would have recovered sufficiently to develop its own nuclear bombs. He could already see that the next generation of nuclear weapons would be far more destructive than the first. His military objective was to help the US get to the next stage of deterrence.

Von Neumann memorably said in 1945: 'if we're going to have to risk war, it will be better to risk it while we have the A-bomb and they don't' (Macrae, 1992, 332). This statement was a classic application of his two-person competitive game theory. His theoretical findings told him bargaining positions could be strengthened if there was full information on both sides—he wanted Soviet leaders to understand that in the first few minutes of a nuclear war an A-bomb would be launched, targeted to kill them all. He also said: 'if you say why not bomb them tomorrow, I say why not today? If you say at 5 o'clock, I say why not 1 o'clock?' Some viewed this statement as warmongering. To von Neumann it was important that it be stated publicly, because the US threat needed to be credible. This became known as the MAD theory, the 'mutually-assured destruction' doctrine, resulting from his application of game theory that would dominate strategic thinking in the Cold War that lay ahead.

Von Neumann was continuing to consult part-time at the Los Alamos laboratories, working ever more closely with the US Military. In July 1946 he received an intriguing invitation: would he travel to the Pacific Ocean to a remote atoll known as Bikini in US Micronesia? There he could observe controlled explosions from the US tests on a new generation of atomic bombs. There were both atmospheric and underwater detonations, some held just offshore from the atoll where von Neumann and other experts stood watching. The most powerful of these tests was an atmospheric explosion that released up to 40 times the explosive equivalent of the Hiroshima bomb. This time the military may have miscalculated: the blast created a major pressure wave, with a huge condensation cloud rising into the air and spreading radioactivity. Basic precautions had been taken to shield the observing scientists and crew from the bomb effects, but it appears that they seriously underestimated the health risks from nuclear fallout. With his encyclopaedic knowledge and photographic memory, von Neumann may have recalled the biblical saying: 'those who live by the sword will die by the sword.'

9

Economists in the Cold War

Money, Computers, and Models, 1946–55

Kung Making Hot Money

Over the next decade the wartime economists transformed into Cold War economists, though each adapted in their own way. Von Neumann was working for the US Military to build a bigger, better bomb to deter the Soviets. Kantorovich was now also working on an atomic bomb project, but for the other side. Schacht had become an economist and spokesman for those caught in between: the non-aligned movement. And Leontief was arguing that military spending was too high on all sides, representing a threat to world peace. In this rivalrous world Kung was leveraging Cold War anti-Communist feeling in the US to raise money for his own cause.

Unlike some other wartime finance ministers, Kung had never attached much importance to economic theory. Instead he was a man of realpolitik and real self-interest. Unlike many of his less realistic Kuomintang colleagues, he now perceived there was little hope of returning to mainland China. He had looked at Taiwan and seen its dictatorial government, its corrupt politicians, and a weariness by the US to keep funding this fight, and he had concluded that Taiwan could not guarantee him and his family the stability, security, and earning opportunities that they sought: Instead he decided to devote himself to the best opportunities offered by a more pure capitalist system, which to him meant Wall Street. Kung settled down to a less dangerous life in the US as a banker, dividing his time between the Riverdale mansion and the Wall Street office of the family-controlled Bank of China, where much of the family's liquid assets were held. It was from this office that the Kungs and Soongs managed their many other financial, property, and commercial interests worldwide.

Yet the Chinese ties still pulled: a considerable amount of Kung's time was now spent lobbying for continued US support to the Taipei-based Government as a bulwark against Chinese Communism. The US continued to fund military aid to the Kuomintang: between the end of World War II and the retreat from the mainland they sent $2.5 billion in military aid. However increasingly the Nationalist Government was seen to be corrupt and self-seeking. For example rumours emerged that Kung's son Louis, a major in the Kuomintang, had been selling precious tin to enemy Chinese Communists, so keen was he to make money under any circumstances.

Kung tried to counter these perceptions of venality by making generous political donations to the US Republican Party. He felt that reputation, like anything else, should be able to be bought. The New York Riverdale mansion became the nerve centre for the new Taiwan China lobby, and there was financial support available for any congressman clear-headed enough to support the Nationalist Chinese cause against Communism. Kung became very astute in understanding and manipulating US executive and congressional politics.

The 1949 retreat of the Kuomintang to Taiwan was followed by the anti-Communist McCarthy hearings in Washington, and the outbreak of the Korean War, soon leading to fighting between US and Chinese troops. In the US there was a political outcry about 'who lost China?' Political pressure funded by the China lobby coordinated by Kung out of his Riverdale mansion pointed an accusing finger at Roosevelt economic advisor Lauchlin Currie amongst others. It has been estimated that the China lobby spent $2 million on the 1948 US presidential election, and more in future years, while also demanding that the State Department and other departments get rid of advisors seen as sympathetic to the People's Republic of China.

Occasionally Kung or other family members would pay a visit to their old Kuomintang colleagues in Taiwan, but the United States was their family home now, and they assumed their Western names. The oldest daughter Rosamond had married a Kuomintang officer, while second daughter Jeanette usually dressed in male clothing and became a mysterious and manipulative advisor to powerful Aunt Mai-ling in her US lobbying efforts. Son David followed Kung into the family bank, and youngest son Louis became a Dallas oilman, marrying glamorous movie actress Debra Paget, and helping to manoeuvre Richard Nixon towards presidential office.

The family had become extremely rich. Concerned by rumours of their wealth and irritated by their financial support of the Republicans, President Truman ordered an FBI enquiry into US Aid and the affairs of the Kung–Soong family. The FBI put the Kung mansion under surveillance, but made limited progress in tracking their financial dealings. Much of the family wealth was held in the Bank of China in New York (controlled by Kung) and the Bank of Canton in San Francisco (controlled by brothers-in-law T. A. and T. V. Soong), and these institutions were not cooperating. The FBI estimated all the family's deposits in US banks at around $US800 million. But in addition there were properties and industrial interests not included in that figure, plus financial assets spread amongst international financial centres. It was very difficult to value such assets and impossible to know whether this really was the richest family in the world. It has been estimated that Kung and Ai-ling's combined wealth was likely worth more than US$1 billion, a massive amount at the time and equivalent to multi-billionaire status today. In frustration President Truman concluded: 'they're all thieves, every damn one of them...They stole $750m out of the [$3.8 billion] that we sent to Chiang' (Seagrave, 1985, 437).

Later in 1959, aged 77, Kung returned to Oberlin, his old college, for a reunion of the Oberlin Shanxi Memorial Association. He endowed a scholarship there, but when asked about his finances, the elderly man said he had lost most of it with the collapse of the Nationalist Government and was now living off meagre savings. This was a huge overstatement.

In 1966 Kung stepped down from his bank directorships, and moved into a new mansion on Long Island. With a severe heart condition his health was deteriorating, and the following year he had a crisis and had to be moved to a New York hospital. He never recovered and died there aged 87. His funeral was attended by a colour guard from Taiwan, Chiang Kai-shek's son and wife, together with many pillars of the US–China lobby, including ex-Vice-President Richard Nixon—the man who a decade later would shock the Taiwan lobby by opening up relations with Communist China. Kung's legacy was not the economy of Taiwan, but his own personal wealth.

Ai-Ling, autocratic and secretive, lived another six years before dying in New York City, still possibly the richest woman in the world.

Von Neumann in the Cold War

A decade after the war, diplomatic temperatures were frigid: the world was in the grip of the Cold War. There was no traditional battlefield, but the war could be seen in the Soviet occupation of Eastern Europe, anti-Communist McCarthyism in the US, the Chinese Communist Party victory over the Kuomintang Government, the Berlin Blockade, the Marshall Plan, the Korean War, the many post-colonial independence movements, the formation of the NATO Alliance in Western Europe, and von Neumann's Mutually-Assured Destruction nuclear doctrine.

Following the death of Stalin in 1953, Khrushchev came to power in the USSR, and in 1956 he shocked the Soviet Communist Party by denouncing Stalin's crimes. However the Soviets still believed in the historically-determined victory of communism over capitalism. The establishment of the Warsaw Pact, the harsh crack-down on the Hungarian Revolution, the tanks sent to suppress Polish dissent, all this demonstrated to the world that the East–West split was still a very deep one. In addition to the geopolitical split there was still little commonality in the roles and views of economists across the divide, and no economic resolution between market economies and centrally-planned ones.

Von Neumann spent his last years closely associated with the US Military, very aware of the realpolitik implications of game theory in the Cold War, and fundamentally pessimistic about its outcome. To him, a game theory outlook implied that the US must stay ahead in the arms race, that it should be prepared to use its nuclear advantage if necessary, and that the Soviet Union must always be convinced that this was a credible threat.

To analyse such a state of credibility, bluff and deterrence required a framework, and von Neumann's game theory provided this. However, political scientists modelling the complex US–USSR nuclear stand-off soon required more realism and sophistication than offered by the pioneering game theory model. Economists had been slow to appreciate von Neumann's advances in game theory. Initially the work was picked up by

Princeton mathematicians, and then by Cold War researchers at Rand Corporation and the US Office of Naval Research. It was not until 1950 when Nobel Prize-winning economist John Nash extended the gaming to derive more generalized equilibrium conditions for (more realistic) non-zero sum, non-cooperative, and cooperative games, that the research entered the economics mainstream and began to be applied more rigorously to market situations.

Other economists followed, modelling particular situations such as multi-player games, coalition games, stochastic games, mixed games, and other more realistic behavioural challenges. Mathematician A. W. Tucker (who had been at Harvard with Leontief, at the 1935 Moscow conference with Kantorovich then later in correspondence with him, and at Princeton with von Neumann) worked on complex nonlinear games and helped derive the well-known 'prisoner's dilemma' (where two prisoners are each offered the chance to confess, each knowing that this would be advantageous only if the other does not). Von Neumann was somewhat sceptical of such variable-sum games that might allow for both conflict and cooperation. Before Nash and Tucker had done their work, he essentially viewed superpower confrontation as a prisoner's dilemma, but one that would not end in Nash equilibrium (Field, 2014).

Von Neumann maintained his close military consulting links over the next decades, working for all three arms of the US Military at various sites across the country, and also with contractors such as IBM, Rand, and other corporations. His world-view of Soviet dangers increasingly coincided with theirs. Most of his work now related to how the US should plan strategic defence in a nuclear age. The left-wingers among his Princeton colleagues disapproved of this military-industrial work, and disliked his increasingly hawkish right-wing views. Von Neumann has been portrayed as the archetypal Cold War warrior. He may have been the inspiration for the lead role of the brilliant nuclear expert scientist in a wheelchair, played by Peter Sellers with a middle-European accent, in the Cold War satire film *Dr Strangelove or How I Learned to Stop Worrying and Love the Bomb,* directed by Stanley Kubrick.

In many respects von Neumann was proved correct in worrying about Soviet intentions and capabilities. The US Administration had not suspected that the Soviet Union had a high degree of nuclear sophistication, and they were taken aback when in August 1949 the Soviet Union tested its first nuclear device, labelled 'Joe-1' by the Americans. The US intelligence community was particularly surprised by this demonstration of nuclear capability, having thought they enjoyed a much longer lead time over the Soviet scientists. The latter (including Kantorovich) had been assisted in their work by having a number of spies and fellow travellers within the US establishment. In particular Klaus Fuchs, the German physicist, had worked with von Neumann at Los Alamos, while all the time feeding information about the US bomb effort back to the Soviet Union. (If the Soviet Union had paid more attention to the von Neumann-Fuchs bomb configuration, they could probably have cut short their own development process.) To von Neumann's surprise Fuchs was arrested and exposed, being imprisoned in the UK the following year. The Fuchs case was headline news, yet the Soviet's espionage exercise went much deeper than just one man: Keynes's Washington colleagues Dexter White and Lauchlin Currie, and other US Treasury officials, and some of his notorious Cambridge fellow students such as Donald Maclean, were also fellow travellers leaking strategic materials to the Soviet Union.

By this time a number of influential people in the NATO countries felt the US should seriously consider an early pre-emptive nuclear attack on the USSR. This included some on the right of politics like von Neumann, but it also included many other influential thinkers across the political spectrum including left-wing British philosopher Bertrand Russell and even American Cold War diplomat George Kennan. Earlier in the Korean War, General MacArthur had pressed for its use against China. Many other strategists developed their own versions of 'preventative war', based on game-theoretic thinking. Presidents Truman and Eisenhower had both seriously considered the possibility of a first strike against the Soviet Union, and the US Military had made detailed plans for this (e.g. in the US National Security Council Report No. 68 sent to President Truman in 1950). Few economists or the military were enthusiastic about a first or unprovoked strike, but they used game theory to model nuclear interactions, investigating operating rules versus discretion, optimal information flows, and probabilistic assessments. Later a similar game-theoretic approach would be used to guide monetary policy.

One side-effect of US nuclear supremacy was that it allowed the US Administration to reduce the post-war Pentagon budget very significantly.

However the outbreak of the Korean War showed that US conventional capability had become badly rundown. It also showed that the ultimate deterrent of a nuclear bomb to cover defence needs was in some ways very limiting. The upshot was a National Security Council report in 1949 that resulted in the Pentagon conventional budget being tripled.

Now that the US no longer had uncontested nuclear leadership and could no longer threaten an un-retaliated nuclear strike, there was considerable pressure to take the next technological steps to develop the hydrogen bomb, which was potentially much more destructive. Arguments about this step split the scientific community. Predictably von Neumann supported developing the H-bomb, though even he was not as strong an adherent as its determined supporters Edward Teller and Ernest Lawrence. This development was roundly opposed by many of von Neumann's Princeton colleagues. Once again the hawks won. By 1954 the US had developed the hydrogen bomb, and just one year later the Soviet Union followed suit. In game theory terms the world was now living in a more equal two-sided competitive game with imperfect information and limited cooperation. Whereas economists like Keynes had placed such weight on international cooperation, von Neumann saw himself as living in a zero-sum world where the choice was to win or lose. And he was not alone: that young Russian economist Kantorovich, who he had met in Moscow two decades earlier, was now actively involved in research on the Soviet bomb; Soviet propaganda also promoted a winner-takes-all world.

The early 1950s was a very testing time, as the Korean War was fought, and the anti-Communist accusatory hysteria of McCarthyism spread across the US academic community. Anyone not supporting a right-wing line could be accused of being a Communist sympathizer. A number of left-wing economists were exposed in the witch-hunt, including Leontief's Harvard and OSS colleague Paul Sweezy and some of the Bretton Woods delegates. Though having one's career ruined was far less harsh than Stalin's punishments, the McCarthy hearings carried a hint of the Soviet trials that Kantorovich had witnessed. Despite his own right-wing views, von Neumann refused to play any part in the McCarthy witch-hunts: when his brilliant colleague Robert Oppenheimer was falsely accused of being a Communist spy, von Neumann organized a group of witnesses for the defence, despite personally disagreeing with Oppenheimer's politics and policies.

In 1953 President Eisenhower came to power and his Secretary of State John Foster Dulles proclaimed a policy of 'massive retaliation' if the Soviets were to try to start a war in line with von Neumann's credible threat theory. For several years von Neumann was the key designer of nuclear credibility strategies for the US. His combination of scientific understanding, his practical approach, his mathematical and economic insight, and his credibility with the military made him the key player in Washington. It was a position that he filled comfortably.

As the arms race escalated and other countries became nuclear powers, von Neumann amended his two-person gaming approach. He now stressed that, in contrast to the end of World War II, 'there has been a complete change in the underlying economic–political–strategic position. Nuclear weapons are no longer expensive, they are no longer scarce, and they are no longer a monopoly of the US' (Macrae, 1992, 358). This completely changed the rules of the game, but his analysis still pointed to the need for a strong US arsenal.

As the nuclear race continued, von Neumann was observing the evolving EDVAC computer design, watching the spread of the von Neumann architecture in computing, and thinking again about how it had been conceptually based on the human brain. He was starting to see that what had been envisaged as a fast computing device might be able to lead to much bigger things for mankind. Computers, he said, could be much more important than bombs.

Von Neumann received a number of offers from prestigious universities to pursue his work on computing. These offers were tempting because von Neumann was now feeling less empathy at the Institute for Advanced Studies. Some colleagues thought practical computing was inimical to serious theoretical science, while Einstein and others felt that von Neumann's work was already too tainted by its military and militaristic connections.

Despite this opposition from academic colleagues, the Institute for Advanced Studies, the RCA Company, and the US Military agreed to jointly fund a lab at Princeton to build a new advanced computing machine based on von Neumann's designs, which promised to do calculations thousands of times faster than existing machines. Initially von Neumann foresaw applications such as better weather prediction, recalling that the crucial D-Day landings had been endangered by poor meteorological forecasts. In addition he thought that such a machine could open up a new approach to empirical economics, eventually allowing economists and others to move on from the oversimplified linear calculations (as used by Leontief and Kantorovich) to more complex but more realistic nonlinear relationships. Von Neumann was very aware that such nonlinear relationships existed everywhere in business and economics, in other sciences, and indeed in life. He had already demonstrated this in his study of bomb shock waves during the war. For the first time, economists would be able to test out their theories in a more realistic way, being at last able to join their scientist colleagues in trying out ideas in the laboratory. Computer simulation was being born.

As with the EDVAC, von Neumann persuaded his military contacts that his IAS computer research should also be openly available. His first report in June 1946 was sent to 275 institutions and researchers in different countries. Over the next half decade many more IAS computer project papers followed. These papers established the 'von Neumann architecture' (with its stored memory, processor, program instructions, and data) that still forms the foundation of computing today.

Despite all his activities, von Neumann was always available to his colleagues for advice, and his mind roamed dazzlingly fast across subjects. An example was the development of linear programming, originally pioneered by Kantorovich. In 1947 US economist George Dantzig visited von Neumann for a chat about optimization techniques. Feeling busy, von Neumann urged him to get to the point of his argument. Dantzig quickly wrote a geometric and algebraic version of his argument on the blackboard. Von Neumann looked at it briefly, and said 'oh that', then gave a 90-minute impromptu lecture on how it might be developed. Dantzig said his independent discovery of linear programming techniques derived from the original insights in this talk.

In 1949 von Neumann designed the first self-reproducing computer program (essentially the world's first computer virus). The IAS computer was finally completed in 1951, and was used by von Neumann for H-bomb calculations. In the meantime other researchers were using the IAS papers to build their own variants, including the MANIAC (to imply something maniacal) at Los Alamos, the so-called JOHNNIAC (named after von Neumann) at Rand Corporation, and eventually the much faster IBM 701 'Defence Computer' machine, which led to the

IBM 714 computer, the first major commercial success. The subsequent computing success of the IBM Company owed a lot to von Neumann's ideas and calculations. These more powerful computers were soon being used for the new applications they offered economists such as Leontief. The Russians were also watching: by the early 1950s the Soviet Academy of Sciences in Moscow had also built a related machine.

In 1955 von Neumann became a commissioner at the Atomic Energy Commission, and he and Klari moved to Washington. Three months later his active and exciting life came to a halt. He developed severe pains in his left shoulder, and after surgery, bone cancer was diagnosed. Initially the doctors hoped the disease could be contained. After a long series of tests he was given some very bad news: he had been diagnosed with bone leukaemia, originating from bone or pancreatic cancer. It is likely (though unproven) that this was due to his exposure to radiation received at the Bikini Atoll bomb test site.

Von Neumann worked feverishly at this time fearing his life was limited, focusing his thoughts on his last work. He had a series of medical treatments, but the condition only worsened: he had lesions on his spine and serious problems walking. It was soon clear that this would be fatal. Von Neumann kept this diagnosis secret from friends and colleagues, and it only served to speed up his work, as he dashed between a frantic schedule of meetings, travel, and research.

Late in life he had developed a new interest: the computer and the brain. Von Neumann was fascinated by the possibility of learning from human biology to improve thinking and computation techniques. This was an interest he had shared with Norbert Weiner (the inventor of cybernetics), and they had jointly organized meetings on the subject (Heims, 1982). He started preparing for a prestigious guest lecture at Yale University on neurobiology: this would compare the human brain with the stored program computer, though he eventually concluded that they were conceptually different, the computer being a sequential processor while the brain operated in parallel. He completed the paper, but sadly was by now too sick to deliver the guest lecture. Increasingly ill, he struggled to complete a book on the subject, which was published after his death as *The Computer and the Brain*. It suggested new types of mathematical approaches, of the sort we would now call artificial intelligence. It also related to early social psychology and the development of 'psyops' or psychological operations used by the military as cerebral propaganda (or 'brainwashing').

What happened over the rest of the year was even more tragic: his brilliant mind began to fade. As he felt the end was approaching, he became first worried and then increasingly terrified that he would run out of time before solving the crucial problems he still had in his mind. His body was failing fast. He made his last public appearance in February of that year seated in a wheelchair as President Eisenhower presented him with the US Medal of Freedom. He was admitted to Walter Reed Hospital in Washington DC in April 1956, where he struggled to continue his work from his bed. There was a constant schedule of visits from colleagues and military men, all eager for his final insights.

His daughter Marina Whitman, by now a famous economist herself, recorded the tragedy of watching this genius die (Whitman, 2012). When he realized he was close to the end his mind panicked: he went through mental terrors—deep fear, psychological breakdown, screaming every night. He was in despair that he was dying too early. In his final days he returned to the Catholic faith. Typically, he said: 'so long as there is the possibility of eternal damnation for non-believers, it is more logical to be a believer at the end.' However his priest with whom he had long conversations about life, death, and God, said that even this renewed faith failed to relieve his terror.

So clever in life, von Neumann did not seem to know how to die. He had to be sedated with increasingly strong painkillers, and the US Military even posted a guard on his ward in case the painkillers made him hallucinate and reveal military secrets. In fact he did start hallucinating, but his rambling was in his birth tongue of Hungarian not English.

Takahashi had died three decades earlier. He had worked in Hiroshima, helping it develop economically, only to be prematurely killed by a right-wing true believer. Von Neumann was himself a right-wing believer who had helped destroy Hiroshima by dropping the atomic bomb. He was prematurely killed, probably by radiation from his work on bombs.

Von Neumann never left the hospital again. On 8 February 1957 he passed away. Hearing of his death, Hans Bethe, his physicist colleague, quoted in *LIFE magazine* said: 'I have sometimes wondered whether a brain like von Neumann's does not indicate a species superior to that of man.'

His wife Klari married again, but always fragile, she committed suicide six years later.

Kantorovich at War and Peace

Von Neumann had been working in academia for the US military on problems of computing and defence. In the post-war years Kantorovich was in a similar position in the USSR. Kantorovich and von Neumann had met in Moscow in 1935, little realizing that they would be pitting their prodigious mathematical talents against each other's country a decade later, a more personalized form of game theory than either might have ever envisaged.

The political arm of the Soviet Government had been persistently hostile to Kantorovich's economic work, but the Soviet Military had recognized his abilities, and they now tasked him with highly confidential work on their atomic programme. From 1948 Stalin had accelerated research into thermonuclear explosions, seeking to counter the US A-bomb leadership. This involved well-resourced teams of top scientists and mathematicians led by Andrei Sakharov. The teams were controlled by the NKVD secret police and assisted by leaked information from a network of sympathizers and spies in the US.

Kantorovich's old colleague Sergei Sobolev had been working on this project for several years, and was now Deputy Director of the Institute for Atomic Energy. He may have suggested his name, for in May 1948 Kantorovich was personally tasked by a directive from the USSR Council of Ministers to head a group of up to 15 mathematicians to assist with calculations for atomic reactors. This was the top-secret project 'Enormoz', the codename for the Soviet Union's urgent request to use covert material from the Anglo-American nuclear weapons work including the US Manhattan Project to build a bomb. Initially his work focused on analysing the leaked US findings and independently checking the leaked US conclusions; after a few years the Soviets were more confident in their own research, and Kantorovich was put to work on calculating the critical mass of the fissionable substance needed for an atomic explosion, estimating concepts such as neutron density and the force needed to move atomic arrangements. (The full details of the work have never been revealed, but the assignment was referred to in 'Top Secret Directive No. 1990-774ss/op, 1948', of the Council of Ministers of the USSR.)

The CIA knew about Kantorovich's role and had kept a file on him. This is known because a copy was seized from the US Embassy in Tehran during the 1971 occupation by students. The file noted that Kantorovich had spent much of his life battling Soviet bureaucracies to win acceptance of the usefulness of his linear programming work. (The de-cyphered 'Venona Project' papers of the time show that the KGB kept a file on von Neumann, following the Manhattan Project involvement of spy colleague Klaus Fuchs.) In 1949 US spy planes patrolling the borders of the Soviet Union picked up traces of airborne radioactivity: the USSR had tested its first A-bomb, much earlier than US analysts had expected. The Cold War was about to enter a new phase.

While in Yaroslavl during World War II Kantorovich had been invited to a seminar in Moscow on the future of calculating machinery. This mainly involved slow analogue machines and old-fashioned electro-mechanical calculators. But nevertheless it sparked an enduring interest, and when Kantorovich returned to Leningrad after the war, he thought deeply about computational problems, and began working on the automation of programming and computer construction.

Kantorovich was interested because he felt that better computation techniques were necessary to improve economic performance. But the first to acknowledge that advanced computing power was actually needed were not Soviet economic planners but rather the Soviet Military: they wanted computing capability for their research into nuclear and missile weapons. During wartime the Soviet Union had kept up to date with American computing developments, having received over 20,000 pages of classified documents from Soviet agents working covertly at large US military-industrial firms. In 1945 Soviet computing pioneer Sergey Lebedev had built a simple analogue computer to solve a set of differential equations, based on what he knew of the American ENIAC and EDSAC designs. Von Neumann's 1946 publication on computer principles had been available in the USSR, although not in open press until the 1950s. Some information about US computing was also accessible from foreign journals as early as 1946. That year a Soviet journal *Advances in Mathematical Sciences* devoted a special issue to analogue computing and the US Bush Differential Analyser. In following years there were articles on US digital electronic computing, including reporting on von Neumann's account of his 'ENIAK' machine. Lebedev reported he had access to data on 18 US machine designs. In 1949 the Soviets published an outline of von Neumann's stored program concepts, but the first Soviet full stored program digital computer (MESM) took several more years to complete.

Kantorovich's Division of Approximate Calculations at Leningrad University had been involved in original research for the USSR atomic project. Initially calculations were carried out on desktop semi-automata that had been seized from Germany as wartime reparations. Rather like von Neumann, Kantorovich brought in punchcard machines that originally had been used to process results of the 1939 USSR Population Census, and he proposed new ways to adapt these, describing the work as 'the paralleling of similar calculations, which made it possible to introduce simple program changes on the plug board (of course by hand)' (O'Connor and Robertson, 2014, 5).

Kantorovich then designed a simple electrical relay calculator which carried out arithmetic operations. Under his instruction a local producer of analogue calculating machines manufactured about 40,000 of these calculators over the next decade, and they were still to be found in commercial use until the 1970s. This calculator allowed the estimation of Bessel functions; calculating Bessel functions was important because it was a standard technique to solve a differential equation system such as found in a modern economic model. Similar work was being done in the US on the Harvard Mark II and ENIAC machines, but the Soviets were proud to have finished their Bessel calculations in 1948 several years before the US had published completed tables. In 1948 Kantorovich and his colleague M. K. Gavurin established a computational mathematics unit within the Mathematical Analysis Department at Leningrad University, and there Kantorovich was among the first in the USSR to teach numerical analysis. Three years later the unit was expanded to become a full Department of Computational Mathematics.

Until the 1950s much of Kantorovich's economic work had been constrained by the need to calculate results by hand. For example in the plywood problem, Kantorovich had estimated there were potentially billions of possible outcomes, and all but the simplest solutions remained beyond the possibilities of manual calculation. He was naturally interested to exploit the evolving possibilities of computation. But, as in much of his research, this did not prove straightforward. Kantorovich had had access to von Neumann's pioneering IAS computing paper, but the latter's new ideas on computing architecture were associated with anti-Soviet American military expansion and were restricted. In addition Soviet propagandists had in 1951 denounced the growing field of cybernetics in the US as the dream of American capitalists who wanted to use automation to replace class-conscious workers. In the post-war Soviet Union cybernetics had been labelled as 'Western' by Stalin, which effectively prohibited its use. The pioneering book *Cybernetics* by Norbert Weiner with some content from von Neumann had been banned in the USSR.

In 1951 the BESM-1 (the first Soviet 'large-scale electronic computing machine') was constructed in Moscow, based on von Neumann's IAS computing machine blueprints. The Soviet Ministry of Machine Building and the Academy of Sciences also unveiled the first large-scale high-speed Soviet machine STRELA. There was some discussion about possible economic applications but it was not until the late 1950s that there were serious Soviet attempts to apply computing to economic planning.

In 1953 Kantorovich gained access to a basic electronic computer at Leningrad University, and reported on automatic programming problems, eventually pioneering an early programming language named PL–I. This was a more generic language than von Neumann's and very flexible in its application. Kantorovich described at as uniquely suitable for any type of intellectual problem, capable of running any type of analogue or digital computer, and capable of automating complex and lengthy problems. Standard processing programs were stored in the computer memory and performed calculations on data, initially at a high level in what he called large blocks, before addressing more detailed calculations (Nitusov, 1997).

Kantorovich then established a class to teach programming skills designed for the new mainframe Soviet computers. Despite the Cold War isolation, the Leningrad computer scientists and mathematical economists were now rapidly catching up with the West, and this time the competitive game was taking place between institutions such as Princeton University and Leningrad University.

Living standards were at last improving in the Soviet Union. Kantorovich's family had survived the war, the children were growing up, and would soon distinguish themselves at university. Photographs show a more relaxed lifestyle: picnics on a beach and a vacation in Crimea. Kantorovich liked to swim, walk, play chess, play an occasional game of ping-pong, and collect wild mushrooms—he had a reputation of consuming even dubious ones.

In 1953 Stalin died. Several years later Khrushchev condemned Stalin's legacy at the historic 20th Soviet Communist Party Conference. Subsequently Khrushchev allowed some liberalization in economic thinking, and the First Secretary of the Communist Party became an active, if unlikely, supporter of mathematical economics. There was one immediate effect: Soviet economic institutes started publishing economic papers and books from the West. Soviet authorities now began to accept that economists such as Kantorovich might be permitted to assist with economic issues. He was tasked with a typical programming problem: the optimal allocation of taxis in Soviet cities. He organized a team of 15 to 20 mathematicians, gave each a separate problem to analyse and a huge amount of data, and then had them report back for a brainstorming session within a week. This allowed him to calculate for the first time price elasticity of demand and to recommend a complete revision of Soviet taxi tariffs, which was subsequently implemented.

Kantorovich had survived the Stalin era, and had kept his independence, refusing to ever join the Communist Party. He had been labelled as 'anti-Marxist', his books had to be prefaced with an explanation and apology for 'errors', and he had not been allowed to hold high positions. This left him very cautious in what he would say even after the Khrushchev thaw. A visit by Ambassador Raymond Pohl to Kantorovich in 1957 reported that he still seemed very nervous about meeting a Westerner, very reticent about expressing his views in halting English. US-Dutch economist T. C. Koopmans wrote to Kayson: 'his contributions are somewhat concealed by self-imposed political cautiousness in the style of writing' (Duppe, 2013, 28).

But changes were afoot: since 1956 Kantorovich had been able to give economic lectures at the Leningrad State University promoting his 1939 and 1942 breakthroughs, teaching a course on 'economic calculation', and enthusiastically participating in seminars. In early 1957, together with some colleagues from Leningrad, Kantorovich was invited to visit the Institute of Economics of the Academy of Sciences in Moscow, described as the citadel of traditional Marxist-Leninist economic theory. He was there to present a paper on planning to a small group of key officials and academics, and for the first time it was positively received. This was an important test of the changing views on the post-Stalin era, and a test of continuing hostility to any theories challenging the primacy of the labour theory of value.

By the following year the repressive atmosphere was lifting: the Academy of Sciences set up a Laboratory of Economic-Mathematical Methods under Kantorovich's colleague Vasily Nemchinov. Kantorovich took a courageous stand and openly criticized orthodox Stalin-era political economy at a 1959 conference. He came under immediate attack from traditional Soviet economists for this position. But times were changing, and this time he received support from colleagues.

The new institute published more freely. Kantorovich was at last allowed to re-publish his original 1939 paper on linear programming and also an expanded book version of his optimal planning work, though only with a lengthy editorial preface by Nemchinov, who praised Kantorovich's earlier linear programming work (and also Leontief's input-output techniques which he described as a useful special case), but was quite critical of his colleague's claims to have extended the techniques to economic planning. He particularly singled out the use of 'objectively determined valuations' (i.e. shadow prices) as being 'inconsistent and incorrect', though he accepted that Kantorovich had at least disassociated himself from the 'concepts of bourgeois economists' (Nemchinov, 1959, vi–xvi).

The only acceptable economic views in the past were those seen as consistent with Marxist socialist theory. In the late 1950s Nemchinov had tried to import Leontief's input-output ideas into the Soviet Union to improve economic planning. He argued that this work had Soviet origins, but despite this, had encountered ideological resistance by officials who saw it as a capitalist tool. Kantorovich did not think input-output was a practical planning tool. Nevertheless, the Soviets became gradually more receptive to Kantorovich's own ideas once they had some exposure to the macro-level input-output tables of Leontief—as a Russian émigré himself, the latter's ideas seem to have been more acceptable to Soviet planners (Katsenelinboigen, 1978, 142). His book *Studies on the Structure of the American Economy* had been translated and circulated in the Soviet Union as early as 1955 (in breach of copyright) though not officially published in Russian until 1959.

By 1960 Gosplan had become involved with the academic community once again, at last declaring their interest in what economists and cybernetics might contribute to the Soviet planning process. A large conference took place in Moscow on the application of mathematical models in economics and planning, and Kantorovich was invited as one of the key participants, delivering a paper on 'Mathematical Methods in Economics'. The arguments were debated noisily, even angrily, but this time Kantorovich took a more assertive stand, criticizing mainstream Soviet economists for their dislike of optimization techniques, and being attacked in turn by hardliners with the poisonous label 'bourgeois' (Gardner, 1990, 639). But his new approach was now being openly condoned by Premier Khrushchev, who believed that mechanization, standardization, and automation were the keys to Soviet modernization. The next year the term 'economic cybernetics' was explicitly declared to be the official party line at the 22nd Congress of the Communist Party. Interest expanded quickly: there were soon more than 40 Soviet research institutes involved in related research. Some of the Soviet scientists were very guarded about the new methods, but a number of younger economists were excited by the possibilities.

With this new toolkit and approval from the politicians, there was now speculation about whether Gosplan could compute a single optimized economic plan based on a large linear program with input-output techniques being used for sectoral composition. Kantorovich had been one of the first to realize the potential of computers to solve such a full economic system, but he understood that in the 1960s there were no computers that could store and process all the data that would be necessary to deliver the hundreds of thousands of shadow prices. Consequently the state's planning committee was slow to adopt the technique on a significant scale.

If the Russians were tracking American economic thinking, the Americans had never stopped tracking the Russians' own economic advances. During the Cold War the US Rand Corporation undertook many research programmes studying the Soviet economy, initially building on Leontief's wartime work. Rand apparently translated Kantorovich's book, but it was not publicly available in English until 1965 (Bockman and Bernstein, 2008, 586). It was only then that it was realized that some of the new Western economic ideas of the 1950s such as input-output, growth models, and development economics had already been receiving Soviet attention.

At the urging of the US Military, the Rand Corporation compiled another report, this one on the state of Soviet cybernetics and its official reception. It noted that a bitter fight had been under way between conservative economists in Moscow and the younger Soviet cyberneticists. Kantorovich was now a leader of this latter group, though Rand reported he was still in party disgrace. (The Rand report was not published until 1963, and the comment on party disgrace was probably out of date by then.)

In 1960 Kantorovich and family made a major move: they transferred to Novosibirsk in Western Siberia. The city had become one of the largest industrial centres in the Soviet Union, as a result of many wartime plants moving eastward out of range of German bombers. As the Cold War intensified it was also seen as safe from Western intelligence surveillance. In the 1950s the government designated as a centre for scientific research, Akademgarodale (literally 'Academic City'), a new research complex 30km south of Novosibirsk. Kantorovich was appointed Deputy Director of the Institute of Mathematics in the Novosibirsk State University at the Siberian Division of the Academy of Sciences, an Institute which had been established by his old colleague Sergei Sobolev. (Not being an approved party member, Kantorovich could not be Director.)

The city was built in the middle of a Siberian forest, and housed 20,000 scientists and support staff working in about 35 research institutes and universities, in well-equipped laboratories, many of them focused on secret defence work. While in the Soviet mind Siberia was still viewed as a place of exile, this location had its attractions: scientists received a supplement on salaries, were allocated comfortable apartments, could buy good supplies of food, their children accessed top schools, and there were excellent sports facilities, concert facilities, and arts venues.

Kantorovich was moving far from the locus of government economic policy: it is unclear whether he was directed to move or whether it was his own decision. No matter how comfortable the new workplace, moving from the historic western capital of Leningrad to a forest beyond an industrial city in far-off Siberia must have been a cultural shock. Yet Kantorovich may have thought that moving from the intense Cold War politics of European Russia would offer him more opportunity to do his economics.

In fact it opened up new horizons for him: at Akademgarodale he was offered new computing facilities and top research students. In his new position Kantorovich led the emergence of a new school of economics, recruiting heavily from former colleagues in Leningrad and attracting younger economists who had technical training rather than older ideologues. This school was not bound to the old style of Marxist-Leninist socialism, but looked instead to a new era of mathematical economics under the label of 'system of optimally functioning socialist economy'. This is what became known as Soviet-style economic cybernetics, focusing on optimization techniques for production, in contrast to the political economy of socialism. It was not revolutionary, but the mathematical approach was less ideological, used advanced computation methods, and was aimed at improving the operation of state enterprises and optimizing economic plans.

In 1960 Koopmans, Kantorovich's correspondence friend, was invited to visit the Soviet Union. He met Kantorovich briefly on arrival in Moscow, then later flew 3,000 kilometres to Novosibirsk. There he met Kantorovich in his laboratory at the Institute of Mathematics and reported that they had fertile discussions about the application of mathematics and economics.

By now Kantorovich had established a top-quality school of economic mathematical modelling at Novosibirsk. As well as doing advanced theoretical research, he and his team worked on a number of practical industrial projects on topics as diverse as the structure of machine tractor parks, the optimization of rolling mill production, an automated management system for the state procurement organization, techniques to improve workflow at the local instrument and turbo-generator factories, the optimization of targets for coal mining by the state mining company, and linear programming methods for rayon manufacture by a local chemical fibre combine.

Kantorovich had already designed an electrical calculator. A few years later he designed a larger device called 'Computer A.M.', a specialized minicomputer processor, described in his work *Computation System Consisting of Universal Digital Computing Machine and Minicomputer.* This embedded in hardware form the multilevel pipeline with direct memory access that he had earlier envisaged in his programming architecture. He received several patents for design elements that were later widely implemented in both Soviet and foreign computers. A pilot A.M. computer was constructed at his laboratory in Novosibirsk, but it was never produced commercially.

Khrushchev's de-Stalinization programme continued, and the academic climate was improving markedly. In 1964, despite not being a party member, Kantorovich was voted on to the elite Academy of Sciences of the Soviet Union, official recognition at last of his unique economic contribution. There were very few full academicians in the Soviet Union, they held an exalted rank equivalent to that of a Soviet general, and in addition they enjoyed many special privileges.

Recognition continued: in 1965, following lobbying from many influential academics, Kantorovich was awarded the Lenin Prize, the highest Soviet academic award, for his originally suppressed publication *The Economic Calculation of Best Use of Resources.* The Soviet Government had now moved from opposition to enthusiasm for economics and planning, which would ultimately lead to the 1960s Kosygin reforms that introduced partial marketization to the Soviet Union, denoting sales and profitability as two market indicators of an enterprise's success. Kantorovich's mathematical model approach suited the needs of this new generation of post-war Soviet leaders who wanted improved efficiency of allocation to meet the demands of a consumer economy, all of which was proving far more complex than wartime production. Ultimately the straitjacket of Marxist-Leninist ideology with its labour theory of value would be loosened sufficiently to accommodate such changes.

Several years later Kantorovich's Lenin Prize was elevated to the Order of Lenin, the highest civil decoration of the Soviet Union. In later years he complained that he would have preferred to receive The Order of the Hero of Socialist Labour, for the very practical reason that in the Soviet Union people recognized this more common award in shops and restaurants, and it could guarantee bookings and better service in this unresponsive economy. After all his hardships during the war and his years as an outsider, Kantorovich was now leading a comfortable life as a respected and respectful member of the Soviet Establishment.

Kantorovich started to receive international recognition: he was awarded a number of economic honours and honorary doctorates initially from Eastern European institutions, then from the West. He began to receive invitations to travel abroad, though continuing Cold War suspicions meant he could not accept these at first. In 1965, after failing to get Kantorovich to visit him, Koopmans made another visit to the Soviet Union, where he met Kantorovich, this time in his private home, an unusually intimate invitation at that time. A few years later Kantorovich organized a large symposium on Models of the National Economy, obtaining permission to offer some invitations to Western economists, so that Koopmans was able to visit once again.

At the beginning of the 1970s there was a further sign of official acceptance: Kantorovich was invited to move back west, this time to Moscow, the heart of Soviet Government. There he was appointed to head the Laboratory for Economic-Mathematical Methods in the Business School, then moved to the All-Union Institute of Systems. In 1971 the Institute of Management of the National Economy was established in Moscow to develop economic mathematical methods and encourage the development of computers and planning. There Kantorovich continued to work on improved computing devices and the automation of programming. The Institute of Economic Management had been set up on the initiative of Premier Alexei Kosygin to train officials in modern management, economic planning, and the use of computers, reflecting the growing Soviet interest in Western management science. Kantorovich's CIA file noted that both Premier Kosygin and Party Secretary Kirilenko attended the opening of the Institute, an unusual honour that signalled official encouragement. The Soviet Government was at last recognizing Kantorovich's economic contribution and wanted him closer to policy decision-making. He was recognized as founder of a new school of thought on the optimal functioning of the Soviet economy, resulting in a considerable amount of economic research, but employing mathematics to sidestep the recurring ideological criticisms (Gardner, 1990, 642). As time passed he received many other invitations, including being asked to serve on the Committee on Prices of the USSR Council of Ministers, somewhat ironic given his early work on prices that had been so technically advanced but so ideologically unsound.

In 1975 there was more exciting news: the Nobel Prize awards were announced, and most unusually the Soviet Union had won two of them. The Peace Prize had controversially been awarded to nuclear scientist turned peace advocate, Andrei Sakharov, whose military work Kantorovich had been involved in. The other award went to Kantorovich himself, named as winner of the Nobel Prize in Economics, jointly with his Dutch-American colleague Tjalling Koopmans for 'contributions to the theory of optimal allocation of resources'. According to one report, the Nobel Prize Committee had decided to award him the prize two years earlier, but Kantorovich had not been confident he could accept and asked that it be delayed (Bockman and Burnstein, 2008, 608). Kantorovich joined the very small elite group of Soviet Nobel laureates, which included such luminaries as Boris Pasternak and Alexander Solzhenitsyn. He was to be the only economist in the Soviet Union ever to be so honoured (though there was one Russian émigré prize winner: Wassily Leontief).

It was a mark of his growing acceptance by the Soviet Establishment that Kantorovich was permitted to travel to Sweden to receive the prize from King Gustav. Although now aged 64 this trip was his first journey outside the Soviet Union. The Awards Ceremony attracted much attention, partly because of the controversy surrounding Andrei Sakharov, the Soviet atomic expert who had become a peacenik, and was denied an exit visa. On the stage in Stockholm, Kantorovich accepted the economics award from the Swedish King and delivered an acceptance speech. He proudly pointed out that the October Russian Revolution had left a unique set of circumstances in the USSR: for the first time in history all means of production had passed into the possession of the people, and hence there was a unique need and opportunity for centralized control of the economy. This meant Soviet economists faced a quite different challenge from Western ones, shifting economic theory from studying markets to systemic control of prices, rents, and interest, both observable and unobservable, in their static and dynamic forms. The result was that Soviet economists developed multi-product linear optimizing models as their dominant approach, a path independently followed by Leontief and von Neumann.

There was an informal reception in Stockholm with several American economics Nobel laureates, and there at last Kantorovich met fellow Petrograd prodigy Wassily Leontief. He attended a seminar in Sweden organized in his honour, and as a result of this he and Koopmans together produced a book entitled *Problems of Application of Optimisation Methods in Industry.*

Next Kantorovich travelled on to the United States where he attended the January Annual Meeting of the American Economics Association in Atlantic City, a vast professional event with over 1,000 economists and several hundred papers ranging across many economic topics. We can only assume he would have been impressed, if not bewildered, by the breadth, openness, and robust criticisms indulged in by American academic economists, to say nothing of the resorts and casinos in Atlantic City. There was a session devoted to the year's Nobel Prize winners: Kantorovich's ex-colleague Stanislav Menshikov presented him to an audience which included Tjalling Koopmans and Lawrence Klein. There was also a session at the conference on input-output analysis and the Leontief Paradox, but it is unclear whether Leontief himself attended this. After he left the United States, Kantorovich travelled on to India, then visited the new International Institute of Systems Analysis which had just been established in Vienna to build scientific bridges across the Cold War divide. There he attended a conference with the world's other pioneers of programming, Koopmans and Dantzig.

Later he was given permission to visit other institutions abroad. Over the next decade he received many international honours, a late recognition from the West of his huge and original achievements. His new opportunities to travel and to see other economic systems left a lasting impression but did not change his fundamental economic thinking about the positive potential of socialist systems.

A lifetime of ideological conformance took its toll; even late in life Kantorovich was very guarded and non-critical in his support of the socialist system. In a 1979 interview he said that in contrast to the Stalin years there was now an understanding that shadow prices should be used to reflect scarcity: critics must remember that the Soviet system was still relatively new and evolving. With mathematical and computing advances the early principles of material balance could now be represented in models that would deliver shadow prices that potentially could be more efficient than in the imperfect 'free' markets of the West (Pizano, 2009, loc. 1749).

During his career Kantorovich had published very widely—over 300 papers and books. He described these as being mainly mathematical with work on optimal planning and prices, and a focus on the economic problems of planned economies. Asked in 1979 what he thought were the most influential economic theories he replied: 'I think that the works of Keynes and his school, the works of Leontief and von Neumann, and the works of Soviet economists in the sphere of the theory of planning and its implementation are the most important contributions' (Pizano, 2009, loc. 1971).

By the 1980s he had retired and he led a comfortable quiet life in Moscow. He held fast to his views on the viability of the Communist system. He outlived the Cold War Soviet leaders long enough to see the first of the glasnost reforms from the new Communist Party General Secretary Mikhail Gorbachev and the first of the peace summits with US President Reagan.

At the peak of his powers, like von Neumann, he found he had contracted cancer. Like von Neumann he had been working on atomic experiments, though there is no evidence that exposure to radiation caused his condition. Despite being able to access good medical services, the disease had taken hold, and it proved incurable. Leonid Kantorovich died in Moscow in April 1986; his hard wartime life had taken its toll—he was aged only 74.

One of his admiring ex-students who was now in a position of some power used his connections with the Kremlin to arrange for *Pravda*, the official organ of the Communist Party, to print an obituary. That announcement at the highest level made it possible for the family to obtain a special burial site at the prestigious Novo-Devichie cemetery in central Moscow. There was a large funeral which was attended by Kantorovich's wife, two children, and grandchildren. (All these four children and children-in-law had followed in his footsteps and become mathematical economists themselves.)

The obituary had been signed by, amongst others, the General Secretary of the Communist Party Mikhail Gorbachev, who more than anyone would be responsible for the eventual breakdown of the Soviet economic system.

Leontief at Peace

If Kantorovich had accepted the Nobel Prize offer earlier in 1973, he would have stood alongside Wassily Leontief on the stage at the Nobel Prize ceremony in Stockholm. Leontief had been awarded the Nobel Economics Prize that year 'for the development of the input-output method and for its application to important economic problems'. In wishing to honour Kantorovich, that other boy from Petrograd that same year, the Nobel Committee had recognized the connections in their work.

At this time Leontief remained very interested in the Soviet economy. His archived papers contain basic input-output charts for the Soviet Union for several years. In contrast to the struggles of Kantorovich, Leontief had led an easier academic life in the US. However he too had encountered a hostile academic atmosphere and had suffered from the constrictive atmosphere engendered by the Cold War, with his own run-ins with McCarthy-era restrictions.

Input-output techniques had been condemned as capitalist in the Soviet Union. In the US they suffered the reverse criticism: they were seen as technologies designed for a planned economy, unsuited to market-based capitalism, fundamentally 'un-American'. Political pressure on the US Government had led to the termination of input-output research funding at the Bureau of Labour Statistics which had built the giant US economy model, and later at the US Air Force, which was modelling tactical economic vulnerabilities. American private companies showed no such ideological reticence, and at this time Leontief was much in demand to model the effects of technical change in a number of industries. He worked for many large corporates and had a retainer with several large consulting firms.

In 1950 Senator Joseph McCarthy made his infamous speech alleging that Communists and sympathizers were endangering the US system; there was an atmosphere of mounting suspicion and paranoia in Washington. Leontief had tried to access some government statistical information for his modelling research, but he was told it was classified and available only to people with a high security clearance. He argued that he had been cleared for his wartime work, but only then found that his OSS security clearance had been revoked, on the basis that he was allegedly sympathetic to Communist front organizations (he had belonged to the Russia War Research organization, a diaspora body), and additionally that he had misinformed the US Government about his birth (which may have been true, as he was unaware of the fact that he had actually been born in Germany). In practice, Leontief's Russian name, his origins, and his increasingly public criticism of the arms race were more likely the real reasons. It was a difficult period, full of rumours and accusations. His wife Estelle claimed Joseph Schumpeter's wife had told the authorities they had named their daughter after Stalin's daughter Svetlana (despite this accusation the Schumpeters remained family friends). The CIA had a file on Kantorovich; now it appeared that the FBI had files on Leontief and his wife.

Leontief was never unwilling to confront authority. Rather than look for ways to access the data which may anyway have been available from other sources, he had the determination, liberty and funds to take a confrontationist approach, hiring a top lawyer and enduring a long and expensive legal process. He collected affidavits about his integrity from colleagues and confronted the authorities at a hearing before the Eastern Industrial Personnel Security Board in New York. The board noted his Russian heritage and accent, and was initially unsympathetic: his name appeared to have been on a number of articles published in Russian economic journals during wartime, and board members accused him of being a Soviet sympathizer. Leontief took a perverse pleasure in demonstrating that the actual author had been a completely different person: another Soviet economist with the same family name. Leontief was a socialist, but like many émigré Russians, decidedly not a Communist: his views had been made public back in 1937 in his paper entitled 'The Significance of Marx for Modern Economic Theory'. In 1954 the US Government eventually reinstated his security clearance.

It was clear from the World War II bombing experience that input-output analysis offered a way to identify and map sectoral vulnerabilities in modern economies, and that would continue to be important for defence purposes. In 1947 Leontief wanted to update the input-output table of the US economy but the Bureau of Labor Studies was facing funding cuts. Leontief's interest was in generating information for economic recovery policies in the United States. Eventually the work was incorporated into a well-funded Air Force Cold War programme entitled SCOOP ('Scientific Computation of Optimum Programs'). By this time the US was concerned about bottlenecks to Cold War mobilization. The research eventually managed to produce a huge input-output table mapping US production, with a quarter of a million cells, which involved far more sectoral detail and a huge increase in data: 450 industrial and 50 other sectors (limited to 42 in Leontief's 1951 published version).

At the end of the war the Strategic Vulnerability Branch of the US Army's Air Intelligence Division was established to pull together material on bombing targets in Europe and Japan. It compiled this information in a 'Bombing Encyclopaedia' covering military installations, important industrial plants, service facilities, and infrastructure, including data on production, employees, and inputs (organized along wartime input-output guidelines and using the bombing concepts of cushion, depth, and substitutability). Initially the database covered the wartime Axis powers. But as Cold War tensions increased, the encyclopaedia was extended to cover potential targets in the USSR.

Game theory told the Strategic Vulnerability Branch that if they were listing Soviet targets, the Soviets were likely doing the same thing for the United States. So the next obvious step was to include US domestic facilities that could be potential targets of a Soviet attack. This database became so huge (70,000 detailed listings by the 1950s) that the main problem was not just sourcing data but organizing it. In 1952 the Univac computer, a development from the ENIAC, become available: the first was produced for the US Census Bureau, the second went to the Pentagon for the USAAF to be used for the Bombing Encyclopaedia. During the 1950s the US Office of Defence Mobilization built more sophisticated models of the effects of projected nuclear attack on the US using input-output techniques. Since then there has been much US military use of input-output models to simulate supply lines, enemy targets, and vulnerable sectors.

While the military continued to pursue their own technical interests in input-output mapping, Leontief was more interested in its civil applications, showing how to connect it to an economic growth model, and how international trade might impact it. He found that the United States, the most capital-abundant country in the world, exported goods that were more labour-intensive than capital-intensive, and this became known as the Leontief Paradox. Between 1944 and 1946 Leontief had written three path-breaking papers using input-output techniques to estimate the effects of a change in final demand on output, employment, wages, and prices of individual sectors. The input-output analysis would play an important role in developing general equilibrium theory in the 1940s and 1950s. Eventually Leontief would go further, constructing open economy input-output models, and by the mid-1970s he had built a simplified model of the world for the United Nations, with 15 regions and 45 sectors.

In 1948 Leontief established the Harvard Economics Research Project which collated regional input-output tables and capital-coefficient matrices to derive the investment implications of changing demand and to generate growth paths. Initially the project comprised Leontief and an assistant with a slide rule. Before long it had become a large programme accommodated in its own sprawling wooden house near Cambridge Common at Harvard. After some years of work Leontief reluctantly conceded that input-output analysis had become so data-intensive that compilation was now a job for official statistical agencies rather than for academics.

In the 1950s American economists had questioned whether Kantorovich had really pioneered linear programming. Now Leontief heard claims from other Soviet economists that input-output analysis was actually a Soviet invention too. This claim was not without some basis given the early work of Soviet planners such as Pavel Popov and his colleagues. The early Soviets did not invent the input-output formulation, though they did invent the row-column representation of inter-industry flows, and it was Popov who seems to have had the original idea of combining a national accounting table with a mathematical model (Akhabbar, 2006, 16).

After the war Leontief had begun a series of annual summer seminars in European locations such as Austria, giving European economists a chance to mix with Americans, designed along the lines of the pre-war Vienna colloquium attended by von Neumann. In 1959 during the opening-up era Leontief had an opportunity to make a three-week visit to Moscow and his old home town, now named Leningrad. A decade earlier von Neumann at Princeton and Kantorovich at Leningrad Universities were on the opposite sides of the deep divide. Leontief's intention was to bridge this divide, devoting his trip to building contacts between Harvard and Leningrad University academics.

On this trip he was impressed by many young Soviet economists and mathematicians, some of whom were also working on input-output techniques. Many of the scholars were postdoctoral colleagues of Kantorovich and Nemchinov. Leontief visited Kantorovich's Institute in Leningrad, and met Kantorovich there. He reported that the Russian, who was about to transfer to Novosibirsk, was considered newly respectable, even being able in public sessions to criticize (the 'meaningless discourse') of the Marxist-Leninist era. In Harvard's *Crimson Magazine* Leontief reported that he could see some partial adoption of Western economic theories including his own, and he felt that might bring the Soviet people substantial economic improvements.

No doubt they had an interesting conversation—for Kantorovich, the de-Stalinization of the Soviet system meant that he had been working on allocation systems which no longer had to be slavishly based on Marxist-Leninist theories of labour value, though his Nobel speech shows he never fundamentally resiled from this foundation stone. Kantorovich had pioneered linear production models within a Marxist-Leninist theory of labour value. In contrast Leontief had pioneered linear production models based on Western labour markets; his seminal paper on wage contracts posited what might be described as a 'property theory of value'. Leontief's work on principal–agent theory in labour markets was to spawn considerable research by other economists: by focusing on sticky markets with imperfect governance, he was exploring the microeconomic differences between capitalist markets and communist systems.

Sticky labour markets had also been an underpinning in Keynes's *General Theory* explaining why macroeconomic markets might not automatically equilibrate. Keynes was by now long dead, but Keynesianism was very much alive and becoming increasingly influential. By the 1950s most Western governments were considering the use of active fiscal policies and monetary policies to stabilize their economies as they rebounded from the suppressed consumption and high debt of the war years. In contrast to Keynesian stabilization of demand, von Neumann, Kantorovich, and Leontief had all focused on supply-side ways to help economies to grow better.

By the 1950s there was interest among economists in other countries in using input-output techniques for development planning purposes. Leontief had a following of younger economists in both Japan and Germany. Ironically in the US the technique had been labelled as too socialist, while in the USSR Kantorovich had dismissed it for planning purposes due to the drawbacks of the technical coefficients, saying he would rather use the Novosibirsk work on dynamic linear programming (Pizano, 2009, loc. 1817).

Leontief was to make several more trips to Leningrad and Moscow. He always looked for opportunities to help young Russian economists, he joined several Soviet economic academies, and in 1991 he helped set up the Leontief Centre in St Petersburg to implement support for transition reforms in Russia. His archives are full of correspondence with Russian academics and proposals for conferences and studies on the Russian economy. For several years he maintained a correspondence with Kantorovich, mainly concerning the publication of the latter's research in the West, and he also contributed to a volume of essays in honour of Kantorovich's colleague, Vasily Nemchinov.

As he became more well known, Leontief received many invitations to travel and advise. In 1969 he had the opportunity to visit Cuba (although US citizens' travel was highly restricted at the time and Leontief claimed the US Government made his trip very difficult). In 1972 (the same year as President Nixon's famous visit) he travelled to China, now much changed from his 1928 trip. In both cases he wrote studies of these centrally-planned economies, very critical of their inefficiencies.

By the 1960s US defence spending had increased significantly, approximately doubling post-war expenditure in real terms. Leontief had become an independent authority on the economic impact of military budgets. He was much less sympathetic than von Neumann to the military build-up, arguing that the military spending of the major powers all needed to be cut. Like Takahashi he saw fiscal control as an important instrument to promote peace. As Leontief continued his work, his military views hardened (just as did von Neumann's), but in his case he had become an avowed pacifist, joining several peace organizations, ironic given the earlier application of his input-output research to wartime bombing.

In later years Leontief's interests spread wider: he contributed to traditional economic topics such as demand theory, international trade, econometric methods, technical change, and economic dynamics; he worked on topics from his earlier life such as socialist economics and economic planning; and he delved into new areas that had not yet been identified by most researchers such as population economics, environmental economics, and disarmament.

Leontief's input-output work had given him a unique insight into the pattern of arms expenditure in the economy. He had been involved in studies with the US Air Force and Rand Corporation estimating the costs, investment implications, and indirect effects of US and international military spending as he documented the implications of the Cold War arms race. These findings increasingly led him to question von Neumann's MAD approach. There was growing interest in the possibility of nuclear disarmament, and Leontief became deeply interested in both its security and economic possibilities. In the early 1960s he attended a number of the Pugwash Conferences (established in Canada under the influence of von Neumann's colleague Albert Einstein and Keynes's colleague Bertrand Russell), presenting papers on the economics of disarmament. Many other disarmament conferences followed, and Leontief became a member of the UN Group on the Social and Economic Consequences of Disarmament. By 1965 he had gathered his views in scholarly form in an article published in the *Review of Economics and Statistics*, entitled 'The Economic Impact of an Arms Cut'.

At that time he also helped establish an East–West Institute dedicated to the study of arms impacts, which he saw as a counterpoint to the International Atomic Energy Agency. This eventually saw the light of day as the International Institute for Applied Systems Analysis in Vienna, where Kantorovich was later able to visit and work. Its work contributed to the historic Strategic Arms Limitation Talks (SALT) and to subsequent nuclear agreements in the 1970s.

All his life Leontief had been dedicated to economics being based on hard data. In his presidential address to the American Economic Association in 1970 he railed against economic models that had been constructed without regard for observable empirical testability. Leontief remained a very energetic writer and a tireless exponent of technology (though he never learned to type). Aged 80 when most are retired, he produced a very modern paper entitled 'The Future Impact of Automation on Workers'.

Colleagues remember him as a marvellous raconteur but 'a member of the awkward squad' because of his frequent and colourful quarrels with colleagues and authority. In 1975 following arguments with colleagues at Harvard he took a perverse pleasure in walking away from his 40-year employer with some of his best students, and joining New York University. This was his protest at Harvard's refusal to award tenure to Marxist economists and to take on student curriculum complaints. To him this remained a dark shadow left over from McCarthyism and the Cold War. By his own admission he did not have many close friends amongst his colleagues, and his wife moved in a more socialist artistic set. Yet colleagues remember him as urbane, witty, and with a sparkling range of conversation.

Leontief's input-output achievements had guided wartime military policy, but his last years were devoted to peace and disarmament. In 1983 with colleague Faye Duchin he published an important new book: *Military Spending: Facts and Figures, Worldwide Implications, and Future Outlook*. This used input-output analysis to analyse the probable effects of different rates of military spending on economic performance for major countries around the world. The results showed that continuing current levels of military production and procurement would likely hold back development in most developing countries. He concluded that reducing military spending would dramatically improve the conditions in the world's poorest regions and the Eastern Block, while even the US would be better off: military spending hurts all, but it hurts Americans less than others.

The Cold War ended a decade later, but only after the US had demonstrated the accuracy of Leontief's predictions by outspending the USSR on nuclear attack systems. Intellectually vigorous until the end, the 93-year-old Wassily Leontief died in 1999 in New York City. After a long and demanding life he had seen his warnings about fiscal constraints come true, he had seen the breakup of the Soviet Union and the re-establishment of his own motherland of Russia, and he had heard the President of the United States acknowledge the end of the Cold War.

10

Annex

Economies in Wartime

Impact of the War on the Major Warring Economies

Much of the military and political history of World War II takes economics for granted, believing battles are won through military tactics and strategy alone. Yet protracted military engagement cannot happen without economic management. Generals need economists and finance ministers too.

The decade of world wars between 1935 and 1945 brought huge yet different economic problems. By many measures it represented the biggest cumulative economic shock in the history of the world. There is a significant literature on the economies of the protagonists during wartime. All the economies were severely disrupted, though in different ways. They had many different economic problems and tried many different economic policies. Can we generalize the impact of World War II on the economies of the major participating countries? The following summary reflects the results of research by Harrison et al. across the major protagonists (Harrison, 1998).

The overall economic impact of warfare on a protagonist country initially depended on the degree of preparation undertaken in preceding years, the industrial structure of the country, the extent of spare capacity, and the allocation and control mechanisms for shifting production from civilian to military uses. Dictators had the advantage of direct control, and the disadvantage of poor individual decision-making. Centrally-planned economies had the advantage of controlling resources, and the disadvantage of poor allocative efficiency.

In all countries investment, especially public investment, increased considerably and it was particularly directed towards armaments, with a high public funding content. Investment for purely civilian ends dropped significantly. Capacity use improved noticeably, and new mass production techniques were used to turn out huge volumes of standardized military equipment. Labour inputs were limited by the demands of the armed forces, and where forced labour was involved there were significant quality problems. Overall there were major disruptions to peacetime production and considerable uncertainty in planning. International trade became costly and dangerous, and it declined in volume, refocused on providing food and war supplies.

Financing of the war effort had to be primarily from domestic sources, as peacetime international capital markets froze up. Domestic taxation increased and public bond issues expanded. National wealth and asset values declined.

Household consumption was crowded out and declined in all countries. There was a reduction in the quality of civilian production, and consumer choice narrowed considerably. Most countries introduced rationing. This reduction in private consumption was the main driver of reduced standards of living during the war. Considerable amounts of private assets were nationalized or confiscated.

There were potentially large economic distributional impacts in the protagonist countries. Occupied and ravaged populations lost land, housing, and other assets. In all countries the taxed and mobilized sectors of the population suffered most heavily. Some industrialists and some skilled labour groups gained during the war. Post-war arrangements could be highly disruptive, with continued rationing, black markets, authoritarian governments, loss of territory, and sometimes revolution. With few exceptions, national debt built up significantly during wartime, then gradually reduced over peacetime (Slater, 2018). By extension, it has only been the ability to raise major debt that allowed major wars to happen at all, putting the burden of funding on to future generations. In a broader socio-economic sense, funding policies such as proposed by Keynes showed that the burden could also be moved between capital and labour, younger and older cohorts, cities and rural areas.

In most countries wartime brought a big increase in public ownership of industry, an increase in the size of the public sector, a more directed allocation system, intense industry policy, more regulation, increased government revenue, public deficits, and mounting public debt. The role of economists changed from their traditional focus on growth and stabilization to building targeted industrial capacity, prioritizing military production, and limiting civilian and household production. This required allocation mechanisms, price stabilization, and income policies. It also meant innovative funding and management of the government's accounts, and involved finding credible ways to postpone the funding burden to future peacetime generations.

After the war, economies returned to a civilian orientation, but they would never be the same again.

Wartime Economic Burdens

Chapter	Population, million	GDP $US bn.	GDP $US bn.	Armed Forces	Munitions Production	Military Spending
	(1938)	(1938)	(1944)	(000, 1944)	($bn, 1944)	(% GNP, '44)
1 Japan	72	320	360	5380	6	76
2 China	412	610	n.a.	4300	n.a.	n.a.
3 Germany	69	667	830	9420	17	70 ('43)
4 UK	48	540	657	5090	11	56
5 USSR	167	684	688	12225	16	69
6/7 USA	131	1520	2848	11410	42	47

The GDP data are in $US, adjusted to 2018 prices. The figures for China relate to the Nationalist Government, excluding Communist China and Manchuria; note that the Chinese data is not reliable.

Source: Harrison (1988, 1998)

Summary of Wartime Policy Approaches

The following table in brief summary form provides a taxonomy of the issues faced by seven economists in the six economies that are the focus of this book.

Economic Issue	Economic Position of Protagonist Countries
Resource Availability:	
• Domestic economic resource availability	US held many resources; Japan heavily dependent on raw material imports
• History of economic management	Japan had a limited tradition of macroeconomic management
• Industrial base	Germany, UK, US all had deep industrial capability
Economic Governance:	
• Dictatorship v. democracy	Political/military dictatorships in USSR, Germany, Japan limited role of economists
• Direct intervention by leaders	Fiscal demands by Hitler, Stalin, Chiang and Tojo interfere with economic management
• Role of economists in government	UK and US had established important economic units in government
• Economist community	US and UK had active economic advice from academic and private economists
• Corruption v. rules	China very corrupt; Germany, Soviet Union had party preferences
Control of Military Spending:	
• Normal budget arrangements	UK, US followed legislated arrangements; Japan over-ruled them; China budgeting was shambolic
• Authoritarian policy	China levied individual groups in ad hoc way; Germany appropriated private savings; Soviet Union collective ownership
• Military requisitioning	Japan, China, Germany, others requisitioned resources as required
Preparation for War:	
• Rearmament in advance	Germany had been covertly rearming for years, USSR had military base
• Economic preparation in advance	USSR had centralized planning in place; Japan had rearmed for its Manchurian expenditure
Financing Expenditure:	
• Wartime taxes	China taxed businesses/peasants in ad hoc way; UK Keynes Plan spread tax burden
• Domestic borrowing	Wartime bonds issued in most countries; compulsory borrowing in China and elsewhere
• Borrowing on international markets	Practised by Japan in WWl, most dictatorships unable to borrow internationally in wartime
• Funding from diaspora	Big contributions from overseas Chinese diaspora,
• Funding from colonies	British Commonwealth contributed to UK Imperial Japan controlled colonies; Germany tried unsuccessfully
• Assistance from Allies	Considerable Lend-Lease aid by US to UK, USSR; targeted military aid to China

Macroeconomic Management:

- Managing aggregate demand — UK (Keynes Plan) suppressed consumption spending; US stimulated through New Deal
- Monetary management — Germany controlled currency and inflation; China completely failed its monetary management

Resource Allocation Mechanisms:

- Market allocation v. central planning — Markets dominant in US; central planning and control dominant in USSR
- Compulsory rationing — All including US practised some forms of price control and quantity control
- Dealing with distributional impacts — Vouchers and special assistance in UK, Germany

International Economic Regulation:

- Extent of openness — Germany had a tradition of open trading; Soviet Union was a closed economy
- Capital controls — Strict controls on outward flows in most countries
- Exchange rate management — Competitive devaluations in many countries; UK, US leave gold standard
- Trade restrictions — Significant controls in most countries, mainly managed by foreign exchange allocations
- Bilateral barter trade — Germany, China, Japan did barter trade deals: commodities for arms
- Breaching embargoed trade — Japan, Germany breached sanctioned trade through third players

Managing Resources:

- Requisition of domestic resources — Most countries requisitioned resources with or without compensation
- Market-based resource allocation — US still maintained most market allocation; UK markets widespread
- Plunder and requisition — Germany plundered in USSR; Japan plundered in China; Soviet Union plundered post-war

Managing Production:

- Production planning techniques — USSR had central control; US largely market-based; others used mixed techniques
- Directing armaments industry — All countries controlled armaments production closely
- Public v. private production — USSR all production was state-owned; US almost all private; UK, Germany mixed; Japan used state-influenced zaibatsu
- Outsourcing production — UK produced arms in US factories; Germany produced in Occupied Europe
- Transport modes — Shipping crucial for island nations: Japan, UK; rail was key in China and Europe

Continued

Continued

Economic Issue	Economic Position of Protagonist Countries

Labour Management:

- Labour force — Wage controls in place in all countries; labour direction in most
- Conscription — All countries conscripted men for military; some also had conscription for certain civilian roles
- Impressed, slave labour — Widely used by Japan, Germany, also Soviet Union
- Role of women — Increased participation in labour force in most countries, but low participation in Germany, Japan

Unblocking Supplies:

- Breaking embargoes — Germany, Japan obtained key resources through third countries, barter trade
- Breaching blockades — UK, USSR kept supplies open with defended convoys
- Outlasting sieges — USSR restricted consumption to near starvation levels

Dealing with Physical War Damage:

- Rapid reconstruction of infrastructure — Germany rapidly rebuilt rail tracks, bridges; China slow to reconstruct
- Alternative housing — UK, Germany, USSR provided emergency housing for bombed-out civilians; huge Chinese homelessness
- Protecting key production — Germany hid factories; USSR moved them east out of bombing range; US largely undamaged; China much disrupted

Economic Aggression on Enemies:

- Disrupting key plants — UK, US bombed key German plants; US destroy much Japanese capacity
- Attacking economic bottlenecks — US, USSR attacked rail junctions, bridges; US cut off Japan supply lines
- Counterfeiting currencies — Germany, USSR both tried flooding enemies with counterfeit currency

Armistice Strategies:

- Demobilization — Slow demobilization in victor countries; continuing Cold War requirements; demob assistance, e.g. US GI Support
- Demilitarization — Rapid enforced demilitarization, trials and constitutional change in Germany, Japan; China embroiled in civil war
- Delayed consumption — Continuing post-war rationing in Japan, Germany, UK

Post-War Strategies:

- Reconstruction and war damage
Germany, Japan, West Soviet Union all rebuild rapidly; China remains disrupted
- Funding wartime debts
US Marshall Pan, US Lend-Lease and Comintern equivalents
- Threats and game theory
US and USSR carried out mutual threats strategy
- Mutually-Assured Destruction:
MAD: an ultimate strategy of the Cold War

Bibliography

Ah Xiang. *Chiang Kai-Shek's Money Trail*. http://www.republicanchina.org/MoneyTrail.

Ahamed, Liaquat. 2009. *Lords of Finance: The Bankers Who Broke the World*. Penguin Books.

Akhabbar, Amanar. 2006. *Social Technology and Political Economy: The Debate on the Soviet Origins of Input-Output Analysis*. History of Economics Research Group. Nanterre University. https://economix.fr/uploads/source/doc/journees/hpe/2006-12-21_Akhabbar.pdf.

Akhabbar, A., G. Antille, E. Fontela, and A. Pulido. 2011. 'Input-Output in Europe: Trends in Research and Applications'. *Oeconomia*. 1 (1), 73–98.

Aroche, Fidel. 2015. *Wassily Leontief, the Input-Output Model, the Soviet National Economic Balance and the General Equilibrium Theory*. Mimeo. http://www.unizar.es%3Earchivos.

Barnett, Vincent. 2005. *A History of Russian Economic Thought*. Routledge.

Baumol, William J. and Thijs ten Raa. 2009. 'Wassily Leontief: In Appreciation'. *European Journal of Economic Thought*, 16 (3), 511–22.

Beaud, Michel and Gilles Dostaler. 1997. *Economic Thought since Keynes: A History and Dictionary of Major Economists*. Routledge.

Bientinesi, Fabrizio and Rosario Patalano (eds), 2017. *Economists and War: A Heterodox Perspective*. Routledge.

Bjerkholt, Olav. 2016. *Wassily Leontief and the Discovery of the Input-Output Approach*. Memo 18/2016. Department of Economics, University of Oslo. sv.uio.no.

Blusiewicz, Thomasz. 2016. *Economics of Foreign Aggression in Nazi Germany, 1936–1939*. Mimeo.

Bochner, S. 1958. *John Von Neumann 1903–1957: A Biographical Memoir*. National Academy of Sciences.

Bockman, Johanna and Michael A. Bernstein. 2008. 'Scientific Community in a Divided World, Economists, Planning and Research Priority during the Cold War'. *Comparative Studies in Society and History*. 50 (3), 581–613.

Bossone, Biagio and Stefano Labini. 2016. *Macroeconomics in Germany: The Forgotten Lesson of Hjalmar Schacht*. Vox CEPR.

Braun, R. Anton and Alan R. Grattan. 1993. 'The Macroeconomics of War and Peace'. *NBER Macroeconomics Annual*. Volume 8.

Brivers, Ivars. 2009. 'Economic Calculation in Non-Monetary Terms – the Forgotten Ideas of Kantorovich and Siroyezhin'. *Bulletin of Political Economy*. 3 (1), 37–49.

Burdekin, Richard C.K. 2008. *China's Monetary Challenges: Past Experiences and Future Prospects*. Cambridge University Press.

Cabral, Maria Joao. 2003. 'John Von Neumann's Contribution to Economic Science'. *International Social Science Review*. 78 (3–4), 1–9.

Cairncross, Alec. 1995. 'Economists in Wartime'. *Contemporary European History.* 4 (1), 19–36.

Cha, Myung Soo. 2000. *Did Takahashi Korekiyo Rescue Japan from the Great Depression?* Discussion Paper A-395. Department of Economics, Yeungnam University.

Chalou, George C. 2001. *The Secrets War: The Office of Strategic Services and World War II.* National Archives and Records Administration.

Chen Hongmin. 2001. 'Chiang Kai-Shek and Hitler: An Exchange of Correspondence'. *Annali di Ca' Foscari.* 40 (3). 281–92.

Chiang Kai-shek. 1967. 'Biographical Sketch of Dr Kung Hsiang-hsi'. *Taiwan Today.* 10.9.67.

Coble, Parks. 2003. *Chinese Capitalists in Japan's New Order: The Occupied Lower Yangzi, 1937–1945.* University of California Press.

Coble, Parks M. 1975. *The Shanghai Capitalists and the Nationalist Government, 1927–1937.* Harvard University Asia Centre.

Cockshott, Paul. 2007. *Mises, Kantorovich and Economic Computation.* MPRA. https://mpra.ub.uni-muenchen.de/6063/1/MPRA_paper_6063.pdf.

Collier, Stephen J. and Andrew Lakoff. 2016. *The Bombing Encyclopaedia of the World.* http://www.limn.it.

Connor, Andrew and Naureen Haque. 2010. *The Defense of Hjalmar Schacht.* Mimeo. studylib.net.

Copeland, Arthur H. 1945. 'Review of the Theory of Games and Economic Behaviour'. *Bulletin of the American Mathematical Society.* 51 (7), 498–504.

Davidson, Paul. 2007. *John Maynard Keynes: Great Thinkers in Economics.* Palgrave Macmillan.

Davies, R. W., Harrison, M., Khlevniuk, O., and Wheatcroft, S. G. 2018. *The Soviet Economy: The Late 1930s in Historical Perspective.* https://ssrn.com/abstract=3166964.

Dean Best, Gary. 1974. *Financial Diplomacy: The Takahashi Korekiyo Missions of 1904–1905.* http://www.asj.upd.edu.ph.

DeBresson, Christien. 2004. 'Some Highlights in the Life of Wassily Leontief – an Interview with Estelle and Wassily Leontief'. Chapter 9 in *Wassily Leontief and Input-Output Economics.* E. Dietzenbacher and M. Lahr (eds). Cambridge University Press.

Dietzenbacher, Erik and Michael L. Lahr (eds). 2004. *Wassily Leontief and Input-Output Economics.* Cambridge University Press.

Dore, Mohammed, Sukhamoy Chakravarty, and Richard Goodwin. 1989. *John Von Neumann and Modern Economics.* Clarendon Press.

Dorfman, Robert. 1995. 'In Appreciation of Wassily Leontief'. *Structural Change in Economic Dynamics.* 6, 305–8.

Duppe, Till. 2013. 'Koopmans in the Soviet Union: A Travel Report of the Summer of 1965'. *Journal of the History of Economic Thought.* 38 (1), 81–104.

Engerman, David C. 2011. *Know Your Enemy: The Rise and Fall of America's Soviet Experts.* Oxford University Press.

February 26 Incident. http://en.wikipedia.org/wiki.

Field, Alexander J. 2014. 'Schelling, Von Neumann, and the Event That Didn't Occur'. *Games.* 5, 53–89.

Fenby, Jonathan. 2009. *Chiang Kai-Shek: China's Generalissimo and the Nation He Lost.* Hachette.

Foley, Duncan K. 1998. 'An Interview with Wassily Leontief'. *Macroeconomic Dynamics.* 2, 116–40.

Fonseca, Goncalo L. (no date) 'John Maynard Keynes, 1883–1946'. *History of Economic Thought.* http://www.hetwebsite.net/het.

Fremdling, Rainer and Reiner Staglin. 2014. 'An Input-Output Table for Germany in 1936'. *Economic History Yearbook.* 55 (2), 187–96.

Gardner, Roy. 1990. 'L.V. Kantorovich: The Price Implications of Optimal Planning'. *Journal of Economic Literature.* 28 (June), 638–48.

Gerovitch, Slava. 2001. 'Mathematical Machines of the Cold War: Soviet Computing, American Cybernetics and Ideological Disputes in the Early 1950s'. *Social Studies of Science.* 31 (2), 253–87.

Gregory, Paul and Mark Harrison. 2005. 'Allocation under Dictatorship: Research in Stalin's Archives'. *Journal of Economic Literature.* 43 (September), 721–61.

Guglielmo, Mark. 2008. 'The Contribution of Economists to Military Intelligence During World War II'. *The Journal of Economic History.* 68(1), 109–50.

Hadley, Eleanor M. 1989. 'The Diffusion of Keynesian Ideas in Japan'. Chapter 11 in *The Political Power of Economic Ideas: Keynesianism Across Nations.* Peter A. Hall (ed.). Princeton University Press. 291–310.

Hagemann, Harald. 2010. *Wassily Leontief and His German Period.* Mimeo. leontief-centre.ru.

Hagemann, Harald. 2014. *The German Edition of Keynes's General Theory: Controversies on the Preface.* Universitat Hohenheim. Mimeo. http://www.uni-hohenheim.de.

Hamilton, John Maxwell. 2003. *Edgar Snow: A Biography.* Louisiana State University Press.

Harrison, Mark (ed.). 1998. *The Economics of World War II: Six Great Powers in International Comparison.* Cambridge University Press.

Harrison, Mark. 1988. 'Resource Mobilisation for World War II: The USA, UK, USSR and Germany 1938–1945'. *Economic History Review.* 41 (2), 171–92.

Harrison, Mark. 1993. 'The Soviet Economy and Relations with the United States and Britain, 1941–1945'. Chapter 4 in *The Rise and Fall of the Grand Alliance, 1941–45.* Ann Lane and Howard Temperley (eds). Palgrave Macmillan. 69–89.

Harrod, Roy F. 1951. *The Life of John Maynard Keynes.* Macmillan.

Hays Parks, W. 1995. 'Precision and Area Bombing: Who Did Which When?' *Journal of Strategic Studies.* 18 (1), 145–74.

Heims, Stephen J. 1982. *John Von Neumann and Norbert Weiner: From Mathematics to the Technologies of Life and Death.* MIT Press.

Hjalmar Schacht. https://en.m.wikipedia.org.

Holler, Manfred J. 2016. 'What John von Neumann Did to Economics'. In G. Faccarello and Heinz Kurz (eds). *Handbook on the History of Economic Analysis.* Edward Elgar Publishing. Volume 1, 581–6.

Hoover Institution Archives Staff. *Inventory of the HH Kung Papers 1917 to 1949.* http://www.oac.cdlib.org.

Howlett, W. P. 1992. *New Light Through Old Windows: A New Perspective on the British Economy in the Second World War.* Working paper 2/92. London School of Economics.

Ikeo, Aiko. 2014. *Tameyuki Amano and the Teachings of Sontoku Ninomiya: The Japanese Foundation of Modern Economics.* International Economic Association, 17th World Congress.

International Military Tribunal, Nuremberg. 1946. *Verdict Hjalmar Schacht.* https://crimeofaggression.info.

Jacobson, Carl. 2011. 'Strengthening China through Education and the Oberlin Spirit'. *Biographies: H.H. Kung.* http://www.oberlin.edu/library.

Johnson, Zdenka. 2017. 'Financing the German Economy during the Second World War'. *West Bohemian Historical Review.* 7 (1), 115–43.

John von Neumann. https://en.m.wikipedia.org.

Josephson, Paul R. 1997. *New Atlantis Revisited: Akademgorodok, the Siberian City of Science.* Princeton University Press.

Kaliadina, Svetlana A. 2006. 'W.W. Leontief and the Repressions of the 1920s: An Interview'. *Economic Systems Research.* 18 (4), 347–55.

Kaliadina, Svetlana A. and Natalia Pavlova. 2006. 'The Family of W.W. Leontief in Russia'. *Economic Systems Research.* 18 (4), 335–45.

Kantorovich, L. V. 1960. 'Mathematical Methods of Organising and Planning Production'. *Management Science.* 6 (4), 366–422.

Kantorovich, L. V. 1965. *The Best Use of Economic Resources.* Pergamon Press.

Kantorovich, L. V. 1968. 'Trends of Development in Automatic Programming Based on Large-Block Systems'. *Steklov Mathematical Institute.* 96, 1–6.

Kantorovich, Leonid Vitaliyevich. 1975. 'Mathematics in Economics: Achievements, Difficulties, Perspectives'. *Sveriges Riksbank Prize in Economic Sciences in Memory of Alfred Nobel.* https://www.nobelprize.org.

Katsenelinboigen, Aron. 1978. 'L.V. Kantorovich: The Political Dilemma in Scientific Creativity'. *Journal of Post-Keynesian Economics.* 1 (2), 129–47.

Katsenelinboigen, Aron. 1979. *Soviet Economic Thought and Political Power in the USSR.* Pergamon Press.

Katsenelinboigen, Aron. 1986. 'Mathematical Economics in the Soviet Union: A Reflection on the 25th Anniversary of L. V. Kantorovich's Book, the Best Use of Economic Resources'. *Acta Slavica Iaponica.* 4, 88–103.

Kemeny, John G., Oskar Morgenstern, and Gerald L. Thompson. 1956. 'A Generalisation of the von Neumann Model of an Expanding Economy'. *Econometrica.* 24 (2), 115–35.

Keynes, J. M. 1920. *The Economic Consequences of the Peace.* Harcourt, Brace and Howe.

Keynes, J. M. 1925. *The Economic Consequences of Mr Churchill.* L. and V. Woolf.

Keynes, J. M. 1928. 'The Financial Reconstruction of Germany: The Men Who Engineered It'. *Sydney Morning Herald.* 13.

Keynes, J. M. 1937. 'The General Theory of Employment'. *The Quarterly Journal of Economics.* 51 (2), 209–23.

Kindleberger, C. P. 1999. 'Some Economic Lessons from World War II'. Chapter 14 in *Essays in History: Financial, Economic, Personal.* University of Michigan Press.

Kirshner, Jonathan. 2007. *Appeasing Bankers: Financial Caution on the Road to War.* Princeton University Press.

Klein, Burton. 1948. 'Germany's Preparation for War: A Re-Examination'. *American Economic Review.* 38 (1), 56–77.

Klein, Daniel B. and Ryan Daza. 2013. 'Wassily Leontief: Ideological Profiles of the Economics Laureates'. *Economic Journal Watch.* 10 (3), 417–28.

Klein, Daniel B., Ryan Daza, and Hannah Mead. 2013. 'Leonard Vitaliyevich Kantorovich: Ideological Profiles of the Economics Laureates'. *Economic Journal Watch.* 10 (3), 385–8.

Kohli, Martin C. 2001. 'Leontief and the US Bureau of Labor Statistics, 1941–54: Developing a Framework for Measurement'. *History of Political Economy.* 33 (Supplement), 190–212.

Kuhn, H. W. and A. W. Tucker. 1958. 'John von Neumann's Work in the Theory of Games and Mathematical Economics'. *Bulletin of the American Mathematical Society.* 3 (2), 100–22.

Kuhn, Harold W. 2004. 'Introduction' in *Theory of Games and Economic Behaviour.* John von Neumann and Oskar Morgenstern. Rev. edn. Princeton University Press.

Kung, H. H. https://en.m.wikipedia.org.

Kung, H. H. 1939. *China's Wartime Progress.* China Information Committee, Chungking.

Kung, H. H. 1945 'China's Financial Problems'. *Foreign Affairs.* 23 (2), 222–32.

Kurz, Heinz D. and Neri Salvadori. 1993. 'Von Neumann's Growth Model and the "Classical" Tradition'. *The European Journal of the History of Economic Thought.* 1 (1), 129–59.

Kutateladze, S. S. 2007. 'Kantorovich's Phenomenon'. *Siberian Mathematical Journal.* 48 (1), 1–2.

Kutateladze, S. S. 2007. 'The World Line of Kantorovich'. *International Society for Mathematical Sciences.* January, 1–9.

Kutateladze, S. S. 2011 *Mathematics and Economics of Kantorovich.* http://www. math.nsc.ru.

Kutateladze, S. S. 2012. 'Mathematics and Economics of Leonid Kantorovich'. *Siberian Mathematical Journal.* 53 (1), 2012–14.

Kutateladze, S. S. et al. 2002. 'Leonid Kantorovich 1912–1986'. *Siberian Mathematical Journal.* 43 (1), 3–8.

Kutateladze, S. S. 2008. *Sobolev of the Euler School.* http://www.researchgate.net.

Lange, Oskar. 1979. 'The Computer and the Market'. *Comparative Economic Systems: Models and Cases.* Morris Bornstein, ed. 126–9, Homewood.

Lee, Changmin. 2013. *The Role of the Private Sector in Japan's Recovery from the Great Depression.* Discussion Paper 2013–11. Department of Social Engineering, Tokyo Institute of Technology.

Leeds, Adam E. 2016. 'Dreams in Cybernetic Fugue: Cold War Techno-Science, the Intelligentsia, and the Birth of Soviet Mathematical Economics'. *Historical Studies in the Natural Sciences,* 46 (5).

Leonard, Robert. 2008. *New Light on von Neumann: Politics, Psychology and the Creation of Game Theory.* CESMEP working papers 200707, University of Turin. *Leonid Vitalyevich Kantorovich.* https://en.m.wikipedia.org.

Leontief, Wassily. 1925. 'The National Economy Balance of the USSR'. *Planowoye Hoziaystvo (The Planned Economy)*. No. 12.

Leontief, Wassily. 1936. 'The Fundamental Assumptions of Mr Keynes' Monetary Theory of Unemployment'. *Quarterly Journal of Economics,* 51 (1), 192–7.

Leontief, Wassily. 1941. *The Structure of the American Economy 1919–29: An Empirical Application of Equilibrium Analysis.* Harvard University Press.

Leontief, Wassily. 1946. 'The Pure Theory of the Guaranteed Annual Wage Contract'. *Journal of Political Economy,* 54 (1), 76–9.

Leontief, Wassily. 1960. 'The Decline and Rise of Soviet Economic Science'. Republished in *Essays in Economics.* M. E. Sharpe, 223–36.

Leontief, Wassily. 1970. Theoretical Assumptions and Non-Observed Facts. *American Economic Review.* 61 (1), 1–7.

Light, Alison. 2008. 'Lady Talky: Review of Bloomsbury Ballerina by Judith Mackrell'. *London Review of Books.* December, 19.

Linz, Susan J. 1984. *World War II and Soviet Economic Growth 1940–1953.* BEBR working paper 1038. University of Illinois.

Littleboy, Bruce. 1996. 'The Wider Significance of "How to Pay for the War"'. *History of Economics Review,* 25, 88–95.

Luke, Rolf E. 1985. 'The Schacht and the Keynes Plans'. *Banca Nazionale Del Lavoro Quarterly Review,* 152, 65–76.

Macrae, Norman. 1992. *John von Neumann: The Scientific Genius Who Pioneered the Modern Computer, Game Theory, Nuclear Deterrence, and Much More.* American Mathematical Society.

Malinovsky, B. N. 2010. *Pioneers of Soviet Computing,* edited by Anne Fitzpatrick. http://www.sigcis.org.

Meek, Ronald L. 1953. 'Stalin as an Economist'. *The Review of Economic Studies.* 21 (3), 232–9.

Miner, Luella and Fei, Ch'i-hao. 1903. *Two Heroes of Cathay, an Autobiography and a Sketch.* Fleming H. Revell Company.

Moggridge, Donald E. 1992. *Maynard Keynes: An Economist's Biography.* Routledge.

Nanto, Dick K. and Shinji Takagi. 1985. 'Korekiyo Takahashi and Japan's Recovery from the Great Depression'. *American Economic Review* 75 (2), 369–74.

Nathan, Otto. 1944. *Nazi War Finance and Banking.* National Bureau of Economic Research.

Nemchinov, V. S. 1959. 'Editorial Preface'. *The Best Use of Economic Resources.* L. V. Kantorovich. 1965 translated edition, vii–xvi. Pergamon Press.

Nitusov, Alexander. 1997. *Leonid Vitalyevich Kantorovich: Mathematician, Economist and Cyberneticist Academician of the USSR Academy of Sciences Nobel Prize Winner in 1975.* Russian Virtual Computer Museum. http://www.computer-museum. ru>english.

Nove, Alec. 1991. *The Economics of Feasible Socialism.* Harper Collins.

O'Connor, J. J. and E. F. Robertson. 2014. *Leonid Vitalyevich Kantorovich.* School of Mathematics and Statistics, University of St Andrews. https://www-history.mcs. st-andrews.ac.uk/Biographies/Kantorovich.html.

O'Neil, William D. 2003. *Interwar US and Japanese National Product and Defence Expenditure.* CNA Corporation.

Ohno, Kenichi. 2006. *The Economic Development of Japan*. National Graduate for Policy Studies, Tokyo.

Peterson, Edward Norman. 1954. *Hjalmar Schacht, For and Against Hitler: A Political— Economic Study of Germany, 1923–1945*. Christopher Publishing House.

Pilkington, Philip. 2013. *Hjalmar Schacht, MEFO Bills and the Restoration of the German Economy 1933–1939*. http://www.nakedcapitalism.com.

Pizano, Diego. 2009. *Conversations with Great Economists: Hayek, Hicks, Kaldor, Kantorovich, Robinson, Samuelson, Tinbergen*. Jorge Pinto Books.

Pollock, Ethan. 2001. *Conversations with Stalin on Questions of Political Economy*. Working paper 33. Woodrow Wilson International Centre for Scholars.

Poundstone, William. 1992. *Prisoner's Dilemma: John Von Neumann, Game Theory, and the Puzzle of the Bomb*. Anchor Books.

Ramsden, Dave. 2015. *The First 50 Years of the Government Economic Service*. Mimeo. King's College London.

Romanovskii, I. V. 2006. 'A Modern View of LV Kantorovich's Work in Software'. *Journal of Mathematical Science*. 133 (4), 1398–401.

Rosenhead, Jonathan. 2003. 'IFORS Operational Research Hall of Fame: Leonid Vitaliyevich Kantorovich'. *International Transactions in Operations Research*. 10, 665–7.

Ruggles, Richard and Henry Brodie. 1947. 'An Empirical Approach to Economic Intelligence and World War II'. *Journal of the American Statistical Association*. 42 (237), 72–91.

Samuelson, Lennart. 2000. *Plans for Stalin's War Machine: Tukhachevskii and Military— Economic Planning, 1925–41*. Macmillan.

Samuelson, Paul A. 1989. 'A Revisionist View of Von Neumann's Growth Model'. In *John von Neumann and Modern Economics*. M. Dore et al. (eds). 100–22. Clarendon Press.

Samuelson, Paul A. 2004. 'The Portrait of the Master as a Young Man'. Chapter 1 in *Wassily Leontief and Input-Output Economics*. E. Dietzenbacher and Michael L. Lahr (eds). Cambridge University Press.

Schacht, Hjalmar. 1922. 'Discount Policy of the Reichsbank'. In *Reconstruction in Europe*. J. M. Keynes (ed). Manchester Guardian Commercial Supplement Number 11. December 7.

Schacht, Hjalmar. 1931. *The End of Reparations: The Economic Consequences of the World War*. J. Cape.

Schacht, Hjalmar. 1956. *Confessions of the Old Wizard: The Autobiography*. Houghton Mifflin.

Schacht, Hjalmar. 1967. *The Magic of Money*. Oldbourne.

Schenk, Catherine R. 2015. 'China and the International Monetary Fund 1945–85'. Chapter 13 in *History of the IMF: Organisation, Policy and Market*. K.Yago, Y. Asai, and M.Itoh (eds). 275–310. Springer.

Schuker, Stephen A. 2014. 'J.M. Keynes and the Personal Politics of Reparations', *Diplomacy and Statecraft*. 25 (3), 453–71.

Seagrave, Sterling. 1985. *The Soong Dynasty*. Harper.

Seneta, Eugene. 2004. 'Mathematics, Religion and Marxism in the Soviet Union in the 1930s'. *Historia Mathematica*. 31 (3), 337–67.

Shabad, Timoddre. 1975. 'Leonid V. Kantorovich'. *The New York Times*. October 15.

Shibamoto, Masahiko and Masato Shizume. 2011. *How Did Takahashi Korekiyo Rescue Japan from the Great Depression?* http://eh.net%3EShibamotoShizume.

Shizume, Masato. 2009. *The Japanese Economy during the Interwar Period: Instability in the Financial System and the Impact of the World Depression*. Institute for Monetary and Economic Studies, Bank of Japan.

Shoah Resource Centre. 2000. *The Historian Albert Fischer on the Minister of Economics and the Expulsion of the Jews from German Economy*. The International School for Holocaust Studies.

Skidelsky, Robert. 1983. *John Maynard Keynes: Hopes Betrayed 1883–1920*. Macmillan.

Skidelsky, Robert. 1992. *John Maynard Keynes: The Economist as Saviour 1920–1937*. Macmillan.

Skidelsky, Robert. 2000. *John Maynard Keynes: Fighting For Britain 1937–1946*. Macmillan.

Slater, Martin. 2018. *The National Debt: A Short History*. C. Hurst and Co.

Smethurst, Richard J. 2007. *From Foot Soldier to Finance Minister: Takahashi Korekiyo, Japan's Keynes*. Harvard University Press.

Smethurst, Richard J. 2017. 'Japan's Keynes. Takahashi Korekiyo'. Chapter 14 in *The Diffusion of Western Economic Ideas in East Asia*. Malcolm Warner (ed.). Economic Books. 266–84.

Smethurst, Richard J. and Masataka Matsuura. 2000. *Politics and the Economy in Pre-war Japan*. Discussion paper JS/00/381, the Suntory Centre, London School of Economics.

Spahn, Peter. 2013. *On Keynes's 'How to Pay for the War'*. University of Hohenheim. https://wipol.uni-hohenheim.de.

Steil, Ben. 2013. *The Battle of Bretton Woods: John Maynard Keynes, Harry Dexter White, and the Making of a New World Order*. Princeton University Press.

Sutela Pekka and Vladimir Mau. 1998. 'Economics under Socialism: The Russian Case'. *Economic Thought in Communist and Post-Communist Europe*. Hans-Jurgen Wagener (ed). Routledge. Chapter 2, 33–79.

Szasz, Domokos. 2011. 'John Von Neumann, the Mathematician'. *The Mathematical Intelligencer*. http://www.math.bme.hu.

Takahashi Korekiyo. https://en.m.wikipedia.org.

Tassava, Christopher J. 2008. 'The American Economy during World War II'. *EH.Net Encyclopedia*. Robert Whaples. http://www.eh.net/encyclopedia.

Tcheremnykh, I. N. (no date) 'Input-Output Models'. Volume 2 of *Systems Analysis and Modelling of Integrated World Systems*. http://www.eolss.net.

Temin, Peter. 1990. *Soviet and Nazi Economic Planning in the 1930s*. Economics working paper 554. Massachusetts Institute of Technology.

Tooze, Adam. 2007. *The Wages of Destruction: The Making and Breaking of the Nazi Economy*. Penguin.

U.S. Government. 1946. Summary Report. *United States Strategic Bombing Survey (Pacific War)*. Government Printing Office.

Vane, Howard R. and Chris Mulhearn. 2009. *Wassily W. Leontief, Leonard V. Kantorovich, Tjalling C. Koopmans and J. Richard N. Stone: Pioneering Papers of the Nobel Memorial Laureates in Economics*. Edward Elgar Publishing.

Vershik, A. M. 2001. *L. V. Kantorovich and Linear Programming*. Steklov Institute of Mathematics. http://www.pdmi.ras.ru.

Von Neumann, John. 1945a. 'A Model of General Economic Equilibrium'. *The Review of Economic Studies*. 13 (1), 1–9.

Von Neumann, John. 1945b. First Draft of a Report on the EDVAC. US Army Ordinance Department/Moore School of Electrical Engineering.

Von Neumann, John and Oskar Morgenstern. 1944. *Theory of Games and Economic Behaviour*. Princeton University Press.

Wakatabe, Masazumi. 2014. Keynesianism *in Japan*. https://jshet.net.

Ware, Willis H. and Wade B. Holland. 1963. *Soviet Cybernetics Technology: I. Soviet Cybernetics, 1959–1962*. Rand Corporation. Memorandum RM–3675–PR.

Warner, Malcolm. 2014. *On Keynes and China: Keynesianism 'With Chinese Characteristics'*. Judge Business School, Working paper 2/2014.

Weitz, John. 1997. *Hitler's Banker: Hjalmar Horace Greeley Schacht*. Little, Brown and Co.

White, Theodore and Annalee Jacoby. 1947. *Thunder Out Of China*. Victor Gollancz.

Whitman, Marina von Neumann. 2012. *The Martian's Daughter: A Memoir*. University of Michigan Press.

Wilson, Thomas and Bryan Hopkin. 2000. 'Alexander Kirkland Cairncross, 1911–1998'. *Proceedings of the British Academy*. 105, 339–61.

Index

For the benefit of digital users, indexed terms that span two pages (e.g., 52–53) may, on occasion, appear on only one of those pages.